JANE AUSTEN

— The Banker's Sister —

JANE AUSTEN
— *The Banker's Sister* —
E. J. CLERY

Biteback Publishing

First published in Great Britain in 2017 by
Biteback Publishing Ltd
Westminster Tower
3 Albert Embankment
London SE1 7SP
Copyright © E. J. Clery 2017

ISBN 978-1-78590-176-8

10 9 8 7 6 5 4 3 2 1

A CIP catalogue record for this book is available from the British Library.

Set in Adobe Garamond Pro

Printed and bound in Great Britain by
CPI Group (UK) Ltd, Croydon CR0 4YY

MIX
Paper from
responsible sources
FSC
www.fsc.org   FSC® C020471

CONTENTS

INTRODUCTION

In 2013 the Governor of the Bank of England, Mark Carney, announced that Jane Austen would appear on the redesigned £10 note, scheduled for issue in 2017 to coincide with the 200th anniversary of her death. There was a flurry of media excitement. Most of it was inspired by the success of the campaign, 'Keep a woman on English banknotes'. Few noted the fact that a £10 'Austen' banknote was already in existence. Her brother Henry had established himself as a banker in 1806, and built up a small empire of country banks with its headquarters in London. A £10 banknote issued by the Alton partnership of Austen, Gray and Vincent is now on display at the cottage where Jane once lived, in the neighbouring village of Chawton. It was here, at the Jane Austen House Museum in rural Hampshire, that the Bank of England governor made his announcement. But Henry Austen went almost unmentioned, for the good reason that Henry Austen had gone bust. His banking enterprise had been swallowed up in the post-war financial crash of 1816, and many clients, including family, friends and neighbours, had suffered terrible losses. This has been an aspect of Jane's life brushed under the carpet by descendants and neglected by biographers. The history of Henry's rise and fall, intertwined with Jane's publishing career and imaginative life as a novelist, is the topic of this book.

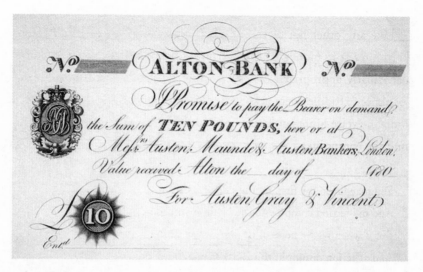

Alton Bank: Austen, Gray & Vincent, £10 Banknote. Reproduced by kind permission of the Jane Austen Memorial Trust.

Henry was Jane's favourite among her six brothers. They were drawn together by temperament, both of them quick and witty, while his boundless optimism and enthusiasm counterbalanced her occasional tendency to low spirits and irritability. Once Jane began writing novels in earnest their connection became professional. His various homes in London were her base of operation for entering the publishing industry. Henry acted as her agent, dealing with publishers and printers on her behalf. After her death he became her literary executor, arranging publication of her final works and presenting to the public the earliest biographical sketch of his sister.

At the time of Mark Carney's announcement I had some awareness of Henry's business activities, having taught the writings of Jane Austen for many years at the University of Southampton. In the line of duty as well as pleasure, I would often make my way to the Centre for Early Women Writers at Chawton House Library, housed in the mansion once owned by Jane's wealthy brother Edward Austen Knight. The contrast between Chawton Great House and modest Chawton Cottage, just ten minutes' walk away, can never fail to be striking.

Like any other fan of the novels, I was also aware of Jane Austen's keen interest in money. This alone makes her appearance on a banknote particularly appropriate. She even wrote a charade based on the word 'banknote'. Riddles were popular in the Austen family, and in this one, a four-line verse hinted at 'bank' and 'note' before requiring the guesser to find the composite:

> You may lie on my first, by the side of a stream,
> And my second compose to the Nymph you adore
> But if when you've none of my whole her esteem
> And affection diminish, think of her no more.

This little ditty was untypical because it suggested that love should remain unsullied by the question of money. Her normal stance was more hard-headed , and once upon a time this was found shocking. It clashed with the image of sweet Aunt Jane which developed in Victorian times. W. H. Auden joked about the dissonance in his 'Letter to Lord Byron' published in 1937:

> It makes me most uncomfortable to see
> An English spinster of the middle class
> Describe the amorous effects of 'brass'
> Reveal so frankly and with such sobriety
> The economic basis of society.

Since then, attitudes have changed and become far more accepting and even appreciative of her insistence on the importance of a good income. There have been excellent overviews of the money factor in her fiction by, most notably, Edward Copeland. Her dealings with the book trade have been explored by Jan Fergus, Kathryn Sutherland, and Anthony Mandel. Recent years have seen essays discussing Jane Austen's relation to theories of political economy in her day, and monographs on the economic contexts of her work by Sheryl Craig and Stephen Mahony. The 'economic basis of society' in the world of Jane Austen's novels has perhaps never been better encapsulated than in Raymond Williams's *The Country and the City*. It is not a simple, static world, Williams insists:

> ...it is an active, complicated, sharply speculative process. It is indeed that most difficult world to describe, in English social history: an acquisitive, high bourgeois society at the point of its most evident interlocking with an agrarian capitalism that is itself mediated by inherited titles and by the making of family names ... An openly acquisitive society, which is concerned also with the transmission of wealth, is trying to judge itself at once by an inherited code and by the morality of improvement.

Yet in all of this critical commentary, the figure of Henry Austen, Jane's most important and direct link with the economic transformations of her time, has been almost entirely absent.

I have long been interested in the conjunction of literature and economics, and the announcement of the Jane Austen £10 note was the spur I needed to make a systematic investigation of Henry's career. There have been two books published on Jane Austen's 'sailor brothers', Francis and Charles. Peter Knox-Shaw's *Jane Austen and the Enlightenment* is in part a tribute to the influence of her scholarly brother James. Linda Slothouber has published a survey of Edward Austen Knight and his Chawton estate. There was no equivalent study of Henry, but I became aware of an extraordinary series of articles on various aspects of his career, first as a militia officer, then as an army agent, and eventually as a banker, published over the past twenty years in the journals issued by the British and North American branches of the Jane Austen Society. Two researchers in particular, Clive Caplan and T. A. B. Corley, have delved into the archives to provide vital new evidence about Henry's activities and associates, and the causes of his downfall. This material, together with the invaluable reference works of Deirdre Le Faye, provided much of the factual foundation for a biographical reconstruction.

Tony Corley himself is of the view that a life of Henry Austen can never be written, due to the paucity of surviving documents. It seems clear that there was a deliberate attempt to wipe the details of his ill-fated business enterprise from the family record. No letters between Jane and Henry were preserved, and by some strange fatality the Bankruptcy Commission report on the bank failure was shredded. Nevertheless, thanks in part to Corley's findings, we now know far more and I have ventured to write a dual biography of brother and sister in the belief that Henry's exploits had a substantial bearing on Jane Austen's life and, most importantly, on her creativity. Conjecture must bridge the gaps in our knowledge. I make constant use of those papers that have survived, but at certain points I allow myself the licence of a biographer to imagine the thoughts and feelings of my subjects or dramatise their actions.

Henry's story has, in fact, the makings of a novel rather more sensational than Jane's best-known fictions. As a teenager, Henry was attracted to a cousin, Elizabeth Hancock, a glamorous figure several years older who was born in Calcutta and benefited socially and financially from the generosity of her godfather Warren Hastings, the first Governor-General of India. She was married to a French aristocrat and Henry went to Oxford to study for the clergy, but the flirtation continued on her visits to England. The French Revolution changed the course of both their lives; Henry joined the militia on the declaration of war in 1793, and Eliza lost her husband to the guillotine. He became a captain and a paymaster to his regiment, wooed Eliza, and after an initial rejection, married her in 1797. With her fortune as capital, Henry left the military and set up in London as an agent managing regimental pay and the sale of army commissions, but from the beginning his career was compromised by the involvement of a shadowy figure, Major Charles James, who acted as a secret partner, and drew Henry into illicit and dangerous practices. Major James was also the 'confidential agent' of the Earl of Moira, a prominent military commander and Whig politician. It was James's role to ease the finances of Moira, a man as profligate and unscrupulous as his bosom friend the Prince Regent.

Henry was drawn like a moth to the epicentre of power and corruption in Regency society. But he was not stupid. He tried to spread his portfolio, developing enterprises independently of Charles James, assembling a network of country banks and eventually gaining the prize position of Receiver General for Oxfordshire, gathering land and income tax which could be used for his own profit before being remitted to the government. He was brought down in the end partly through forces beyond his control, but most immediately by his fateful connection with the Prince's Carlton House set. The wealthiest members of the Austen clan had stood surety for the receivership and when Henry was unable to hand over the tax revenue were forced to pay tens of thousands of pounds. The whole extended family was brought to breaking point.

Where does Jane fit into this picture? As a young girl, she was fascinated by the attachment between this adored older brother and her captivating cousin, even titling one of her first literary efforts *Henry and Eliza*. During his years in the militia and the early period in London as an army agent she could see relatively little of him, although it was through his mediation that her first novel was sold in 1803. In 1809 the widowed Mrs Austen and her unmarried daughters settled in Chawton Cottage, owned by Edward but crucially also neighbouring one of Henry's banks, in Alton. It was at this point that Jane entered the slipstream of Henry's endeavours, and successfully found a publisher for *Sense and Sensibility* thanks to the shady Major James. He lurked ominously behind the scenes of Jane's debut, as well as the establishment of Austen & Co. Henry, habituated to risk, encouraged Jane to take the unusual route of publishing on commission, gambling on her publications rather than selling copyright outright. She was anxious but persuaded by his promise to underwrite any losses, and followed this speculative practice for all but one of her later works with mixed results.

Jane began to make regular trips to London to stay with Henry and Eliza once her literary career had been launched. She enjoyed their sociable and cultured way of life, and met constantly with Henry's business associates. After Eliza's death in 1813, she visited Henry even more frequently, staying with him over the bank premises in Covent Garden and later nursing him through a dangerous illness. Letters home to her sister Cassandra report on Henry's doings, and glory in his successes.

The closeness between brother and sister is also reflected in her novels. Versions of Henry appear frequently in her fiction, not least his namesake, the charming but unscrupulous Henry Crawford in *Mansfield Park*, master of the fashionable card-game Speculation. But the untoward fate of the fictional Henry also suggests a degree of critical distance. In the final novels Jane worked through her increasing doubts about the speculative mindset and, following the 1816 crash, the shock caused by the collapse of Henry's enterprise, in which she suffered losses along with the rest of the family. She loved him too much to blame him, however, and even in her last unfinished novel *Sanditon*, which promised to be the chronicle of a comparable collapse, financial risk-taking is treated with indulgence.

Certain aspects of Austen's life appear very differently alongside Henry's banking career. The relationship with her brother Henry offers a vital source for recapturing her experience of Regency modernity. The standard assumption has been that her environment was rural, traditionalist and staunchly Tory. Placing Henry and his banking business in the foreground gives a radically revised view of her awareness of contemporary events, ideas, and public figures. Equally, Henry's affairs provide a window onto a dynamic new England, galvanised by a long period of war, centred on a metropolis which was in the process of becoming the world's financial capital. He may have been just a small player in this setting, but his ventures were perfectly attuned to the spirit of the times. They also have striking resonances in the present day.

It is only now, following the crash of 2008 and the consequent scrutiny of the culture of banking, that we can fully appreciate the extent of Jane Austen's links with 'the economic basis of society'. This is a case of one age of speculation acknowledging another. In 1797, due to an acute shortage of metal coinage and fears that a French invasion would lead to a run on the banks, the British government enforced the first universal paper money economy, and national credit became an imperative just at the moment of greatest economic instability. The world of banking was deregulated, expanded, and internationalised, with the corrupting proviso that the continuation of the war meant profit. Innovative methods sometimes involved dubious morality. There were rapid cycles of boom and bust, hyperactive investment and enterprise and waves of bankruptcy. For a time, Henry thrived in this climate. He was the early nineteenth-century embodiment of the 'animal spirits' identified by John Maynard Keynes as the mainspring of capitalism. At times he displayed the 'irrational exuberance' identified by Alan Greenspan, chairman of the Federal Reserve, as the chief symptom of a bubble on the point of bursting.

This book counters the stereotype, still widespread, of the spinster tucked away in a Hampshire village, detached from the great historical changes of her era. The prologue sketches the origins of the bond between brother and sister; the epilogue addresses Henry's influence on Jane Austen's legacy, and the recurrences of the banking theme in her afterlife, up to the present. The rest relates the story of the linked careers of Henry and Jane, and the ways in which their common cause was manifested in the novels. By the end, readers will see the decision of the Bank of England to put Austen on the £10 banknote as a knowing wink from destiny.

A NOTE ON TITLES AND QUOTATIONS

The titles of all Jane Austen's works, whether published in her lifetime or after, are presented in italics.

Quotes from her writings and other works from the period have been modernised by removing capitals at the start of nouns. Quirks of spelling have been silently corrected. In some contexts accuracy is essential, but here the aim is to avoid the impression of period quaintness.

A NOTE ON MONEY

I have not tried to convert the monetary values of Jane Austen's time into present-day equivalents in the course of this book. The cost of living has changed in so many respects that any attempt at precision would be misleading. Edward Copeland, however, has provided valuable guidelines to the lifestyle implications of different levels of income in his book *Women Writing About Money: Women's Fiction in England, 1790–1820* and his essay 'Money' in *The Cambridge Companion to Jane Austen*. An income of £800–£1000 per year, enabling ownership of a carriage and employment of four servants, is the threshold for something approximating our notions of a comfortable middle-class existence. If one takes as a measure the 'sufficiency' of sensible Elinor Dashwood in *Sense and Sensibility* – £1,000 – one could use a multiplier of sixty or seventy to arrive at a 'good' income in early twenty-first century south-east England. The website 'Measuring Worth' proposes a range of comparators for assessing value historically. The debts of the Earl of Moira which stood at nearly £100,500 in 1804, when Henry Austen first began lending him money, would today equate to just under £8 million in terms of 'historic standard of living' value, but almost £94 million with respect to 'labour earnings'.

PROLOGUE: HENRY AND JANE

When Jane Austen was a girl she wove stories with the crazy logic of dreams around those closest to her. Aged twelve, she began preserving them for posterity. She was the youngest but one of eight children, and anxious to impress. In her literate and literary family effusions of wit and fancy were highly valued, and skits, charades and comic poems were common currency. A substantial number of Jane's efforts in this mode were copied in fair hand in three hardbound books inscribed with the jokingly imposing titles *Volume the First*, *Volume the Second*, and *Volume the Third*.

In late December 1788, having just turned thirteen, Jane wrote a story featuring a stolen banknote titled *Henry and Eliza*. The heroine was a foundling, discovered beneath a haycock as a baby and taken into the care of Sir George and Lady Harcourt. Possessed of enchanting graces and adored by her benefactors Eliza lived a life of uninterrupted happiness until the age of eighteen, when she was detected stealing a £50 banknote. She was immediately turned out of doors, but knowledge of her own excellence supported her spirits. Thanks to the good offices of an innkeeper friend, she was placed as the companion to the Duchess of F. Before long, her bewitching loveliness had stolen the heart of Henry, the fiancé of the Duchess's daughter. The chaplain, being very much in love with Eliza himself, obliged her by secretly uniting Henry and Eliza in marriage. The couple took flight to the Continent, pursued by the enmity of the Duchess. In France, Eliza gave birth to two boys, but three years later Henry died and she was left a widow, thousands of pounds in debt. She returned to England only to be shut in Newgate Prison through the Duchess's machinations. Ever resourceful, she escaped with the aid of a small saw and a rope ladder carelessly left in the corner of her cell. Her two sons being too small to climb down, she tossed them out the window, cushioning their fall with a pile of clothes. They were unharmed but she had no means to feed them, as she was reminded when she discovered they had bitten off two of her fingers. She determined to return to her old friends Sir George and Lady Harcourt who greeted her with open arms. Their joy was completed by Lady Harcourt's sudden recollection that she had placed an infant daughter in a haycock while Sir Harry was absent in the American war, and that Eliza must therefore be their own child. The theft of the banknote was freely forgiven, and Eliza and the children taken back to Harcourt Hall. Unable to forget the wrongs she had endured at the hands of the Duchess, Eliza now took the opportunity to raise an army and demolish Newgate and by that act, gained the blessings of thousands, and the applause of her own heart.

This comic tale of high passion and petty larceny was written in honour of Jane's cousin Eliza, Comtesse de Feuillide, the most exotic personage ever to have crossed the threshold of the shabby rectory in the Hampshire village of Steventon. Born in Calcutta, Eliza had been given a fortune by the famous Warren Hastings of the East India Company and performed with *éclat* in court theatricals at Versailles. Jane's little *jeu d'esprit* may have arisen from wordplay relating to Eliza's maiden name, 'Hancock', and the haycock under which the fictional Eliza is found, with a subliminal emphasis on the second syllable. At Christmas the previous year the Austen household had crackled with sexual tension when worldly Eliza, an accomplished and unapologetic flirt, arrived to participate in the seasonal amateur dramatics.

Petite with exquisite features and large languorous eyes, Eliza was twenty-six, married, and the mother of an eighteen-month-old boy, but she was anything but matronly.

Miniature portrait of Eliza Hancock, c. 1780, by an unknown French artist.
Reproduced with kind permission from the owner.

The tithe barn over the road was fitted up as a theatre, a space of metamorphosis, and James, the eldest Austen son and master of the revels, love-struck, immediately awarded Eliza the main role in their chosen play. It was a racy comedy by Susanna Centlivre, *The Wonder! A Woman Keeps a Secret* from the unbuttoned days of Queen Anne. Eliza was Violante, a Portuguese beauty and the wonder of the title, who shields her friend from paternal tyranny and champions a woman's right to choose her partner. Henry, then sixteen, cut a manly figure as he spoke the lines of the prologue written by James, with suggestive praise of 'lov'd Eliza's golden reign', an attack on Puritan morality, and celebration of the return of Stuarts along with 'loyalty & wit', an era when even old age has its 'vigour' half restored. The theatricals in the deep night of the year were a withdrawal from quotidian propriety, 'a dream, a pleasant dream' as Henry's namesake in *Mansfield Park* reminisces, recalling his dalliance with the 'lovely Maria', a sparkling fantasia quickened with desire, an interval of 'exquisite pleasure ... We were all alive' (II.v).

Eliza once quipped to her confidante, cousin Philadelphia Walter, 'I always find that the most effectual mode of getting rid of temptation is to give way to it.' She cultivated an epigrammatic style in her letters. Like the indomitable Eliza in Jane's story, she had glimpsed her quarry. The fact that he was ten years her junior did not signify. In the spring of 1787 she had put off a visit from Phylly because Henry was coming to stay with her and her mother in Orchard Street, London.[1] A plan was hatched that he should chaperone them back to France the following year. But this enticing prospect was cruelly dashed when a fellowship became available that would allow Henry to begin his studies at Oxford University. And so instead, in August 1788, Eliza came to visit James and Henry in Oxford, where James had already completed a degree in preparation for taking clerical orders and Henry was about to take the same path. Phylly received an appraisal of the gardens at St John's College and of Henry aiming to impress with his fashionable air – his *bon ton* – and looking dangerously seductive: 'I do not think you would know Henry with his hair powdered & dressed in a very ton-ish style, besides he is at present taller than his father.'[2]

The journey to France had to be undertaken in mid-September without him. Eliza, suffering from disordered nerves, trapped in Paris by '*conjugal duties*' (as she darkly underlined) and a 'rude and riotous' toddler, would reflect yearningly on the Steventon theatricals and report to Phylly that Henry was apparently 'taller than ever'.[3] Height in a man is a great aphrodisiac, Jane would later concur. Mr Darcy in *Pride and Prejudice* instantly impresses at the Meryton Assembly with his 'fine, tall person'. Emma Woodhouse feels the first stirrings of physical attraction when she notices the 'tall, firm, upright figure' of her brother-in-law and neighbour Mr Knightley 'among the bulky forms and stooping shoulders of the elderly men' at the Highbury ball. She dexterously procures a dance with him, for 'you know we are not really so much brother and sister as to make it at all improper'. To which he can only reply, 'Brother and sister! – no, indeed' (III.ii).

Henry and Jane were brother and sister indeed, but this could not prevent her from fantasising about improprieties. As she entered adolescence her notions of passion were formed by the spectacle of her older brothers in thrall to Eliza. The spell cast by the play-acting of Christmas 1787, when make-believe fused with reality, lingered as the calendar brought round the next Steventon production. Henry was this time cast in the lead role in Isaac Bickerstaff's *The Sultan; or, A Peep into the Seraglio*. With Eliza absent, he played opposite another cousin, seventeen-year-old Jane Cooper, in the part of the rebellious English slave Roxalana who, a forerunner to Elizabeth Bennet, cocks a snook at male supremacy and wins the day. It was to Jane Cooper that *Henry and Eliza* was formally and 'humbly' dedicated by the young Jane Austen. The latter, not yet old enough to join in the acting, had been busily scribbling during rehearsals and no doubt the two Janes giggled together over the coupling. *Henry and Eliza* had been preceded by the chronicles of *Frederic and Elfrida*, *Jack and Alice*, and *Edgar and Emma*, but now daringly, outrageously, family names had been incorporated while the scenarios remained as wild as ever.

Stolen banknotes were a prominent feature of the stories most closely connected to Eliza. The wanderings of the fictional Eliza begin when she is discovered stealing a banknote from the Harcourts, and they end when she is forgiven following the revelation that they are her true parents. In *Love and Friendship*, a much more ambitious satire on sentimental conventions dedicated to Eliza in June 1790, genteel robbery is rife. The life story of the unfortunate Laura is related in a series of letters to Marianne, the daughter of her childhood friend Isabel. Laura is whisked away from the idyllic retirement of her parents' cottage in the Vale of Usk by young Edward Talbot, determined to marry in defiance of the wishes of his father Sir Edward. The small difficulty of a complete lack of funds is outweighed by the exalted claims of love.

Throughout *Love and Friendship*, the higher order of beings marked out by their 'delicate feeling, tender sentiments, and refined sensibility' think nothing of thieving from the brutish older generation. Excessive emotion is mingled with ruthless economic self-interest. Thus another young rebel, Augustus, 'gracefully' purloins a substantial sum of money from his unworthy father prior to eloping with Sophia. Soon Augustus and the like-minded Edward Talbot are imprisoned for debt, and Laura joins Sophia in taking refuge in the home of the latter's cousin, Macdonald. He is another despotic father as they see it, bent on marrying his young daughter to a respectable but woefully unromantic man. Consequently, the fugitives agree, they are fully justified in filching the banknotes hidden in a private drawer in his library. Sophia is unfortunately caught 'majestically removing the 5th banknote from the drawer to her own purse', and the two heroines take to the road again.[4]

Eventually Laura happens upon two cousins, Philander and Gustavus, kindred financial predators, who have run off with their mothers' combined fortune of £900 'always kept in a drawer in one of the tables which stood in our common sitting parlour, for the convenience of having it always at hand'.[5] Untouched by the news that the mothers have subsequently starved to death, they embark on a career as travelling players. It is in this guise that they lift two banknotes worth £50 each from Sophia and Laura while both ladies are prostrated by their habitual fainting fits. Poor Sophia indulges in one fainting fit too many and dies of a cold caught while lying unconscious outside as the dew falls, but Laura survives to be awarded a generous annuity by Sir Edward after the death of her husband in a carriage accident.

Bad behaviour is by no means unusual in Jane Austen's childhood writings. In *The Beautiful Cassandra*, a tribute to Jane's beloved older sister of

the same name, the heroine on the rampage in London is a serial offend-
er. At a pastry shop she devours six ices, refuses to pay for them, coolly
knocks down the pastry cook and walks away. Her next lark is a round
trip by hackney carriage to Hampstead. When the coachman demands
payment she places her bonnet on his head and scarpers. Capital crimes
feature in some short sketches presented to an infant niece. The hero of
a comic drama blithely declares his intention of supporting himself in
London with a 'bad guinea' – passing counterfeit coins was classed in
the criminal code as treason and carried the death penalty. *A Letter from
a Young Lady, whose feelings being too Strong for her Judgement led her into
the commission of Errors which her Heart disapproved* encompasses multi-
ple murders, a forged will and lying under oath in one medium-length
paragraph. But the theme of misappropriated banknotes seems to have
been uniquely attached to Eliza. Why?

Eliza Hancock was born on 22 December 1761, the daughter of a
surgeon in the employ of the East India Company and his wife Philadelphia *née* Austen, sister of the Reverend George Austen. The Hancocks
had returned to England in 1765 under the wing of their friend Warren
Hastings, the future Governor-General of Bengal. After three years, Dr
Hancock, short of funds, returned reluctantly to India, while his wife and
daughter remained, staying chiefly in London. Letters between England
and the subcontinent took six months or more to arrive. Dr Hancock
maintained contact with his wife as far as the uncertainties of weather
and shipping allowed, sending money and other valuables for her support, but he never regained a fortune sufficient to return to England and
died in 1775 without seeing his family again.

From the wreck of Hancock's financial affairs Eliza and her mother
emerged apparently unscathed. They led a peripatetic life in Germany
and Flanders for two years, and reached Paris in 1779 as Eliza turned
eighteen. There, they moved in the best circles. Eliza mingled with royalty
on several occasions, and in late 1781 married an officer of dragoons, Jean-
François Capot de Feuillide, who styled himself 'Comte de Feuillide' and

dazzled her with his high connections and expectations of an estate in Gascony, south-west France.

Her uncle the Reverend George Austen disapproved of the match, which he saw as a threat to her Protestant faith and to her fortune, held in trust for her by Mr Austen himself. The fund was a gift to Eliza from Warren Hastings, co-managed by his brother-in-law Mr John Woodman, yielding interest which gave her an annual income of around £600. At that time George Austen was raising a family of eight on a similar sum. In contrast to her magical inheritance, his income was laboriously acquired through church livings at Steventon and Deane and from farming of glebe and rented land, supplemented by tutoring boarders.

Jane was fascinated by one shocking aspect of the Hancock family history in particular. She incorporated experiences belonging to Eliza's mother, Philadelphia, into another of her early stories, *Catharine; or, The Bower*. The heroine's childhood friend is forced by the death of both her parents to accept the offer of a relative to finance a voyage to the East Indies. The objective was to find a rich husband. Catharine grows heated when her friend is casually described as 'lucky' to have been backed in this desperate gamble, and demands whether it could be considered 'lucky, for a girl of genius and feeling to be sent in quest of a husband to Bengal, to be married there to a man of whose disposition she has no opportunity of judging till her Judgement is of no use to her, who may be a tyrant, or a fool or both for what she knows to the contrary. Do you call *that* fortunate?'[6] Young women spent the perilous eight-month journey to Bengal anticipating an essentially involuntary union with a man who might be double their age. Marry or starve. The fictional Cecilia Wynne is trafficked to the personnel of the East India Company, just as the orphaned Philadelphia Austen had been in 1752.

These female migrants, dubbed the 'fishing fleet', landed marriage partners according to luck, looks and connections. Philadelphia's match with fretful melancholic Tysoe Saul Hancock, prematurely aged although only six years her senior, was probably helped along by her uncle Francis

Austen, who acted as Hancock's business agent in England. Hancock could not be considered a prize catch but the marriage was not a complete disaster, thanks to the network of 'fishing fleet beauties' who had sailed with Philadelphia aboard the *Bombay Castle*. One of them, Margaret Maskelyne, wed an ambitious young clerk turned soldier and administrator, Robert Clive, who would be chiefly responsible for the ruthless and rapacious imposition of British rule in the subcontinent. Another of her companions on the voyage out, Mary Elliot, married an officer who met an untimely fate in the Black Hole of Calcutta, imprisoned following the capture of Fort William by the Nawab of Bengal in 1756. But Mary's next husband, Warren Hastings, another clerk in the Company, went on to become one of the most powerful men in the world at the head of a great multinational corporation. Thanks to the intervention of Clive, Hancock was in 1759 appointed surgeon at Fort William, moving from Madras to Calcutta. It was there that he and Philadelphia became intimates in the circle of Hastings, when she nursed Hastings's wife, her old friend, through her final illness only a few months after the relocation. It was there that the Hancocks' first and only child, Elizabeth, was born in 1761, known in childhood as Betsy.

Warren Hastings stood as Betsy's godfather, but the intensity of his friendship with Philadelphia led to rumours that the relationship with her child was a nearer one. After the widowed Hastings and the Hancocks departed for England together in January 1765, a member of the Calcutta community, the wife of Clive's secretary, spread the scandalous report that Philadelphia had become Hastings's mistress. Lord Clive himself wrote to his wife in the home country to avoid keeping company with Mrs Hancock 'for it is beyond a doubt that she abandoned herself to Mr. Hastings'.[7] Hastings was not spotless when it came to women. A sentimental infidelity of exactly this kind occurred with the Baroness von Imhoff under the nose of a neglectful husband when she supported Hastings through a dangerous malady on his return passage to India in 1769. As Hancock would himself remark, 'Debauchery under the polite name of gallantry is the reigning vice of the settlement.'[8] Hastings would eventually marry the Baroness following divorce proceedings in 1777.

Other evidence that supports the idea that Hastings had fathered Philadelphia's daughter, perhaps with Mr Hancock's complicity, includes the eight years of childlessness before the Hancocks' move to Calcutta, the naming of the girl after Hastings's daughter who had died in infancy in 1758, and his unusually active lifelong interest in Betsy's well-being and financial support. He made extravagant monetary gifts to Betsy of £5,000 in 1772 and another £5,000 in 1774, which Hancock accepted on her behalf without demur. It has been objected that Hastings was given to acts of generosity, and that Philadelphia may well have had miscarriages prior to Elizabeth's birth. Certainly those most closely involved carried on the connection down the years with no apparent consciousness of guilt or shame. Yet one is struck by the warmth of the language in the confidential letters that passed between Hastings and Mrs Hancock; he addresses her as 'my dear and ever-valued friend' and she many years later, diffidently approaching him concerning business matters after a period of silence, drifts into intimacy, 'knowing your heart as I know it and being convinced that in spite of appearances it is not changed for your friends'.[9]

Such rumours or suppositions could not have been unknown to the Austens, whose own connection with Warren Hastings was of long standing. According to family tradition, Hastings's sickly young son had been sent to England and at Philadelphia's suggestion entrusted to the care of her brother the Reverend George Austen at Steventon in 1761. Sadly he had died there of 'a putrid sore throat', probably diphtheria, and it was said that George's young wife had grieved for the boy as if he were one of her own.[10] The story has been substantiated by records in Hastings's papers of a salary of £100 paid to 'Mr Austin' along with expenses for young George. Warren Hastings appears not to have held the loss of his child against the Austen family. He approved the appointment of George Austen as one of the trustees of Eliza's inheritance. Later he would do his best to pull strings in aid of the Austen sons.

In return, the Austens took a partisan interest in Hastings, who had been appointed Governor-General in India in 1773. A chequered series of military clashes with native rulers and widespread disgust at the profiteering of the East India Company had undermined his position and he arrived back in England in 1785 to face impeachment on charges of maladministration, corruption and extortion. A marathon trial followed, lasting from 1788 until his acquittal in 1795, during which the most celebrated political orators of the day regularly denounced him as a tyrant and a thief in the House of Commons. Philadelphia Walter, referred to here by her nickname 'Phylly' to avoid confusion, went to stay with Philadelphia Hancock and Eliza in London in April 1788. There she met Mrs Hastings and attended the trial for a full day from ten in the morning till four in the afternoon, particularly admiring the eloquence of Fox 'but not to our satisfaction as he is so much against Mr Hastings who we all here wish so well'.[11]

Echoes of these events would certainly have reached young Jane in Steventon in hushed exchanges and cryptic allusions. The rumours surrounding Hastings and his god-daughter may have provided inspiration for an unfinished comedy, designed to be presented as an afterpiece to the family theatricals of 1788. *The Mystery*, dedicated by Jane to her father, is wholly composed of enigmatic broken conversations, unfinished sentences and whispered revelations not shared with the audience: 'Are you convinced of its propriety?', 'You understand me, my love?', 'And what is to become of...'.[12] Jane seems to have been in the unsettling tradition of precocious adolescent girls who voraciously study the manners and morals of adults, piecing together the evidence and passing judgement. She was described at the time by Phylly Walter as 'not at all pretty & very prim, unlike a girl of twelve'.[13] Like Fanny Price in the opening volume of *Mansfield Park*, Jane looked without expecting to be looked at.

There was a *mystique* about Eliza and she cultivated it, describing herself as 'your outlandish cousin'.[14] She affected a humorous scepticism about the institution of marriage, once declaring 'I have an aversion to the word *Husband* & never make use of it.'[15] Her style was the coquette, rather than the operatic lover. Eliza's first choice of marriage partner could not be described as mercenary. The depredations were on the other side. But it was governed by a worldly desire for stability, rank and title rather than strong affection. The pattern of marital absenteeism set by Eliza's parents was continued into the next generation. Like young Jane, Eliza was an anti-sentimentalist when it came to affairs of the heart, and we can suppose she relished the mockery of high romance in *Love and Friendship*, where stolen kisses are funded by stolen banknotes. Sexual impropriety and financial impropriety stand in metaphorical relation.

Sometimes, however, a banknote in Jane Austen is just a banknote. The *Juvenilia* is full of startling satire on wealth and power. Take the opening of *Henry and Eliza*, which sees Sir George and Lady Harcourt 'superintending the Labours of their Haymakers, rewarding the industry of some by smiles of approbation, and punishing the idleness of others, by a cudgel'.[16] In both *Henry and Eliza* and *Love and Friendship* in 1788 Jane Austen registers an unruly force in modern British society, 'fictional' money, a disembodied substitute for precious metal. The poet Shelley would call it the 'ghost of gold'.

'Running cash notes' as an alternative to hard cash had been in use in Europe since the sixteenth century. Goldsmiths, the forerunners to bankers, issued hand-written notes promising to pay the bearer a specific sum in coinage on demand. The device was more convenient than carrying a bag of coins, and facilitated foreign trade and larger transactions. The issuing of banknotes commenced as a national enterprise with the founding of the Bank of England in 1694. The Bank was a private joint-stock company, designed to raise funds for King William III's war against France by providing receipts for deposits as legal tender. But the use of such new-fangled instruments was as yet restricted to a small monied elite and the authorities were keen to keep it that way. After the Great Recoinage of 1696 when the vast pool of clipped and devalued silver coins was melted down and legitimate coinage reissued, the minimum value of banknotes was raised to £50. At the same moment, in 1697, the forging of banknotes became a capital offence. Since the average yearly income was less than £20, the majority of people in the first half of the eighteenth century would have passed their lives without ever coming into contact with a banknote.

However, the trend was towards wider use of paper money. Nowhere was that better understood than in north-west Hampshire, in the vicinity of Winchester. In 1723 the Portal mill at Laverstoke was awarded a contract by the Bank of England to produce the fine rag paper required for its banknotes. Its founder Henry Portal, a French Huguenot refugee, had perfected the technique of the watermark. The Laverstoke paper was recommended to the Bank by William Heathcote, Portal's friend and neighbour. His nephew, Sir Gilbert Heathcote, presided as Governor of the Bank of England at the time when it began issuing partly printed notes for completion by hand. The era of mass-produced fixed denomination banknotes was imminent. The Portal family grew rich from the banknote trade and became leading figures in the county. They built a fine neo-classical villa designed by Joseph Bonomi, an architect who would gain a mention in *Sense and Sensibility*. Laverstoke was just five miles from Steventon, and James Austen was to preach at the church of St Nicholas in the parish, and meet and marry his first wife there. The Portals were among the dance partners of the Austen girls and Jane teased Cassandra about Benjamin Portal 'whose eyes are as handsome as ever', while their friend Mrs Lefroy recorded a visit to view the mill in 1801.[17]

With the spread of paper money came the risk of abuses and additions to the criminal code. Hanging was the sentence for passing, or 'uttering', forged notes, even if the crime was committed unknowingly. The severity of the punishment is a measure of the anxieties regarding control of this new financial medium. The financial system was coming to depend on banknotes and their legitimacy needed to be protected at any cost. Not until the 1830s, when the production and circulation of banknotes was more fully regulated, was the death penalty for forgery and uttering converted to transportation or life imprisonment. By 1745 notes were being part printed by an increasing number of small private banks in round sums ranging from £20 to £1,000, often using paper produced by the Portals, but David Hume in 1754 still spoke of 'this new invention of paper money'.[18]

From 1759, there were gold shortages caused by the Seven Years' War; the war that would deliver the Indian subcontinent to Britain. The Bank of England was forced to issue a £10 note for the first time. Smaller denominations brought banknotes into the lives even of the working poor. This major cultural shift can be charted through the literary fashion for 'it-narratives', novels in which objects or animals relate their experiences as they pass from one hand to another. The most famous and successful work in the genre was Francis Coventry's *The History of Pompey the Little* (1751), which takes a lapdog as its main protagonist. Pompey runs the gamut of owners from high-born Lady Tempest to a blind beggar and back again, introducing a wide range of satiric scenes. Money lent itself beautifully to these histories of social circulation. The earliest excursions in this mode took metal coins as hero, old-fashioned currency, capable of moving freely down as well as up the social scale: *The Adventures of a Halfpenny* appeared in the periodical *The Adventurer* in 1753, while *Chrysal: or, The Adventures of a Guinea* by Charles Johnstone was published in 1760, with an additional instalment in 1765.

The Adventures of a Bank-Note (1770–71) by Thomas Bridges, himself a failed banker, represents a conscious new departure. A poet receives thirty guineas from a publisher for a manuscript. After paying off his rent arrears and his debts to tradesmen, he finds he has twenty-one pounds, six shillings and ninepence, and three farthings left. Not enough to purchase a knighthood; and so as the next best thing, he decides to 'raise his dignity' by depositing £20 at the bank in exchange for a banknote. He intends to keep it, but is soon forced to change it for coins with a grocer, Mr Raisin-stone. Soon it is changing hands with dizzying velocity: 'by the Yorkshire clothier, I was paid to a wool-stapler; he paid me to a Nottingham weaver; the weaver changed me with the landlord at the Bull in Bishopsgate-street; the landlord paid me to the one-eyed Norwich warehouse-keeper; from him I went to a gingerbread-baker for gingerbread sent by the waggon into the country. By Timothy Treaclebread the gingerbread-baker, I was paid to Mrs. Coppernose, a rich brazier's widow, for rent: all this was performed in less than three hours. The duce fetch these men of business, says I to myself, they give very little rest, either to money or bank-notes.'

What is new here is the way the banknote, even one for as large a sum as £20, is able to pass readily in all walks of life. Paper money had become common currency. However, Bridge's depiction also has its old-fashioned side. The banknote storyteller distinguishes himself from money, on the grounds that he has an identifiable parent for 'the person that deposits cash for a bank-note may properly be called its father'. This banknote revels in the distinction of having a *poet* for a father, since 'the generality of bank-notes are noblemen's stewards, placemen's gentlemen, city user-ers, knowing stock-jobbers, bankers' clerks, and bishops' toll-gatherers'. The signature of the original depositor, 'Timothy Taggrhime', marks it out. In Henry Fielding's celebrated novel *Tom Jones* (1749) the return of lost or stolen banknotes to their original and rightful owners was a prominent plot device.

When in 1758 a cashier at the Bank of England refused to redeem a banknote that turned out to be stolen, although tendered unawares, it triggered the landmark lawsuit *Miller v. Race*. The judge Lord Mansfield ruled that the note must be considered as equivalent to cash, regardless of any original title to it. Banknotes 'are as much Money as Guineas themselves'; once a banknote enters into currency, the original owner has no further claim to it.[19] The fact that the case came to court in the first place showed that many still struggled with the idea that banknotes could circulate anonymously and impersonally, just as coins did. The ease with which banknotes are passed illicitly in *Love and Friendship* was a peculiarly modern phenomenon.

In *The Adventures of a Rupee* (1782) by Helenus Scott, an employee
of the East India Company, the peregrinations of the coin are sympto-
matic. Less than midway through the novel the rupee arrives in England
in the pocket of a sailor, never to return to India. 'Every rupee of profit
made by an Englishman', Burke was to tell the parliamentary inquiry
into Company corruption, 'is lost forever to India'.[20] Untold riches
would follow the same route, extracted with brutal efficiency from native
rulers and peasants alike through a mixture of military force and bribery.
The conquests of the 1750s gave birth to the culture of the 'nabobs', the
Anglo-Indian term for those who had succeeded in becoming obscenely
rich in the East Indies. This was the world into which Betsy Hancock was
born. Dr Hancock resigned his medical post with the Company in 1761,
the year of Betsy's birth, in order to set up private trade with Warren
Hastings, speculating in salt, timber, carpets, rice and Bihar opium.[21]

Tysoe Saul Hancock felt that a life of leisure and luxury was his due
in return for the many years of exertion, ill health and loneliness spent
in a godforsaken foreign land, but he never came near to acquiring the
stockpile of £44,000 that would yield the necessary annual income. After
just three years in England he went back to India in 1768 to try again.
Early expectations were dashed by the tragic loss of an outward-going
vessel, which simply vanished after leaving Cape Town. He was initially
barred from obtaining a *dustuck*, a licence to trade under Company protection and avoid local tolls, and unwillingly accepted another medical
post at Calcutta in order to qualify. Remitting money payments to Britain proved to be impossible, and he had to rely on Hastings in Madras
to act as go-between. Rough diamonds sent in the keeping of a ship's
captain were an easier means of transferring wealth. Hancock raged
against the dilatory accounting of Francis Austen, the uncle of Philadelphia and George; 'by his management I may be a fourth time ruined'.[22]
In August 1774 he lost 40,000 rupees, the equivalent of £5,000, due to
failed contracts and a shipping accident. When his wife, anxious about
his ever-worsening health, urged him to rejoin her, Hancock simply

observed that their capital of £20,000 would yield only £700 a year. As Philadelphia later reflected in a letter to Hastings, 'some people are born to be unfortunate'.[23]

The forty-three letters that have survived from Tysoe Hancock to Philadelphia and Betsy present an engrossing account of the colonial operation in microcosm. During the voyage back to India he had been considering seven-year-old Betsy's education and this becomes a constant theme. Should she be raised as a lady, given his bleak prospects? After consulting with Hastings, he decided that no expense should be spared. There had to be music and dance tutors, horse-riding and a good address in the fashionable West End of London. Just as the transported convict Magwitch in Dickens's *Great Expectations* endures the hardships and deprivations of colonial Australia, scrabbling to raise a fortune so that he can make a gentleman of his young benefactor Pip back in England, so Hancock struggled and contrived with every ounce of his waning energies to make his daughter a lady, knowing that he would probably never set eyes on her again. While Betsy bloomed and thrived in green, temperate Albion, he and everything around him turned to dust. Like Pip, Betsy at times recoiled from acknowledging the life-sapping sacrifices of this demanding stranger, as he became. Hancock complains that she never writes to him and when she does he complains about her poor handwriting. He describes piteously to his wife the slow destruction by heat and humidity of the miniature portrait of Betsy, which he has cherished like an icon in his solitude even though he found fault with the drawing. He begs her to keep Betsy's recollection of him alive. In Calcutta he keeps his expenses to a minimum; he sees no one and goes nowhere. But Philadelphia must not stint: no second-hand furniture, no economising on tuition, despite their expenditure being double their income. Betsy Hancock is the product of credit, which is derived in turn from the burgeoning empire in the East. Her upbringing exemplifies the dynamic between Britain and its colonies.

Betsy was intended to be ornamental, but she also had to understand money. The importance of learning arithmetic is another running theme in the correspondence. Hancock was exasperated by Philadelphia's ignorance of accounting. In April 1771 he sent Betsy, aged nine, a gift of 'four gold mohars' and turned it into a lesson in division and currency conversion: 'They are worth six pounds, eighteen shillings (6.18s) ... let me know how much each gold mohar is worth, & what you lose or gain by exchanging them.'[24] His purpose was fixed. He referred again to the 'mohars' in a letter dated eighteen months later, dismayed to learn that Betsy was still innumerate. He repeatedly urged his wife to advance Betsy's study of arithmetic as well as writing, and continued to send his daughter gold and silver coins as encouragement.

The girl's inheritance involved complex financial mechanisms. The first monetary gift from Warren Hastings to Betsy in 1772 took the form of 'a Respondentia bond for 40,000 rupees to be paid in China'. Hancock wrote to Philadelphia, 'I have given directions for the amount, which will be about £5,000 to be immediately remitted home to my attorneys.'[25] Respondentia is a type of loan which allows the lender to recover their capital with interest on the safe arrival of commodities by ship; a form of futures contract. In this instance, the commodity in question would have been opium. The following year Britain overtook Portugal as the lead supplier of opium to China. In spite of attempts by more than one emperor to ban the drug, trade was booming, driven by the desire of European powers to reduce the trade deficit with China. Hancock asked his wife to tell no one of the gift, 'not even the dearest friend you have'.[26]

A capable accountant was essential for dealing with remittances of various kinds from far-flung sources. Hancock insisted that Philadelphia keep large sums in the bank and make withdrawals as occasion required. He advised her to open an account with Gosling & Clive, at 19 Fleet Street. Instead she followed the lead of her brother George, and opened an account at Hoare's, one of the oldest private banks, where generations of Austens were to hold deposits. As Hancock felt death approaching in the course of 1775, he redoubled his efforts to make the family financially secure, sending a bank bill of £150, and setting up a trust fund with a further gift of £5,000 from Hastings, appointing Mr Woodman and George Austen as trustees. From his sickbed, he imagined every step to be taken: an indenture must be drawn up, George Austen must come to town, and the costs of his journey reimbursed. The interest would give Philadelphia a present income, and ensure a substantial fortune for Betsy in the long term. His last act was to send Betsy a gift of pearls and a filigree blotter.

Dr Hancock died aged fifty-two on 5 November 1775, a month before Jane Austen's birth. His legacy in the family can be found in *Sense and Sensibility* where Marianne and Willoughby regard Colonel Brandon as just such a tiresome East India hand as Hancock, forever explaining the 'existence of nabobs, gold mohrs, and palanquins' (I.x). News of his death only reached England in June 1776. He died in debt and Warren Hastings as executor would have the job of sorting out the confusion over many years.

John Woodman and George Austen lost no time in purchasing South Sea Annuities and Consols, government bonds, as interest-yielding investments for Philadelphia. They arranged the sale of rough diamonds for £3,939.3s.6d, set up the account at Hoare's Bank, and purchased further Consols the following year. In 1777 Betsy, now fifteen and preferring to be called Eliza, departed with her mother for the Continent, where the cost of living was cheaper. Their movements for the next two years can be traced through bank correspondence. In June 1778 Hoare's Bank wrote to Philadelphia in Brussels with notification that they were sending her bills of exchange for £200 drawable from a branch of Herries & Co. and a £200 letter of credit to Sir John Lambert in Paris. Expatriates on the move needed to be conversant with methods of bank transfer, and had to keep in close contact with bank agents.

The Reverend George Austen has often been represented as almost a self-sufficient yeoman farmer, overseeing harvests, tending poultry and appraising pigs at the local market when not reading a book or preparing the next sermon in the retirement of his study. But the history of Eliza shows him in a rather different light, as a man of affairs conversant with finance, and this is borne out by the high level of activity in the ledgers of his own account at Hoare's Bank, over which he seems to have maintained tight control. Based on the ledger records, Deirdre Le Faye's *Chronology of Jane Austen and Her Family* notes frequent transactions on the stock exchange. There is no indication there that he ever went into the red. His wife Cassandra Austen appears to have been similarly methodical, keeping careful household accounts. As early as 1760, aged twenty-nine and still a proctor at Oxford University, George became the trustee of a slave plantation in Antigua at the request of one of his former pupils, James Langford Nibbs. Dr Hancock naturally turned to him when seeking a safe pair of hands for Eliza's fortune. Soon after, in 1778, he was appointed as one of the commissioners to oversee the construction of the Basingstoke Canal.

Where George and Cassandra Austen were profligate was in the number of their offspring relative to income. The gloomy Dr Hancock protested against the 'violently rapid increase' of their family, on learning from Philadelphia of the birth of Henry, their fourth child.[27] James had been born on 13 February 1765, a tidy nine months after the wedding day. Then on 26 August 1766 came George; on 7 October 1767, Edward; 8 June 1771, Henry; 9 January 1773, Cassandra. Mr Austen had already sold off in parcels his £800 worth of South Sea Annuities, and it was at this point that the overstretched Austen family finances reached a crisis. Mrs Austen's brother James Leigh-Perrot came to the rescue with a money order for £300 paid into the Reverend Austen's account in February 1773. A more permanent increase came the following month with the presentation, courtesy of Uncle Francis Austen, of the clerical living in the neighbouring village of Deane, worth £110 yearly. That summer, too, the Austens began taking in regular boarders, three or four at a time, to be tutored for university entrance for fees ranging from £35 to £65 a year. The family continued to grow: on 23 April 1774, Francis; 16 December 1775, Jane; and finally, Charles on 23 June 1779.

A family of eight, like the family of ten described at the start of *Northanger Abbey*, must always be called a fine family where there are heads and arms and legs enough to go around. But while all the children were healthy, there were fears soon after the birth of George, the second son, that something was lacking. He had a mental disability, was subject to fits, and may have been a deaf mute. It was the additional cost involved that gave Dr Hancock concern, particularly given his role as the boy's godfather. Before long, young George was exiled from the family and delivered to the care of the Culhams in the nearby village of Monk Sherborne, to join his 'imbecile' uncle Thomas Leigh. He remained there until his death at the age of seventy-two. His upkeep had been paid first by his father and then by his brother Edward, but he had never been readmitted to the family circle. The solution was relatively humane by the standards of the time, for the struggles of a large and impecunious family with only a tenuous grip on gentility involved a focus on the survival of the fittest that could be ruthless.

By this measure Henry was early on the source of great pride. Mrs Austen wrote to Mrs Walter on 20 August 1775, marvelling at the way he seemed determined to bridge the gap with his next oldest brother: 'Henry has been in breeches some months and thinks himself near as good a man as his brother Neddy, indeed no one would judge by their looks that there was above three years and a half difference in their ages, one is so little and the other so great'.[28] Neddy was to have the fairy-tale future. Adopted by childless relations at the age of fifteen, he eventually became the owner of a great estate. But in the Reverend Austen's view, Henry outstripped him in natural abilities. Anna Lefroy was to reflect in later years, 'My Uncle Henry Thomas Austen was the handsomest of his family, and, in the opinion of his own father, also the most talented … Brilliant in conversation, and like his father, blessed with a hopefulness of temper, which, in adapting itself to all circumstances, even the most adverse, seemed to create a perpetual sunshine of the mind.' Anna adds that some 'considered his abilities greater in show than in reality' (her own father, the eldest brother James, had less showy talents), but that 'for the most part he was greatly admired'. Henry shared his father's sanguine temperament, and also inherited a striking physical feature, eyes of 'a peculiar and bright hazel'. 'None of the children had precisely the same excepting my uncle Henry', Anna recalled, although 'aunt Jane's were something like them'.[29]

The pairing of Henry and Jane was standard in the family; a response to some kind of innate bond which went beyond kinship or external characteristics. Mrs Austen was struck by it from the moment Jane was born. She wrote to Mrs Walter on the day after, 'We have now another girl, a present plaything for her sister Cassy and a future companion. She is to be Jenny, and seems to me as if she would be as like Henry, as Cassy is to Neddy.'[30] When Phylly Walter met Jane at age twelve and judged her 'not at all pretty' she also remarked that she was 'very like her brother Henry'.[31] If the likeness didn't extend to good looks, then the observations must have been occasioned by inward or metaphysical qualities. The two were cosmically linked, facing each other across the year, June and December, summer solstice and winter solstice, complementary opposites.

The short stories, dialogues, and unfinished novels Jane wrote as a girl represent her own commentary on the dynamics of her familial circle. Each of them is graced with an elaborate mock-dedication to some family member or close friend. Four are dedicated to her beloved sister Cassandra, destined to be her constant companion through life. The appreciation of each for the other was profound. Cassandra was to write with passionate eloquence after Jane's death, 'She was the sun of my life, the gilder of every pleasure, the soother of every sorrow, I had not a thought concealed from her, & it is as if I had lost a part of myself.'[32] Jane eulogised Cassandra in one of the childhood dedications, and certainly meant it: 'Madam, You are a phoenix. Your taste is refined, your sentiments are noble, and your virtues innumerable.'[33] Cassandra was a collaborator as well as dedicatee of one of Jane's most substantial early works, *The History of England*, providing amusing illustrations to accompany the comic text. *Catharine, or the Bower*, in which we can find the first traces of Jane's mature style, was also dedicated to her.

The two youngest brothers, Frank and Charles, were each presented with two comic skits, designed to cheer them as they underwent naval training far from home. The two eldest nieces Anna and Fanny, daughters of James and Edward respectively, were both given at birth nonsensical 'scraps' and 'morsels' in the guise of moral instruction. In addition to *Love and Friendship*, her cousin Jane received one of the best dedications, for *A Collection of Letters*, a graceful tribute composed almost entirely of words beginning with the letter 'C' in honour of her surname 'Cooper'. The rest of the clan had to make do with just one dedication among the works handed down.

Lesley Castle, the sole early piece dedicated to 'Henry Thomas Austen Esqre', was composed as late as 1792 when she was seventeen and he twenty-one, still at Oxford preparing for ordination as a clergyman. It is the second of the works, copied neatly into *Volume the Second*, following *Love and Friendship*. The dedication reads, 'I am now availing myself of the liberty you have frequently honoured me with of dedicating one of my novels to you', suggesting that either Henry had also written novels and dedicated them to her, or had been the beneficiary of several of Jane's earlier efforts. In either case, the works have been lost or destroyed, like the many letters she wrote to him, and he to her, over the coming years. In subsequent biographical accounts the relationship of Henry and Jane has remained muted, partly owing to the loss of direct dialogue between them. The one survival is this dedication, which is answered on the same page by a playful acknowledgement written and signed by Henry: 'Messrs Demand and Co – please to pay Jane Austen Spinster the sum of one hundred guineas on account of your Humbl. Servant. H. T. Austen. £105.0.0.'[34] It is a nice bookkeeping flourish that the one hundred guineas in payment are precisely converted into pounds sterling. The sum must have seemed to them both at the time a magnificent one.

At a stroke, Henry prophesied his own diverted course into a career in

finance, and his role in launching his talented sister as a professional paid
writer. She, of course, had already prophetically fantasised his improbable
future with Eliza.

Henry and Eliza was only one of several early stories that featured
family names. There are a scattering of characters called George, James,
Edward, and Charles, as well as *The Beautiful Cassandra*. Henrys pre-
dominate, however, with the peculiarity that they are all rapidly killed
off. This is such a marked feature that it must have been a private joke.
Eliza's Henry dies just four paragraphs after his first introduction. It may
seem like cheating to include in this survey the five Henrys from *The
History of England from the reign of Henry the 4th to the death of Charles
the 1st*, but the principle of selection creates, especially at the start, the
effect of a succession of dead Henrys, each allotted paragraph ending on
an insistent down-note: 'the King died' (Henry IV); 'Inspite of all this
however he died' (Henry V); 'The King was murdered' (Henry VI); 'His
Majesty died' (Henry VII); 'The King's last wife contrived to survive him,
but with difficulty effected it' (Henry VIII).[35]

Dead Henrys in English history are a matter of course, but Jane then
went on to add three more fictional ones to the inventory. In *Evelyn*,
a bewilderingly convoluted tale, we are given the story of Rose, the
grief-stricken sister of the main protagonist Mr Gower. Only belatedly
is it revealed that the husband whose untimely end in a shipwreck off
the Isle of Wight eventually leads to hers is a Henry. Eventually it emerges that the report of Rosa's demise was false but Henry, alas, remains
dead. The second instance, surprisingly, was in the very work dedicated
to Henry Austen. The action is dated 1792, the year it was written. The
first we hear of Henry Hervey in *Lesley Castle*, he has been thrown from
his horse, fractured his skull and been 'pronounced by his surgeon to be
in the most eminent danger' [*sic*]. He fulfils the prediction and promptly
dies, just days before he was to have married Eloisa (doubtless another
teasing reference to Eliza). The tragedy is related in a letter to a friend by
Eloisa's sister Charlotte Lutterell, who is an obsessive cook and far more

distressed by the wasted wedding feast than the loss of the bridegroom: 'what in the name of Heaven will become of all the victuals!'[36] The focus of the unfinished tale soon shifts towards the antics of Sir George Lesley who takes as his second wife a vain young woman primed to tyrannise her stepdaughters. Yet a gleam of genuine pathos regarding ill-fated Henry escapes the framework of folly and satire. Margaret Lesley observes that 'there never were two young people who had a greater affection for each other than Henry and Eloisa'.[37] And Eloisa confides to a friend, 'The possibility of being able to write, to speak, to you, of my lost Henry will be a luxury to me, and your goodness will not I know refuse to read what it will so much relieve my heart to write.'[38]

There is a similarly lost Henry in *A Collection of Letters*. Here the strangeness is magnified by the fact that he was the husband of a charming woman who goes by the name of 'Miss Jane'. When she is induced to tell her story, she reveals that having married Henry Dashwood without the consent of her father, she contrived to keep it a secret even after bearing two children by passing them off as the children of a brother. After Henry was killed 'fighting for his country in America', and the children and then her father died in quick succession, there seemed no reason to reveal her true marital status.[39]

As in *Henry and Eliza*, Jane seems to have been mischievously pairing Henry with an older female cousin; in this case, Miss Jane Cooper, the dedicatee of the piece, who was the same age as Henry and had played opposite him in the Steventon theatricals. But the fact that Henry Dashwood has an equivocal identity as husband and brother of Miss Jane suggests that the author may have been unconsciously trespassing in forbidden regions. Could the unhappy endings of these various fictive marriages have been a form of wish fulfilment?

On 1 July 1788, Henry, aged seventeen, took up his fellowship at Oxford University. James had been there since 1779, having been admitted at the early age of fourteen, but in spite of cherishing literary ambitions and producing his poems and theatrical epilogues, it wasn't until the

galvanising arrival of Henry that he actually ventured into print. On 31
January 1789 the brothers launched an Oxford-based periodical titled *The
Loiterer*, inspired by Samuel Johnson's journal *The Rambler* and similarly
devoted to the observation of contemporary manners and morals. Each
issue was composed of an essay or narrative. James wrote twenty-seven
of them, Henry contributed ten and the rest were the work of student
friends, including Benjamin Portal. The journal had some success; the
sixty numbers were collected and republished in two volumes, reaching a
readership beyond the university. This development must have electrified
Jane; her brothers had broken into the literary public sphere. Over the
course of *The Loiterer*'s fourteen-month lifespan a good deal of the planning, discussion and composition would have taken place at Steventon,
where she could participate.

Traces of Jane's influence have been discovered in the pages of *The
Loiterer*, and one item in particular has been confidently attributed to
her. Issue number 9, published 28 March 1789, includes a letter from
'Sophia Sentiment' complaining that the journal had nothing to offer
female readers, and James wrote a tongue-in-cheek reply. The question of
whether this letter represents Jane's public debut has been debated and
on balance the evidence suggests that it does, given overlaps in style and
substance with *Love and Friendship*. A factor that hasn't previously been
taken into account is Jane's relationship with Henry. The letter specifically finds fault with the previous number: 'The Confessions of a Profligate
Undergraduate', written by Henry and signed 'H. Homely'. Sophia Sentiment protests that although the story was 'good enough' there was 'no
love, and no lady in it, at least no young lady', and she goes on to suggest
a number of appropriately turgid plot twists. She ends by insisting that
melodrama and fatalities are essential ingredients if the author wants to
please the ladies, and offers assistance. But if her wise words are ignored,
'may your work be condemned to the pastry-cook's shop', where it will be
used to wrap pies and pasties, 'and may you always continue a bachelor,
and be plagued with a maiden sister to keep house for you'.[40]

A threat, or a promise? The idea of keeping house for a bachelor brother was the dream of many a maiden sister at the time. Marriage was a lottery; every pregnancy a dangerous game of chance. For a girl like Jane, vigilant against romantic nonsense, without any prospect of independent means and with ardent aspirations as a writer, what could be better than living with a beloved brother who also published? Dorothy Wordsworth would live that dream with her brother William in the 1790s.

Caroline Austen, James's younger daughter, recollected that although Jane was an affectionate sister to all her brothers, 'one of them in particular was her especial pride and delight'.[41] She remained steadfast in that 'especial pride and delight', regardless of circumstances, to the end of her life. On one occasion she told Cassandra that she had expended 'wit & leisure' writing to Henry because 'he desired to hear from me very soon' and had sent a letter to *her* that was 'most affectionate & kind, as well as entertaining; - there is no merit to him in *that*, he cannot help being amusing'.[42] We can take it on trust that there were many such exchanges, and that he reciprocated her preference. Although for a long while his attention was focused on career and courtship, and he would always be prone to the social distractions that naturally arose as a consequence of his sunny and gregarious temperament, it was Henry who recognised the necessity of getting Jane's novels into print, and had the drive and knowhow to make it happen. His affection for her included an apprehension of her genius keener than that of anyone else in the family. To make the world take notice of her work eventually became a mission, even an obsession.

The prophetic scribblings of their early years suggest a recognition that he was her future, and she was his. Each would somehow aid the other to escape their modest provincial destinies and enter the public stage. This is the story of Henry and Jane.

CHAPTER 1

DEAD MEN'S SHOES:
LADY SUSAN, ELINOR AND MARIANNE, FIRST IMPRESSIONS (1793–1800)

Louis XVI, the deposed King of France, was publicly executed in Paris on 21 January 1793. Ten days later the new French Republic and Great Britain were at war. On 8 April, Henry Austen enlisted as a lieutenant in the Oxfordshire Militia and set out to join his unit at Southampton.

The French Revolution, that seismic shift in European politics, abruptly created a new opening in Henry's life. He had been on the brink of ordination as a clergyman. His father, the Reverend George Austen, a penniless orphan at the age of six, owed his present income and social credit to the lifeline of a scholarship awarded by his school at Tonbridge, allowing him to attend St John's College, Oxford. A degree from one of the two ancient universities was the essential qualification for entering the clerical profession. In the next generation, the two most bookish sons, James and Henry, were to be given the chance of pursuing the same quietly respectable career. Their Oxford scholarships came thanks to the fact that through their mother, Cassandra Leigh, they were 'founder's kin', descendants of one of the grandfathers of the founder of St John's College. Irene Collins, in her study *Jane Austen and the Clergy*, has explained the thinking behind this privilege. It was considered as im-memorial compensation to descendants for the diversion of wealth that might otherwise have been handed down to them. The scholarships were called 'fellowships' and provided residence and an allowance for as long as the incumbent chose to remain single and earned below a certain limit. But there were only six available. Aspirants must wait until one of the existing fellows graduated and moved out, married, or died. The system was known as 'waiting for dead men's shoes'.

St John's College had been from the moment of its foundation a beacon of bourgeois orthodoxy. The founder was Sir Thomas White, a leading member of the Merchant Taylors Guild and Lord Mayor of London, who in Mary Tudor's time had endowed the college to train clergymen who would counter the heresies of Calvin and Luther. But it opened its doors as Elizabeth began her Protestant reign, and became instead a factory for Anglican ministers. It continues to possess famously extensive gardens that must then have been welcome to country boys like James and Henry. Their journal *The Loiterer* contained a spirited defence of commerce by an anonymous friend, who remarked 'that more than one of our colleges derives its chief support' from men of trade, a class typically despised by the students who benefited from their largesse.[1]

With placid diligence Henry had followed in the footsteps of his brother James, who by 1793 was installed as rector of Sherborne St John and Cubbington. Henry began his studies aged seventeen, was awarded his BA qualification after the standard four years, and then fulfilled the residence requirements in the normal way for a further three, tutoring undergraduates. On 8 June he would turn twenty-four, the door to the Church would open, and he would enter. But with the outbreak of war another door appeared where none had existed before and Henry walked through it, with no fixed idea of where it might lead.

The Oxfordshire Militia was a newly formed regiment. Its command-ing officers were looking to fill the lower ranks and prepared to overlook an inability to fulfil the property requirements, should the right sort of man come along. Henry was expected to provide evidence of income from land to the value of £50 per annum, half of it being held in the county, but got round the conditions and gained an officer's commission through connections and recommendations.

The change of plan seems to have caused little surprise or dismay at home. Mr and Mrs Austen already had a son in the armed forces, for Frank was now a lieutenant in the navy. Charles was in the second year of training in the Naval Academy at Portsmouth, and would go to sea the following year. Furthermore, the militia was something like a home guard, a volunteer force, distinct from the regular army. It was unlikely that Henry would see action abroad and most believed the war would be short-lived. How long could the upstart French Republic resist the combined might of the major European nations now including Britannia, ruler of the waves? But the British campaign got off to a ragged start, France went from success to success on the Continent, and for the remainder of the decade England lived with the constant fear of invasion. Henry's Oxfordshire regiment was occupied with training new recruits, escorting prisoners of war captured by the fleet to inland prisons, helping to quell mutiny in the navy and dealing with riots in its own ranks, even undertaking a year-long tour of duty in Ireland following the large-scale rebellion there in 1798. But above all, guarding the coastline against invasion – which meant several not unpleasant sojourns by the seaside at Southampton, Brighton, Portsmouth, Yarmouth and the Isle of Wight. There was plenty of socialising with the locals, dancing, gaming and philandering, especially during the inactive winter months, when the officers and troops were billeted at inns.

In the early years, Henry was able to obtain leave of absence for up to two months at a time on several occasions in order to complete his academic qualifications at Oxford, to visit family, or to join a shooting party. He was keeping his options open and might still eventually return to the clerical fold. His relationship with the commanding officer, Corporal Lord Charles Spencer, the second son of the third Duke of Marlborough, was amicable from the start and turned into an enduring friendship. One of these periods of leave allowed him to miss at least some of the most disturbing episodes in the regiment's history in the spring of 1795, when food shortages and appalling conditions in freezing unfinished barracks near Brighton led to rioting among the rank and file in the company. The soldiers had to purchase their own food supplies, and their daily pay (1s. 1/2d) was now only equivalent to a loaf of bread. Privates from the regiment joined local men in seizing shipments of grain in Newhaven, enraged by stockpiling and profiteering. Henry was recalled from Oxford, but pleaded illness. He was present, however, to witness the exemplary punishment, an eerie event in a vale outside Brighton where massed ranks of men stood in silence while two of the ringleaders were shot over their coffins by firing squad, and four others were flogged almost to death, 300 lashes each. A handbill was passed around nearby Lewes with the revolutionary message in verse to 'arise and revenge your Cause,/ On those bloody numskulls, Pitt and George':

> Haste soldiers now, and with intrepid hand
> Grasp sword and gun to save thy native land
> For see your comrades murder'd, ye with resentments swell
> And join the rage, the aristocrat to quell...[2]

There was feverish anxiety among the ruling class concerning the spread of French Jacobinism, and the Oxfords were threatened with disbandment or even transportation. The government, seriously alarmed, responded with brutality but also took some constructive action to reduce discontent in the ranks. Regular rations replaced cash allowances and the barrack-building was expedited. It is likely that Henry and other liberal-minded officers comforted themselves with these improvements.

Jane, at home in Steventon, was keeping a close eye on Henry's progress as she prepared to launch her own career. His decision to take the King's shilling seems to have been her cue to put aside childish things. The period of her literary apprenticeship, writing the skits and sketches of the *Juvenilia*, ended on 3 June 1793 when she added into *Volume the*

First a final item, the 'Ode to Pity'. It was a burlesque on the melancholy clichés of pre-Romantic poetry, replete with moonbeams, nightingales and mouldering abbey. But there was a surprise at the head of the second of the two verses:

> Gently brawling down the turnpike road,
> Sweetly noisy falls the Silent Stream[3]

Henry's regiment was at that moment 'gently' or not so gently 'brawling down the turnpike road', guarding 250 prisoners on the way from Southampton to Salisbury. The roads of the southern counties were alive with redcoats. She would march in step with him. She started building up her storytelling stamina with a novella in the form of letters, *Lady Susan*. Her next attempt would be a serious strike at publication. She began drafting, also in letter form, a story around two sisters, Elinor and Marianne, geographically divided in the standard way, each reporting to the other her trials and tribulations.

In November of 1794, the Oxfords went into winter quarters in east Hampshire and Henry took three weeks' leave and spent time with his family. He was able to be at the rectory on Jane's nineteenth birthday, to see her receive the gift from her father of a mahogany writing desk with a drawer for paper and a 'glass ink stand complete': the tools of her intended trade.[4] And he had excellent news to share and mull over with his parents and sisters. He had been appointed acting Paymaster, purely on merit. It was a position of responsibility and trust, which involved handling all the financial business of the regiment and supervising the distribution of an annual payroll of £15,000 per year. Quite by accident, Henry had discovered his vocation. He quickly developed a flair not only for keeping accounts, but also for charming clients. And before long, he awoke to the opportunities for increasing personal profit by acting as private banker to other officers.

Now feeling himself a rising man, Henry plucked up courage while on leave at Oxford in April 1795 to write and congratulate Warren Hastings after he emerged victorious from the show trial on his alleged abuses in India. Henry's eagerness to make a good impression was apparent in the stilted formality of his prose:

Dear Sir,

An humble, and hitherto a silent spectator of national concerns, permit me at the present interesting moment to transgress the strictness of propriety, and though without permission, I hope without offence to offer you the warm & respectful congratulations of a heart deeply impressed with a sense of all you have done & suffered. Permit me to congratulate my country & myself as an Englishman; for right dear to every Englishman must it be to behold the issue of a contest where forms of judicature threatened to annihilate the essence of justice.

Engaged as you must be by those who are more relatively though not more abstractedly interested in this late decision than myself, I dare not take up more of your leisure, for intruding on any part of which I already owe an apology, though I have none to offer except that the many instances of your kindness shewn to me have long since justified the sincerity of that respect & esteem with which I now take the liberty of subscribing myself

Your much obliged and
much attached humble Servt
Henry Thos Austen[5]

It is easy to imagine that this convoluted missive cost Henry agonising effort, and more than one sheet of paper crumpled and tossed aside. His anxiety to gain favour probably had less to do with Hastings's renewed political influence or Henry's career advancement than with an event which had taken place early the previous year. On 22 February 1794 the Comte de Fueillide, Eliza's husband, was taken from his prison cell to the guillotuine in the Place de la Révolution in Paris.

During the 1780s, the Comte had pursued land reclamation schemes at the ancestral home, Le Marais near Guyenne. James Austen had visited in 1786 and admired his agricultural improvements. But the draining of the marsh had been resented by the local peasantry, who lost access to common land and wildfowl, and come the revolution this put the Comte in a vulnerable position. He moved back to Paris in 1792 intending to travel onwards to England, but found himself trapped and under surveillance as a would-be *émigré*. At the height of Robespierre's Reign of Terror he attempted to bribe a functionary into releasing a titled friend and ended up on the block himself. The news only reached Eliza in June, accompanied by strange rumours. It was said that in a frantic bid to evade the death sentence he had attempted to persuade the court that he was a mere valet who had murdered the true Comte de Feuillide and assumed his identity.[6]

Eliza left London and paid an extended visit to friends in Northumberland. But she was not absent from the minds of certain Austen family members. *Lady Susan* is transparently inspired by Eliza's anticipated comeback as a merry widow. Jane had a hunch that the Comte's untimely end would not subdue her lively spirits for long. The widowed Lady Susan Vernon is not an exact portrait, for Eliza in reality does not seem to have been particularly mercenary and manipulative, but Jane gave her the same rakish letter-writing style. Jane also bestowed on the fictional character physical traits borrowed from her cousin. Lady Susan is 'delicately fair, with fine grey eyes and dark eyelashes', in her mid-thirties but with the allure of a woman ten years younger.[7] Jane understood that for Eliza flirtation was a form of stoicism and a psychological survival tool. They would share this English version of *Les Liaisons Dangereuses*, the most famous fictional portrayal of amatory power play, and laugh together. Eliza had once jokingly explained to her cousin Phylly the nature of her affinity to the younger of the Austen sisters: 'My heart gives the preference to Jane, whose kind partiality to me, indeed requires a return of the same nature.'[8]

Henry was also thinking of Eliza as he laboured to compose an

ingratiating letter to her godfather Warren Hastings, the only parent
remaining to her since her mother's death two years earlier. The enchantment of that acting Christmas had never been dispelled. Towards the end
of his time as a student at Oxford, there had been the threat of a terrible
rift, but she had forgiven him. As was her custom, she confided in Phylly:

> Henry is now rather more than six foot high I believe, he also is much im-
> proved, and is certainly endowed with uncommon abilities, which indeed
> seem to have been bestowed, tho' in a different way, upon each member of
> this family. – As to the coolness which you know had taken place between
> H. and myself, it has now ceased, in consequence of due acknowledge-
> ments on his part, and we are at present on very proper relationlike terms,
> you know that his family design him for the church.[9]

She had added, 'Pray do not neglect burning this.' The question may
be asked why a long letter mainly concerned with unsensational news of
the Austen family should need to be destroyed? The oblique reference
to the coolness between Eliza and Henry suggests an answer. Eliza was
estranged from her husband; there may have been a move or declaration
of some kind from Henry, something that deviated from 'proper relationlike terms' and earned a rebuke from her.

All the while Eliza continued to eye Henry in something other than a
'relationlike' way. Now he was twenty-three, no longer a growing boy, it
was less easy to pass off continuing exclamation over his height and other
attractions as mere cousinly monitoring. And given Eliza's dim view of the
clerical life, the abrupt statement in the letter: 'You know that his family
design him for the church' could be taken as both a guilty admission that she
had been entertaining thoughts of him as a potential mate, and reassurance
to herself rather than her correspondent that he had been ruled out. Henry
knew of her aversion to the clergy and preference for an officer's uniform.
In spite of the hopelessness of his cause this knowledge may have played a
part in his decision to join the militia soon after their quarrel was mended.

After leaving Oxford in 1790, the aspiring author James Austen had subsided into a hunting, shooting country clergyman, in possession of two parishes just as obscure as Steventon and living in the village of Deane adjacent to it. Following morning service at Sherborne St John he stayed to dine at the Vyne manor house with his patron, the notoriously backward-looking William Chute, who refused to mend the muddy road to his house because he preferred to enjoy the winters in seclusion with his horses and hounds. James's comfortable existence was ruptured by the sudden death of his wife Anne Mathew in May 1795. His thoughts, too, quickly turned to Eliza. Documentation is lacking, but the family tradition has it that in the autumn of 1795 both James and Henry were courting Eliza, and she flirted happily without any intention of submitting to matrimony again in a hurry. Although keen to visit country cousins, she was ensconced in London among wealthy French émigrés and returned nabobs, lodging in the district above Oxford Street and south of the present-day Marylebone Road. Henry actually proposed at this point, but she turned him down.

In the early part of 1796 James also made his intentions plain. Eliza stalled and her friends teased her, Phylly dropping hints about 'domestic retreat', and Sophia Burrell, a talented poet, writing 'To Eliza, a Dialogue between Inclination and Prudence.' 'Prudence' favours the 'gilded bait' and scorns both the 'quartered Captain' whose 'paltry pay can scarce produce, Enough for regimental use' and the church minister in his 'parsonage by yew trees bounded, And with infernal roads surrounded' doomed to 'be a drone for life'. But 'Inclination' can't help but dwell on the pleasures of rural retirement.[10] Lady Burrell could afford to entertain romantic ideas of love in a cottage with a cultivated clergyman. She was the daughter of the East India Company magnate turned banker Sir Charles Raymond, the heiress to £100,000, with a town house in Harley Street and an estate in the country. Prudently, she had married a wealthy cousin twice her age, lately deceased. No sooner had she buried him than she gave her heart to the Reverend William Clay twelve years her junior, tutor to one of her sons, and moved to the Isle of Wight.

In *Love and Friendship*, the father of the heroine Laura had been 'bred to the Church' and therefore considered himself qualified to conduct a marriage service, although he had not actually taken holy orders.[11] Now aged twenty, Jane was ready to consider more deeply the question of men's vocations and, by extension, women's options when deciding on a husband. She had seen her brothers channelled one by one into their allotted places in life; all apart from Henry, who although bred to the Church remained unfixed. In her latest work in progress, *Elinor and Marianne,* she introduced another such young man still reviewing the alternatives although as the eldest son in a wealthy family he has the luxury of not working at all. Edward Ferrars, in the revised version of the story published many years later as *Sense and Sensibility*, rules out the army – 'too smart for me'; the law is 'allowed to be genteel enough' but he has no inclination for it; the navy 'has fashion on its side'; while the Church, his preference, is 'not smart enough for my family' (I.xix).

Being the daughter of a clergyman Jane was naturally biased towards the clerical profession; she arranges for three of the six heroes in her published novels, including Edward Ferrars, to take the cloth. Nonetheless she was fully alive to the perceived disadvantages, and would place the most outspoken objections in the mouth of a character often assumed to have been based on her cousin Eliza. 'A clergyman is nothing,' Mary Crawford tells Edmund Bertram in *Mansfield Park*, chagrined to find that the man she had been looking upon with favour is about to be ordained, 'You really are fit for something better.' Everyone knew that clerical orders often meant a humdrum existence among narrow provincials on an insufficient income; 'I thought *that* was always the lot of the youngest, where there were many to choose before him.' With her own brother-in-law in mind Mary concludes damningly, 'A clergyman has nothing to do but be slovenly and selfish – read the newspaper, watch the weather, and quarrel with his wife. His curate does all the work, and the business of his own life is to dine' (I.ix).

'Soldiers and sailors are always acceptable in society. Nobody can wonder that men are soldiers and sailors', is another of Mary Crawford's dictums (I.xi). With such ideas doubtless echoing in his head, Henry continued in his erratic course. Jane's first surviving letter, dated 9 January 1796, includes two reports on Henry that perfectly illustrate his vacillating state of mind. He had tried and failed to buy an adjutancy, the next step up in the militia, and was now 'hankering after the regulars', thinking of trying for an officer's commission in the 86th, 'a new raised regiment, which he fancies will be ordered to the Cape of Good Hope' on the trade route to India. Jane ends this report by remarking to Cassandra, 'I heartily hope that he will, as usual, be disappointed in this scheme.' She was facing the departure of Tom Lefroy, the visiting nephew of her friend Madame Lefroy and the first dance partner to excite her interest seriously, and could not bear the loss of another 'most agreeable young man', namely Henry.[12] Postings abroad were full of peril, and the Austens in Steventon perpetually combed the newspapers and navy lists for tidings of Frank and Charles. Cassandra's fiancé, Tom Fowle, was about to sail to the West Indies as private chaplain to the Colonel of the 3rd Regiment of the Foot. The following April they would learn that he had been struck down by yellow fever before arriving.

In the same letter Jane mentions that Henry was off to Oxford to be awarded his Master's degree, in line with the original clerical scheme intended for him. With the encouragement of his wealthy older brother Edward, he was exploring the idea of buying the succession to the living at Chawton, a pleasant village not far from Steventon on the main road from London to Gosport. A 'living', also known as a benefice, was an appointment accruing income gained from tithes, 10 per cent of all earnings or produce in the parish, and the use of 'glebe' land belonging to the church. In the period 7,000 livings out of 11,342 in England and Wales were gifts to be distributed by aristocrats and gentry. The Chawton living had been owned by Thomas Knight II until his death in 1794, and while most of his property had gone to his nominated heir, Edward Austen, the Chawton living was inherited by another distant relative, David Papillon,

an excise commissioner and landowner in Kent, whose son John Raw-
storne Papillon was already a vicar at Tonbridge in that county.

It was not unknown for more fortunate clergymen to hold up to four
or five livings at a time, and to pocket the tithes and income from glebe
land from all of them while paying a curate a fixed wage to fulfil the
duties. But under the influence of the evangelical movement this kind of
non-residency and delegation was increasingly frowned upon and Edward
and Henry made the offer on the basis that the Papillons might prefer
cash in hand. The present incumbent at Chawton, the Reverend John
Hinton, was still very much alive and there was something repugnant
about covert haggling over the succession to the rectory. But that was the
order of things. Whether an Anglican clergyman or the heir to an estate,
it was a matter of waiting to step into 'dead men's shoes' and dead men's
houses. Benefices were sometimes advertised for sale in the newspapers
along with estimates of their value and hints regarding the age and state
of health of the incumbent minister. The average value of a living at the
time was £120, barely enough for a single man to keep up genteel appearances, but Chawton was worth more. Edward and Papillon negotiated on
price but in the end no agreement was reached and in 1802 John Papillon
would succeed to the Chawton living and move to Hampshire.

While negotiations were still ongoing, Henry, on the rebound from
Eliza, began courting Mary Pearson, the daughter of a naval captain residing in Greenwich. He took leave to spend time with her family in
the summer of 1796 while the Oxfordshire regiment was stationed at
Yarmouth barracks. With fortunate timing, he was able to miss another
spate of rioting. Ninety armed sailors from a nearby man-of-war invaded
a meeting in the town held by the well-known radical John Thelwall, and
attacked both speaker and audience. However on this occasion the militia were able to stay out of trouble. The magistrates, disliking Thelwall's
politics, ignored appeals to call in the soldiers to restore public order.

Politics were not uppermost in Henry's mind as he constantly revolved
plans for the future. He reflected on the way his great-uncle Francis had

somehow beaten a path to riches and prestige after being left destitute at an early age. Francis's father, John Austen IV, had been expected to inherit the Kent estate of his grandfather, John Austen III: the very names assumed a steady cascade of wealth down the generations, and he made no special provision for his growing family, which included five sons. But John IV died of consumption the year before his father, and although the grandfather made the eldest of the boys (another John) his heir, he disliked his daughter-in-law and left her and the other children to their fate. The widowed Elizabeth Austen resourcefully found work as the housekeeper of the Master of Sevenoaks Grammar School, allowing the younger boys to receive an education without charge. The second son, Francis, was bound apprentice to an attorney in 1714 for a premium of £140. As Henry later passed on the story to one of his nephews, the progress of Francis was down to a mixture of determination, charm and powers of persuasion, on the basis of only a modest leg-up. He 'set out in life with £800 & a bundle of pens, as attorney, & contrived to amass a very large fortune, living most hospitably, and yet buying up all the valuable land' around the town of Sevenoaks. He managed to marry 'two wealthy wives' in succession and to persuade 'the godmother of his eldest son, Motley Austen, to leave to her said godson a small legacy of £100,000'.[13]

The arbitrary order of birth and of death seemed to decide most matters of importance in a hierarchal society based on landed property, with only the occasional deviation, like Thomas Knight's decision to adopt Edward. Henry also thought wistfully of a clerical living very different from hard-scrabble Steventon, a 'very desirable & pleasant Rectory of West Wickham situated in a very fertile & cheerful part of West Kent, about 5 miles from Croydon'. Another Henry Austen in the previous generation, first cousin of his father, had also been 'destined for the Church', and because he was the son of an older brother he received the rich living while George Austen had to struggle to provide for his family in Hampshire. Old Reverend Henry Austen was a useless rector, an absentee with non-conformist sympathies. But primogeniture, the right of succession according to order of birth, 'with all its ramifications', counted for more than aptitude or hard work in those days before the Reform Bill, Henry explained to his nephew.[14]

Jane was evidently in sympathy. The legend of the improvident father John Austen IV and the crotchety grandfather John Austen III fed into the narrative she had been constructing under the title of *Elinor and Marianne*, and she highlighted the peculiar disadvantages of women within the system. The Dashwood mother and daughters are cut adrift from home and fortune due to just such a calamity as befell her great-grandmother Elizabeth Austen; a calamity that had continued with all *its* ramifications to her own generation. She could not help but reflect bitterly at times on the twists of fate that distinguished the Kent Austens from the Hampshire Austens. 'People get so horridly poor & economical in this part of the world that I have no patience with them,' she wrote to Cassandra, '—Kent is the only place for happiness, everybody is rich there.'[15]

Like Elizabeth Austen at the start of the eighteenth century, George Austen made the best of the hand life had dealt him by prioritising education. When he and his two sisters had been left orphans, Uncle Francis had given him the basis of a gentleman's education in the form of tuition at Tonbridge Grammar School, and hard study had led to the fellowship at Oxford University and ordination. The grafting of his impoverished line onto that of the wealthy Knights was a great and unexpected stroke of good fortune, an event commemorated by a silhouette from 1783 showing young Edward being ceremoniously handed over. Although Thomas Knight's widow had a life interest in the estate, Edward was heir to a range of properties including great houses at Chawton in Hampshire and at Godmersham in Kent, and a scattering of parishes and farms in both counties. In the event that Edward in turn died without heir, the estate would pass down to each of his brothers in succession. But there seemed little chance of that. Edward married Elizabeth Bridges in 1791 and by 1796 had two sons and a daughter; he would go on to have eleven hardy children in all. Aside from Edward, none of George Austen's sons were likely to inherit much in the way of financial or landed capital, and his daughters would have almost no dowry. But all his children would have the benefit of cultural capital in abundance, and at least a modicum of social capital through family and friends, though it had to be energetically cultivated and along with the hopes came some sharp disappointments. Above all, the brothers and sisters would help each other along. 'We must not all expect to be individually lucky,' says the heroine of Jane's unfinished novel *The Watsons*, 'The luck of one member of a family is luck to all.'[16]

In August 1796 it was Jane's turn to visit Rowling, Edward's home while his adoptive mother remained at Godmersham. With Edward and also Frank, who was home on shore-leave, she stopped over in Cork Street in the fashionable West End of London, her first recorded visit to the capital, giving her the chance to familiarise herself with the London streets named in the recently completed *Elinor and Marianne*. Henry was there to greet her in Kent and she had a chance to scrutinise Mary Pearson, perhaps on a day trip to Greenwich. Although she was willing to fall in with Henry's plan that Mary should travel back to Steventon with her to meet the parents, she was not impressed. 'If Miss Pearson should return with me, pray be careful not to expect too much beauty,' she confided to Cassandra, 'I will not pretend to say that on a *first view*, she quite answered the opinion I had formed of her. My mother I am sure will be disappointed, if she does not take great care.' What girl could be worthy of the darling of the family? In the event, her travel plans were thrown in the air by Henry's decision to go back to Yarmouth for some medical treatment. Jane remained stranded without a brother to act as escort on the return journey, not for the last time. She resigned herself to the delay with good humour, only remarking pointedly to Cassandra that it was not unlike 'waiting for *deadmen's shoes*'.[17]

Jane put the time she *had* managed to spend in conversation with Henry to profitable use in her next novel project, *First Impressions*, begun once she finally arrived home in October and occupying her for the better part of a year. *First Impressions* in its original form has not survived. But in *Pride and Prejudice*, the revised version, the representation of the militia suggests that Jane was not impressed by what she learned. There is no sign in the published work of any very vital defensive role in the national war effort. The officers are seen chiefly at play, lounging in their winter quarters, flirting with the local girls. It is of course a woman's eye view; the heroine's consciousness remains, as always in her narratives, paramount. However Jane also placed words into the mouths of men, and the main incentive for joining a regiment it would seem is 'the prospect of constant society – and good society'. There are traces of Henry in the charming Lieutenant George Wickham (his surname taken from the parish lost to George Austen). He is a 'disappointed man' who declares 'the church *ought* to have been my profession – I was brought up for the church'. He claims to have gone into the military after being deprived of the living promised to him by Mr Darcy's father, his patron (I.xvi). But although Henry would later be regarded as a reckless speculator by some, he was certainly not a rake, a liar or a swindler in the Wickham mode.

Pride and Prejudice has been called Jane Austen's 'militia novel' and praised for its exact depiction of the old system of quartering troops among civilians used for the last time in the winter of 1794–95 before being replaced by the mass-construction of barracks.[18] But beyond offering a documentary record, what the published novel and presumably its manuscript precursor showed was a society shaken up by the requirements of war, and most immediately the effervescent presence of mobile militia units. They may not be presented as a force for good, but they are certainly seen to be an agent of change. England at war saw unprecedented mobility and new social configurations. The relatively static communities of Meryton, Pemberley, or Rosings collide with moving objects in uniform. There are stark juxtapositions of pleasure and violence relayed in the gossip of the officer-mad younger sisters Kitty and Lydia: 'several of the officers had dined lately with their uncle, a private had been flogged, and it had actually been hinted that Colonel Forster was going to be married'

(I.xii). In wartime England a bankrupt villain can insinuate himself into respectable society concealed by a fine uniform and a rich landowner can be jolted into a sense of social responsibility and of connectedness with the denizens of Cheapside. Anything could happen. An obscure young woman might flout the lady of the manor and end up marrying a great man from a noble line with a splendid fortune.

The fourth son of a country parson could even marry a French countess. This is what came to pass on 31 December 1797, when Elizabeth, Comtesse de Feuillide, gave her hand in marriage to Captain Henry Thomas Austen of the Oxfordshire Militia. The ceremony took place at Marylebone Church, where Lady Sophia Burrell had wed her William in May.

What changed Eliza's mind? Pity may have been a factor. In November 1796 Henry turned up at her door following the break-up of his engagement with Mary Pearson. He seemed thin and ill. Her diagnosis, with a pun on 'Pearson', was that he had been wounded by the intolerably flirtatious behaviour of the 'pretty wicked looking girl with bright black eyes which pierce thro' & thro', no wonder the poor young man's heart could not withstand them', she wrote to Phylly.[19] Eliza might see herself as a combatant in the eternal battle of the sexes but when a long-standing *beau*, her own cousin, was brought in as the casualty of another woman, she could not help but feel protective.

Then again, she had her own worries over health. She realised that Hastings, her only child, would never be fully well or live independently. He continued to suffer from fits and she was sure he was epileptic. Henry was a kind man and seemed fond of the boy, and it was becoming a matter of urgency that she shared the responsibility. Her mother had died from breast cancer, and now Eliza was suffering worrying symptoms. As always she confided in Phylly and ran the risk of wearying her with details of the condition and the treatments she had to endure, including the repeated application of leeches, and surgery on a swelling after a poultice failed to reduce it.

Eliza bravely contrived to give such accounts a comic turn, describing
for instance the 'two smart young men' in the doctor's waiting room who
'opened eyes as wide as barn doors' when she entered. Old habits would
never die, and she continues her rattling talk, of 'a reasonable quantity of
beaux the present hard times considered'. Learning from Phylly in Kent
of an attentive military man she urged her to 'send Captn. Anderson to
me with all speed for his £100,000 will suit me wonderfully well' and
protested that it would be 'very unfair in such a disinterested being as
yourself to make such conquests, you ought to leave them to those females who like myself have a great relish for all the pretty things that are
not to be had without plenty of cash'.[20]

The consideration that weighed most with Eliza may have been the
two promotions Henry received early in 1797. On 18 February he was
made adjutant, supervising the internal management of the Oxfordshire
regiment and directing the men's training, a role usually given to an officer
from the regular army. As a mark of his colonel's esteem, on 29 March he
was also elevated to the intermediate rank of 'Captain Lieutenant'. This
brought the courtesy title of 'Captain' but without the necessity of a property qualification. The post of Paymaster also remained his. Eliza wrote
delightedly to Phylly on 3 May, 'Captn. Austen has just spent a few days
in town; I suppose you know that our Cousin Henry is now Captain, Pay
Master & Adjutant, He is a very lucky young man and bids fair to possess
a considerable share of riches & honours...' And she added, significantly,
'I believe he has now given up all thoughts of the Church, and he is right
for he certainly is not so fit for a parson as a soldier.'[21] Along with the new
conviction that Henry was destined for riches and honours, may have
come a flattering sense of her own importance with him. In *Mansfield
Park*, Mary Crawford is mortified and resentful on discovering that, in
spite of her disapproval, Edmund Bertram still planned to take orders;
'she had thought her influence more' (II.vi). Henry recognised that Eliza
could not stoop to the situation of parson's wife, and it seemed that her
influence had prevailed.

These possible explanations of Eliza's change of heart are based on evidence that has long been available, but there is a curious clue not previously considered. Bank ledgers speak a secret language of their own. In the ledger records for the account held by Henry in Hoare's Bank from 1795 to 1798, there appears the deposit entry for 25 February 1796 'By Countess of Feuillide £156'. Why would Eliza give Henry a large sum of money at a time when, according to family tradition, she had just rejected his initial marriage proposal? It is possible that the two of them had parted amicably, and that Henry, with his growing financial know-how, had undertaken to invest the money for her or carry out some other transaction. He bought a considerable number of government-issued bonds in June. Alternatively, it seems possible that she had advanced him the money to help pay for his advancement in the militia. Henry had previously attempted to gain an adjutancy, and learned of his failure in January 1796. In the autumn of 1796, immediately after the engagement with Mary Pearson had been called off, he was in London visiting the army agency Cox & Greenwood, which dealt in the sale of commissions. On 22 October Colonel Spencer ordered him back to Yarmouth and the muster role recorded: 'Austen, Paymaster, absent to attend the Colonel of the Regiment on particular business.'[22] He may now, after some hesitation have taken the opportunity to conduct business of his own, for the ledger records state on 15 October: 'To Cox & Greenwood £300.' Could it be that Eliza had been investing in her own happiness, helping to boost Henry to a rank which would make him marriageable in the eyes of her godfather, and betting on his potential for gaining 'riches and honours'?

Now that Eliza had resolved to marry Henry, she set to work putting her financial house in order. For although she was to reassure Warren Hastings that Henry was 'in possession of a comfortable income', in fact his annual pay, after the promotions, would still only have been a meagre £281 a year, certainly not enough to keep the carriage to which she was accustomed.[23] Any attempt to recover the French property was out of the question for the duration of the war. By early June 1797 Eliza had consulted a lawyer and written to Mr Woodman with the intention of taking the trust fund established by Warren Hastings into her own hands. Mr Woodman explained the need for proof of the Comte's death, and he and the Reverend George Austen in turn consulted Warren Hastings. Eliza visited her godfather and his wife that summer at their country house Daylesford near Cheltenham, but made no mention of the imminent marriage. In September 1797 a legal release was drawn up to place the stock holdings in Eliza's hands. On her behalf, John Woodman and George Austen had put her £10,000 towards £5,517.1s of Consols 3 per cent and £6,000 of Old South Sea Annuities. By the end of October, the business was completed.

The marriage plans were still a secret, even from Phylly. Eliza may have been sensitive to the appearance of a conflict of interest between George Austen's role as trustee of her fortune and his position as father of the bridegroom. Perhaps she also expected disapproval, given their close kinship, the age difference, and Henry's still modest income. Writing to Phylly, she denied plans for a liaison with Henry over the summer: he was posted to Norwich and she was on her way in the opposite direction to Cheltenham in Gloucestershire. By late September however she had drifted north-east to Lowestoft, where her son had been sent under the care of her trusted servant Madame Bigeon for reasons of health. She rejected Phylly's 'wicked surmises' – Lowestoft was a full twenty-eight miles from Norwich. But it was only ten from Great Yarmouth where Henry's division was actually posted.[24]

Eliza broke the news to Warren Hastings on 26 December, just five days before the wedding. Her justification for taking the step, in addition to his 'comfortable income' was 'the excellence of his heart, temper, & understanding, together with his steady attachment to me, his affection for my little boy, and disinterested concurrence in the disposal of my property, in favour of this latter', and she mentioned too that he had waited for her acceptance for more than two years.[25] The letter that informed Phylly has been lost. Mr Austen did have advance warning, and gave the couple £40 for wedding celebrations with the Oxfordshire Militia, a generous amount twice the annual allowance received by Cassandra and Jane. There was excitement in the neighbourhood of Steventon over this fairy-tale development. When Mr Austen refurbished his carriage the following year, it was assumed that the family crest on the panelling was a coronet, because of the son who had married a countess. No one in the Austen family seems to have attended Henry's town wedding and this was probably due to the fact that it had been hastily arranged. The country was in a desperate state of upheaval and leave was now difficult to obtain.

Great Britain felt like a nation under siege, now at war with Spain and the Netherlands as well as France. In December 1796 a French fleet had sailed for Ireland and only been prevented from landing by bad weather. In February 1797 another French force of 1,400 troops succeeded in landing at Fishguard, on the south-west tip of Wales, with the intention of marching on Bristol as part of a three-pronged attack. French soldiers clashed with local yeomanry and civilians before being forced to surrender after two days. Later in the year, British sailors, the first line of defence, launched mutinies for fair pay and better conditions at Spithead and Nore. At the start of 1798 a full-scale invasion still seemed only a matter of time. In February, Eliza, writing to Phylly about a projected visit to Steventon, dealt light-heartedly with the threat.

I mean to send my servants &cc by the stage and let Henry drive me because it will save post horses, for you must know that I am become excessively stingy and am scraping up all I can against the arrival of the French who will of course deprive me of every thing but the few guineas which I may have contrived to hoard. I suppose you have seen a print of the rafts on which they mean to reach us.[26]

The mood remained jittery. The Fishguard invasion had provoked a run on the banks that threatened the stability of the British economy as a whole. The total face value of the notes in circulation at the time, £10,865,050, was almost double the gold reserves of £5,322,010. To restore order and prevent a repetition, Prime Minister William Pitt took an unprecedented step. Until further notice the Bank of England could dispense with the obligation to convert banknotes into gold on demand. It cancelled the promise which appeared and continues to appear on each individual paper note, signed by the chief cashier of the Bank, 'I promise to pay the bearer on demand' the sum specified in 'real' money. Payment in coinage, also known as 'specie', was suspended in order to protect the gold bullion vital to the war effort.

The Bank Restriction Act of 1797 was originally intended to last for weeks rather than years, but was renewed by Parliament again and again as an essential safeguard until its repeal in 1821 and the establishment of the gold standard. It was called a 'restriction' act, but its effect was to unleash economic activity. Without the need to back banknotes with bullion there was a massive proliferation in the production and usage of paper money and with it, an expansion of credit. The first £5 notes had been introduced in 1793 at the start of the war and from 1797 the Bank of England began issuing £1 and £2 notes. Coins became scarcer than ever. There was a dramatic shift to a full-scale paper money regime, and with it came a mushrooming of note-issuing banks outside the metropolis. The Bank of England only operated in London. Country banks, almost entirely unregulated, assumed much of the responsibility for managing the circulation of banknotes further afield.

The parliamentary opposition, the Whig party, were loud in their denunciation of the uncoupling of paper from silver and gold. Richard Brinsley Sheridan, in a speech to the House of Commons, described the Bank of England as 'an elderly lady in the City ... who had unfortunately fallen into bad company', inspiring the caricaturist James Gillray's celebrated image of the 'Old Lady of Threadneedle Street'. In this print, the Bank, a crone clothed in a gown made up of one and two pound notes, is seated stubbornly on a chest containing gold bullion, her arms waving in alarm while Pitt, pictured as a scrawny seducer, puckers up for a kiss while reaching into her pocket for guineas. 'Murder! – Murder! – Rape! – Murder!' she cries in the speech bubble, 'O you villain! – what have I kept my honor untainted so long, to have it broke up, by you at last?'

James Gillray, *Political-ravishment, or The Old Lady of Threadneedle Street in Danger!*, 1797. © The Trustees of the British Museum.

The Whigs argued that the government was putting Britain's public credit at risk by tampering with the currency. They were taking up the cry of the radicals outside Parliament, initiated the previous year by Thomas Paine's diatribe *The Decline and Fall of the English System of Finance* (1796). Paine, better known as the author of *The Rights of Man*, had been found guilty of seditious libel in absentia after fleeing to France in 1792. From Paris he predicted the imminent doom of the British economy, citing currency depreciation, inflated prices, and the fragility of public credit, as millions of pounds worth of paper circulated while backed by, allegedly, a mere £1 million worth of bullion in the bank vaults. British war policy was being sustained by a confidence trick, he declared. John Thelwall, who crossed the path of the Oxfordshire Militia for a second time when he returned to lecture in Norwich in the late spring of 1797, had similarly prophesied national bankruptcy in his published account of the troubles in Yarmouth the previous year:

> Our population is exhausted, our manufactures are palsied, our commerce is threatened with annihilation, our public credit is shaken to its foundations, our specie is vanishing, paper circulation maintains its standard with difficulty, our loan contractors are reduced to every shuffling expedient to fulfil, or to postpone, their engagements with the Government...[27]

The radicals were, in effect, strategically contributing to the collapse in public trust that they envisaged. It was vital for the government to rally support against this collapse, and fast. In the *Reading Mercury* for 1 March 1797 there appeared a list of worthies in the Basingstoke area – tradesmen, gentlemen and clergymen – who, following the stoppage of payments by the Bank of England, publicly announced their willingness 'to receive, as usual, the notes of the Bank of England, and those issued by the Basingstoke Bank of Messrs. Jeffreys, Toomer and Legg'. Among those named were George and James Austen.[28]

With the future uncertain and public anxiety rife, Jane decided to seize the day and attempt to get her newly finished novel, *First Impressions*, into print. The previous year 'Miss J. Austen, Steventon' had appeared in the subscription list for *Camilla*, the third novel of the celebrated Frances Burney. Her name can be found among 1,058 others, headed by royalty, all willing to subscribe one guinea upfront to reserve a copy. Publishing by subscription was an early form of crowd-funding, and by the late eighteenth century was generally employed either to raise charity for a needy author or else, for the more brazen writers, as an attempt to maximise profits. Burney in fact shrank from the self-exposure involved in drumming up subscriptions, but she had recently married an impoverished

French émigré, General D'Arblay, and badly needed to boost her income. The scheme was a great success. *Camilla* cleared £1,000 through subscription, and another £1,000 through sale of the copyright to the consortium Payne, Cadell & Davies. Not only was Jane an ardent fan of Burney – classing her novels among those in which 'the greatest powers of the mind are displayed' (*NA*, I.v) – but she had a personal connection through her mother's cousin Cassandra Cooke, who had befriended the great writer when she came to live in the house opposite at Great Bookham in Surrey.

This sense of connection may have been the slender link that led Mr Austen to write on 1 November 1797 to Cadell & Davies, Burney's publisher, offering the manuscript of *First Impressions*. It was normal for a male relation to conduct business negotiations on behalf of a female author. Burney's brother Edward had sought a contract for her first novel *Evelina* in heavy disguise, in order to preserve her anonymity. The Austens had no useful contacts in the London book trade, and on the evidence of George Austen's letter, little clue as to how to get a book into print. It begins, 'Sirs, I have in my possession a manuscript novel, comprised in three vols. about the length of Miss Burney's Evelina.'[29] He offered to send the manuscript and enquired about the expense of publishing 'at the author's risk', which would entail paying the production costs and giving the publisher a percentage of the profits. He also sought an opinion on the value of the copyright, which normally involved outright sale of the manuscript with no share for the author in future profits.

Mr Cadell rejected *First Impressions* by return of post, sight unseen. There was nothing in the naive overture to suggest the firm would be missing out on a masterpiece. Jane swallowed the disappointment and valiantly set to work again, redrafting *Elinor and Marianne*. The letter-form in which it had originally been written was now out of fashion. Burney had employed it in her debut, *Evelina*, published in 1778. Burney's later novels, *Cecilia* in 1782 and now *Camilla*, confirmed a popular shift towards third-person narration.

Jane endeavoured to prepare herself for publication and fame by honing the discreet and ironic narrator's voice that would become her trademark. In the meantime, economic conditions in the country continued to worsen. Eliza declared she was 'almost ruined with the hard times', struggling to pay the income tax introduced as a temporary measure to support the war, complaining piteously that the 'new taxes will drive me out of London and make me give up my carriage'. The costs of renting and keeping servants were also rising steeply.[30] Across the Channel, a French 'Army of England' under the young commander Napoleon Bonaparte was gathered at the start of 1798 and in May a revolt of 30,000 armed peasants broke out in Ireland, eventually backed by a party of French troops that landed at Killala Bay in County Mayo.

There was a call for volunteers to restore British control in Ireland, and the Oxfordshire Militia including Henry answered it. But for the moment they were retained on guard duty in Ipswich. It was not until the start of 1799 that they were summoned to relieve the companies who had already succeeded in suppressing the rebellion. Eliza remained in England with her son while in April, Henry was on his way to Ireland, suffering an appalling crossing in bad weather before being posted to patrol the coast and post road north of Dublin. In late August the opportunity arose to get a commission in the regular army without purchase. Many in the militia took it. But Henry stayed on in Dublin along with half his regiment in advance of the Act of the Union, the completion of the 'pacification' process.[31]

On the whole, the Austen boys in uniform were making the best of the footholds afforded to them by the war. Under mysterious circumstances Henry gained a captaincy in November 1798. The family had no idea who had provided the property qualification. His role as acting paymaster became a full appointment on Christmas Day 1798, and at the same time came the news that Frank had been promoted to Commander of the HMS Petterel. Charles had been made a naval lieutenant the previous year.

In 1797 Mrs Knight had determined that Edward should take possession of the estate in her lifetime rather than waiting to inherit after her death, and he moved into Godmersham the following year. Jane, suffering an increasingly pinched existence at Steventon, found the disparity hard to bear. She wrote to Cassandra, who was visiting Kent, 'Poor Edward! It is very hard that he who has everything else in the world that he can wish for, should not have good health too.' She could not help being equally barbed about Mrs Knight retaining a substantial income and Edward getting the rest: 'I am tolerably glad to hear that Edward's income is so good a one as glad as I can at anybody's being rich besides you & me.'

A year or so later she applied herself to read Robert Henry's *History of Great Britain*, offering to share it with her friend Martha Lloyd by relaying the contents in seven parts. 'The Friday's lot, commerce, coin & shipping, you will find the least entertaining,' she wrote to Martha.[32] With her latest literary production, set in the money-minded resort of Bath, she was very sure she had mastered the way to make economic matters a source of amusement.

CHAPTER 2

MODERN TIMES: *NORTHANGER ABBEY* AND *THE WATSONS* (1800–1805)

The year 1800 saw great changes in the lives of both Jane and Henry. The Henry Austens and the George Austens were to launch into the new century with new social identities and new economic outlooks. The Reverend George Austen decided to retire and take his wife and two unmarried daughters to live in Bath. Henry resigned his commission in the militia with the intention of moving to London with Eliza and young Hastings and setting up as a private army agent.

Although Eliza had enjoyed flirting with Henry's brother officers in camp at Ipswich immediately after the wedding, she had, she declared to Phylly, 'entirely left off trade' and with her son's health precarious, she was keen to establish a more permanent home among old friends in London.[1] The War Office was now scaling back the home force, offering six months' pay to militia officers for voluntary retirement. Henry felt the time was ripe to put his newfound skills in accounting to more profitable use. He was granted leave for much of 1800, preparing for the transition to civilian life, but rejoined the troops on the Isle of Wight at the end of November to learn gratifyingly that the official auditor was 'perfectly satisfied with the accounts, and wished he could always make as favourable a report'.[2]

With cutbacks to personnel, militia regiments were more inclined to outsource the functions performed by regimental paymasters. Henry would continue to administer pay and half pay for the Oxfords at a rate of two pence in the pound for the whole payroll, plus pay of one soldier at sixpence a day, and could also provide banking services for its officers including lucrative interest on loans. Half pay for inactive or retired officers was distributed on a semi-annual basis, and to avoid the inconvenience of a trip to London, recipients could appoint a half-pay agent to collect it at a rate of 2.5 per cent commission. Commission brokerage promised more substantial returns. Henry, through his efforts to secure his own promotions, had gained a valuable insight into the under the counter dealings with Cox & Greenwood, the biggest and most successful private army agency.

On rare occasions it was possible for a man to rise through the ranks without money. Non-purchase commissions sometimes became available when manpower was at a premium and new regiments were being raised. Vacancies created by death in action were filled on merit, not sold. But for the most part commissions for any rank from ensign to lieutenant colonel, whether in the regular army or the militia, were commodities. The logic was that the commission served as a cash bond for good behaviour with the additional benefit of ensuring exclusivity in the officer class. Officers had a stake in maintaining the status quo, and their money would eventually be returned as capital for an honourable retirement. In theory the purchase system was transparent with set prices attached to different branches of the army, the Life Guards being the most expensive and the Infantry the least. New officers had to swear an oath that only the listed amount had been paid. But in reality posts in the most desirable regiments could go for double the official rate and even be sold, covertly, at auction. It was technically illegal to extract private profit from the transaction, but malpractice of this kind was customary and had long been overlooked.

It is unlikely that Henry was entirely open about these expectations when he stopped over at Steventon on 22 November 1800, on the way to the Isle of Wight for his final period of military service. However the talk of new schemes was contagious. Mr Austen caught Henry's restlessness, then Mrs Austen. The following week, while Jane was on a visit to Ibthorpe to stay with Martha Lloyd, and Cassandra was in Kent, her father resolved to retire and go with his wife and daughters to live in Bath. Steventon rectory was to be handed over to James, who would be paid to officiate as curate while Mr Austen continued to receive the income from tithes. James with his second wife Mary Lloyd, Martha's sister, would welcome a change from the cramped conditions at Deane, now they had two children. Jane was greeted with the decision on her return, and family tradition had it that she fainted on the spot. Letters written to Cassandra at this time show that she had severe misgivings, yet she would have understood the thinking in favour of the move.

The age and increasingly fragile health of both Mr and Mrs Austen, now sixty-nine and sixty-one, were the primary concerns, and for that and other reasons Bath had much to recommend it. The elderly couple had a sentimental attachment to the spa town as the place where they had courted and wed; there were close relations living there and good transport links for visiting and receiving visits; and if after all either of the girls were tempted to try matrimony there could be no better place to find a husband. It is also possible that Jane's parents believed they were helping her to fulfil her vocation as an author. Jane had begun her third novel, set in Bath, in August 1798. When she had read aloud from her work in progress, it was clear that she had soaked up details of the spa's places, habits and visitors from recent stays there.

For nearly a month, from late November to early December 1797, Jane, Cassandra and their mother had stayed with Mrs Austen's older brother James Leigh-Perrot and his wife at their Bath residence, No. 1 Paragon Buildings. The sensations of the fictional heroine 'all eager delight' on first arrival, looking 'here, there, every where' as she approached the city's 'fine and striking environs,' surely must have borne some relation to Jane's own experience (I.ii)? In the summer of 1799, the novel then

known as *Susan* and later published under the title *Northanger Abbey*
was nearing completion and Jane leapt at the chance to return to Bath
with Mrs Austen, in the company of Edward, his wife Elizabeth, two
children and a pair of servants. They had lodged in old-fashioned but
elegant Queen Square, and while Edward took the waters and even tried
the experimental application of electricity for incipient gout, Jane was
enjoying walks in the beautiful countryside and observing the fashion
for trimming hats with fruit decorations. Would not city life expand her
knowledge of modes and manners and better qualify her as a novelist?
Perhaps Mr and Mrs Austen had noticed the avidity with which Jane had
listened to Henry's plans for establishing himself in the metropolis. 'Oh!
Who can ever be tired of Bath?' Jane's heroine exclaimed. They may have
misread the sentiment as her own.

Henry was on hand to soothe Jane at the start of January. 'He was
as agreeable as ever during his visit,' she wrote to Cassandra at Godmersham, adding 'I get more & more reconciled to the idea of our
removal'. Away from Steventon, they would be mobile, light-footed, free
of encumbrances. Open to change and varied society like Henry and
Eliza, they could spend future summers billeted by the sea or in Wales;
'we shall now possess many of the advantages which I have thought of
with envy in the wives of sailors or soldiers.'³ Jane paused in her writing
and reflected before inserting 'often' before 'thought of with envy'. Eliza's
advantages had frequently crossed her mind.

Still, Jane could not help shrinking from the idea of Bath as their main
place of residence. It was a strange phenomenon, this ebullition of the
modern on the site of an ancient Roman spa, nestled in the verdant Avon
valley. Bath was pure surplus, a consumerist fantasyland constructed from
the over-abundant time and money of society's winners, and organised
around the diseases of prosperity and the hectic pursuit of pleasure. Its
rebirth as a health resort began in the 1720s and its fashionable heyday
was the third quarter of the century, when George Austen and Cassandra
Leigh had married there. Although the city was now past its prime as a

magnet for the social elite, the established rituals of the Pump Room and the ballroom continued unabated, as Jane scrupulously recorded in the Bath novel that would become *Northanger Abbey*. In that narrative, she presented the spectacle of hedonism from the perspective of an excited and impressionable young girl, an *ingénue*, as Burney had done with the sights of London in *Evelina*. The spectacle amused Jane herself, as an analyst of manners.

All the same, after two short sojourns Jane knew she would find the constant ebb and flow of visitors energy-sapping. The new-built terraces of pale cream Bath stone and stucco created a painful 'white glare', as she refers to it in *Persuasion* (I.v). Writing to Cassandra on arrival in May 1801, she describes a sensory assault. 'The first view of Bath in fine weather does not answer my expectations; I think I see more distinctly thro' rain. – The sun was got behind everything, and the appearance of the place from the top of Kingsdown, was all vapour, shadow, smoke & confusion.'[4] The same scene of arrival, replayed in her final novel *Persuasion*, is suggestive of unresolved trauma. As Anne Elliot enters the city, persisting 'in a very determined, though very silent, disinclination for Bath', she 'caught the first dim view of the extensive buildings, smoking in rain, without any wish of seeing them better' (II.iii). The question of whether the ordeal was worse in fine weather or foul was evidently a close-run thing. Jane attributed to the later heroine her feelings on becoming a permanent resident: 'She disliked Bath, and did not think it agreed with her – and Bath was to be her home' (I.ii).

Mr and Mrs George Austen and their daughters were to join the flow of migration from country to city. The British population had undergone rapid growth in the preceding century, from 5 million in 1700 to 9 million in 1801. At an ever increasing rate, people sought work and other opportunities in towns. By the turn of the century, London, with more than a million inhabitants, was by far the largest city in Western Europe, rivalled only by Peking (Beijing) and Edo (Tokyo) in the Far East. Bath, with 40,020 inhabitants at the time of the 1801 census, was one of the most sizeable urban centres outside the capital. Although the nation was still predominantly rural and most towns remained small, urban experience was becoming the measure of a good life. Cities were being recast in brick and stone and ambitious speculative building developments spun out featuring squares, parades, colonnades and crescents. With the growth of retail outlets, shopping became a favourite pastime, and theatres, concert halls, ballrooms, art galleries, museums, and print culture burgeoned. Of necessity there was constant interaction between town and country, and an urban hub could bring wealth to the agrarian hinterland that supplied its needs.

Cities were alternatively often denounced as parasitical. A Hampshire man, the radical journalist William Cobbett, would dub the growing metropolis the 'great Wen', a carbuncle on the face of the nation. William Cowper, the favourite poet of Marianne Dashwood in *Sense and Sensibility*, coined the famous aphorism, 'God made the country, Man made the town.' While he acknowledged in *The Task* that cities are 'nurseries of the arts', he didn't stint in voicing commonly held suspicions regarding their immoral nature using as metaphor the challenge of waste disposal that represented a logistical nightmare when many bodies were densely gathered together:

In proud and gay
And gain-devoted cities; thither flow,
As to a common and most noisome sewer,
The dregs and fæculence of ev'ry land.
In cities foul example on most minds
Begets its likeness. Rank abundance breeds
In gross and pamper'd cities sloth and lust,
And wantonness and gluttonous excess.
In cities, vice is hidden with most ease,
Or seen with least reproach; and virtue, taught
By frequent lapse, can hope no triumph there
Beyond th'atchievement of successful flight.

The Austens, notwithstanding such warnings, prepared to transfer what wealth they had from the country to the city. Jane wrote to Cassandra, 'My father is doing all in his power to increase his income by raising his tithes, &c, & I do not despair of getting nearly six hundred a year'.[5] In early May, most of their worldly possessions, the substance of their Steventon existence, went under the auctioneer's hammer. They would take the proceeds and begin again, as town-dwellers.

By the day of the auction Jane and her mother had already arrived to stay with the Leigh-Perrots at the Paragon. Mrs Austen's brother James had added 'Perrot' to his name on inheriting the estate of his maternal great-uncle. His wife Jane was the daughter of Robert Cholmeley, the owner of an estate in Barbados, and had been sent back to England for her education. They married in 1764 and had no children. There was an expectation that in due course one of the Austen sons might be made heir to their estate, Scarlets, near Wargrave in Berkshire, where they spent half the year.

The first consideration on coming to Bath was to buy a new dress. This is what Catherine's chaperone Mrs Allen does in *Northanger Abbey*, after spending several days 'learning what was mostly worn' (I.ii). And this is what Jane did in May 1801. Any period of residence in a town as fashion-conscious as Bath meant catching up with the latest look, or appearing singular and risk being excluded. The next most pressing concern for the Austens was to find permanent accommodation. They felt stifled under the roof of the Leigh-Perrots with their inadvertently high-handed ways and tiresome small parties. And the Paragon was a decidedly urban address, pinched between two busy streets on a steep slope above the river. Mother and daughter were discouraged by the poor quality of the housing on offer. Damp was a common problem, and poor construction and small rooms were others. Real estate speculators were more concerned with splendid show than convenience or solid workmanship. In the end they opted for 4 Sydney Place, an address just off the wide stylish thoroughfare of Great Pulteney Street which stretched their budget of around £650 per annum to the limit. It was almost new, a tall narrow two-bedroomed house with room in the attic for servants and the advantages of an open-front aspect near the southern edge of town with ready access to the pleasure grounds at Sydney Gardens, and the disadvantage of a short lease of three-and-a-half years.

Getting to grips with the housing market was just one of the new skills to be learned. Country-dwellers, with their kitchen gardens, barter arrangements and 'make do and mend' philosophy were relatively self-sufficient. In town, money was king. All goods and provisions must be paid for by cash or credit, and the sheer abundance of retail options was simultaneously exhilarating and overwhelming. Anyone reading Jane Austen's letters is likely to be struck by the frequency of involved discussion of small purchases at linen-drapers, haberdashers and hosiers. When she and Cassandra were separated there were usually opportunities for shopping either in transit, particularly during stopovers to and from Godmersham, or else during longer stays in the city. In 1801, the future stretched out oppressively as one long shopping expedition. The move to Bath was bound to alter Jane's economic horizons.

She had been warned. As we know from *Northanger Abbey*, she regarded Frances Burney's *Camilla* as a work in which 'the most thorough knowledge of human nature' is 'conveyed to the world in the best chosen language' (I.vi). It was a novel that dealt at length with the alienation felt by a country girl transplanted to the spa towns of Tunbridge Wells and Southampton. In one of Jane's earliest letters, dated September 1796, she described herself as 'just like Camilla'. Stranded in Kent without Henry to escort her homewards via London, her situation was that of Burney's heroine stuck in a half-built summer house when her annoying brother takes the ladder away.[6] But in one crucial respect she was determined not to resemble Camilla Tyrold: she would scrupulously avoid running up debts in town. As she wrote of one of her own heroines, 'She had not Camilla's youth, & had no intention of having her distress.'[7] Jane, like her mother, kept careful accounts.[8]

Mr Tyrold, the father of Burney's Camilla who happens to be a Hampshire parson, gives his young daughter a personalised sermon in preparation for her entrance into the world. It is of no practical use whatsoever in guarding the heroine from the accidents and temptations of fashionable society. When Jane came to stage a comparable scene at the start of *Northanger Abbey* she debunked high-flown moralising of this kind. Mrs Morland simply says to her daughter, 'I beg, Catherine, you will always wrap yourself up very warm about the throat … and I wish you would try to keep some account of the money you spend; – I will give you this little book on purpose.' Catherine's clergyman father, with similar pragmatism, does not give her 'an unlimited order on his banker' or even a £100 bank bill, but only ten guineas with the promise of more if needed (I.ii).

Catherine, like Camilla, is mistakenly believed to be an heiress and similarly attracts fortune-hunters. She differs from Camilla in escaping the attention of moneylenders. Burney described with heart-rending minuteness the way in which the entire Tyrold family becomes entangled in a web of credit charged at extortionate rates. Mr Tyrold is arrested for his daughter's debts and actually incarcerated in Winchester Prison. On learning of this disaster Camilla faints on the spot, and recovers only to despair: 'Her reason felt the shock as forcibly as her heart; the one seemed tottering on its seat, the other bursting its abode.' The scene became iconic, a parable for modern times. In Chawton Great House, once the property of Edward Austen Knight and today a library dedicated to early women's writing, there can be seen a contemporary illustration of Camilla's Calvary. The painting by Henry Singleton, *Camilla Fainting in the Arms of Her Father*, resembles nothing so much as a pietà, with the heroine's inert form illuminated in a white muslin gown like a winding sheet, supported by Mr Tyrold while a surrounding group look on in fear and wonder. She is the symbolic victim of consumer culture. Many others in reality died on that altar.

Henry Singleton, *Camilla Fainting in the Arms of Her Father*, 1796. Reproduced with
kind permission from Chawton House Library.

On 8 August 1799, Mrs Leigh-Perrot stepped into Smith's haberdashery
on the corner of Bath and Stall Streets to buy some black lace to trim
a cloak while her husband went to the Pump Room for some of the
mineral water to treat gout. She handed over a £5 note for the card of
lace, and waited for her £1.19s change. Lace was an expensive item. Half
an hour later the Leigh-Perrots passed the shop together and the shopkeeper, a Miss Gregory, stepped out and asked if she also had a card of
white lace, unpaid for. Mrs Perrot denied it, and when a card of white
lace was found along with the black in her paper parcel she assumed it
must have been a mistake on the part of the shop-assistant, Charles Filby.
Six days later, however, Mrs Leigh-Perrot was arrested, taken before the
mayor and magistrates, and committed to the county gaol at Ilchester
to await trial at the County Assizes in Taunton the following March.
The Austens and other friends and relations were dismayed and full of
sympathy at this extraordinary turn of events. Mrs Austen offered to

send one or both of her daughters to keep her sister-in-law company, but Mrs Leigh-Perrot could not 'let those elegant young women' be 'inmates in a prison', though she wrote appreciatively of the support she received from James Austen in particular, and Henry took leave from his regiment on 15 March, probably with the intention of offering additional aid.[9]

Hanging was the punishment for the theft of any item above 12s in value. If Mrs Leigh-Perrot was found guilty and spared the death penalty, the sentence would be commuted to transportation to Botany Bay in Australia. Her husband had begun settling his affairs in order to accompany her in that eventuality. At the Taunton Assizes five prisoners were sentenced to death before her case came before the judge, including a fourteen-year-old boy charged with burglary. In the end Mrs Leigh-Perrot was saved by a combination of factors. On the one hand, a long series of witnesses for the defence, from gentry neighbours to tradesmen, vouched for her respectability and honesty. On the other, unsavoury information about the haberdasher's business began to surface. It had been bankrupted and was now being run by creditors; the shopkeeper and the 'assistant' Mr Filby, a bankrupt thrice over, were lovers; and the trick of including unpaid-for goods in a customer's parcel had been used at least once before. The judge took almost an hour for his summing up, but the jurors dismissed the charges in less than fifteen minutes. Rumours circulated that Mr Leigh-Perrot had bought off the prosecution but it was the general opinion that he and his wife had comported themselves with dignity, and they took up their place again in Bath society vindicated.

Mrs Leigh-Perrot's near-fatal decision to buy a bit of black lace for trimming taught the lesson that a shopping trip could end at the gallows. And while with *Northanger Abbey* Jane did not write a shopping and hanging novel, she nevertheless probed some of the tensions in a modern acquisitive society. The novel has generally been described as a satire on the Gothic novels then popular. It would be truer to say that it is a satire on consumer society, and that the craze for Gothic horror was simply one especially sensational instance of consumerism in the late 1790s, at the time the novel was first composed.

This documentary intention is borne out by the short 'Advertisement by the Authoress' prefixed to the work when it was finally published in 1817: 'The public are entreated to bear in mind that thirteen years have passed since it was finished, many more since it was begun, and that during that period, places, manners, books, and opinions have undergone considerable changes.' Gothic fiction is just one among an array of historically precise commodities that feature in Catherine Morland's adventure, and it had a particular quality which suited the purpose of the author beautifully. The Gothic genre, at least in the work of its foremost practitioner Ann Radcliffe, was an enlightenment vision of a distant past in which romance and criminality flourished together. Catherine, Jane Austen's naive heroine, is so immersed in the 'horrid' novels of Radcliffe and her followers that she begins to see the present-day world around her through the veil of the Gothic past, only to have that veil snatched away repeatedly. It is the act of switching between past and present that allows 'the modern' to appear so strikingly *as* modern, not as taken-for-granted everyday normality.

The majority of the novel is not set at Northanger Abbey but in what is called 'the Bath world' (II.x). Since originally the title featured the name of the heroine and not the Abbey, the reader was to look for continuities between the two locations she passes through rather than wait for the 'Gothic' plot to begin. What stands out about Bath from the start is that it is a bubble, an isolated economy, in which individuals can circulate at face value, unmoored by knowledge of their history or circumstances. Everything in Bath is about superficial display, whether it is the facades of the houses or the spectacle of the shop windows. And in this Bath world the members of the leisured class go round and round. 'Every morning now brought its regular duties', touring the shops, going downtown or uptown, attending the Pump Room to 'parade up and down for an hour', attending assemblies in the Lower Room and the Upper Room, attending the playhouse (I.iii).

It is an economy in which fraud can thrive, and the Thorpes exhibit to the reader their spurious values. 'I hate money', Catherine's Bath friend Isabella falsely declares, and in doing so confirms her resemblance to a worthless forged banknote (II.ii). Her brother John manifests inflationary tendencies. His boasts are designed to boost not only his own value, but that of anyone with whom 'he was, or was likely to be connected'. Hence his exaggerated notion of the wealth of his friend James Morland, who is engaged to Isabella, 'doubling what he chose to think the amount' of his father Mr Morland's clerical income, 'trebling his private fortune, bestowing a rich aunt, and sinking half the children'. For James's sister Catherine, his own target, 'he had yet something more in reserve, and the ten or fifteen thousand pounds which her father could give her, would be a pretty addition to Mr. Allen's estate'. He then 'adds twice as much' for the 'grandeur of the moment' since his confidante is General Tilney. The General has no acquaintance with Thorpe but this being Bath, 'never had it occurred' to him 'to doubt the authority' of the report, and he instantly determines to secure Catherine for his own son (II.xv).

The crucial stages in the education of the naive and guileless heroine occur when she learns not to take characters at their own valuation. This happens fairly quickly in the case of John Thorpe. Nevertheless, it requires courage for her, with all the 'civility and deference of a youthful female mind', to entertain the 'bold surmise' that with his 'idle assertions and impudent falsehoods' he might not be 'altogether agreeable' (I.vii; I.ix). She clings far longer to the idea of Isabella's genuine worth before being forced to abandon it in the face of overwhelming evidence to the contrary. The biggest puzzle of all is General Tilney, who possesses all the trappings of honour and dignity. He is seriously rich already and expresses 'most generous and disinterested sentiments on the subject of money' (II.xi). He is the father of her adored Henry, and seems not only to like her but to be actively courting her as a potential daughter-in-law. And yet

Catherine's intensive training in the conventions of Gothic enable her to divine that he is a counterfeit.

There are formidable barriers to the realisation that criminality in the Gothic romance style can co-exist with the modern. Northanger Abbey, the General's country seat, has been thoroughly modernised and boasts every new-fangled luxury and convenience. She is wrong in her anticipations about the Gothic building, and Catherine blushes at her own suspicions regarding the owner. Henry himself lectures her eloquently on the subject when he catches her searching for clues in the bedroom where Mrs Tilney had died abruptly, apparently unmourned by her husband.

> Does our education prepare us for such atrocities? Do our laws connive at them? Could they be perpetrated without being known, in a country like this ... where every man is surrounded by a neighbourhood of voluntary spies, and where roads and newspapers lay every thing open? Dearest Miss Morland, what ideas have you been admitting?

The answer of course is that such atrocities could be perpetrated, and the laws do connive at them, and this is tacitly admitted by the rhetorical mode of the questioning. Eventually Catherine hears enough 'to feel, that in suspecting General Tilney of either murdering or shutting up his wife, she had scarcely sinned against his character, or magnified his cruelty' (II.xv). He may not be a bandit chief but he is unquestionably a modern-day domestic tyrant and an economic predator, Ann Radcliffe's Montoni updated for Regency England.

There has been a substantial amount of research done on Austen's choice of recognisable and sometimes notorious names for her characters. Janine Barchas, for instance, makes the case for a reading of Catherine's exploits in Bath with Mr and Mrs Allen through the well-known history of Ralph Allen, the fabulously wealthy 'postal entrepreneur' and 'stone mogul' whose name was indissociable from the spa town.[10] It seems plausible to suggest that allusion to celebrities enhanced the works for the general reading public of the day. But what of the use of Austen family Christian names? These have not been much considered. Why, in *Sense and Sensibility*, did Jane name the somewhat inadequate hero 'Edward' and include two ill-fated young women called 'Eliza'? What might she have intended when she used her own name for the disagreeable sister-in-law of the heroine of *The Watsons*, or the gentle, beautiful sister in *Pride and Prejudice*, or the enigmatic Jane Fairfax in *Emma*, with her superlative piano-playing, her poverty, and her good looks? Granted, most of the Christian names in the Austen family were commonplace ones, but on the other hand, there were many other less personal choices available. Perhaps there was something in the mood or music of names which played a part in the selection process. It must have been difficult, after so many years of thinking of her first Bath novel as *Susan*, to change the heroine's name to 'Catherine' during the 1816 revisions because another novel had since appeared with the original title.

We can't be certain that the hero's name was 'Henry' in that first version, but when Henry was preparing the novel for publication under the title *Northanger Abbey*, immediately after Jane's death, he must have felt every fond repetition of his name like a ghostly caress. 'Henry's smile' has a therapeutic effect on the fond heroine (II.v). As in *Collection of Letters*, one of the skits Jane had written in her youth, a 'Henry' features both as brother and lover, and the line between the two is sometimes blurred. Eleanor Tilney scolds her brother for playfully quizzing Catherine: 'Miss Morland, he is treating you exactly as he does his sister' (I.xiv). In *Pride and Prejudice* Mr Darcy is only ever thought of as 'Mr Darcy' by Lizzy, in spite of her impudent treatment of him. In *Emma*, although hero and heroine are brother-and-sister-in-law and he has known her from birth, Emma declares that she cannot call him anything but 'Mr Knightley', except when required by the marriage ceremony (III.xvii). Mr Tilney is a stranger when they first meet, but he is 'Henry' in Catherine's mind from chapter ten of the first volume, at which point their acquaintance is aided and abetted by the friendship between Catherine and Eleanor. As a brother, Henry is notably attentive and empathetic; it is he alone who makes Eleanor's life with her father bearable. As a lover, Henry is remarkably fraternal, teasing and protective rather than amorous. It is only with difficulty, if ever, that the reader is brought to think of him as an ardent suitor in the final chapters. And he falls into banking metaphor, either an adoption of Henry Austen's habit or a broad hint: 'I am come, young ladies, in a very moralising strain, to observe that our pleasures in this world are always to be paid for, and that we often purchase them at a great disadvantage, giving ready-monied actual happiness for a draft on the future, that may not be honoured' (II.xi).

'O what a Henry!' Jane was to exclaim on hearing from Cassandra that their brother had been invited to the event of the London season to celebrate the victory of the allies in 1814.[11] Evidently she felt there was such a thing as 'a Henry' and it seems to have been a matter of charm; a gift that could be mobilised for social advantage. *Northanger Abbey* contains a flattering portrait of a Henry, witty and charismatic, while in *Mansfield Park* Henry Crawford shares these characteristics in a minor key. Henry Crawford is a master of picturesque taste, called upon to give his advice on the new modelling of the grounds at Sotherton. Henry Tilney is similarly expert, giving Catherine a crash course on the analytical appreciation of landscape during a walk round Beechen Cliff. Henry Austen, it has been revealed, may have moonlighted as a drawing instructor. In August 1805, Jane wrote to Cassandra in Kent asking her to bring back with her 'Henry's picture of Rowling' for some neighbours to see.[12] In the same year Fanny, Edward's eldest child, recorded in her diary that 'Papa went to Canterbury to fetch Aunt Harriet to take drawing lessons of Uncle H. A.' The most interesting mention of this talent for landscape sketching, with direct relevance to Henry's army agency business, is Lady Morley's reminder to her sister-in-law Theresa Villiers, many years later, that 'Mr Austen was y'r drawing master.'[13]

The reference is telling because it is evidence of the importance of social skills to the success of an army agent. Henry may first have become acquainted with John Parker, then the 2nd Baron Boringdon and later the 1st Earl of Morley, at Oxford University where they were contemporaries. Alternatively it could have been after they had both become militia officers, since Lord Charles Spencer, lieutenant colonel of Henry's regiment, was the uncle of one of Parker's closest friends, Lord Henry Spencer, son of the fourth Duke of Marlborough and another contemporary of Henry Austen's at Oxford. Parker was gazetted Lieutenant Colonel of the North Devon Militia regiment in 1794. He had a great estate, Saltash near Plymouth, and could easily manage the property qualification to get his foot on the ladder. In 1799 he became colonel, with the finances of the regiment in his gift. In 1803 he was to present the agency for the North Devons to Henry. A charm offensive, which might involve some private tutoring in landscape drawing for the sister of a patron, was part of good business practice.

An army agent could rise to any height if he played his cards right. Cox & Greenwood were cousins and business partners based at Charing Cross and known as the 'Bankers of the British Army'. They not only handled military pay, but dealt in delicate matters of regimental transfer and promotion involving even members of the royal family. Charles Greenwood, the more extrovert of the two, became a trusted friend and confidante to Prince Frederick, second son of George III, Duke of York and Albany and Commander-in-Chief of the British Army. On one occasion, the Duke of York introduced the army agent to the King as 'Mr Greenwood, the gentleman who keeps my money', at which Mr Greenwood remarked 'I think it is rather his Royal Highness who keeps my money.' The rejoinder greatly delighted old King George, who cried, 'Do you hear that? Frederick, do you hear that? You are the gentleman who keeps Mr Greenwood's money.'[14]

Jane may have had in mind such covert financial connections when she named Captain Tilney 'Frederick' and made him an officer in the 12th

Light Dragoons, a superior division which had been given the title the '12th Prince of Wales's Regiment of Light Dragoons' in 1768 by George III. The fact that his father General Tilney is 'obliged to go to London for a week' is another show of inside knowledge of Henry's trade. It has been ingeniously proposed by Clive Caplan, first, that the very fact that the General seems to be unemployed at the height of the war may indicate that he has bought his way to the top, and second, that his departure to visit London at a critical moment in the campaign to acquire Catherine and her fortune for his younger son, points to another shabby possibility. Promotion to the rank of general 'could cause the loss of the value of a commission, which was £3,500 for a lieutenant-colonelcy'.[15] General Tilney may then have opted to keep the rank of lieutenant colonel for pay purposes while holding the rank of general by retiring on half-pay, and furthermore seems to have opted to collect it from London in person, cutting out the middle man.

It was on a visit to the Royal Pavilion at Brighton in 1832, while playing a rubber of whist with his old friend Duke Frederick, by then redubbed William IV on inheriting the throne, that Charles Greenwood collapsed and died in his eighty-fourth year. Greenwood's executor and heir, a nephew, discovered that instead of inheriting a large fortune he was liable for £25,000 in debts, partly due to Greenwood's 'contributions to impecunious royalty'. He was no 'pound-shilling-and-pence-agent' but rather a generous benefactor his eulogist proposed, perhaps tongue in cheek; 'the able advocate and judicious counsellor of officers, whose want of family influence seemed to require an easy and unembarrassed medium of communication with the Commander-in-Chief'.[16]

Eliza, like Henry, understood the importance of an aristocratic patron, and following their marriage immediately set to work on Colonel Lord Charles Spencer. She may have 'left off *trade*' in the sense of collecting admirers on her own behalf, but she could still contribute to Henry's prospective business, writing languishingly to Phylly of Lord Charles 'if I was married to my third husband instead of my second I should still be in love with him – He is a most charming creature so mild, so well bred, so good, but Alas he is married as well as myself and what is worse he is absent and will not return to us in less than a month.'[17] Spencer was fifty-eight years old and an unlikely love object. He had, however, stellar ties to the government and the court. At the time he was busy organising plump sinecures for his sons, and hoped to raise his own income by the same method, casually asking his cousin Earl Spencer to lobby for a place 'which would make up the whole about £2,000 a year, a *lord of the Admiralty*, or some such thing'.[18] There was every reason for Henry and Eliza to want to hitch their wagon to his star, and their combined efforts paid off. Although Spencer resigned and was replaced as colonel by William Gore-Langton in 1798, thanks to his continuing influence Henry was appointed the London agent for the regiment. On 24 January 1801, Henry mustered the troops one final time, issued pay to officers and to sergeants for distribution to the rank and file, and collected the receipts. The commanding officer and adjutant examined and certified his returns, they were signed off, and his army career was at an end. The next month the pay list of the Oxfordshire Militia carried the entry: 'Agent: H. T. Austen & Co.'[19]

Henry moved from one chain of command to another, according to Eliza. She assured Phylly, 'Henry well knows that I have not been much accustomed to control & should probably behave rather awkwardly under it, and therefore like a wise man he has no will but mine'.[20] But the bank ledger tells a different and more comradely story. On 30 September 1797, Eliza de Feuillide, having taken charge of her own finances following the dissolution of the trust fund, opened an account in her own name at Drummonds Bank, at Charing Cross. In March 1798, after the wedding, Henry closed his personal account at Hoare's, and on 4 July opened a new personal account at Drummonds Bank, credited with £576.17s. On 11 December Eliza closed her account and Henry transferred the balance of £644.5s from his account and together they opened a joint account at Drummonds Bank. These centripetal steps spoke of mutuality in their life together as well as in business. The money was gleaned from war and empire, and the fact that the account served for both the army agency and Eliza's expenses seems surprising. Yet the integration of business and romance at first promised well.

As with Henry's decision to join the militia and to marry Eliza, no evidence remains to indicate what the Austen family thought of his move into finance. There must at least have been relief that he would not now end up in the regular army and be shipped overseas. In 1801 news arrived that William Fowle, a medic and the brother of Cassandra's deceased fiancé, had died in the Egyptian campaign. He left a wife and two young children of five and four. Much ink has been spilt over Jane's apparently heartless remarks on massive British casualties following the battle of Corunna in 1809 ('Thank Heaven! we have had no one to care for particularly among the troops') or the Battle of Albuera in 1811 ('How horrible it is to have so many people killed! And what a blessing that one cares for none of them!'), but fervent thankfulness that Henry had left the military as well as Cassandra's bereavement and sympathy for stricken friends provide the most ready explanation.

When Cassandra stopped over with Henry and Eliza on the way back from Godmersham in January 1801, Jane was avid for news of their London life and particularly interested in the business premises: 'I hope you will see everything worthy of notice, from the Opera House to Henry's office in Cleveland Court; and I shall expect you to lay in a stock of intelligence that may procure me amusement for a twelvemonth to come.'[21] Henry had set up shop at Cleveland Court, a distinguished address on the doorstep of the palace of St James and fashionable Pall Mall, but most significantly, just around the corner from Warren Hastings's sister and brother-in-law who lived in Cleveland Row. John Woodman, an attorney who acted for Hastings and who, with George Austen, had overseen the finances of Philadelphia Hancock and her daughter, was evidently ready to help the new enterprise get off the ground. In terms of topography as well as London social contacts, Henry was building on foundations provided by Eliza.

The location of their home, too, was dictated by Eliza's prior attachments. They leased a house at 24 Upper Berkeley Street, a recently built terrace in the familiar patch near Portman Square, north of Oxford Street. Here they settled comfortably with Eliza's beloved French domestic staff, Madame Bigeon and her daughter Marie Perigord, joined by a chef, Monsieur Halavant. Phylly Walter visited them in June and found them living 'quite in style', but also rather like two children playing house. She noted that Eliza talked sentimental nonsense about retiring to Wales and Henry agreed straight away. Eliza preferred to refer to Henry as 'my cousin' ('I have an aversion to the word *husband* & never make use of it'). When Henry became very ill, 'a cough, hectic pain in the side and in short every thing which denotes a galloping consumption', their bond became even tighter. Eliza watched over Henry anxiously for five months, missing the signs that the condition of her son Hastings was rapidly deteriorating.[22]

The death of Hastings de Feuillide aged fifteen on 9 October came as a severe shock. He was buried five days later in Mrs Hancock's grave, in the churchyard at St John-at-Hampstead. At the end of the month Eliza wrote to Phylly thanking her for her condolences, and reporting that Henry was better, cured by a prescription from the fashionable physician Dr Matthew Baillie. She mentioned that Henry was not at home. Tomorrow she would go to Godmersham to pay a visit without him. This is the last we hear of Eliza's vivacious confidential voice. Philadelphia Walter preserved no more of their correspondence. Was it because the letters spoke of continuing unhappiness? Did Eliza come to feel that marrying Henry had been a mistake? She turned forty on 22 December 1801, still in theory of child-bearing age, but there would be no more children. Neither would she and Henry become one of those married couples who live only for each other, like the Leigh-Perrots, or the fictional Admiral Croft and his wife so winningly depicted in *Persuasion*. Henry and Eliza would holiday and visit together from time to time, but for the most part they led parallel lives.

At the start of the marriage Eliza had been certain of 'all the comfort which can result from the tender affection & society of a being who is possessed of an excellent heart, understanding & temper'. It is impossible to know where the blame lay for the distance that grew between them. The Hancocks' pattern of marital absenteeism may have been passed down to Eliza, or else Henry's enthusiasms may not have accorded with the quiet existence she now wanted. All we know is that an estrangement took place, noted by Jane after Eliza's death.

At the end of October 1801 news of peace preliminaries began to circulate. Britain had been at war for eight years, and Henry's prospects were still tied to the conflict with Napoleon just as surely of those of the sailor brothers, Frank and Charles Austen. Peace would reduce the prospects for advancement for the latter two, and very likely halve their pay. Henry could expect less in the way of fees for handling the regimental payroll; there would be fewer officers in service and fewer loans to arrange. All the more reason to focus on the trade in commissions. In peacetime they could then be treated purely as merchandise and posed less of a risk to health.

On 23 November 1801 Henry and his official partner J. Henry Maunde, a former fellow-officer who had served as paymaster of the Oxfordshire Militia after Henry's resignation, entered into a speculative scheme involving the clandestine sale of commissions. It was initiated by a contract composed of eight articles. The draft copy owned by the Jane Austen Memorial Trust announces that these were 'secret articles'. Henry Austen and Henry Maunde were to 'make themselves responsible for due attendance at the office and correct management of accompts'. Another signatory, one Charles James, was to remain in the background. His involvement in the partnership would never be made public, but he would have 'at all times a perfect right to enter the said office, & inspect all papers and accompts relative to the joint concern' and was 'invited to make such inspection as frequently as he chooses, for the sake of mutual satisfaction'. The three partners would equally divide the expenses and the profits. The contract also left room for each of the partners to venture their own capital in order to purchase vacant commissions 'for speculation' and take 10 per cent of the profit before the division of spoils. The draft copy bears the signatures, 'Henry Thomas Austen' and 'Charles James'.[23]

Who was this Charles James? He too had served in the militia, and it has been suggested by T. A. B. Corley that he and Henry Austen may have met at Colchester Barracks, when the North York Militia was quartered there along with the Oxfords during the winter of 1796–97.[24] According to a laudatory obituary, which reads very much as if it were the work of his own hand, 'Few men ever evinced more activity in all the transactions of life.' That was no lie. He was a prolific writer, beginning in the late 1780s with a translation of a play by Beaumarchais, several volumes of verse, and a response to Edmund Burke's *Reflections on the Revolution in France* (1790) expressing sympathy for the revolutionaries. His personality, like his list of publications, seems full of contradictions. At the time he signed the agreement with Henry he was specialising in military reference works. His pocket *Regimental Companion* went through numerous editions, and a handsome 1,000-page *Military Dictionary* boasted a dedication by permission to the Commander-in-Chief, the Duke of York.

At any moment, Charles James was liable to dash off a political pamphlet on a burning issue of the day, usually in connection with the reform of the militia, and more often than not with some reference to his personal grievances. He was obsessive regarding slights and criticisms to the point of monomania, boasting of his own remarkable integrity, fiercely justifying his conduct and rounding rancorously on detractors. This habit would grow with the crackdown on army corruption later in the decade. The engraved portrait that appears on the frontispiece of the *Military Dictionary* accompanied by some belligerent lines from one of his poems shows the face of a pugilist, rather than that of the sensitive man of letters he purported to be.

Portrait of Charles James, frontispiece, *Military Dictionary* (T. Egerton, 1802).

The publications also make apparent Charles James's gift for servile flattery towards great men. He had need of this talent for he had been born an outsider, the son of a Warwickshire merchant, very likely Catholic since he was educated abroad at Jesuit colleges in Bruges and Liège. The dedications to his works make clear that he was close to Major-General Francis Rawdon, Earl of Moira. James's obituary states that he served for a time as Moira's 'confidential secretary'. From 1802 at the latest he in fact acted as Moira's 'principal man of business', contracting loans on behalf of this notoriously spendthrift aristocrat, and attempting to keep him out of the bankruptcy court.[25]

Since Lord Moira was to be in some degree Henry's nemesis, it is worth pausing to review his career up to this point. Towards the end of the 1780s, Lord Rawdon, as he then was, after coming back a hero from the American war and taking his seat in the House of Lords, had endeared himself to the sons of George III. He became the public champion of George, Prince of Wales, proposing that the heir be made Regent during the King's first bout of madness in 1788, and doing his best to persuade Parliament to pay off the Prince's gargantuan debts. By 1795 the sum had climbed to an astounding £630,000, tens of millions in today's money. The outbreak of war with France did nothing to curb George's extravagance.

Lord Moira was himself in possession of an income that would have satisfied some princes. He inherited an estate from a maternal uncle yielding £3,000 per annum in 1790, and three years later acceded to the earldom, with the addition of £18,000 annually. High living and frequent loans to the Prince of Wales, however, plunged him deep in debt . 'Moira and I,' George would say, 'are like two brothers, when one wants money he puts his hand in the other's pocket.' In fact the transfer of funds seems to have been all in one direction, and the Prince 'never repaid a single pence'. By the spring of 1804, 'Moira was in debt to his bankers for the mind-boggling sum of £100,494.19.7', an amount that could never realistically be repaid.[26] He speculated in iron smelting and coal mining, and was driven to selling off portions of his inherited estates in Ireland and in England. Parliamentary immunity protected him, but it was with fellow feeling that he repeatedly pressed for reform of the laws which put debtors in prison.

The Prince of Wales failed to honour his personal debts, but endeavoured to repay Moira in other ways. In 1790 Moira had been appointed Grand Master of the Freemasons by his royal friend. Freemasonry was the epitome of the workings of power and influence in the land; invisible networks, whether of kinship, armed service, social clubs, or church and political clientage, operating silently for the most part. George favoured the Whig party largely because his father preferred the Tories and inter-generational conflict was a firm tradition in the royal family. When Tory hegemony was broken in 1806 and a coalition government formed, Moira was rewarded with high office and a large salary and could then dispense patronage in turn, distributing more minor posts to followers like Charles James. Moira remained loyal even as the Prince's reputation was dragged through the mud on an almost daily basis. He had invested too much to be able to draw back now.

The Treaty of Amiens was agreed on 25 March 1802. It was to be an interlude lasting only fourteen months, but at the outset Henry felt an urgent need to find new sources of income and evidently applied to Warren Hastings, perhaps for a loan, and was turned down. In a subsequent letter to Hastings on 5 June he made the best of it, praising the former Governor-General as 'the preserver of India, & the special saviour of the British Empire', and describing 'sensations little short of horror' at 'the possibility of appearing to you capable of meanness or rapacity'. Henry declared his own 'innate sense of independence' and lamented 'the ingratitude of that kingdom which had prevented the powers of your benevolence from equalling the wishes of your heart', signing off 'your friend and servant'.[27] Eliza must have told him that requests of this kind would be fruitless. She had said so three years before when Phylly asked if Mr Hastings could be induced to pull strings on behalf of one of her brothers.[28] Nevertheless, the letter must have served its purpose. In time the former ruler of Bengal did exert himself to help the husband of his god-daughter.

Eliza had already bade Warren Hastings an affectionate farewell in March, in a note announcing that she and Henry would join the flow of travellers taking the first opportunity in nine years to visit France. Their object was to reclaim the Guyenne estate of her first husband. On 28 June they were issued with passports, along with a friend Mrs Marriott, who had stood witness at their wedding. Although the mission was unsuccessful, Henry established commercial contacts that led to a sideline in wine smuggling. He returned to England alone in March 1803, and in April stayed for two nights with Warren Hastings at Daylesford. Eliza and Mrs Marriott were still in France when war broke out on 16 May, and raced to the coast to avoid internment.

In their absence, Jane had also experienced drama. She and Cassandra alleviated a tedious Bath winter with a visit to Catherine and Alethea Bigg at Manydown House near Steventon. On the evening of 2 December, their brother Harris Bigg-Wither made a proposal of marriage to Jane. In contrast to John Thorpe's proposal to Catherine Morland in *Northanger Abbey*, there could be no mistaking it, although it was equally unexpected. Jane, caught off guard, accepted. She was not in love with Harris, who was five years her junior and likeable enough, but simply an overgrown, slightly uncouth presence in the background of the friendship with his sisters. However, the match would mean escape from city purgatory and return to familiar rural society, greatly enhanced social status and a life of relative luxury not only for Jane, but for Cassandra, and their mother also should Mr Austen die before her. Jane spent a night tormented by the opposing demands of aspiration and prudence, and the next morning retracted her consent, and departed with her sister. They arrived in tears at the Steventon Rectory, insisting that James take them back to Bath immediately.

According to her niece Caroline Austen, Harris Bigg-Wither made a perfectly decent husband to another woman in due course: he 'went through life very respectably, as a country gentleman', siring ten children. That prospect was exactly what Jane turned her back on. Caroline commented in her reminiscences,

> I have always respected her for the courage in cancelling that yes ... All worldly advantages would have been to her – & she was of an age to know this quite well – My aunts had very small fortunes & on their father's death they & their mother would be, they were aware, but poorly off – I believe most young women so circumstanced would have taken Mr W. & trusted to love after marriage.[29]

In the event of Mr Austen's death, the women's situation would be bleak indeed. Mrs Austen had independent investments yielding approximately £190 per annum, and Cassandra's fiancé had left her a legacy of £1,000, giving her an income of £50 on which to scrape by. Jane would have nothing at all and be wholly dependent on the charity of the rest of the family. She was jolted into the need to become an economic agent in her own right, and made another attempt to enter the literary marketplace. In the spring of 1803 William Seymour, Henry's lawyer and business agent, successfully arranged the sale of *Susan* for the rock-bottom price of ten pounds.

Jane's acceptance of this pitiful sum must have been an act of desperation: anything to make a start; next time she would do better. The payment for her first work represents an extraordinary contrast to the amounts regularly flowing in and out of Henry's bank account, or the prize money awarded to her sailor brothers on top of their salaries. Yet £10 to £20 was the standard rate offered by the Minerva Press, the first publisher to attempt the mass-marketing of popular fiction. Many in its stable of authors were needy widows or spinsters. *Susan* was now in the hands of Crosby & Co., at No. 4 Stationers Hall Court in the printing and publishing quarter of the City of London, close to St Paul's Cathedral. The title was advertised, but the novel did not appear. Why this should be, Jane never learned; it was a mystery as impenetrable as the inventions of Mrs Radcliffe. The manuscript would remain hidden in a cupboard, untouched and unseen for the next thirteen years, as useless as the collection of washing-bills found by its heroine, while all around whirred the ceaseless activity of typesetting, inking, printing.

In Westminster, Henry moved the office from Cleveland Court to No. 2 Cannon Row, Parliament Street, well situated near the Houses of Parliament and the War Office and began canvassing energetically for new agency business. On 20 May 1803 he wrote to Colonel George Purefoy Jervoise of the newly re-embodied North Hampshire Militia, following up an overture by his brother James, in an attempt to poach a client from London's most illustrious army agency. He argued that while the loss of one regiment could matter little to Cox & Greenwood, with 'one hundred regular battalions' on its books, the acquisition of a second regiment would make an enormous difference to Austen & Maunde. If the colonel transferred he would be helping another 'Hampshire man' to raise his credit and persuade other militia companies to give him their patronage.[30] Henry argued that a smaller agency could offer superior promptness and accuracy, and assured the colonel that Messrs Cox and Greenwood, whom he knew well, had borne him no grudge for taking over as London agent for the Oxfordshires. The reply was terse, in spite of the fact that Colonel Jervoise had had the pleasure of dancing with Jane four years earlier. The Jervoises, she had commented, were 'apt to be vulgar'.[31]

Henry could make little progress through his own efforts. The assistance of his secret partner Charles James and the influence of Lord Moira turned out to be vital to expanding the operation. On 24 July 1803, Henry's firm became London agents for the Nottinghamshire Militia under Colonel Edward Thoroton Gould who had served in America with Moira. There must have been rejoicing in the Austen family at this breakthrough, and Jane was to immortalise the name of Gould's residence, Mansfield Woodhouse, in two separate novels. Success followed success, as Henry had anticipated. Having added a second company to his books, he could utilise Lord Charles Spencer's connection with Colonel John Parker, Lord Boringdon, to acquire the North Devon Militia. On 24 September the North Devons transferred from the agency Ross & Ogilvie of 37 Argyll Street, who had run into financial difficulties and were on the verge of bankruptcy.

The aid of Charles James came at a substantial price. Not only does the Drummonds' bank ledger for Austen & Maunde show frequent money transfers to James, but by the autumn of 1803 Henry had agreed to make a series of loans to Lord Moira. As Stuart Bennett has uncovered through examination of the Moira papers in the Huntingdon Library, Moira and James were in constant dialogue on the former's chronic debt problems, and in this period James makes a number of allusions to the 'pecuniary accommodation' promised by 'Mr. Austen'.[32] It is vital to an understanding of Henry's ethos and the reaction of his family after his downfall to

note that this perilous involvement with James and Moira wasn't solely
for his own benefit. The loans coincide with reminders from James to
Moira to pull strings at the Admiralty on behalf of Frank and Charles
Austen. In Charles's case these persistent efforts yielded success when he
was offered command of the sloop, HMS Indian, stationed in Bermuda,
in October 1804. The previous month, Austen & Maunde relocated to
a courtyard apartment in the refurbished Albany in Piccadilly, formerly
the town house of the Duke of York, while Charles James took one of the
bachelor apartments in the house itself.

Jane, meanwhile, had begun work on a new novel, and if the central
theme of poverty and blighted prospects of single women is anything to
go by, she did so in an anxious state of mind. It is generally agreed that
this manuscript fragment, later given the title *The Watsons*, was abandoned because the subject matter was too close to her own circumstances.
Dialogue dominates, and it is often very funny, but the fear of becoming
an object of ridicule is also prominent. Elizabeth, the oldest of four unmarried sisters, introduces the theme in the opening scene as she drives
the youngest, Emma, to the winter assembly in a nearby market town in
an 'old chair', an inferior open carriage,

> ...you know we must marry. – I could do very well single for my own part
> – a little company, and a pleasant ball now and then, would be enough for
> me, if one could be young forever, but my father cannot provide for us,
> and it is very bad to grow old and be poor and laughed at.

Emma Watson's expectations had been very different. She was raised by
wealthy relations and had stood to inherit a fortune of eight or nine thousand pounds until her uncle died and her aunt took an Irish adventurer
as her second husband. She cannot yet submit to the idea of marriage
'merely for the sake of situation': 'Poverty is a great evil; but to a woman
of education and feeling it ought not, it cannot be the greatest. I would
rather be teacher at a school (and I can think of nothing worse) than

marry a man I did not like.' Elizabeth counters that to her knowledge nothing could be worse than being a teacher at a school and the opinion, both comical and fathomlessly bleak, 'I should not like marrying a disagreeable man any more than yourself; but I do not think there *are* many very disagreeable men; I think I could like any good-humoured man with a comfortable income.'[33]

The Austens in Bath were also facing the unknown. The lease on Sydney Place was coming to an end and Mrs Austen had suffered a brush with death. There was a late summer idyll of walks and fine weather on the Dorset coast in 1804, when Henry and Eliza joined them at Lyme Regis, and then took Cassandra with them to Weymouth, leaving Jane with her parents. On their return in October they fatefully rented a cheaper house at Green Park Buildings, a location rejected during the previous search due to its reputation for rising damp and 'putrid fevers'. On 21 January 1805, George Austen died at the age of seventy-three of a sudden feverish complaint, and the funeral took place five days later at St Swithin's Church, Walcot, where he and Cassandra Leigh had married.

The brothers, with kindly intent, immediately set to work agreeing annual contributions to replace, at least in part, the revenue from the living at Steventon and a small annuity, both lost at Mr Austen's death. Frank offered £100 but Mrs Austen would accept only £50. James also gave £50, as did Henry 'so long as my present precarious income remains'. They expected that Edward would contribute £100, and that when added to the small investments of Mrs Austen and Cassandra Austen, the total would be 'a clear £450 *per annum*'.[34]

But the great injustice of dependency remained. The brothers could act, could seek their fortune, and increase their incomes, while the opportunities available to educated women were close to non-existent. 'Female economy will do a great deal,' says Emma in *The Watsons*, 'but it cannot turn a small income into a large one'. And then there was the ghastly spectacle of the men managing affairs over the heads of 'our dear trio'. 'By Heaven! a woman should never be trusted with money,' Robert

Watson tells his sister Emma. Henry wrote to Frank that his mother
would remain at Green Park Buildings until March and then 'probably
reduce her establishment to one female domestic & take furnished lodgings', adding that with a 'smaller establishment ... I really think that
my mother & sisters will be to the full as rich as ever'. And James wrote
similarly to Frank, who was on duty at Portsmouth:

> I believe her summers will be spent in the country amongst her relations &
> chiefly I trust among her children – the winters she will pass in comforta-
> ble lodgings in Bath. It is a just satisfaction to know that her circumstances
> will be easy, & that she will enjoy all those comforts which her declining
> years & precarious health call for.[35]

He makes no mention of the sisters, seemingly condemned to remain
appendages.

The bereaved women undertook two money-saving moves in Bath in
the next five months, first to lodgings in Gay Street and then to noisy
and noisome Trim Street in the centre of town. Soon, however, a lifeline
appeared. Frank was to be married to Mary Gibson in July 1806. He
proposed that his mother and his sisters set up house together with him
and his wife. Southampton was conveniently close to the naval dockyards
in Portsmouth; they would be able to keep Mary company while he was
away at sea. They gladly accepted. In 1806 Jane permanently departed
from Bath 'with what happy feelings of escape'.[36]

CHAPTER 3

HENRY TURNS BANKER: *LADY SUSAN* AND THE POPHAM POEM (1806–1809)

William Pitt the Younger had dominated the political scene as Prime Minister since 1783, almost without interruption. In January 1806 he died and the Tory government was replaced by a coalition, the 'Ministry of all the Talents'. The patrons Henry had cultivated during his years as a militia paymaster and army agent were almost all attached to the Whig party, the former opposition. His former colonel in the Oxfordshire Militia, Lord Charles Spencer, became Master of the Mint. Lord Moira was given the plum role of Master-General of the Ordnance, which included control of military supplies, and Moira in turn promoted Henry's secret partner, Charles James, to the rank of major in the Corps of Artillery Drivers. Benefits trickled down to Austen & Maunde. In December 1806 the business acquired two more agencies: the Derbyshire Militia led by Colonel Lord George Cavendish, brother of the Duke of Devonshire, and the 4th Garrison Battalion, a newly formed unit, with Sir Charles Hastings at its head. Lord Moira, who was cousin to Charles Hastings and probably helped to arrange a baronetage for him, may have pointed him in Henry Austen's direction, but Warren Hastings also had a hand in the matter. He was a close friend of Sir Charles, not a relation in spite of the shared surname, and wrote to thank him for his 'benevolent and effectual services to my friend Austin [*sic*]'. Hints had evidently been dropped: 'you anticipated my solicitation in his behalf, so as to leave me a mere passive expectant of the good which you meditated for him, and I ardently desired'.[1]

It was at this favourable moment, with the income from the agency growing and the likelihood of more ministerial favours to come, that Henry took the step of becoming a partner in three new country banks, at Alton and Petersfield in Hampshire, and Hythe in Kent. These were the counties he knew best; he had contacts, and opportunity beckoned. The Bank Restriction Act of 1797 restricted convertibility of banknotes to bullion, but stimulated the circulation of paper money and credit, and led directly to the opening of hundreds of small private banks across the country. The war, which necessitated increased government spending and taxation, was also a powerful stimulus for the banking sector. With regard to banknotes, the Bank of England served mainly as a 'Bank of London'. Country banks met the urgent need for the issue and receipt of bank-notes in the provinces, but they required a link to the London money market. Henry positioned himself to benefit all round, with a stake in the provinces and the capacity to act as London agent or 'correspondent'.

Hampshire was having a good war. Alton and Petersfield were small but bustling market towns, and a substantial part of the business of the new banks was the provision of loans to farmers and landowners who were benefiting from an agricultural boom. Due to the difficulty of importing provisions, food prices remained at record levels. Henry set up premises at No. 10 in the High Street at Alton in partnership with Edward William Gray, a twenty-year-old wholesaler recently established in the town. Gray had probably been brought to Alton by the marriage of his brother Frederick to Mary Ann Clement, daughter of the influential local attorney Thomas Clement. There was no effective regulation of private banks, and a later Prime Minister would complain of a state of affairs in which '[a]ny petty tradesman, any grocer or cheesemonger, however destitute of property, might set up a bank in any place'.[2] He could easily have been referring to Gray at Alton, who was indeed a grocer and cheesemonger, although his wholesale business was presumably adequate security for a banking enterprise. Experience was provided by Henry and by a third partner, William Vincent, Gray's uncle, who was already a partner in a bank in nearby Newbury, while Thomas Clement was the leaseholder of the premises at No. 10 in the High Street. The likelihood is that Henry came to know Clement and the Grays by way of his brother Edward's property holdings in the area, or else through the Terrys and Digweeds who were lifelong friends of the Austen family at Steventon and connected by marriage with the Clement family at Alton.

Henry's connections in Petersfield, thirteen miles south of Alton, may have been formed in the militia years. Henry's former regiment had been quartered at Petersfield in the winter of 1794–95, giving him the opportunity to make the acquaintance of William Blunt, who had recently opened a bank there. Now, in 1806, Austen and Blunt went into partnership at 13 Market Square, with William Stevens Louch as a third partner.

Louch was from Kent, and soon left Petersfield to undertake the opening of a bank in partnership with Henry Austen at 93 High Street in Hythe on the south Kent coast, seventeen miles from Godmersham. At Petersfield he was temporarily replaced by Henry Clement, presumably a relation of Thomas Clement. The local sponsor in Kent was probably William Deedes, Member of Parliament for Hythe from 1807 to 1812, married to the younger sister of Edward Austen's wife Elizabeth Bridges and therefore Edward's brother-in-law. When in Kent, Jane socialised with the Deedes and had dined at their home, Sandlings, in September the previous year.

The town of Hythe was a hive of activity in the war years, situated near both a prime smuggling operation and the headquarters of the Royal Staff Corps, an engineering unit engaged in building a military canal. Since May 1806, following the defeat of Napoleon's navy at Trafalgar, both sides had escalated economic warfare, disrupting the trade of the enemy through naval blockades. In November, Napoleon inaugurated his Continental System, banning British trade with Europe, and Britain would retaliate the next year with the Orders in Council of 1807, intended to stop neutrals, notably the United States, from trading with France. Smuggling had always been rife along the south coast of England, but now it was almost the only way to maintain any form of cross-Channel trade. Meanwhile, from 1804 to 1809, fears of invasion led to the construction of the government-financed Royal Military Canal running from Hythe to Rye across Romney Marsh, employing up to 1,500 men. The new bank would thrive on these developments.

Austen & Maunde, at around the same time, was appointed the London corresponding bank for two other country banks, both of them connected with another feature of the wartime economy: the craze for home resorts created by the exclusion of British subjects from the Continent. The Horwood Well Bank was set up to serve the new Horwood Well Spa in Somerset, a speculation dreamt up by French prisoners on parole at nearby Wincanton and promoted by a local barrister Richard Messiter and his business partner William Gapper. The spa was advantageously located on the Bath to Weymouth road, and boasted a direct coach service to London and several inns. There were rumours that the Duke of York's former mistress Mary Anne Clarke had a hand in the scheme, having moved temporarily to Devon after the break-up with her royal lover, the Commander-in-Chief of the British Army. Mrs Clarke, it would soon emerge, had been actively involved in the black market in military commissions. The army agent Charles Greenwood was one of her confederates, and she was also acquainted with Charles James. It may have been by this route that Austen & Maunde came to act as agents for the bank at Horwood Well.

The Buxton and High Peak Bank served the elegant Derbyshire spa town known as the 'Bath of the North'. Buxton was first promoted as a health resort in the 1780s by the 5th Duke of Devonshire, whose country seat was nearby at Chatsworth, using profits from his copper mines, and the efficacy of its waters had been endorsed by the physician and luminary of the Midlands Enlightenment, Erasmus Darwin. Henry Austen's connection to the Duke and his pet scheme came courtesy of the Duke's brother, Lord George Cavendish, who was Colonel of the Derbyshire Militia and the latest addition to the list of clients at the Austen & Maunde army agency. The partners in the Buxton bank were George Goodwin, a former captain with the Derbyshire Militia, and his son.

Jane had not previously given much thought to banking. Although banknotes abounded in her childhood writings, there was only one reference to banking services. At the conclusion of *Evelyn*, Mr Gower is sent 'a draft on our banker for 30 pounds' by the ridiculously bountiful Mr and Mrs Webb, the parents of his deceased wife, in thanks for informing them of their daughter's demise and his swift remarriage. Where did a banker register in the social scale? What ideas were associated with banking by the Austen family? It was not a profession traditionally chosen by sons of the gentry. Negative references to moneylenders and stockjobbers abound in the literature of the eighteenth century. But come the war and the expansion of the financial sector, the profession became more respectable. Walter Bagehot, the son of a banker who became the editor of *The Economist* from 1860, reflected that in this earlier period the name 'London banker' had a 'charmed value', and was taken to represent 'a certain union of pecuniary sagacity and educated refinement which was scarcely to be found in any other part of society'. Bagehot regarded banking as a hereditary calling, but his remarks show why it might have been attractive to newcomers. A man could live in affluence and yet have mind to spare for other more intellectual pursuits, if he chose. The banker-poet Samuel Rogers, friend of all the literary celebrities of the day, was a case in point. 'There has probably very rarely ever been so happy a position as that of a London private banker,' Bagehot concluded, 'and never perhaps a happier.'[3]

In *The Watsons*, Jane glanced at the new prominence of providers of financial services in rural communities. Mr Tomlinson the banker could claim to have the 'best house' in town, outdoing more genteel residents, but prefers to think of his 'newly erected' dwelling as a country mansion, since it boasts a shrubbery and carriage sweep. Jane evidently shared the assumption that a banker is bound to be rich.

'When a man has once got his name in a banking house he rolls in money,' Lady Susan asserts. None of Jane's letters from August 1805 to January 1807 have survived, but around this time she made a fair copy of *Lady Susan*, her short novel in letter form, and it may have been in honour of Henry's latest endeavour that she decided to make Mr Charles Vernon, the brother-in-law of the eponymous villainess, a banker. He, like Henry, is a gentleman banker, the younger son in a family of ancient lineage. Vernon Castle, the family seat, was inherited by the elder son, Lady Susan's late husband, but sold to pay debts incurred by the profligate couple. Lady Susan prevented Charles from buying it, but sweet-natured Charles bears no grudge, however, and is willing to offer her hospitality when she writes, at the start of the narrative, expressing her yearning for country seclusion in the bosom of her family. On arrival she sends a sharp appraisal of the Vernons' standard of living to Mrs Johnson, her equally worldly friend in town: 'The house is a good one, the furniture fashionable, and everything announces plenty and elegance. Charles is very rich I am sure.'⁴

Charles Vernon may be rich but where Lady Susan is concerned he is a soft touch, ignoring his wife's well-founded suspicions. In the course of the story he is thoroughly outmanoeuvred. Lady Susan, on the other hand, has calculating charm and acquisitive passions to spare, as she weighs the benefits of potential husbands for her daughter and herself. The idea that she could be based on Eliza de Feuillide has been a subject of dispute. Certainly Eliza's tendency to refer to flirtation as her 'trade' and to joke about mercenary marriages fits the bill, but jokes about money and greed for it were something of a tradition in the Austen family. Some years later Jane would write to her niece Fanny Knight with regard to the reception of *Mansfield Park*: 'tho I like praise as well as anybody, I like what Edward calls *pewter* too'.⁵

The opening letter of *Lady Susan* is like a word-game involving the use of as many money metaphors as possible. Lady Susan writes to Charles

Vernon, 'My dear brother, I can no longer refuse myself the pleasure of *prof-iting* by your kind invitation, when we last parted, of *spending* some weeks with you at Churchill.' She expresses her eagerness to 'secure an *interest*' in the hearts of his children and laments the way in which her husband's long illness 'prevented my *paying*' due attention to her own daughter, who instead was consigned to a governess 'unequal to the *charge*'. Jane early on sensed the rising spirit of capitalism, and had epitomised the insight in an astonishing sentence in *Edgar and Emma*, written at the age of twelve: 'Mr Willmot was the representative of a very ancient family and possessed besides his paternal estate, a considerable share in a lead mine and a ticket in the lottery.'[6] In this way, she described the layering of economic life in her time, the simultaneity of residual feudalism, industrial capitalism and speculative finance. In *The Watsons*, she showed the way the mental habits of the speculative economy were infiltrating even the most remote recesses of the countryside through the vogue for card games based on banking and finance. Mrs Robert Watson responds to a proposal to play a round game by remarking '*Speculation* is the only round game at Croydon now, but I can play anything.'[7] Four years later, in a letter to Cassandra, Jane would declare herself the patron of Speculation and bemoan its eclipse in popularity at Godmersham by another card game, Brag, in a comic poem. There will be more to say about the dramatic episode featuring a game of Speculation in *Mansfield Park*.

Full-dress fictional portraits of bankers and financiers can be found in the works of Balzac, Dickens, George Eliot and Anthony Trollope. They are rarely glimpsed figures in Romantic-era fiction, but the fact that in 1785 the Marquis de Sade made one of the four libertines who preside over the horrors of *120 Days of Sodom* a banker, alongside three other wealthy authority figures: an aristocrat – a bishop and a judge – is a backhanded testament to the new status of banking as a prestigious choice of career.

The banking system was diverse. At the top of the hierarchy, bankers were firmly installed as part of the political establishment. The Bank of

England had been founded to pay for a war at the end of the seventeenth century and assumed its modern function as a central bank at the end of the eighteenth century, as the result of another war. In its original form it was a temporary private syndicate with a charter to lend money to the Crown for twelve years, but it gradually took on the functions of a permanent branch of government. The Bank was situated in the City of London, at some distance from the Houses of Parliament in Westminster, but it held government cash, issued government bonds, arranged loans and bought silver and gold for the government, and handled government business overseas. It also issued banknotes that circulated mainly in the metropolis, and acted as private banking house for the London business community. Austen & Co. would open a Drawing Office account there. The premises in Threadneedle Street acquired the symbolic importance of a bastion of national economic security.

To the country at large, the Bank of England at times appeared alien and even threatening. There was widespread unease at its political intervention in 1797 when a paper money regime was imposed. Throughout the war years, the architect Sir John Soane was at work doubling the site of the bank to three-and-a-half acres, and enclosing it within a secretive windowless facade. Somewhere in its shadowy and labyrinthine interior, the monstrous National Debt was tended, doubling in size between 1793 and 1802, and then doubling again by the end of the conflict with France in 1815 to a peak of £1 billion; more than twice the value of all the economic activity in the country. The number of clerks employed there swelled accordingly, from 300 in 1792 to 900 by 1813.

In *Northanger Abbey* a misunderstanding occurs when Catherine alludes to a keenly awaited Gothic novel as 'something very shocking indeed, that will soon come out in London ... more horrible than any thing we have met with yet', at which Eleanor Tilney grows seriously alarmed. Henry clears up the confusion by explaining to Catherine that Eleanor has been 'picturing to herself a mob of three thousand men assembling at St. George's Fields; the Bank attacked, the Tower threatened, the streets of London flowing with blood' (I.xiv). His reference is to the Gordon Riots of 1780 when popular resentment at the repeal of anti-Catholic laws exploded into days of violent protest against the backdrop of economic hardship resulting from war in America, with the Bank of England targeted as an emblem of tyranny.

Now, in the midst of even worse economic conditions for the labouring poor caused by war with France, the Bank was itself seen by its critics as a Gothic nightmare with murderous intent. The small denomination notes for £1 or £2 produced by the Bank of England were of poor quality, easily counterfeited, and the counterfeits all too often 'uttered' by poor innocents. The cartoonist George Cruikshank, after seeing a woman hanged for inadvertently passing a bad £1 note, produced a gruesomely satirical *Bank Restriction Note* featuring the figure of Britannia devouring an infant, garlanded with skull and crossbones. Alongside is a row of men and women hooded, nooses round their necks, praying before execution. The banknote is signed on behalf the government and the Bank of England not by the chief cashier, but by Jack Ketch the legendary hangman.

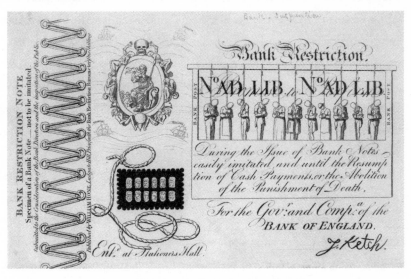

George Cruickshank, *Bank Restriction Note*, 1819.

Entirely distinct from the Bank of England were the London private banks. The most distinguished of them had developed from goldsmiths' businesses in the course of the seventeenth century: Child's, Coutts, Drummonds, Hoare's. Their role was to manage the money of members of the royal family, the aristocracy, the gentry and a few select organisations; keeping cash deposits, making short-term loans and reluctantly agreeing mortgages. By the latter part of the eighteenth century they had stopped issuing banknotes and they avoided commercial dealings, preferring to maintain their air of exclusivity.

It must have been gratifying to Reverend George Austen and his family to have the distinction of holding accounts at Hoare's Bank, the oldest in the kingdom, founded by Sir Richard Hoare in 1679. David Garrick, Lord Byron and Eton College also banked at 37 Fleet Street, although at the time the names of customers were a carefully guarded secret. Service was deferential, and they could expect personal attention from the director himself, always a Mr Hoare down through the generations. Hoare's Bank had risen to great heights in the mid-eighteenth century during the reign of Sir Richard's grandson Henry II, nicknamed 'Henry the Magnificent' for his charisma and patronage of the arts. A substantial part of his enormous wealth went towards adornment of the family estate at Stourhead, including the celebrated neo-classical gardens. Yet Mrs George Austen was pleased to refer to his successors, Harry Hoare of Mitcham and his family partners, as 'those blundering Hoares', complaining that, 'so many of us bank with them that it sometimes puzzles their heads'.[8]

At Drummonds Bank at the sign of the golden eagle at Charing Cross, Henry and Eliza Austen, and Henry Austen & Co., were in the company of such account holders as Isambard Kingdom Brunel, Robert Adam, Capability Brown, Josiah Wedgwood and, as the result of a royal tiff, King George III. The King removed his patronage from Coutts Bank, provoked in part by the use of his personal account to pay off some of his son the Prince of Wales's bills. The founder of the bank was the Scottish goldsmith Andrew Drummond, who migrated to London and set up his business in 1712. His first customers were mainly Scottish gentry and army agents, but the number of customers grew steadily, from 400 in 1744 to 3,200 in 1795, with profits approaching £30,000 per year.

Caution and trustworthiness were the watchwords of such 'West End' banks. Their priority was to maintain high cash reserves. They served the 'Town' and their counterparts in the ancient business quarter to the east, similarly cautious, served the 'City', discounting bills of exchange for merchants and industrialists, lending to stockbrokers, and lending 'on call' with the guarantee of rapid repayment. Both the West End banks and the City banks were reluctant to tie up their assets in long-term investments.

The country banks and their London agents were by contrast the daredevils of the financial world. The country banks multiplied in periods of growth, and although they had a tendency to drop like mayflies during a reverse, they were now an essential feature of the commercial landscape, taking risks on industrial development, agrarian reform, and the rise of consumer culture. In *Letters on Regicide Peace* (1796), Edmund Burke recalled that when he first came over from Ireland in 1750 the country at large almost entirely lacked 'those machines of domestick credit'; there were at most 'twelve banker's shops at that time out of London'. But now they could be found 'in almost every market town' and this circumstance, he concluded triumphantly, 'demonstrates the astonishing increase of private confidence, of general circulation, and of internal commerce'. While country banks flourished, proud Britons could avoid negotiating with the vile regicides across the Channel. But even so Burke feared that such exuberant expansion in the sector 'might be carried to an excess'. L. S. Pressnell, the authority on country banking during the Industrial Revolution, concurs with Burke that around 1750 there were a mere handful of country banks in England and Wales, but by 1784 there were about 120, and by the start of the 1790s around 300. The advent of war in 1793 caused a short sharp decline, but the suspension of cash payments in 1797 inaugurating the era of paper money, credit expansion, and inflation provided ideal conditions. By 1801 the number of country banks reached 'almost 400, and not far short of 800 at the peak in 1810'.[9]

The country banks were a vital resource for the nation at large, yet by law they were restricted to six or fewer partners and thereby vulnerable to shocks. Early in the eighteenth century the Bank of England had been awarded a monopoly on joint stock banking. Other note-issuing banks in England had to remain small-scale concerns (Scottish banks were exempt from this statute). Yet, in contrast to the state of affairs in other European countries, no provision was made for public regulation of their practice and multifarious activities, 'their note issues, their cash ratios, their reserves, cheque transactions or expansionist credit policies'.[10] It was a recipe for instability.

Henry's London office has been described as a West End bank since it was 'relatively small and specialized' and conducted business with senior officers and aristocrats.[11] It was also, of course, located in the West End, at first operating from Albany on Pall Mall. But his business was different from the established West End institutions in a number of ways, in spite of some overlap in clientele. First of all, regimental accounts and commission brokerage remained an important component, and lending to upper-class officers was simply an extension of its origins as an army agency. Secondly, Austen & Maunde had grown by expanding their role as London agents from the militia to country banks. London corresponding banks, sometimes called 'country bankers' themselves, provided Bank of England notes when required, kept reserves and arranged overdrafts, managed the flow of bills of exchange between the provinces to the capital, and generally maintained the level of confidence needed to enable the local banks to issue their own currency. Most of these activities were outside the remit of West End banks, which were London-centric and no longer associated with the issuing of banknotes. Furthermore Henry, individually, was engaging in a problematic practice known as 'pig on pork', acting as a London correspondent for satellite banks while at the same time joining three of them as a partner to create an interlocking structure. This involved a blurring of responsibilities and liabilities which would have been anathema to a prudent West End banker. Their houses had evolved from the possession of large stocks of solid gold bullion and it shaped their character. Henry's attitude to risk was more closely akin to that of the opportunistic, fly-by-night spirit of many of the country banks.

The inexperience of Austen & Maunde was apparent in initial blunders during 1806. They were, after all, learning on the job. The most bizarre took place when Henry Austen was away establishing the branch in Alton. Henry Maunde issued a promissory note for £200 to an individual calling himself 'Count Stuarton'. The Count promptly vanished taking the £200 with him. A reward notice was issued after a year and distributed to coffee houses which the Count was known to have frequented. Charles James kept a copy of it bound up with other papers. The wording of the note was reproduced in full:

Five Guineas Reward

Whereas the Drawer of the following Promissory Note has absconded, whosoever will give notice at Mr. Withers's, Palsgrave-place, Temple-bar, of his present abode or dwelling, so that he may be arrested, shall receive Five Guineas for such information.

24 October 1806.

£200.00

Three Months after Date I promise to pay to Mr. Henry Maunde, or his Order, Two Hundred Pounds, for Value received. Signed Ct. Stuarton.

Payable at Messrs. Austen, Maunde, and Austen, Bankers, Albany.

The description of the culprit which follows is like a page out of a comic novel by the popular mid-eighteenth-century writer Tobias Smollett. The 'Count' was 'ill-looking; marked with the small pox; large red nose' and 'of late dressed in black, in consequence of the death of Cardinal York, having passed himself for a descendant of the Royal House of Stuart'. He 'speaks very full and quick, with a Dutch or German accent; is continually mouthing out extravagant expressions of loyalty, and saying, that he is persecuted by Bonaparte and the French government'. It is difficult to imagine how Maunde gave credence to such a clownish figure; one gets the impression from this incident and another similar misstep a few years down the line, which was to have far more serious consequences, that he was genial but a bit dim. Jane, during future visits to Henry, mentioned other bank staff in her letters but, curiously, never Maunde. Close study of novels might have sharpened his wits and made him a better judge of character.

The promissory note itself resurfaced after nearly two centuries, discovered in the catalogue of a rare books dealer by David Gilson, the author of *A Bibliography of Jane Austen*. On the reverse was an addendum, 'H. Maunde. Pay the Contents to Hugh Moises M. D. Value in Account. Cha: James.' This suggests that the Count may have been appointed as a go-between for Charles James and a third party, Mr Moises, making Maunde's error more comprehensible. James kept some strange company, and played out his own life as a torrid melodrama.[12]

Before long, another mishap occurred relating to the Alton banking house. Olive Burlton, a widow residing in Poole, sent Austen & Co. in London a cheque for £92.18s issued by Austen, Gray & Vincent of Alton. This cheque had originally been directed to Thomas Clement at Alton, but was now endorsed to Mrs Burlton. She requested that the banknotes be sent directly to her, cut in half, with the second set of halves posted separately after the first set had been received, a common security measure. Austen & Co. ignored her instructions and transferred the money to the Poole Bank, where it was retained against a debt. She vehemently denied the debt, and sued Austen & Co. in the Court of the Exchequer. No record remains of the outcome.[13]

There were signs of strain in the secret partnership. On 7 February 1806 a Mr Woodcock, closely connected to Charles James, wrote to him to complain about the refusal of Austen and Maunde to lend him £200. Around this time, they declined to make further advances of money to Lord Moira, although they stopped short of demanding repayment of existing debts.[14] The 'Count Stuarton' affair must also have created internal tension. Furthermore, the illicit dealing in army commissions, Charles James's area of specialisation, was on the brink of becoming a national scandal. In 1806 the relationship between the Duke of York and Mary Anne Clarke ended, and the cast-off mistress immediately threatened to publish details of her relationship with the Commander-in-Chief of the British armed forces. She was silenced for the moment by an annuity, but a storm was brewing. Charles James would be caught up in it when it broke three years later, and Austen & Co. would only barely escape.

Those who have done the most to excavate the outlines of Henry Austen's army agency and bank business have sometimes been inclined to make sweeping criticisms of his judgement and methods. However, it should be acknowledged that when it comes to archival sources it is the mistake, rather than the routine good practice, that looms largest in the records. Austen & Co. enjoyed fifteen years of prosperity. This record looks relatively impressive when seen against the broader picture of scandal-hit army agents and disaster-prone country banks. Henry opted to ride the rollercoaster of the wartime economy and was subjected to numerous ups and downs. Yet, for a while, he managed to stay on the tracks and did it with some flair. There may have been good judgement, as well as luck, in his decision to move away from Charles James and army commission brokerage.

On 24 January 1807 Austen, Maunde & Austen took out a lease for 10 Henrietta Street, Covent Garden. The rent was £110 per annum, payable quarterly, and the contract was signed by Henry and Frank Austen and by Henry Maunde, witnessed by George Lefroy and James Austen. Frank had joined the business after belatedly receiving prize money for the capture of four enemy vessels seven years before, and his involvement must have changed the dynamic of the partnership. He was practical and methodical, and had high moral standards. While he was on shore leave and monitoring affairs it seems unlikely that he would have tolerated Charles James's shady presence, and Henry may have invited him to become a partner for just this reason. For a time Maunde continued to live at No. 1 The Courtyard, Albany, but the new trading name created the impression of a fresh start. The relocation to Henrietta Street brought the agency closer to the City and to the major private banks lining Fleet Street and the Strand. The proximity of the river and its bridges made for easy communication with the satellite banks in Kent and Hampshire.

Jane now had two banker brothers, and as of March 1807 she was sharing a permanent home with one of them. Frank Austen rented a house at No. 2 Castle Square in Southampton to accommodate his wife, mother and two sisters during his absence on convoy duty to India and China. There would have been constant talk of Austen & Co. in the Southampton household, and of its prospects as they were affected by the events reported in the newspapers. Jane's heightened responsiveness to economic shocks was registered in a short poem 'On Sir Home Popham's sentence – April 1807'.

> Of a Ministry pitiful, angry, mean,
> A gallant commander the victim is seen.
> For promptitude, vigour, success, does he stand
> Condemn'd to receive a severe reprimand!
> To his foes I could wish a resemblance in fate:
> That they, too, may suffer themselves, soon or late,
> The injustice they warrant. But vain is my spite,
> *They* cannot *so* suffer who never do right.

Like Shelley's famous sonnet, 'England in 1819', which begins with a cluster of contemptuous epithets – 'An old, mad, blind, despised, and dying King...' – this short philippic is in the caustic tradition of Juvenalian satire. The ministry she berated with such indignation was the coalition

government dissolved the previous month, led by the Whig Lord Gren-
ville. The occasion was its treatment of the naval hero Sir Home Popham
over his conduct in South America.

Popham had been commissioned to patrol the Cape of Good Hope in
Africa, but went rogue to investigate an insurrection in the Spanish American colonies. There were high hopes in Britain that Spain's loosening grip
on its empire could open up new trading opportunities for British goods.
While there he learned of the delivery of a large consignment of Peruvian
specie to Buenos Aires and a contingent of British troops marched into
the town virtually unopposed, requisitioning the gold. At a time when
bullion in the British Isles was in chronically short supply, a shipment
of more than a million dollars had great symbolic importance. It arrived
in September 1806 and was taken in state to the Bank of England accompanied by cheering crowds and bands playing 'Rule Britannia' and
'God Save the King'. Back in Buenos Aires, however, the inhabitants had
risen up against their new rulers, and the British troops were captured and
imprisoned. Popham returned home in disgrace and was court-martialled
on board HMS Gladiator at Portsmouth on 6 March 1807, the day after
the Austens' move to Castle Square.

There was a personal reason for Jane's interest. Eliza's dear friend Lady
Burrell had a son, a captain of dragoons, who was killed in the affair.
When it came to the prosecution of Popham Jane's ire may have been
raised as much by her brothers' banking concerns, as by the Austens' naval
connections or attachment to the Tory party. Investors were in constant
search of a good return on their capital, and Popham's adventure had
raised hopes of a boost to the economy which were then dashed when
the ministry declined to send prompt military reinforcements. Brian
Southam has conjectured that Henry Austen may have had a 'direct interest' in prospects for trade in South America, due to the fact that the Earl
of Moira was a friend of Popham and an ardent supporter of his venture
in Rio.[15] We have seen that the link with Moira, via Charles James, had
resulted in new clients for the Austen & Co. army agency, and that in

return Henry had loaned money to the perpetually cash-strapped Earl. Now that Moira was Master-General of the Ordnance he had immediate access to the First Lord of the Admiralty, and had agreed to help Frank Austen gain command of a frigate. In February 1807 Jane reported to Cassandra the disappointing result of this renewed effort: 'the first Lord after promising Ld Moira that Capt. A. should have the first good frigate that was vacant, has since given away two or three fine ones'. Frank had 'no particular reason to expect an appointment now', but Jane and the rest of the family did not blame Lord Moira.[16] He was bosom friend of the Prince of Wales, he owed Henry large sums of money, and the Austens continued to cherish hopes that his influence would serve their interests.

The nature of Jane Austen's political opinions has long been a moot point. Most clergymen were Tories and Jane's nephews and nieces, who had little interest in the matter, assumed that she shared the 'feeling of moderate Toryism that prevailed in the family'.[17] But on social questions there are many indications that she held progressive views and she was always ready to satirise the pretensions of wealth and power. Party politics on the whole was an unedifying spectacle. The Whigs claimed to be the guardians of liberty and progress but once they got a partial hold on power in 1806 their patrician leaders more closely resembled pigs at the trough. The one uplifting achievement was the abolition of the slave trade in 1807, forced through Parliament by the joint efforts of the evangelical Tory William Wilberforce and the veteran radical Whig Charles James Fox. In the early autumn of 1806, James and Frank Austen were diligent in attending political meetings in support of the re-election of the staunchly Tory William Chute, though Jane herself seems to have disliked him. Loyalty was expected of James, as the rector in a parish controlled by Chute. But Lord Moira was a Whig, and he too was cultivated by the Austen brothers. In this period political allegiance was dictated more by economic interest and external factors of birth and geography than by personal belief or ideology. Higher up the social scale Lord Charles Spencer, Henry Austen's main patron, was notorious for his shifting party loyalties, wholly dictated by the quest for remunerative government sinecures. The reforming Whig politician Francis Horner was to remark of him and his tribe, 'The Marlborough family supports every ministry, but it is always bought'.[18] Jane's family, with better justification, given their difficulty in keeping a foothold in genteel society, were similarly flexible in their sympathies.

On 22 June 1807 Frank set sail with a convoy bound for South Africa, China and the East Indies, leaving his family in Southampton. His wife had given birth to their first child in April, and Mrs Austen was a semi-invalid. Martha Lloyd, following her mother's death, had come to live with them and shouldered some of the domestic burden, but Cassandra was often at Godmersham lending a hand, leaving Jane with the major share of responsibility at Castle Square. There was no time for writing, and little opportunity for travel: the most that could be managed that year was an excursion to stay at Edward's grand Hampshire property Chawton Great House, recently vacated by a tenant. In December 1807, as Jane turned thirty-two, she drew up her cash account for the year. She had received a legacy of £50 from a friend of the Leigh-Perrots, and £6.4s.6d remained. The greatest expense, £13.19s.3d, had been clothing, and second the laundering of clothes, £9.5s.111/2d, she noted precisely. The following year it would be Jane's turn to visit Godmersham, and she seized the opportunity to spend a month with Henry and Eliza.

Henry collected Jane from Steventon in the middle of May 1808 and brought her to No. 16 Michael's Place, Brompton. Since 1804 he and Eliza had been living on the south-west outskirts of London, just off the ribbon development which would later be renamed Brompton Road and distinguished by the great museums of Victoria's reign. The house was somewhat cramped, Jane reported; it may be that they were trying to save money while the bank business was getting established. The area had long attracted artists and actors and the bohemian ambience probably pleased Henry and Eliza. Their address no longer exists. St Michael's Place was an unsuccessful development perhaps, it has been suggested, because 'the site was low-lying and damp'.[19] Some of the forty-four terraced houses were still unfinished shells when it was swept away at the end of the nineteenth century to be replaced by mansion blocks in renamed Egerton Gardens.

No letters survive to suggest how Jane passed the time in London, but soon after her arrival at Godmersham, Jane wrote to Cassandra that she had left Henry in reasonable health and 'the brewery scheme is quite at an end: at a meeting of the subscribers last week it was by general, and I believe very hearty, consent dissolved'.[20] This remark relates to Henry's part in the largest speculative bubble since the South Sea Company crash of 1720. Plans for joint stock companies to promote new products proliferated in the wake of the disappointment over the South American export trade. Henry and his partners were keen to launch a company producing genuine 'Old English Ale' rather than the poor-quality adulterated variety commonly available. His interest had perhaps been piqued by his Hampshire associates; Alton was home to two important breweries. The scheme collapsed because competition for funds was fierce, and potential investors feared exposure to unlimited liability should things go wrong. It was also overtaken by global events. In May 1808 the people of Madrid rose up against their French overlords and the Spanish revolt was sparked. Prospects of access to Spanish American markets were renewed, and speculative investors turned in that direction once again.

Jane now had a scheme of her own that may have been hatched during the visit to London. In the autumn she wrote to Cassandra who had taken her place at Godmersham, 'I depended upon Henry's liking the Alton plan, & expect to hear of something perfectly *unexceptionable* there through him.'[21] Henry's Alton bank partnership had suggested the idea that Mrs Austen, her daughters and Martha Lloyd could move there, closer to Steventon and with the promise of regular visits from Henry himself. At Castle Square they received two generous food hampers which they assumed came from Henry, though they came without any sign of his handwriting 'even as a direction to either', and the present of a pheasant and a hare from Henry's partner Edward Gray and his brother; 'Is this to entice us to Alton, or to keep us away?'[22]

It has been assumed that the move to Chawton village, one mile south of Alton, was instigated by Edward Austen Knight, with the offer of the cottage which he had inherited as part of the Knight estate. However Jane's remarks suggest that she took the initiative of asking Henry to seek out rented accommodation for them in Alton, and that Edward's offer was a subsequent development. In October, Edward's wife Elizabeth Bridges died after giving birth to their eleventh child and he encouraged them to move to Kent, perhaps hoping to have his spinster sisters on call at all times. But without much hesitation, and in spite of their affection for Edward and his children, they chose Chawton, because of its proximity to Steventon, relative freedom and independence, and the benefits of the nearby bank. In addition to bringing Henry frequently into Hampshire, the house of Austen, Gray & Vincent would serve as their post office.

'The progress of the Bank is a constant source of satisfaction,' Jane wrote to Cassandra in January 1809. She was delighted to hear from her sister, who had stopped over in Brompton on her way to Kent, of Eliza's good health and Henry's 'increasing profits'. Perhaps now he wouldn't need to work his poor bank clerk, nicknamed 'High-diddle', so hard.[23] Waiting for the move to Chawton Cottage that would take place in the summer, Jane was fired up and ready for another attempt on the publishing industry. After six years of silence from Crosby & Co. following their purchase of the copyright to *Susan*, she finally wrote in an attempt either to spur them into publication or reclaim the manuscript, disguising her identity with the pseudonym 'Mrs Ashton Dennis'. She assumed they had 'by some carelessness' lost the novel. If so, then she could supply another copy by August. Should they fail to reply, however, 'I shall feel myself at liberty to secure the publication of my work, by applying elsewhere.' She signed off meaningfully, 'I am Gentlemen &c &c, MAD–'. The reply which came two days later was a crushing blow.

We have to acknowledge the receipt of your letter of the 5th inst. It is true that at the time mentioned we purchased of Mr. Seymour a MS novel entitled Susan and paid him for it the sum of 10£ for which we have his stamped receipt as a full consideration, but there was not any time stipulated for its publication, neither are we bound to publish it. Should you or anyone else we shall take proceedings to stop the sale. The MS. shall be yours for the same as we paid for it.

She was being asked to redeem the manuscript as if from a pawnbrokers. It was as if some strange fatality was blighting her ambitions. She knew that her novels were better than the general run of fiction that was printed and sold every day of the week. How could her precious first work have fallen into the hands of a villain who vindictively thought it 'worth while to purchase what he did not think it worth while to publish'? This is how the enigma was stated in the 'Advertisement' prefixed to *Northanger Abbey* once it was finally published in 1818. The reply from the publisher had been signed 'For B. Crosby & Co I am yours etc., Richard Crosby'.[24] We need look no further for the explanation of the private joke attached to Mr Morland in the first paragraph of *Northanger Abbey*, 'a very respectable man, though his name was Richard'.

Cassandra seems to have destroyed letters that Jane sent her when in low spirits. There is a gap in the correspondence after the move to Bath, and also between April 1809 and April 1811 that may have had some relation to this humiliating frustration of her desire for authorship. Yet the relocation to Chawton, which took place on 7 July 1809, was cause for happiness. Frank's wife had moved at the same time to Rose Cottage in Alton, and given birth to a second child. Jane wrote a celebratory letter-poem to Frank, who was back at sea convoying East India ships to China, rejoicing not only in the arrival of a son who would inherit Frank's own admirable qualities, but also the arrival at 'Our Chawton home': 'convinced that when complete, / It will all other houses beat'.

The Chawton home has often been represented as a retreat into the familiarity of a small rural community after the alienating and disruptive experience of urban life in Bath and Southampton. But there was a feature of the village of Chawton that set it apart from a quiet hamlet like Steventon: the road. In 1753 an Act of Parliament had transformed Chawton High Street, widened and henceforth maintained by a turnpike trust with powers to collect road tolls from travellers. It had been turned into one segment of an arterial highway. Chawton Cottage was located yards from the point where the main road from London forked: one route leading west to Southampton via Winchester, the other continuing due south past Chawton Great House, the mansion owned by Edward Austen Knight, to Fareham and Gosport on the coast.

Jane's new home had been bought in 1769 by Thomas Knight II, and became a coaching inn until it was converted into a residence for the steward of the Chawton estate in 1787. The traces of its commercial use can still be seen on the streetside elevation, where there is a blocked up hatch 'through which barrels were unloaded into the cellar'.[25] The garden was once the yard for horses and coaches. The front of the house was situated hard against the road, so close to the traffic that palings were built to protect the walls from the danger of a runaway vehicle.[26]

In *The Watsons* Jane had perfectly evoked the approach of an unknown vehicle in a remote village such as Steventon: 'A sound like a distant carriage was at this moment caught; everybody listened; it became more decided; it certainly drew nearer. It was an unusual sound for Stanton at any time of the day, for the village was on no very public road, and contained no gentleman's family but the rector's.'[27] The soundscape at Chawton could not have been more different. By Caroline, James Austen's younger daughter, the busy road was fondly remembered from visits to her grandmother and aunts: 'Collyer's daily coach with six horses was a sight to see! And most delightful was it to a child to have the awful stillness of night so frequently broken by the noise of passing carriages, which seemed sometimes, even to shake the bed –.'[28]

The road gave life at Chawton Cottage a public dimension. Until a

fence was constructed screening the front, the Austen ladies were on display. Old Mrs Knight in Kent wrote to her granddaughter Fanny soon
after the move, 'I heard of the Chawton party looking very comfortable
at breakfast, from a gentleman who was travelling by their door in a
post-chaise.'[29] Seven years later, Jane had not tired of looking out onto
the world in motion, and described the termly migration of pupils from
London to Winchester College in a letter to a nephew: 'We saw a count-
less number of postchaises full of boys pass yesterday morning – full of
future heroes, legislators, fools and villains.'[30]

Alton too, although it consisted of only three or four streets, offered
animation and interest. It could be reached on foot along the turnpike
road in twenty minutes. It was easy to call on Mary in Lenten Street or
enquire for letters at Henry's bank in the High Street. The town was
a transport hub, with several regular services for London and the rest
of Hampshire operating on a daily basis. These services named for the
coachman or the manager – Collier, Falknor, Yalden – would crop up
in Jane's letters with some frequency. The coaches and the London road
along which they travelled would acquire before long a vital significance.
'I want to tell you that I have got my own darling child from London,'
she would one day write of *Pride and Prejudice*, 'on Wednesday I received
one copy, sent down by Falknor, with three lines from Henry'.[31]

News similarly travelled fast from London. At the start of 1809 the
Mary Ann Clarke affair erupted. It featured prominently in the press
for the rest of the year, and Austen & Maunde were to receive some
unwelcome publicity. In January 1809 Colonel Gwyllym Wardle, a newly
elected MP, accused the Duke of York of involvement in the sale of army
commissions. He brought evidence that the Duke's former mistress
had been trafficking military appointments with the complicity of the
Commander-in-Chief, and his motion of censure was seconded by the
leader of the small band of radicals in Parliament, Sir Francis Burdett. An
inquiry was called, and Mrs Clarke was publicly questioned at length in
the House of Commons, revelling in the limelight and freely implicating

the Duke. Although he was acquitted of complicity, the stink of corruption forced him to resign. Wardle was hailed as a hero by supporters of economic and political reform, but by June Mrs Clarke had been paid £10,000 and awarded an annuity of £400 by the government in return for York's letters and the destruction of her tell-all memoirs, and was ready to turn on her former collaborator. She persuaded an upholsterer to sue Wardle for non-payment of a bill for furniture for her London house, with the implication that he had bought her testimony with new furnishings. Wardle was now on trial and forced to pay the bill and costs, and in December his attempt to clear his name by proving his accusers guilty of conspiracy failed.

Wardle was ruined and soon left politics. His efforts, however, blew the lid on the sale of army commissions. Public outrage was stirred by the accusation that while moneyed nonentities could bribe their way into the officer class, long-suffering veterans were left by the wayside. Charles Greenwood, of Cox & Greenwood, a name that appears constantly in the ledger of Henry's business account, was named and shamed in the many satirical prints inspired by the scandal. Charles James, too, was heavily involved, and ridiculed in a pamphlet by Thomas Hague, 'A Letter to His Royal Highness the Duke of York'. The 'Letter' lampooned James's pretensions as a major in the Corps of Artillery Drivers, implying that the promotion had merely been bought with favours:

> I do not question his dexterity as a trickster, his cold closeness as a *bargain driver*; but, as a *gunner driver*, I may be permitted to speak of him; to ask what are *his* claims to the rank he bears, and the pay he receives? Do they arise from foreign service, wounds, or exploits?

It also insinuated that James, having been educated at a foreign Jesuit college, was a closet Catholic and a likely traitor. Major James's copy of the pamphlet can be found in the British Library collection, covered in furious annotations rebutting the charges levelled by that 'venereal cripple' Hague.

Austen & Maunde were named in the proceedings of the parliamentary commission on 9 February 1809. Back in Mary Ann Clarke's heyday
the two Henrys had hoped to be appointed the agents of a new regiment
and gave Jeremiah Donovan, a go-between, a list of under-the-counter
prices for commissions in the unit. Donovan had been an army surgeon
in the American war, and was acquainted with the Earl of Moira. He
forwarded applications for commissions to Mrs Clarke, who was paid
premiums of hundreds of pounds for making recommendations to her
lover, the Duke of York.

It was further revealed in Parliament that the illicit dealings of Austen
& Co. included the sale of positions in the East India Company. Jeremiah
Donovan was again a co-conspirator. When a buyer came forward for a
clerk's post – a 'writership' – with the Company, the interested parties met
at the Henrietta Street bank, where the covert payment was deposited and
then apportioned into pay-offs.[32] The identity of the East India Company
insider was not disclosed. The aim of the exercise was to expose the scale of
the corruption rather than pursue individual prosecutions. Austen & Co.
had merely been named as participants in a universal culture of bribery,
but the experience must nevertheless have been an embarrassment and a
rebranding exercise was in order. They acquired another new partner.

James Tilson was the brother of Lieutenant-Colonel John-Henry
Tilson, a former fellow-officer in the Oxfordshire Militia. He came trail-
ing a history of bankruptcy, having been a partner in the Dorset & Co.
Bank in New Bond Street which failed in 1803, but to offset that he had
an impeccably respectable family background, including another brother,
Christopher, with the rank of major-general in the regular army, and
a paternal grandfather who, according to a descendant, had been the
'personal friend and constant companion of King George the Second'.[33]
Moreover, James Tilson and his wife were charming company. Henry and
Eliza were soon meeting them socially on a daily basis, having moved in
July 1809 to No. 64 Sloane Street, close to the Tilsons' residence in Hans
Place, Chelsea. A new chapter was beginning for Henry, as well as Jane.

CHAPTER 4

THE SELF-MADE AUTHOR:
SENSE AND SENSIBILITY
(1810–1811)

Jane wrote to Cassandra from Henry and Eliza's home in Sloane Street in a state of euphoria. Two years had passed since the humiliating reply from the publisher Richard Crosby regarding his refusal to publish *Susan*. The next surviving letter, dated 18 April 1811, was written in a perfect holiday of spirits as she awaited the publication of *Sense and Sensibility*. 'I have so many little matters to tell you of, that I cannot wait any longer before I begin to put them down...' She was engaged in a continuous social round, visiting and being visited, and fitting in an excursion to a museum or gallery here and there, and shopping:

> I am sorry to tell you that I am getting very extravagant & spending all my money; & what is worse for you, I have been spending yours too; for in a linen-draper's shop to which I went for checked muslin, & for which I was obliged to give seven shillings a yard, I was tempted by a pretty coloured muslin, & bought ten yards of it on the chance of your liking it; but, at the same time, if it should not suit you, you must not think yourself at all obliged to take it; it is only 3s. 6d. per yard, and I should not in the least mind keeping the whole.

Trimming and silk stockings had been purchased in the crush of Grafton House. There was only an item from Wedgewood's elegant showroom still to be ticked off the list, though she continues to hanker after a straw hat like Mrs Tilson's. In contrast to the 'stupid parties' of the Leigh-Perrots at Bath, she finds the constant 'little parties' involving the Tilsons at Henry's very congenial. Although she has a cold, she loves the walking and the coaching in London.

Eliza was busy preparing for a great musical party. Eighty guests had been invited, and there would be five professional singers '3 of them Glee-singers' and amateurs besides. Henry was busy making enquiries about Frank and Charles at the Admiralty and working at the bank, but also found time to arrange theatre tickets. Jane and Henry were to have gone to the theatre on Saturday night – Eliza resolved to stay at home to save her strength for the party – but unfortunately there was a last-minute change of programme: 'Hamlet instead of King John' and 'Our first object to day was Henrietta St to consult with Henry'. They would now be going to *Macbeth* on Monday; she need not explain to Cassandra the disappointment of missing Sarah Siddons in the iconic role of Constance in *King John*.

Jane was stricken with guilt at a couple of points in the long letter which recounts the doings of four days, exclaiming 'I am a wretch, to be so occupied with all these things, as to seem to have no thoughts to give to people & circumstances which really supply a far more lasting interest – the society in which you are – but I do think of you all I assure you.'[1] Yet she couldn't help herself. She was entirely caught up in the whirl of London, resistless.

The reason for her heedless excitement? That is apparent at the start of her next letter, in which she replies to a question in the letter just received from Cassandra,

> No indeed, I am never too busy to think of S&S. I can no more forget it, than a mother can forget her sucking child; & I am much obliged to you for your enquiries. I have had two sheets to correct, but the last only brings us to W.s first appearance...

Although she'd been in London since the end of March with the express purpose of dealing with the proof sheets of *Sense and Sensibility*, they were slow in coming. Cassandra passed on Mrs Knight's regrets that she would have to wait till May to receive the published novel, and Jane explained that even June now seemed unlikely. She would have to leave London in less than a week but, 'Henry does not neglect it; he *has* hurried the printer, & says he will see him again today', and when he in turn leaves London on business 'It will not stand still during his absence, it will be sent to Eliza.'[2]

'I can no more forget it, than a mother can forget her sucking child.' Jane was now thirty-five, and although she preened when Mrs Knight's brother Mr Wyndham Knatchbull called her a 'pleasing looking young woman' at Eliza's musical party, she could be very certain that literary offspring were the only sort she would ever have. That did not grieve her, now publication was finally underway. The shock of the death of Edward's wife following childbirth was still raw. Even before that event she had anxiously responded to the news that Mrs Tilson, then a new acquaintance, was pregnant with the comment 'poor woman, how can she be honestly breeding again?'[3] Frances Tilson was thirty-three, and this was to be her eighth child out of a total of eleven. Four Tilson daughters had been born in quick succession, a year apart. Jane, now that she had a legitimate union with a publisher, intended her progeny to arrive with equal dispatch.

How had this first successful birth transpired? Henry, in the 'Biographical Notice' he attached to *Northanger Abbey* and *Persuasion* when they were published in 1817, explained the process in the following terms:

Neither the hope of fame nor profit mixed with her early motives. Most of her works ... were composed many years previous to their publication. It was with extreme difficulty that her friends, whose partiality she suspected whilst she honoured their judgement, could prevail on her to publish her first work. Nay, so persuaded was she that its sale would not repay the expense of publication, that she actually made a reserve from her very moderate income to meet the expected loss. She could scarcely believe what she termed her great good fortune when 'Sense and Sensibility' produced a clear profit of about £150. Few so gifted were so truly unpretending. She

regarded the above sum as a prodigious recompense for that which had
cost her nothing.[4]

He might as well have been explaining that babies were brought by
storks; as if the manuscript put by for so long had magically become
print simply as a result of the earnest solicitations of Jane's circle. And he,
more than anyone, knew better.

He was often at Alton on bank business, and after his mother and
sisters with their friend Martha Lloyd had moved to Chawton Cottage,
he stayed with them there. Seeing Jane more frequently, he became aware
of her muted grief at the failure to get her work published. How could
he have been so remiss? He, like his brothers, had been intent on making
his own way in the world and spared little thought for the aspirations
of his talented sister. Yet Henry's own lawyer William Seymour had
placed *Susan* with Crosby & Co. – why had he not been more active in
putting the wrong to rights? With hundreds, sometimes thousands, of
pounds, flowing through his bank accounts, how could the £10 needed
for reclaiming *Susan* present a difficulty? Presumably, for the time being
Jane wanted nothing more to do with Crosby or *Susan*: the parody of
Gothic was now out-of-date and her pride had been severely wounded.
There were, however, the other novel manuscripts, *Sense and Sensibility*
and *First Impressions*, often brought out to delight the family circle, and
with Henry's encouragement she began to work on a revised fair copy of
the first of these to present to a publisher. This time Henry would try to
make a better job of placing her work, but he was a money-man and had
no direct literary contacts. He knew someone who did, however: Charles
James, for whom publication was as natural as breathing.

There has long been puzzlement about how Jane Austen came to forge
the unlikely connection with the bookseller Thomas Egerton, who published almost no novels and whose products often bore the imprint 'AT
THE MILITARY LIBRARY, NEAR WHITEHALL.' Egerton's office was
close to the Austen & Co. bank in Covent Garden, just five minutes' walk

away at Charing Cross where it neighboured Drummonds Bank and the army agency Cox & Greenwood, both frequent destinations for Henry. He recognised the name. *The Loiterer*, the journal produced by James and Henry when they were students at Oxford, had been distributed in London by Egerton. However, that was back in 1789–90, twenty years ago and these days Egerton was, after all, a military publisher. The answer probably lies with two of his bestsellers: the *Regimental Companion* (1799), an officer's guidebook that ran through seven editions by 1821, and the 1,000-page *Military Dictionary* (1802) with its dedication to the Duke of York, both of them authored by Charles James. This is a connection that has hitherto been considered only by the bibliographer David Gilson.[5]

In spite of the Mary Anne Clarke scandal, Henry had not entirely given up either Charles James or the covert brokering of commissions. In April 1811 he wrote to Major James asking for help in procuring an exchange from one regiment to another for the son of an agency customer, William Gore Langton, Lieutenant Colonel of the Oxfordshire Militia. At some point in 1810, Henry entered the bookseller's office. Would Egerton do a favour for the banker friend of one of his most lucrative authors? *Certainly sir, as long as there is no risk attached to me.*

Henry approached the contract as if it were another financial speculation. He agreed to *Sense and Sensibility* being published 'on commission'. This was a system whereby the author took responsibility for purchase of paper, printing and advertising while the publisher oversaw the accounts and distribution, charging the author a 10 per cent commission on every copy. It has been well described as a 'royalty in reverse'.[6] But if sales were inadequate, the author was still liable for the publisher's production costs. Henry was comfortable with the idea of paying a commission, after all this was how he made most of his own money. He was also comfortable with risk. His 'Biographical Notice' makes it clear that Jane, with her £20 per year allowance, was at first terrified by it even though Henry was acting as security. The gamble paid off, yielding a modest profit. But since the production costs were approximately £155 for 750 copies plus £24 for advertisements, Henry had wagered £179 on a possible gain of £140 for the first edition.

Publishing 'on commission' was an unusual step for a novelist to take at the time. Only thirty-four of the 662 novels published in Britain in the 1810s were described on the title page as, like *Sense and Sensibility*, printed 'for the author'.[7] But similarly to subscription publishing, which involved direct payment to the author from readers, it gave the writer a degree of independence, and an alternative to the often paltry copyright payments offered for novels. It seems remarkable that neither of Jane's first two publishers were remotely interested in the quality of the work she put before them. However fiction was frequently dealt with as a disposable commodity, valued by the number of volumes, good for a few rounds in the commercial 'circulating libraries' that now proliferated in the towns and spas, until the bindings cracked and the novel was forgotten. Moreover progress in the bargaining position of the author had been painfully slow. The book business was expanding and becoming more competitive. Marketing and distribution became more sophisticated and towards the end of Austen's life there was the innovation of steam-driven paper-making and printing. But where was the author's slice of the action?

Until the early eighteenth century, authors had barely figured in the financial arrangements for book production. They would be paid by a wealthy patron for their labours, if at all. Copyright was a matter for feuding booksellers, some of whom clung to the old custom that literary property was theirs in perpetuity and others, up and coming, who challenged it and insisted on the provisions of the 1710 Statute of Anne, also known as the Copyright Act, which decreed a limited term of fourteen years, renewable once, after which the work fell into the public domain. The Donaldson vs. Beckett case, fought in 1774, found in favour of the new guard. As usual no one was very interested in the author's rights, but nevertheless the author was recognised as originator of the disputed goods in this legal battle, and gradually the notion of intellectual property became attached to authorship. By the late 1810s writers like William Wordsworth and Robert Southey were putting the case for perpetual copyright but this time as the 'natural inheritance' of the author, rather than the bookseller.

For Henry and Eliza, Jane's authorial debut was cause enough to celebrate. Who could have predicted that the hilarious jottings which had formed part of their holiday amusements at Steventon Rectory would have this result? Jane told Cassandra that the musical party arose from a dinner invitation to a couple of their friends. It could have nothing to do with the forthcoming novel, because she had sworn the family to secrecy over her authorship. But Henry was bursting with pride and Eliza wanted to recapture some of the magic of the theatrical days of their youth. They were too old for costumes now, and so Eliza was determined to stage-manage the reception rooms. She set out off into town on errands, sometimes alone and sometimes with Jane, purchasing flowers and chimney lights and borrowing a great looking glass for the mantelpiece to magnify the effect.

Jane reported to Cassandra that in spite of the inevitable 'solicitudes, alarms & vexations' the party had gone off 'extremely well'. The musicians arrived in two hackney carriages at half-past seven and the back drawing room filled with company, with just a few seeking relief from the heat and press of people in the second room and connecting corridor. It was all 'delight and cordiality of course', and the music 'extremely good'. Jane could never prevent a note of irony creeping into her accounts of social interaction, but nevertheless she felt embraced by this great gathering of family and friends, 'surrounded by acquaintance ... quite as much upon my hands as I could do...', transported by the glitter of the lights, the fragrance of the flowers, the harmony of the music.[8]

The novelties and festivities did not end there. Eliza knew that Jane enjoyed the company of the Tilsons and brought them together almost daily. It was easy enough as they lived just around the corner from Sloane Street in Hans Place. Both were located in 'Hans Town', a speculative project of the late 1770s built on land owned by Lord Cadogan and named in honour of the founder of the British Museum, Sir Hans Sloane. It was the first and most fashionable of the satellite developments that would

spring up to house the professional class, closer to the West End than the
Brompton address, but separate from the urban core and still surrounded
by fields. Jane wrote of walking 'into London'. They needed to take the
carriage to visit émigré friends, the Comte d'Antraigues and his wife,
formerly a celebrated opera singer, with a musical son who performed for
them. Eliza was renewing her intimacy with Jane and taking it further,
into the lost world of her French youth. Jane was charmed by its strangeness and touched by Eliza's eagerness to please.

At the same time, what Jane saw at Sloane Street was at times troubling. There was a fragility about Eliza, physical and emotional. When
one of the horses jibbed at Hyde Park Gate on the way to visit the d'Antraigues in Barnes and they had to get out of the carriage and stand in
the night air for a few minutes while the harness was adjusted, Eliza
caught a cold in her chest which she couldn't seem to shake off. And
when Jane departed at the end of April, she left Eliza poised in indecision
over whether to invite James Austen's eldest daughter, now aged eighteen,
to stay. Jane had encouraged her, assuring Eliza that Anna was a kindred
spirit, amusing and clever. Eliza hesitated. There were tangled feelings.
If she had accepted James's marriage proposal rather than Henry's, she
would have been Anna's stepmother and could perhaps have had more
children of her own. In the end she did invite Anna but the invitation
was refused. This was probably due to the hostility of Mary Lloyd Austen,
the woman who *had* accepted James's hand in marriage, and who would
not trust her unsteady charge in London with the frivolous Frenchwoman. The rejection increased Eliza's sense of alienation from the Austen
cousins who had once been so dear to her. She almost never accompanied
Henry on his many visits to Godmersham and when she did, felt she was
there merely on sufferance. It was obvious that Fanny Knight, Edward's
eldest daughter and the lady of the house, disliked her. Jane, concerned
by Eliza's seeming isolation, invited her to stay at Chawton Cottage that
summer, but the visit was only a partial success, eclipsed halfway through
by the sudden arrival of jolly sailor brother Charles, home at last after

seven years in the West Indies, with a wife to introduce to his mother and sisters and two small lively daughters.

If Jane's three letters from Sloane Street in April 1811 were a snapshot, Henry would feature as a blur. He was a man constantly in motion. Since the untimely death of Hastings de Feuillide ten years earlier, the India fortune that had once been set aside for the child was now theirs to spend, and therefore largely Henry's. The money had given him wings, made him another Icarus. The frequent solo visits to Godmersham were part of this picture: they enabled him to live the high life, indulge in some hunting or merry-making with the children without the responsibilities of a property owner or parent, and to cultivate banking contacts. At 64 Sloane Street, Henry always had one foot out of the door. When he wasn't on the way to the bank he was setting out on other business. But Jane cherished his presence. During her visit, there had been a perfect Sunday afternoon promenading in Kensington Gardens, with Henry and two friends and neighbours, Mr Tilson, and Mr Smith the local apothecary; 'everything was fresh & beautiful'. Jane found herself as much at ease in the company of these money-minded men as she was with Eliza and Mrs Tilson talking about hats.

Almost immediately Henry was away off to Oxford. He wrote to Jane from Wheatfield Park House, the nearby mansion of Lord Charles Spencer, whose son John was Receiver General of Taxes for Oxfordshire. Joy! Henry had gained the appointment of deputy receiver. Jane sent Cassandra his Oxford address, so she could get a first-hand account. Eliza was still recuperating at home, and it may have occurred to Jane that Henry's single-mindedness sometimes verged on selfishness. However, Henry's selfishness was certainly not that of a John Dashwood. He could be loving and thoughtful. Jane, being fond of Eliza, must have felt slightly torn, but ultimately she would always be loyal to Henry, marvelling at his energy and vision and ability to stay one step ahead of the game.

Henry's move into tax collecting appears to have been another effort to spread his risks and reinforce his credit by boosting reserves and cash flow. The context was the worst economic crisis in the crisis-ridden course of the war, involving an epidemic of country bank failures. He had laid the ground by carefully maintaining the goodwill of his former commander in the militia, Charles Spencer, ever short of cash. On 9 March 1810 Austen & Co. had lent £2,000 to Lord Charles. Henry preferred to think of it as a prudent step rather than a bribe, though the odds for repayment were not promising.

The following year, Lord Charles was in a position to return the favour by offering Henry a lucrative new sideline. There were sixty-six receivers general in England and Wales, responsible for travelling throughout their county on a quarterly or semi-annual basis, generally in April and October, to receive the proceeds of the Land Tax and any other government-assessed taxes from parish collectors and to draw up accounts. Deputies might carry out some or all of these duties, and be awarded a share of the official recompense of around one to two thousand pounds annually. The receiver also had the right to hold the tax money for six weeks and use it for loans or investment, and some contrived to hang onto it for two years or more before handing it over to the Treasury. In this way public money stimulated private enterprise and generated private profit. It was a highly desirable perquisite.

From July 1810 an economic crisis escalated, but it was as if nothing could touch Henry. The combined effects of trade blockades with their damage to exports and manufacturing, unemployment, poor harvests and food shortages, galloping inflation and a bleak military outlook, all undermined confidence in financial institutions. The findings of a Parliamentary Select Committee inquiry into the shaky paper currency contributed to the sense of doom. The Bullion Report, published in June, predicted dire consequences if the Bank of England failed to restore convertibility and resume cash payments. Paper money lost a third of its purchasing power in the course of the Suspension period, and the committee feared that the surplus of banknotes would prove a threat to public credit and therefore to the continuation of the war effort. Yet during the crisis Austen & Co. and Henry's three country banks remained buoyant. Frank Austen, one of the Henrietta Street partners, arrived home from convoy duty in the Far East, receiving the formal thanks of the Admiralty and the tangible reward of one thousand guineas and silver plate from the East India Company, on top of a generous pay packet. He had brought back from China ninety-three chests of bullion to defray the freight expenses. In some quarters there was no shortage of precious metal.

During the summer of 1810 twenty provincial banks went under, among them one of Henry's clients, the partnership of Edmund Griffith, Donovan & Co. who ran the Horwood Well Bank in Somerset, although the Buxton bank survived. In Manchester no fewer than five firms were bankrupted, while in London, six banks stopped payments. Bankruptcy was a common occurrence in Georgian England, but in 1810 the rate trebled. Charles Lamb, visiting his friend William Hazlitt near Salisbury, vividly described the impact of a failed bank on the wider community:

> The city of Salisbury is full of weeping and wailing. The bank has stopt payment; and every body in the town kept money at it, or has got some of its notes. Some have lost all they had in the world. It is the next thing to seeing a city with a plague within its walls. The Wilton people are all undone; all the manufacturers there kept cash at the Salisbury bank; and I do suppose it to be the unhappiest county in England this, where I am making holiday.

A country banker, James Oakes, having discovered losses of £36,430 after his crooked London agent committed suicide in the spring, came to the metropolis to investigate and in July 'found the City under the greatest alarm & bankers & merchants coming up to town from all quarters to gain information'. Yet Austen & Co. and its associated country banks calmly carried on trading and issuing banknotes as usual. Unused notes for £10, £5, and £1 from Petersfield New Bank in the period 1810–13 have survived. They are elegantly stamped with the signatures of the partners Austen, Vincent & Clement, and their initials are linked in an oval frame surrounded by a laurel wreath: the insignia of unruffled creditworthiness; no hint of the anxieties contorting the country.

William Cobbett, the Hampshire firebrand, was very sure where the blame lay for imminent national ruin. Writing from a cell in Newgate prison, he launched a campaign against the financial elite, the 'Paper Aristocracy' as he had dubbed it. In the spring of 1810 he had been forced to leave his beloved farm in the village of Botley, just twenty-two miles south of Chawton, to be tried and imprisoned for his seditious condemnation of flogging in the militia in the pages of the *Weekly Political Register*. Now, at the end of August, Cobbett's new campaign was spurred by indignation at the plight of those ruined by the Salisbury crash.

Paper money had again become a topic of hot political contention, as at the time of the Bank Restriction Act in 1797. Pamphlets on the Bullion Report, for and against, poured from the press. The liberal journals ran page after page of reviews and articles, all urging ministers to stop the inundation of paper money and prevent further debasement of the currency by building up stocks of bullion to restore public confidence. The government and the Bank of England counter-attacked, insisting that the data was illusory and the gloom-mongers were mischievous, friends of Napoleon, talking down the pound. Cobbett maintained a regular column on the subject in the *Political Register* until August of the following year. He brought the language of experts down to earth in order to speak to the widest possible audience. The country was on a precipice, and one false step would plunge it into a gulf from which it could never rise. This war was a test of financial strength as much as military power. If British credit was lost, everything was lost, Cobbett claimed as he whipped up public anxiety. But his real target was the credit system itself, which upheld the rotten, ruling elite at the expense of the exploited majority. He anticipated a collapse at the top, not the fall of the nation as a whole.

At the end of September Cobbett was handed a gift. The Perceval ministry's response to the downturn in trade had been to take out another in a series of massive loans as the cost of the war multiplied. The Bullion Report had criticised this reliance on international loans which involved the export of large quantities of gold and had an inflationary effect. Earlier in the year a syndicate of merchant bankers, Goldsmid and Baring, had been awarded a contract to raise £12 million. But the volatile times were creating liquidity problems for international finance.

Unease turned into panic on 27 September 1810 when Abraham Goldsmid shot himself in the grounds of the palatial mansion in Morden. Following news of his suicide the City of London was in turmoil and trading on the stock exchange came to a standstill. *The Times* reported the vertiginous fall in stocks and lamented the loss of a pillar of the City, while *The Courier* asked 'whether peace or war suddenly made ever created such a bustle as the death of Mr Goldsmid'. The Prime Minister Spencer Perceval called an emergency meeting of ministers and Treasury officials to decide on steps to restore confidence. Cobbett rejoiced in the death of this Shylock, the Jewish moneylender in his new guise of rootless international financier. Goldsmid was emblematic of the deceitful paper money system that maintained a corrupt government.

It was in the midst of this economic crisis, which was also a crisis of political legitimacy, that Jane Austen carried out the final revisions to *Sense and Sensibility* and produced a fair-hand copy for Egerton & Co., conscious of the fact that Henry was a minor princeling among the 'Paper Aristocracy'. If the paper money system was profoundly immoral and unjust, and constructed upon an unsustainable foundation of monetary abstractions, then Henry was among the guilty. The letters that might have revealed her attitude to events in 1810 are missing, but her awareness of it is evident from a ditty she penned during her visit to London, addressing one of the casualties of the economic depression, the 'Weald of Kent Canal Bill', which Edward had personally opposed.

The year 1811 opened ominously. King George III entered a final and irreversible phase of madness and was formally replaced as head of state by the bloated and dissolute Prince of Wales. The new Prince Regent promptly turned his back on erstwhile liberal Whig associates and threw his massive weight behind the political status quo in all its severity. The Great Comet, clearly visible from April through to the middle of January 1812, was taken

as a dark omen. Joanna Southcott, the self-styled prophetess of the Apoc-
alypse, published a *Communication* in which she expressed her confidence
that 'mockers' would be silenced by this unmistakable sign from God.

Satirists had a field day with the gloomy 'prophecies' of the Bullionists;
those who wanted to restore the currency to a standard set by precious metals.
Samuel Taylor Coleridge, on the side of the government and opposed to the
Bullionists, intervened with a series of editorials in May 1811, dismissing
'*alarm*' as 'the true source of nine-tenths of the whole calamity'. But Cobbett kept up the pressure, denouncing the paper money system week after
week until August, when he signed off with the reassurance that even if the
'total destruction' of the paper money regime was fast approaching,

> the corn and the grass and the trees will grow without paper-money; the
> banks may all break in a day, and the sun will rise the next day, and the
> lambs will gambol and the birds will sing and the carters and country girls
> will grin at each other, and all will go on just as if nothing had happened.

In Cobbett's reckoning, paper money was mere illusion. For Jane Austen it
meant something very real. It was on the paper dealings of Henry and his
associates that her own paper-based career as author was founded, in the
most literal and material way. When *Sense and Sensibility* was published, on
the title page of each of its three volumes appeared, 'Printed for the Author,
by C. Roworth, Bell-yard, Temple-bar.' Charles Roworth had been the
printer responsible for the reward notice issued by Austen & Co. for information leading to the fraudster 'Count Stuarton', back in 1806. The paper
for the novel and the reward notice issued from the same firm, impressed
with letters formed by the same type, with ink rolled on the same printing
presses. Roworth was to be responsible for the printing of both editions of
Sense and Sensibility, volume one of the first and second editions of *Pride
and Prejudice*, volume two only of the first and second editions of *Mansfield
Park*, volumes one and two of *Emma* and the two posthumous volumes of
Northanger Abbey and *Persuasion*. The association of Austen and Roworth,

which began in the early days of the secret partnership with Charles James, lasted beyond Jane's death.

It was not until the very end of October 1811 that *Sense and Sensibility* was published. It appeared during a deep economic depression, and could be described as Jane Austen's 'austerity novel'. The reader is immediately and rapidly plunged into the details of inheritance in the Dashwood family. Norland Park is a fine estate in the county of Sussex, owned by a bachelor who lives with his sister. When the sister dies, he invites his nephew and his second wife and three daughters to share the home. They care for the old gentleman devotedly but when he dies and the will is opened, it is found that the nephew rather than being named heir has only a life interest, and the estate will eventually go to his son by his first marriage, and in turn to the firstborn grandson, now a beguiling infant.

In this telescoped account, packed into the first few pages, no sooner is the nephew Mr Henry Dashwood introduced than he expires, just one year after his rich uncle; another dead Henry, after the habit Jane formed in the *Juvenilia*. As a consequence his second family are cast out into the world, dispossessed of their beloved Edenic home, to begin again with an income on the perilous edge of what was considered to be a civilised existence. They have a combined total of £10,000, including legacies to the daughters of £1,000 each, invested in stocks or bonds at the 5 per cent interest standard at the time to yield a yearly income of £500. This is a drastic fall from grace and contraction of life chances. It allows for two maids and a manservant, but no carriage or sociability, and probably means the daughters will not marry well if at all. The son, John Dashwood, is enriched by £4,000 a year, on top of the annual £2,000 derived from his late mother and his marriage to Fanny Ferrars (worth £10,000), and can enter the upper echelons of wealth.

The novel was first written in letter form under the title *Elinor and Marianne* and then recast into something closer to its final form before the end of the 1790s. But there would have been further revisions before publication to update it for the early 1810s and Jane was still considering changes as the proof pages came to her. 'The *incomes* remain as they were,' she wrote to Cassandra, 'but I will get them altered if I can'. This is surely a hint that she was adjusting the numbers to take into account the present rocketing rate of inflation, aided by a stay in London with a financial expert, her brother Henry, on hand. Jane Austen is of course famous or notorious for the preoccupation with annual incomes in her fiction, and the precision with which she calibrates social standing in accordance with income. This computational quality is found in all her novels, but in none more so than *Sense and Sensibility*, in which monetising of the characters takes on the dimension of a topical allegory.

Men and women alike have valuations stamped on them. After the opening chapter the figures are mostly supplied by two of the characters, cold-hearted and mercenary John Dashwood and warm-hearted and gossipy Mrs Jennings, who in differing ways join together to form a chorus of financial appraisal. They are aided and abetted by, respectively, his wife Fanny and her son-in-law Sir John Middleton. The brilliant second chapter features a conversation between John Dashwood and his grasping wife, in which his promise to his father to make financial provision for his half-sisters is whittled down from three thousand pounds to 'presents of fish and game and so forth, whenever they are in season'. Mrs Henry Dashwood and her daughters Elinor, Marianne and Margaret then begin a new life in a cottage in Devon owned by her relation Sir John, and their navigation of this unfamiliar terrain is aided by a new set of financial coordinates.

Mrs Jennings, a wealthy widow staying with the Middletons at the big house near the cottage, is able to inform the Dashwood women that Colonel Brandon's estate at Delaford 'was never reckoned more than two thousand a year', while Sir John rates Willoughby's estate 'at about six or seven hundred a year' and is pretty sure his expenditure exceeds it, but his position as heir to Allenham Court excuses it (I.xiv). It is a given in this world that almost everyone is a rentier living off unearned income from land or invested stock. Edward Ferrars, Elinor's love interest, sighs for a profession but is discouraged by his snobbish family from pursuing one.

Elinor and Marianne can only dream, one of an establishment of £1,000 a year, the other for £1,800 or £2,000.

In this social milieu men are like bullion. Their value seems to rise regardless of innate worth. The avarice of John Dashwood is rewarded. Willoughby can wench and gamble, fritter away time and money on hunting and plunge headlong into debt but his rate of exchange as a marriage partner only increases, allowing him to acquire Miss Grey with a fortune of £50,000. Robert Ferrars is described pointedly as a man whose looks manifest 'strong, natural, *sterling* insignificance' (II.xi). Even when marrying a penniless nobody to spite his domineering mother, Robert comes up trumps and is eventually reinstated as heir, in place of his older brother Edward. It is true that Edward and Colonel Brandon struggle with money difficulties not of their own making, but at the end of the day they have reserves of inherited assets and remunerative options open to them.

In contrast, women, like banknotes, are liable to depreciation. This insight is most starkly conveyed by John Dashwood when, following Marianne's harrowing discovery of Willoughby's betrayal and her consequent physical decline, he confides to Elinor, 'I question whether Marianne *now*, will marry a man worth more than five or six hundred a year, at the utmost' (II.xi). Women's value is external, skin deep, paper thin.

The same moral is enforced by the tale of the two Elizas related by Colonel Brandon to Elinor. The first, Eliza Williams, was an orphaned relative his own age, a playfellow from infancy raised in his father's house, 'I cannot remember the time when I did not love Eliza' (II.ix). With time sibling attachment turned to passionate love. But she was an heiress and must therefore marry the eldest son. A plan to elope was discovered and Eliza was forced into a cruel marriage. She eventually fled her unkind husband and fell into the hands of a libertine. After divorce her legal allowance was managed by an agent and withheld. She was then passed around before landing in a 'spunging house'. This is a place where debtors were temporarily kept to be pressed like a sponge for any residual monetary value before being moved to more permanent confinement.

It is there that Brandon, after returning from a three-year term in the military branch of the East India Company, found her: 'So altered – so faded – worn down by acute suffering of every kind … the remains of the lovely, blooming, healthful girl, on whom I had once doated.' A note so debased cannot be returned to circulation, and so although he removes her from imprisonment, her rapid death by consumption can only be a comfort to him.

Colonel Brandon then takes charge of her three-year-old illegitimate daughter, little Eliza. Because of his military duties and bachelor status, she is placed in a school and then, from the age of fourteen, at a boarding house with other girls under the care of a respectable woman. She continued there until around the time when the action of the novel starts, when she is given permission to stay with a friend in Bath, a place which features here as a devaluation zone for unwary ingénues as Brighton does in *Pride and Prejudice*. She is debauched by Willoughby and left in solitary despair. Little Eliza is now a 'poor girl', 'poor and miserable'. She in turn has reproduced illegitimately and been withdrawn from circulation like a counterfeit bill, into an unnamed place in the country 'and there she remains' (II.ix).

As Eliza Austen checked the late-arriving proof pages of *Sense and Sensibility*, after Jane's return to Chawton and during Henry's business excursion to Oxford, what could she have made of the duo of unfortunate and disgraced Elizas? The constellation of ideas was unmistakable. Sexual impropriety, economic disaster, these had featured in the juvenile writings Jane had linked to her alluring and worldly cousin. The fact that Colonel Brandon is suspected of fathering a love child and the gratuitous introduction of the East India Company into the proceedings made it apparent that there was a message. But what did it mean? The Eliza narratives could be taken as a nod to a fellow aficionado of hackneyed fictional conventions, just as *Love and Friendship* had been. They are twice-told tales, and follow lines familiar from many a turgid sentimental novel of the late eighteenth century. Heart-breaking accounts of fallen women were ten a penny, and the manly tears shed by Colonel Brandon had similarly flowed in celebrated works of Laurence Sterne and Henry Mackenzie, beloved by an earlier generation. Jane would restrict such melodramatic matter to the sidelines of her chronicles of modern life, preferring a realism inflected by irony.

At the same time Eliza Austen may have detected in the Eliza subplot a hidden seriousness of purpose, even a tacit sympathy for her own plight. Had she not fallen? Fallen from the pedestal on which she had been placed in her youth? Was she not the shadow of her former self? True, she was a respectable married woman who could take tea with friends and gad about the streets of London on shopping trips. But something along the way had been grievously broken and lost. Marriage to Henry had been an attempt to make permanent the enchantment of their first encounters but also to find shelter and draw close to what remained of her extended family. Instead she had experienced a growing sense of exclusion. Cousin Phylly Walter, once her loyal confidante, had not even written to tell her directly when she married George Whitaker in the summer of 1811. The news only reached Eliza through Cassandra. But Jane spoke to Eliza elliptically through the double echo of her name, as one intelligent childless middle-aged woman to another, and said she understood the way life as it was then organised could hollow out the identity of even the most gifted and apparently fortunate of the female sex.

How were women to compete in such an unequal contest? All the most solid and enduring assets were on the other side. Mrs Jennings' idea of an excellent match is the standard one: '*he* was rich, and *she* was handsome'. Outspoken and precocious Marianne, aged seventeen, recognises the imbalance and declares that she would rather have 'no marriage at all' to 'a mere commercial exchange, in which each wished to be benefited at the expense of the other' (I.viii). Mrs Dashwood is similarly sensitive to the suspicion that an unmarried girl's motives must always be mercenary: 'Men are very safe with us, let them be ever so rich' (I.ix). The reader is assured that in Mrs Dashwood's mind 'not one speculative thought' was raised by the prospect of Marianne wedding Willoughby, with 'his prospect of riches' (I.x).

Fictional characters with integrity must of course deny entertaining any mercenary motives, but Jane herself found greed fascinating and amusing, and revelled in its depiction. Lucy Steele, like Isabella Thorpe in *Northanger Abbey*, is a wolf in the clothing of a sentimental maiden. She is fraudulent currency. Steel is not a precious metal but a powerful alloy, good for a rapier or the dagger to the heart suggested by Lucy's 'sharp little eyes' as she evaluates Elinor's reaction to the news that Edward Ferrars has already been taken. The poor but cunning Lucy Steele 'steals' into the confidence of Elinor and then 'steals' into the good graces of the Ferrars family. The panic in the London town house when her sister foolishly lets slip the secret engagement between Lucy and Edward is the equivalent of the discovery of a burglary, or rather, a swindle. Mrs Jennings reports Fanny Dashwood falling 'into violent hysterics immediately, with such screams as reached your brother's ears, as he was sitting in his own dressing-room downstairs, thinking about writing a letter to his steward in the country'. John Dashwood soon arrives in Upper Berkeley Street where his half-sisters are staying with Mrs Jennings, to give the full story.

> I hope the storm may be weathered without our being any of us, quite overcome. Poor Fanny! she was in hysterics all yesterday ... She has borne it all, with the fortitude of an angel! She says she never shall think well of anybody again; and one cannot wonder at it, after being so deceived! (III.i)

Lucy steals Edward, but when he is disinherited for persevering in the engagement she abandons the swag and steals his vain foppish brother Robert instead. Lucy, with her steely resolve, is well matched to the man of 'sterling insignificance'. They honeymoon in her native Dawlish where she had 'many relations and old acquaintances to cut' (III.xiv).

Jane Austen had a poetic appreciation of the bottom line. It stirred her imagination and stimulated her wordplay. The very idea of convertibility, the substitution of banknotes for bullion, the number one economic issue of the period in which she revised and published *Sense and Sensibility*, had a literary quality to it. It was a like a metaphor, but one that the government and the Bank of England obstinately persisted in banning. Other transmutations, however, could still take place. Henry stopped at Chawton Cottage with Mr Tilson in June 1811 on a flying visit to oversee the Alton bank's move of premises to 10 High Street and relinquish control to Gray; with the deputy receivership he had more than enough business on his hands. Jane took them for a walk through the estate of Chawton Park and recorded for Cassandra's entertainment that 'Mr Tilson admired the Trees very much, but grieved that they should not be turned into money'.[9] *Grieved*; it is the deft touch of hyperbole with which she garnishes the anecdote that shows her own deep appreciation of Mr Tilson's mercantile wit, as if he were a modern-day capitalist Ovid.

James Tilson outdid even her own creation, John Dashwood, who proposes only to turn a grove of walnut trees into a greenhouse. There is a suggestion of Ovid's tale of Danaë, into whose lap Zeus falls in the form of a shower of gold, when Mr Dashwood enthusiastically tells impoverished Elinor of Mrs Ferrars putting 'bank-notes into Fanny's hands to the amount of two hundred pounds' on their arrival in London; 'And extremely acceptable it is, for we must live at great expense while we are here' (II.xi). Chapter eleven of the second volume is a key chapter for any consideration of the economic themes of the novel, in which John Dashwood accidentally encounters his half-sisters in Gray's jewellers in Sackville Street, one of only two real shops mentioned in Austen's fiction, located a stone's throw from Henry's former office in Albany, Piccadilly. Being well-intentioned, according to his own lights, he seeks a tête-à-tête with Elinor in order to regale her with news of his own family and give her tips about husband hunting.

It is no accident when Mrs Jennings mentions John Dashwood sitting in his dressing room 'thinking about writing a letter to his steward in the country'. He is full of schemes, bent on extracting every ounce of profit from the Norland estate. He has applied to enclose Norland Common, a practice encouraged by Parliament to increase corn yield and which benefited rich landowners at the expense of smallholders who had used common land to graze their animals. He has also been expanding his terrain by purchasing a neighbouring farm; the farmer will now be a tenant. He complains to Elinor about the cost of the property, 'the stocks were at that time so low, that if I had not happened to have the necessary sum in my banker's hands, I must have sold out to very large loss'.

John Dashwood's mounting assets lead him to consider himself something of a philosopher and he proceeds to patronise Elinor during another private conversation. He is very ready to rebuke her for 'ignorance of human nature' when she ventures to comment on the apparent contradiction that Mrs Ferrars, having cast off her son Edward, can nevertheless demand sympathy when he marries against her wishes. He is himself baffled, however, by the altruistic behaviour of Colonel Brandon who has freely offered Edward a clerical living at Delaford worth £200 a year when he might have sold it on the market for £1,400; 'Well, I am convinced that there is a vast deal of inconsistency in almost every human character' (III.v).

The reader is expected to concur with Elinor, that happiness has much to do with wealth, but that a moderate £1,000 a year will suffice. The penitent Willoughby berates himself for believing 'false ideas of the necessity of riches' which have lost him Marianne. But the narrator mischievously presents an anti-moral, of the kind that also features in the conclusion of *Northanger Abbey*. Lucy Steele's behaviour 'may be held forth as a most encouraging instance of what an earnest, an unceasing attention to self-interest, however its progress may be apparently obstructed, will do in securing every advantage of fortune, with no other sacrifice than that of time and conscience' (III.xiv).

The only possible place to bring about the crisis of economics and conscience in *Sense and Sensibility* was London. And not just London, but that part of London most closely connected with the Austen representatives of the moneyed interest, Eliza and Henry. Jane followed their trail resolutely.

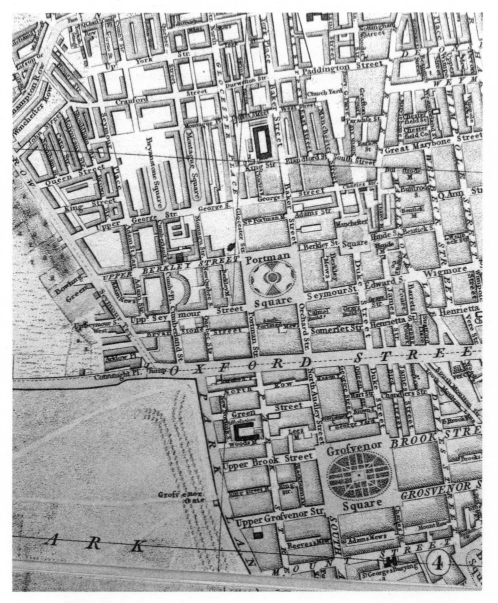

From Carey's New and Accurate Plan of London and Westminster (1810). Courtesy of
Robert Clark.

Their first London address together had been 24 Upper Berkeley Street, the other side of Portman Square from the fictional Mrs Jennings in Berkeley Street. There she has established 'a settled habitation of her own' after the death of her husband 'who had traded with success in a less elegant part of the town'. The house is 'handsome and handsomely fitted up'. Jane no doubt aimed to raise an uneasy private laugh when she had John Dashwood describe Mrs Jennings as 'the widow of a man, who had got all his money in a low way' (II.xi). Philadelphia Hancock, the widow of the East India Company physician and trader Tysoe Saul Hancock, had set up house with her daughter Eliza in Orchard Street, just around the corner. In 1788 the love-struck sixteen-year-old Henry Austen had planned to visit them there.

Jane positioned Mr and Mrs John Dashwood in Harley Street, five minutes' walk from Portman Square and in the same district just north of the great Oxford trunk road. This was another street name with strong resonance for the Austens. Harley Street was an address dear to Eliza's heart; her close friend Lady Sophia Burrell lived there when in town. She could never afford a lodging there herself, but she rented houses as near as she could. Harley Street also had a more sinister family association. Lord Saye and Sele, related by marriage to Mrs George Austen, cut his throat in a fit of depression in a house in Harley Street in 1788. A colonel in the Scots Guards, he had been responsible for protecting the Bank of England during the Gordon Riots eight years previously. Jane was to have 'many a good laugh' when she met his scatty and garrulous widow at Stoneleigh Abbey in 1806.[10]

Every district in London has depths of economic character. It was in the seventeenth and eighteenth centuries that the region west of the City of London was carved up into estates mainly distributed among the higher nobility and favourites of the court. As the town sprawled from the palace of Westminster on the north bank of the Thames, the noble landlords saw their estates soar in value and yield ever more lucrative rental income. The West End represented the urbanisation of aristocratic capital. By gradually paving over the fields beyond Westminster in a series of speculative building developments, the power-broking dynasties of the pre-modern era literally cemented their influence, updating their assets for a new age based on the national primacy of the metropolis.

Wealthy leaseholders put down roots and the north-west outskirts of the West End became the particular preserve of individuals enriched through the East India Company from the 1770s, joined in the 1790s by a substantial number of exiles from revolutionary France. Indian curries and French *ragout* were customary fare in Marylebone households, and Eliza was equally at home with either. Henry had launched his career in the financial services sector with the help of East India Company money and influence while residing in the metropolitan heartland of the nabobs.

Most recently, Portman Square had appeared in the news for another reason linked to Henry and his business. The Duke of York had his town house in Portman Square and had ensconced his mistress Mary Anne Clarke in a four-storey residence in nearby Gloucester Place. While the inquiry into bribery and corruption in the sale of army commissions was in process there was constant press exposure of the numerous personal notes that passed between the two addresses. The grand precincts of the Harley-Cavendish estate, named for princes, dukes and earls, had been thoroughly besmirched by the revelations of this royal soap opera. It was typical of Jane Austen's love of *risqué* allusion that she placed such emphasis on this compromised quarter in her first published novel.

The itinerary of *Sense and Sensibility* crosses Oxford Street southwards to reach Hanover Square, one of the earliest of the great London squares, the address of Mr and Mrs Palmer. It then snakes through the shopping district including Conduit Street, where the Middletons can be found, and Bond Street, where Willoughby is lodged. This is the route to Henry's first three offices, all located in the area concentrated around St James Street and Pall Mall, where Colonel Brandon and Edward Ferrars respectively take lodgings. As one drew closer to the royal epicentre, the ancient Palace of St James and nearby Carlton House, the residence of the Prince of Wales (about to undergo another lavish refurbishment to mark his Regency), the degree of elitism intensified.

Henry, like Mrs Jennings whose money comes from trade, was an outsider in this world. But as a provider of loans and a purveyor of army commissions with a link to the Prince's favourite, Lord Moira, he knew the denizens of Mayfair and it was part of his business to understand the topography of fashion and wealth. Just as Frank and Charles would later give Jane advice about correct naval terminology, so Henry could help her place her fictional characters in London. Thus, Mrs Ferrars is left in splendid isolation in Park Street at the furthest and most fashionable west end of the West End (a coinage of the early nineteenth century).

Mayfair in this period has been described by the innocent term, 'urban village'. Its inhabitants indeed formed a remarkably homogeneous community, with the highest concentration of noble titles in the land, joined by inter-marriage, social ritual, and duties at the royal court and Parliament. Against the background of the French Revolution, the West End assumed the air of a stockade from which the traditional British ruling class successfully defended their hold against the encroachments of the rising commercial middle class, or the threats of the discontented poor.

In 1810 the fortress of privilege had been temporarily breached. Public anger had boiled over when the Prime Minister Spencer Perceval moved to arrest Sir Francis Burdett, the champion of free speech. He had challenged the attempt by the government to stifle debate on the Walcheren campaign, a botched military manoeuvre that had resulted in the deaths by fever of 4,000 soldiers with many thousands more invalided back to England. Burdett barricaded himself inside his house in Piccadilly and theatrically read the Magna Carta to his young son. Crowds rioted in the playground of the rich as soldiers broke through Burdett's ground floor window and dragged him off to the Tower of London.

It was back to normal in salubrious Mayfair, however, by 30 October 1811 when *Sense and Sensibility* finally saw the light of day, priced at fifteen shillings, in a print run of 750 or 1,000 copies. Due to a printer's error, fortuitous or deliberate, the novel was enthusiastically taken up by the beau monde. The attribution on the title page was 'By A Lady', but some of the advertisements identified the author as 'Lady —' or 'Lady A—'. Jane urged the family to maintain a strict silence on her authorship, and rumours flowed unchecked. The precise representation of the West End setting must have supported the idea that it had been penned by an aristocratic bluestocking. The Countess of Bessborough, daughter of Earl Spencer and therefore a cousin of Henry's patron Lord Charles Spencer, called it a 'clever novel' and reported to her former lover Lord Granville that they 'were full of it at Althorp'. A fellow-Hampshire authoress Mary Russell Mitford recorded the theory that it was the work of Frances, Lady Boringdon, the cultivated wife of another associate of Henry's, an attribution that persisted after the publication of *Pride and Prejudice*. The Duke of York, believing gossip that *Sense and Sensibility* was the work of Lady Augusta Paget, presented it to his niece Princess Charlotte, aged fifteen, second in line to the throne. She was entranced, writing to a friend, 'it certainly is interesting, & you feel quite one of the company. I think Maryanne & me are very like *in disposition*, that certainly I am not so good, the same imprudence, &c, however remain very like'.[11]

Finally, after more than a decade of waiting, Jane's career as a professional author, albeit an anonymous one, was launched and her stories would become books. *Pride and Prejudice* would be the follow-up, and almost immediately she began planning an entirely new work: *Mansfield Park*.

CHAPTER 5

WHIG HISTORY: *PRIDE AND PREJUDICE* (1811–1813)

There was no time to be lost. Even before the manuscript of *Sense and Sensibility* had been delivered to the publisher, Jane had begun thinking about revisions to her next novel, now to be *Pride and Prejudice* after one of those hack novelists at the Minerva Press stole her original title, *First Impressions*. No matter. In addition to the benefit of creating a 'brand' identity through its similarity to the title of her first work, the formula 'Pride and Prejudice' had pedigree, having appeared prominently in the concluding chapter of Burney's *Cecilia*. From the summer of 1811 right through the first half of 1812 Jane was absorbed in rewriting, 'chopping and lopping'. In addition to the distraction of household duties she did, however, spare the occasional moment to glance at the newspaper. And what she read there was almost invariably disturbing.

The confrontation between Britain, France and the United States over trade blockades was escalating, with a new front in the war likely to open with America. In England, a three-way battle was also being fought: between the government, the trading and manufacturing interest, and workers of the Midlands and the north. The international and domestic conflicts were linked. The merchants and manufacturers blamed the government for not doing more towards negotiating peace or at least appeasing the Americans by repealing trade restrictions with the Continent. The workers, in particular the skilled frame knitters who supplied

the important export trade in textiles, blamed their employers for introducing machinery to reduce costs, laying off men in favour of cheaper
unskilled female labour, and also blamed government ministers for the
economic mismanagement of which they were the principal victims.

We know that Jane Austen sometimes read the *Morning Post* while in
town. She found there an account of Eliza's notable party, and also the
item on the delay to the Weald of Kent Canal Bill, which her brother
Edward opposed. In *Sense and Sensibility* itself casual references to the
presence of newspapers are part of the realistic texture of her created
world. The newspaper was an important prop in dramatising the dys-
functional marriage of Mr and Mrs Palmer: while she babbles merrily of
the charms of Barton Cottage, he barely lifts his eyes from a newspaper
he has picked up from a table in the parlour. It plays a comparable role
when Mr Darcy begins reading in order to end an awkward conversation
with Elizabeth Bennet, or Tom Bertram shirks his duties at a ball. But
the newspaper was never considered to be the sole preserve of men. Its
presence in the all-female Dashwood household is proof of that. It is
there courtesy of the ever-generous Sir John Middleton, who evidently
thought to be of service to them in passing on the latest issue.

Public and private sometimes intersected in the pages of a newspaper.
Members of the elite would browse the pages, expecting to find news of
each other. In *Sense and Sensibility*, 'the newspapers announced to the
world, that the Lady of Thomas Palmer, Esq. was safely delivered of a son
and heir' (II.xiv). Given the slaughter resulting from the conflict in the
Spanish Peninsula, a sizeable number of newspaper readers were liable
to hear the most unwelcome news of all by way of the lists of casualties.
Jane referred in a letter to Cassandra on the heavy casualties at Albuera,
having seen the battle reported in the *Hampshire Telegraph* in May 1811.
They both knew what it was to consult the naval reports fearfully from
day to day, when Frank and Charles were at sea.

The clearest indication of Jane Austen's investment in contemporary events was the decision to plot *Pride and Prejudice* against the

calendar for 1811 and 1812. To provide this kind of strict timeline for her modern-day Cinderella tale was a remarkable decision. It was first composed in the late 1790s and its appeal has proven to be timeless. Yet as she undertook revisions she recognised it could be timely, concerned with one facet of the socio-economic conflict that flared up in the years 1811 to 1812. We have no information about the changes that were made at this stage, but she must have recognised the utopian implications of a fable which brings about the union of Elizabeth Bennet, an obscure young woman from a downwardly mobile family tarnished by the liability of an uncle in commercial Cheapside, and Fitzwilliam Darcy, the aristocratic Derbyshire estate owner and one of the richest men in the land. Through the reconciliation of trade and landed wealth, Jane would provide an account of what the condition of England *should* be. Immediately after publication she was to describe *Pride and Prejudice* as 'rather too light & bright & sparkling' and suggest that perhaps it needed to be padded out with 'solemn specious nonsense, about something unconnected with the story; an essay on writing, a critique on Walter Scott, or the history of Buonaparté' something that would give it 'shade' and offset delight with the dull weightiness of serious social commentary.[1] But to imagine that the novel as it stands is escapist would be a mistake. It required no supplements or digressions to make it relevant. The topicality is built into the airy infrastructure of the narrative.

When Elizabeth declines to marry her obnoxious cousin the Reverend Mr Collins the plot opens out to allow an exogamous romance to unfold. The conclusion of *Sense and Sensibility* had been a quasi-incestuous tangle: Elinor marries her brother-in-law; Colonel Brandon marries Marianne, a substitute for his deceased sister-in-law, whom he had first loved as a foster sister; the loathsome Fanny Dashwood is now Elinor's sister-in-law twice over and the romantic rival Lucy Steele has been triumphantly installed in her family circle. But *Pride and Prejudice*, along with *Northanger Abbey* and *Persuasion*, has the distinction of telling outward-facing love stories. It is assumed by some of the chief characters that caste must be preserved and property consolidated. Mr Darcy's aunt Lady Catherine De Bourgh is adamant on this score as she expounds to Elizabeth the philosophy of inbreeding:

> My daughter and my nephew are formed for each other. They are de-
> scended on the maternal side, from the same noble line ... Their fortune
> on both sides is splendid. They are destined for each other by the voice of
> every member of their respective houses; and what is to divide them? The
> upstart pretensions of a young woman without family, connections, or
> fortune. Is this to be endured! But it must not, shall not be. If you were
> sensible of your own good, you would not wish to quit the sphere, in
> which you have been brought up. (III.xiv)

Lady Catherine's efforts, of course, provoke the reverse of the desired effect, and Elizabeth's daring and spirited resistance to her aristocratic creed constitutes the dramatic climax of the novel. Lizzy is one heroine who would not marry an approximation of a brother and the romance plot is the stronger for it. But Henry Austen's influence is no less pervasive than in other works, and here it takes a new direction, quite literally. The time Jane had spent with him and his associates had given her a clearer grasp of the extent of his dealings and his network of patronage. It had opened her eyes, and lifted them northwards. Austen & Co. was the London correspondent for the Buxton and High Peak bank under the patronage of William the Duke of Devonshire. The firm was also the London agent for the Derbyshire Militia with the Duke's brother Lord George Cavendish at its helm. These connections added the Midlands to her mental map. A claim has been made that she actually travelled in 1811 to see the Duke's Chatsworth estate and stayed in the market town of Bakewell, on which 'Lambton' may have been modelled, though hard evidence is lacking.[2] The furthest north she is known to have reached was her cousin the Reverend Edward Cooper's parish of Hamstall Ridware in south-east Staffordshire between Birmingham and Stoke-on-Trent during a brief excursion in 1806. Now, in her imagination she ventured further afield than she would ever do again.

Derbyshire is Elizabeth's destined home. Mr Bingley and his bride Jane Bennet will also settle there. Enough has been said already about Henry's career path to suggest the importance of the division into counties as an organising principle, militarily, politically, socially and for the purposes of taxation. The county of Derbyshire was seldom out of the news in 1811. In March the first act of militant frame-breaking took place in Nottingham as the result of a cut in wages at a time when food prices were rapidly rising and unemployment increasing. Flour from another poor harvest produced loaves with crusts like husks and the texture of gruel within. Activism among knitters in the hosiery industry quickly spread into Derbyshire, with several outbreaks in the Ilkeston area at the end of that month. The London newspapers reported the acts of industrial sabotage at the time Jane was there seeing *Sense and Sensibility* through the press, linking them to the threatened collapse of trade with America. With Europe blocked off by Napoleon's Continental System, the United States was the most important export market for British goods. However, the American government resented British interference with their commerce in France, and retaliated with blockades of their own, leading to an 83 per cent fall in the value of exports; from £10.9 million in 1810 to £1.8 million in 1811.

One of the men responsible for restoring law and order was Henry's client, Lord George Cavendish. Not only was he the head of the Derbyshire Militia but he was also the elected Member of Parliament for the county from 1797 to 1831, a role he assumed as his birthright. The Cavendishes of Derbyshire were at the heart of the Whig establishment. The enormous wealth of Lord George's brother the Duke of Devonshire (whose aristocratic title came from a south-west county while his property base was in the Midlands) made him one of the great power brokers of the political scene, wielding influence from the House of Lords through his protégés in the Commons. The Derbyshire Militia was a substantial body of 4,000 men in five regiments but it was ineffective in bringing the miscreants to justice. The frames were too scattered to be guarded, and the communities closed rank to protect their own. Soldiers were dealing with a guerrilla force that generally struck by night and had a perfect knowledge of the terrain.

It was one more minor humiliation for Lord George. A cornucopia of wealth and privilege could do nothing to make him effective. In 1831, just before his death, he was made Earl of Burlington for no particular reason other than loyalty to his friend King George IV, with whom he had shared the courtesan Elizabeth Armistead in the days of their youth. Another claim to fame was the Burlington Arcade, the first covered shopping mall, constructed to stop passers-by throwing rubbish over the wall of his Piccadilly town house. The best that can be said of him is that he was a staunch defender of civil liberties, regularly voting against punitive measures against political radicals. In a speech opposing the introduction of imprisonment without trial in 1817, he argued that the existing powers of magistrates had been perfectly sufficient in dealing with the Luddite rebellion in Derbyshire.

There was a resurgence of frame-breaking throughout the Midlands and Yorkshire towards the end of 1811, and by now it was well known that the perpetrators left cryptic anonymous notes at the scene of the crime claiming to be acting under the orders of 'General Ludd'. The term 'Luddite' has come to mean an irrational dislike of new technology, but those who adopted the label at the time began dismantling machinery only after reasoned and repeated appeals for redress to Parliament had failed. They called on the government to abandon the policies that had led to the downturn in trade, and to protect them from the practices of unscrupulous employers who were laying off skilled textile workers unnecessarily in the pursuit of profit. Frame-breaking was a bargaining mechanism at a time when 'combinations' of workers were banned. The main target of the Luddites in Derbyshire was the wide frame, used to produce 'cut ups', cheaply made and substandard gloves and socks. Their motto was 'Full Fashioned Work at the Full Price'. By the end of December Derbyshire workers had achieved some success: wages were raised by two shillings per dozen items and the 'cut up' trade was checked for the moment, alleviating economic distress.

In February 1812 the first review of *Sense and Sensibility* appeared in the venerable *Critical Review*, founded in 1756 by a fellow comic novelist, Tobias Smollett. It was lengthy and wholly appreciative, showcasing her talents with large chunks of quotation. Jane read it again and again and once she had it almost by heart, probably leafed through the rest of the issue. Since she was ever alert to family interests, her eye may have been caught by two short reviews of pamphlets with a bearing on Henry's concerns. In each, the critic blamed the government for the present economic crisis, and called for a more diplomatic, less belligerent, approach to foreign conflicts. In answer to one aggressively militarist pamphleteer, the critic asked if peace would have given rise to any of the evils that now plagued the country: 'Would it have caused the stagnation of foreign trade, the accumulation of bankruptcies, the depreciation of bank notes, and the disappearance of all the gold coin of the realm?' Would peace with Napoleon prove so detrimental? It was an experiment that had yet to be properly tried. Meanwhile the nation was on the road to ruin through 'the *excessive* issue of bank notes'.[3]

Henry, as a partner in three note-issuing country banks in the relatively prosperous south-east of England, was not just surviving the downturn but thriving in it. Nevertheless, his views on the present crisis would have been informed by his economic interests, aligned with those of his clients. They were almost invariably staunch Whigs, opposed to the government's policies and inclined to exploit its present difficulties. In addition to tribal Whig grandees like Lord Charles Spencer and Lord George Cavendish, Henry had principled Whigs on his books like the current lieutenant colonel of the Oxfords, William Gore-Langton, known to be a 'thick and thin' who could be relied on to vote with the Whigs on any issue.[4]

The moneyed interest was traditionally allied with the Whigs when it came to questions of trade. The Whigs, from their beginnings as a political faction in the late seventeenth century, had welcomed the blending of the ruling class and the rising class, and included many prominent bankers in their ranks. In the current crisis the merchant banker Alexander Baring became one of the party's leading spokesmen in the Commons. He was chief partner in the firm Baring Brothers, a leading broker of government loans, one of the directors of the Bank of England and a member of the Bullion Committee. In 1803 Alexander Baring, in collaboration with the Dutch firm Hope & Co., had issued $11,250,000 in bonds to finance the United States' purchase of the Louisiana Territory from France. He belonged to a class of super-bankers, with the power to alter the course of wars and the destiny of nations through finance. Nathan Rothschild would soon emerge as another in the same league.

The Baring dynasty had German origins and strong American interests. In England they had established themselves in Hampshire, in the Austens' neighbourhood. The founder of the bank, Sir Francis Baring, before his death in 1810, bought Stratton Park near Winchester. The mansion house was remodelled by George Dance in the purest Greek Revival style and became the admiration of the county, a chaste temple constructed from the profits of transatlantic trade and international finance. It was inherited along with the baronetcy and a fortune of £500,000 by the eldest son, Thomas Baring, who had gained his business experience with the East India Company in the 1790s at the time of Warren Hastings's trial. There were, therefore, points of overlap and although evidence of an acquaintance between the Barings and Austens has yet to emerge, we know that Alexander Baring owned *Emma*. A copy with his bookplate and the stamp of his country residence, 'Melchet Court, Romsey', is now in the collection of the University of Illinois.

Alexander Baring's speeches in Parliament were regularly reported in the papers, and Henry would have been aware of his arguments. So highly respected was his opinion on economic matters that even the Tory

Prime Minister, Spencer Perceval, had heeded his cautions on the Bullion
Report and resisted the immediate resumption of cash payments by the
Bank of England. Another Tory Prime Minister, Benjamin Disraeli, was
to call him 'the greatest merchant England perhaps ever had'. A liberal
Tory, Edward Littleton, would remark in 1819:

> I know no individual who gives me more the idea of a perfect mercan-
> tile character than Mr Baring – liberal and consistent in his politics
> – leaning to the side of the oppressed in all countries, having intimate
> communication with the great merchants of all parts of the world; generous
> and manly in pursuit of public interests – candid but discreet in pursuit
> of his own.[5]

In 1812, however, the Tories would have had less enthusiasm for his views.
In March he called for an investigation into the effects of the British
trade blockades on the national economy. He had joined forces with the
progressive Whigs in a campaign to overturn the Orders in Council and
avert war with the United States. His motives were partly humanitarian
– he had sympathy for the protesters in the northern counties – and
partly self-interested and pragmatic. Trade with America was crucial to
the Barings' business.

Another name appears in the parliamentary records of the debate on
trade blockades, a name which in full has strong associations for any
reader of Jane Austen's works: Lord Milton, otherwise known as Charles
William Wentworth Fitzwilliam. He was the son and heir of Earl Fitzwilliam, the richest man in England. In early 1812 the West Riding of
Yorkshire was at the eye of the Luddite storm which had spread from
the Midlands, and Earl Fitzwilliam was Lord Lieutenant of the region.
Lord Milton, like Alexander Baring, was a frequent speaker for the Whigs
in the Commons. On 3 March he briefly stated that he had been given
a petition signed by many thousands of the manufacturing population
complaining of deep distress and praying for relief. The petition was

addressed with urgency to the Prince Regent and he observed that the Prince had not held a public levee for three weeks. In this observation there was implied criticism of the selfish indolence of Prince George.

A number of Austen scholars have observed the crop of names borrowed from the Fitzwilliams of Yorkshire, who not only passed down 'Wentworth' as a given name, but had their main seat at Wentworth Woodhouse. They ask if there is significance in the fact that names from this patrician source turn up variously in *Pride and Prejudice*, *Emma*, and *Persuasion*. Margaret Ann Doody has dubbed the phenomenon the 'Great Surname Matrix'.[6] She, like Donald Greene in his study of Austen's attitude to the peerage, supposed that the intent must have been satirical on the basis that Jane was a Tory by inclination. In *Jane Austen's Names, Riddles, Persons, Places*, Doody remarks of Mr Darcy's Christian name that, owing to this association with a prominent political dynasty, it 'reeks of successful Whiggery and Gargantuan wealth'.[7] The fourth and present Earl Fitzwilliam had indeed inherited a magnificent mansion set in 1,500 acres of parkland with a further 14,000 acres in the West Riding worth nearly £20,000 per annum, double Fitzwilliam Darcy's fabulous estimated income. However, Mr Darcy's wealth is not the target of any very severe critique in the novel, and Mr Darcy himself is eminently redeemable. While his character is flawed at the start by pride of birth, this is not enough to explain why the otherwise attractive romantic hero should be allotted a name with such powerful Whig resonance.

Non-political suggestions have been made. Elizabeth Jenkins discovered that for a prank someone, probably Jane herself when a young girl, linked her name in the Steventon Marriage Register with 'Henry Frederick Howard Fitzwilliam of London'. It seems reasonable to suppose that at one level she simply liked the grand rolling syllables. On the other hand, 'Jane Austen of Steventon' is also married off on the same page to 'Arthur William Mortimer of Liverpool' and 'Jack Smith'.[8] More recently Janine Barchas has proposed that the name-checking of famous aristocrats was part of her wider preoccupation with celebrity. Knowledge of Henry Austen's network of professional contacts suggests alternative possibilities.

The Whig aristocrats were a tightly knit group. Lord Charles Spencer, prominent in the story of Henry's career, was the cousin of Henrietta, Lady Bessborough, a notable figure in high society, who had enthused about *Sense and Sensibility* remarking, 'They were full of it at Althorp.' Althorp was the Northamptonshire seat of her father, Earl Spencer. Her response to *Pride and Prejudice* is not known, but she must have been struck by the fact that Mr Darcy's sister shared a name with her sister, who had been until her death in 1806 the wife of the Duke of Devonshire, both the real and the fictional Georgiana presiding over a great house in Derbyshire. The Duke had a connection with Henry on two counts, through the Buxton bank and the militia regiment led by his brother. In 1806 the son of his friend, Charles Augustus Bennet, Lord Ossulston, formerly a private customer of Henry's, was married at the Duke's town residence in Piccadilly, Devonshire House. Lady Bessborough's husband, meanwhile, was the brother of Lady Charlotte, the wife of Earl Fitzwilliam. Putting the complexities of these interrelationships to one side, the main point is that for any of the inhabitants of Althorp or Wentworth Woodhouse or Chatsworth, the family names found in *Pride and Prejudice* and the later novels would be taken as a ready clue to the author's political sympathies. For anyone, indeed, with an interest in current affairs, the information that Colonel Fitzwilliam is the younger son of an earl, the subject of one of Elizabeth Bennet's witty sallies during her stay at Hunsford, would be understood as a topical reference, and probably as a display of Whig affinity.

If there was any such affinity on Jane Austen's part, it was mediated by her attachment to Henry. His fortunes were bound up with the Whig elite by direct patronage, and ultimately by a shared reliance on that thoroughly unreliable font of good things, the dilatory and capricious Prince Regent. Henry's secret partner Charles James continued to act

as a business agent for Lord Moira. And Moira remained part of the
inner circle of 'Prinney' although the strain caused by the Prince's failure
to implement a handover of power to the Whigs, his former political
allies, his friends, his old drinking, gambling and whoring partners, was
beginning to tell.

Once *Pride and Prejudice* is reconsidered in the light of the many
connections between the Austens and the great Whig families, the immediately topical slant of its romance plot becomes apparent. The love
story of Fitzwilliam Darcy and Elizabeth Bennet is also about the ruling
aristocratic elite reconnecting with the commercial middle class. Lizzy,
when provoked by Lady Catherine, may call herself 'a gentleman's daughter' and therefore a suitable wife for Mr Darcy, but when earlier in the
novel she considers what his 'strong objections' might be to the match
between his friend Mr Bingley and Jane Bennet, she is pretty sure it was
down to the Bennet girls 'having one uncle who was a country attorney,
and another who was in business in London' and the insulting terms of
his first proposal to her soon confirm it (III.xiv; II.x).

Jane Austen's decision to give the Bennets a commercial hinterland is
intriguing. The crux of the plot, the problem over the entail of the father's
estate in a family with five daughters and no son, could have remained
the same without it. The name 'Bennet' has an aristocratic ring, but Jane
would have known through Henry's dealings that the lord who possessed
it had married Emma Colebrooke, from a well-known banking family
based in City of London. The fact that the Bennets in the novel also
have 'low' City connections, in addition to the prospect of poverty, was
a careful and deliberate choice. It was this additional dimension of their
predicament that gives rise to a great set-piece scene, soon after the arrival
of Mr Bingley and his entourage at Netherfield Park, a grand estate in
the vicinity of Longbourn. Bingley's sisters share information about the
Bennets in the drawing room at Netherfield, while Elizabeth, a guest,
attends to her sister, lying ill upstairs.

'I think I have heard you say, that their uncle is an attorney in Meryton.'

'Yes; and they have another, who lives somewhere near Cheapside.'

'That is capital,' added her sister, and they both laughed heartily.

'If they had uncles enough to fill *all* Cheapside,' cried Bingley, 'it would not make them one jot less agreeable.'

'But it must very materially lessen their chance of marrying men of any consideration in the world,' replied Darcy. (I.viii)

The sisters, wary of the charms of the Bennet girls, play up the hilarious incongruity of the niece of a Cheapside merchant aspiring to marry a man 'in possession of a good fortune'. Cheapside, we are to understand, represents social death in the eyes of fashion.

Soon after, with Bingley and Jane drawing nearer to an engagement, and Darcy increasingly drawn to Elizabeth, Miss Caroline Bingley engineers a group decampment back to London and the safety of the Hursts' house in Grosvenor Street in Mayfair, just off New Bond Street. Mr Gardiner, the infamous uncle, lives in Gracechurch Street in the City of London and in topographic terms, Grosvenor Street and Gracechurch Street could hardly be further apart. On contemporary maps Grosvenor Street appeared at the furthest point of westward urban expansion, end-stopped by Hyde Park, while Gracechurch Street was at the outer edge of the old City quarter in the east. London was a single conurbation made up of two cities, representative of frequently opposed interests and perspectives. Robert Southey, in a travelogue published in 1807, suggested there was an 'imaginary line of demarcation' between the western and eastern ends of the town and observed that a nobleman could not possibly be found residing in the City 'unless he should be confined for treason, or sedition in Newgate or the Tower'.[9]

'Cheapside' connotes 'trade', derived from the Old English term *céap*, a place for buying and selling. The reader is told that Bingley's forebears made a fortune in trade in 'the north of England', but now the son and

heir is looking to purchase an estate, leaving behind those trade origins.
He is already consorting with the old landed gentry. His friend Darcy
may not have a title but he has a family seat, and a library handed down
through generations, and names which, like 'De Bourgh', date from William
the Conqueror. The Bingley family's capital acquired by trade is
being invested in social climbing. One can assume that it is the dowry
of his sister Mrs Hurst that has made possible the lease of a residence in
exclusive Grosvenor Street, since she has 'married a man of more fashion
than fortune' (I.iv). Chatting with Charlotte Lucas, Elizabeth denies
that Jane is angling to catch Mr Bingley, and remarks pointedly that
four social evenings with card-playing have 'enabled them to ascertain
that they both like Vingt-un better than Commerce' (I.vi). Be that as
it may, commerce is the game from which the Bennet family cannot be
dissociated.

Another conversation, this time between Elizabeth and Mrs Gardiner,
wife of the Cheapside uncle, confirms the toxicity of the City of London
location from a 'fashionable' perspective. Mrs Gardiner is concerned that
Jane in her lovelorn state may not agree to visit her given that Mr Bingley
is also in London.

'I hope,' added Mrs Gardiner, 'that no consideration with regard to this
young man will influence her. We live in so different a part of town, all
our connections are so different, and, as you well know, we go out so little,
that it is very improbable they should meet at all, unless he really comes
to see her.'

'And *that* is quite impossible; for he is now in the custody of his friend,
and Mr Darcy would no more suffer him to call on Jane in such a part of
London! My dear aunt, how could you think of it? Mr Darcy may perhaps
have *heard* of such a place as Gracechurch Street, but he would hardly
think a month's ablution enough to cleanse him from its impurities, were
he once to enter it; and depend upon it, Mr Bingley never stirs without
him.' (II.ii)

The horror of contamination Elizabeth attributes to Mr Darcy is her recognition of a taboo of miscegenation which is expressed territorially. It speaks to the tribal mentality displayed in the earlier conversation between Bingley's sisters and in Caroline Bingley's pointed letter to Jane, an attitude which Elizabeth assumes Darcy shares. Miss Bingley's designs are insular, aimed at a double alliance: her brother must marry Georgiana Darcy; she herself must marry Fitzwilliam Darcy. The social body based in the elite stronghold of Mayfair must be protected. Given that trade is a feature in the family backgrounds of both the Bennets and the Bingleys, it is the very fragility of the boundary between them that gives rise to a defensive horror which Elizabeth scarcely exaggerates.

Momentarily there appears a possibility that the barrier could be breached. Chance takes Jane near Grosvenor Street and she pays a visit, but it is not returned for two weeks and when Caroline does arrive in Gracechurch Street, she gives Jane to understand that her chances with Bingley are hopeless. Although he apparently knows she is in town, he makes no attempt to visit her, and it is unlikely that he will ever return to Netherfield again.

Lying behind the great Regent Street project of 1817–23 is a fear of contamination of the kind Elizabeth Bennet describes. It could be classified as an instance of epidemiological town planning. John Nash's proposal for the construction of a new major south–north thoroughfare from Carlton House in Pall Mall up to the new Regent's Park was passed by an Act of Parliament in 1813, the same year that *Pride and Prejudice* was published. It has typically been represented by architectural historians as a triumph of public works in the grand style, an act of courage by Nash or of characteristic self-indulgence by the Prince Regent, who intended to build a new palace in the park. But it was at the same time, unmistakably, a *cordon sanitaire* which below Oxford Street 'hugged' (Nash's term) the inner contour of the West End, leaving its geometric plan of wide streets and squares intact while demolishing the outer edge of the unsavoury, heterogeneous district of Soho. The design was surgical in its precision;

'the only logical and "biologically" correct line', in the architectural historian John Summerson's words.[10]

We can gather that the Mayfair perspective was not one that Jane Austen herself shared. The fact that she opted to make the Gardiners stalwart residents of the City, at a time when it was becoming more exclusively commercial and the number of residents was diminishing, is a feature as striking as the invention of a West Indian context for Sir Thomas Bertram in *Mansfield Park*. The favourable depiction of the Gardiner aunt and uncle, educated, cultivated, judicious and, in the case of Mrs Gardiner, with a playful wit akin to that of Elizabeth, suggests that the reader is intended to form a very different idea of their immediate environment than that assumed by the Bingley sisters. The implicit championing of trade was not new in Jane's work. The heroine of *Catharine, or The Bower* written in 1792, the first Austen character to display a moral conscience, is a merchant's daughter.

Mr Gardiner is a merchant, and although we do not learn the nature of his trade, he would have belonged to the dynamic, innovating Cheapside represented in a pictorial 'view' in *The Repository of the Arts* in 1813. This journal, documenting and shaping changes in taste and fashion, was published by the cultural entrepreneur Rudolph Ackermann, a German immigrant who ran a print shop and drawing school in the Strand, close to Henry's bank in Covent Garden. In precisely the period of Austen's writing career, it published more than seventy prints of architectural landmarks and street scenes across London, collected in a volume entitled *Select Views of London* in 1816. Ackermann's publications ignored supposed divisions between east and west. The lengthy commentary that accompanies the engraving of Cheapside in the *Repository* details the commodities sold in each of the warehouses and shops – luxury goods such as silks and muslins, hosiery, furs and silverware – along with news of refitted and newly installed retailers. Cheapside was evidently not always cheap; nor did it suffer from the deprivations affecting the northern counties.

View of Cheapside from *The Repository of the Arts* (1812).

Another factor that belies the notion of Cheapside as a commercial back-water or forbidden zone, beyond the pale of elite consciousness, is its continuing importance as a metropolitan transit zone. Three major east–west arteries converged at Cheapside. The result was a source of wonder to visitors. The German poet and journalist, Heinrich Heine, declared that here you could 'hear the pulse of the world beat audibly'. Richard Rush, the American Minister to Britain, painted the scene in the district of Cheapside vividly in 1817:

> The shops stand side by side for entire miles. The accumulation of things, is amazing; it would seem impossible that there can be purchasers for them all, until you consider what multitudes there are to buy ... In the middle of the streets, coal wagons and others as large, carts, trucks, vehicles of every sort, loaded in every way, are passing. They are in two close lines, like great tides, going reverse ways, and reaching farther than the eye can see. The horses come so near to the foot pavement which is crowded with people, that their hoofs, and the great wheels of the wagons, are only a few inches from the people. In this manner the whole procession is in movement with its complicated noise; it confounds the senses to be among it all...[II]

Gracechurch Street, just east of Cheapside, was a main north–south axis, connected to London Bridge. In a letter of 1808 Jane told Cassandra that James had caught the stagecoach into Kent from the Cross Keys in Gracechurch Street, the rest of the family having crowded into James's private coach on a visit to Edward. For Elizabeth Bennet, the street is a convenient stopping-off point as she travels from Hertfordshire to Kent to see her friend Charlotte, now Mrs Collins, and again on the way back. Many coaching inns were located there and in Bishopsgate, its continuation to the north.

Henry would sometimes visit this area on his way to the Bank of England to manage the charge account of Austen & Co. The walk from Henrietta Street to Threadneedle Street took him through Cheapside. Beyond Soane's majestic new Bank premises lay two other important commercial institutions with special significance for him, both of them near the top of Gracechurch Street. East India House, with its splendid neo-classical facade, was situated around the corner at the junction of Leadenhall Street and Lime Street, on the site of the present-day Lloyd's Building. This was the palace that Warren Hastings's endeavours had built. It would not be inappropriate for Henry to go and pay homage on occasion. He ultimately owed his own present prosperity to the East India Company. It was Hastings's gift to Eliza that had provided the security for Henry's move into finance. Hastings may at some time have given him a tour of the interior, to see the capacious Directors' Court Room with the bas-relief panel by Rysbrack of *Britannia Receiving the Riches of the East* and, because the theme was pleasing and to the point, the oval ceiling painting in the great Revenue Committee Room of *The East Offering Its Riches To Britannia*. He would probably not have visited any of the 'pent-up offices, where candles for one-half the year supplied the place of the sun's light' as one of the underlings, the essayist and Company clerk Charles Lamb, described them.

Crossing Gracechurch Street in the direction of Leadenhall Street, Henry could have glimpsed on his left the anonymous front of Barings

Bank spread over three houses, at No.'s 6 to 8 Bishopsgate. The Barings dealt in sums on a scale beyond the dreams of a minor adventurer like Henry Austen. Sir Francis Baring had been director and then chairman of the East India Company in addition to running his own thriving merchant bank. In 1963 the Georgian structure was to be demolished by John Baring, the 7th Baron Ashburton, whose heavy hand with the family's architectural heritage earned him the nickname 'Basher Baring'. Eventually a dark grey skyscraper would be constructed in its place and thirty-two years later the family firm itself would vanish into history courtesy of the rogue trader Nick Leeson.

On his way back to Henrietta Street, Henry would have passed through St Paul's Churchyard, the heart of the bookselling trade, bordering the north side of the Cathedral. He might then have reflected on his and James's early exploits in authorship. What an irony that Jane, without the benefit of a university education, had achieved literary success. He only wished she wouldn't insist on anonymity. For now, the best he could do was to make sure a copy of *Sense and Sensibility* fell into the right hands.

The route along Ludgate Hill led past Stationers Hall Court on the right, and one time or another must have jogged his memory. One of these days he must call in at Crosby's, do something about the Bath novel of Jane's, the satire of Radcliffe and the horrid novelists. The manuscript was still there, gathering dust. But hearing the clock on St Dunstan's Church strike the hour as he approached Hoare's Bank at Fleet Street, he realised he must hurry. He had dallied too long in the City. Striding towards Temple Bar he was comforted by the sight of Roworth's print shop. Very soon *Pride and Prejudice* would be ready for the press. This would surely be the one to make Jane's fortune, and reflect glory on him and the rest of the Hampshire Austens.

Now Henry was back in the Strand, in the neighbourhood of Henrietta Street. It is here that Jane had decided to locate the crisis of her latest work. For at the very moment when Elizabeth and Darcy are drawing together during her visit to Derbyshire with the Gardiners, they are divided

again by the news contained in a letter from Jane. Reckless Lydia, the
youngest of the Bennet sisters, has eloped with Lieutenant Wickham after
accompanying her friend Mrs Forster, the wife of the militia colonel, to
dissolute Brighton. Initially the family imagine they must have travelled
north to Gretna Green, where couples could marry without a licence or
parental permission. But it soon becomes apparent that the runaways
have diverted to London, and therefore to the iniquity of cohabitation
without vows from which there could be no return to respectability.

Lydia disappears with Wickham into the jumble of streets in the
middle of town, and the narrator becomes appropriately vague regarding
their whereabouts. Since concealment is the issue here, Jane Austen, with
nice wit, conceals from the readers the exact location of their lodgings.
Mr Darcy tracks Wickham down by going to an 'Edward Street' (there is
more than one), the doubtful address of the shady former governess who
had almost succeeded in delivering his sister into Wickham's clutches.
When it comes to the den of vice itself Mrs Gardiner's report to Elizabeth
is censored: 'At length…,' Mrs Gardiner writes, 'our kind friend procured
the wished-for direction. They were in – street' (III.x). A strong hint,
however, is provided by the unexpected and joyous news that Wickham
and Lydia have actually been married at St Clement's Church in the
parish where they had been lodging. Here again, there is some room
for doubt. It could be St Clement's Eastcheap, not far from Cheapside,
but this would surely be too close to the Gardiners to serve as a logical
hideout. Commentators agree that the church in question must be St
Clement Danes, on the Strand.

The parish of St Clement Danes extended either side of the Strand,
south to the river and up to Lincoln's Inn Field with Drury Lane as its
western boundary and Covent Garden and Henrietta Street close by.
The district was densely populated, with a headcount of 12,000 in 1801
(compared to 350 in tiny St Clement's Eastcheap parish) and was socially
miscellaneous, a mixture of commerce, imposing waterfront residences and deep poverty in its alleys and courtyards. This neighbourhood

offered anonymity and an abundance of cheap lodgings with, should it be needed, one of the best parish relief systems in the metropolis. After a scandal some years earlier, when it was discovered that the mortality rate for pauper children in the care of the parish stood at 90 per cent, the system had been reformed. Abandoned and illegitimate infants were now sent out to nurse in the country and, when grown, were 'apprenticed' in substantial numbers in one of the 'dark satanic mills' of the north. A frequent destination was a factory in Backbarrow in Cumberland. Had things worked out differently, the product of Lydia's frolic might have joined the ranks of children powering the Industrial Revolution.

The Lydia–Wickham imbroglio appears to be the very realisation of the sneers about Cheapside voiced early in the novel. It epitomises the expected fate of the Bennet girls, cruelly exposing their lack of market value, and confirming the idea of the institution of marriage as a market exchange. Lydia was not worth marrying for herself; Wickham had to be bribed into it, at a price which Mr Bennet judges to be not less than £10,000, the very sum that had been attached to Miss King, a recent quarry of Wickham's. It is a mercenary match that confirms the idea that the distance between Cheapside and the West End cannot be bridged.

And yet, it turns out that this disaster finally humbles both Darcy and Elizabeth sufficiently to remove all the obstacles represented by pride and prejudice.

Trade emerges as an alternative source of integrity and refinement. Mr Darcy is ultimately able to shake off his 'abominable pride', the tribal mentality characteristic of Grosvenor Street. It is when he returns to London from Pemberley to join with Mr Gardiner in facilitating the marriage of Wickham and Lydia, and actually dines at Gracechurch Street, that the possibility of a happy ending has finally arrived. Both Mr Darcy and Elizabeth are humiliated by impossible relations, socially high and low, but they are united in their love of the Gardiners. In the final lines of the novel, the City merchant and his wife offer the common ground for reconciliation.

With the Gardiners, they were always on the most intimate terms. Darcy, as well as Elizabeth, really loved them; and they were both ever sensible of the warmest gratitude towards the persons who, by bringing her into Derbyshire, had been the means of uniting them. (III.xix)

The taboo of trade is dismissed as a shibboleth. Contemporary readers were left with an allegory in which, along the lines of the Whig campaign against the Orders in Council, the traditional ruling class unite with the commercial middle class to ensure harmony and future prosperity.

Jane was continuing to refine this vision of regeneration in May 1812 when news arrived from London that the Prime Minister Spencer Perceval had been shot dead in the lobby of the House of Commons by John Bellingham, a bankrupted Liverpool merchant. Although Bellingham's grudge against the government went back many years, the fact that he was in trade and came from Liverpool, the main port for transatlantic trade and a hotbed of protest, could not fail to be understood as an extension of Luddite insurgency into the very heart of Westminster. In London and in the north the labouring poor rejoiced, horrifying Tory loyalists. Coleridge, a former radical turned fervent defender of the status quo, dashed off a hagiographic editorial on Perceval for the government-backed *Courier* newspaper. In Cumberland his friend and brother-in-law Robert Southey wept and lamented, anticipating civil war.

Elsewhere the response was more laconic. Mrs James Austen in Steventon, writing her diary entry for 11 May, noted simply 'Mr Perceval was shot as he entered the House of Commons', before adding as an aide-memoire, 'he was the prime minister'.[12] Edward and his daughter Fanny arrived on the 11th to stay with Henry and Eliza in Sloane Street, after visiting family in Hampshire and Oxford. The following day Fanny recorded in her diary trips into town for shopping and the theatre at Covent Garden as if nothing had happened.

A fortnight later at Carlton House, the Prince Regent's opulent palace in Pall Mall, scenes took place that would settle the succession to Perceval,

and indirectly, the fate of Henry Austen. Lord Moira, formerly one of the
Prince's closest intimates, was summoned. The two had been estranged
by George's unexpected failure to form a Whig government following his
accession to the Regency, and in particular by his strange intransigence
over the question of Catholic emancipation, the Anglo-Irish Moira's red-
line issue and a cause his royal friend had previously supported. Thomas
Creevey, an ally of Henry Brougham on the radical wing of the Whig
party and an avid gossip-monger, sent a vivid report to his wife from
Brooks's club in St James's Street:

> ...late last night Prinney sent for Moira and flung himself upon his mercy.
> Such a scene I never heard of; the young monarch *cried* loud and long;
> in short he seems to have been very nearly in convulsions. The afflicting
> interview was entirely occupied with lamentations over past errors, and
> delight at brighter prospects for the future under the happier auspices of
> his old and true friend now restored.

Moira, attempting to steady the blubbering Prince, told him 'generally of
the distressed state of the country'. The Prince professed astonishment,
ministers had concealed it from him, and he had not seen a newspaper
for three or four weeks. At last Moira 'suggested to him that perhaps he
would wish to be more *composed* before they went further into detail'.
Another two meetings followed, but the Prince's state became no calmer.
He was dithering between a government led by Moira or by Lord Welles-
ley, brother of the Duke of Wellington, who was more hawkish on war
policy. But both of them were adamant on the need for Irish Catholic
relief and that was something he was now reluctant to concede, due – he
claimed – to new-found filial devotion for his stricken father and his
anti-Catholic views.

On the 28th, another of George's closest friends, Richard Brinsley
Sheridan, reported that the Prince himself was approaching a mental
breakdown; 'I begin to think that his reign will end in a day or two in

downright insanity.' Come the first day of June, the suspense continued. Creevey said of the Prince, 'The more one sees of the conduct of this most singular man, the more one becomes convinced he is doomed, from his personal character alone, to shake his throne.' A Whig-dominated ministry still seemed within reach and Creevey was thrilled to hear from Samuel Whitbread that Moira had produced a programme of reforms: 'his plan for revoking Orders in Council, conciliating America by all manner of means, the most rigid economical reform, nay, parliamentary reform if it was wished for: in short every subject was most agreeable and satisfactory'.[13]

Then on 8 June came the thunderbolt. Negotiations had broken down. Moira could not rally sufficient support from liberal Tories. Instead Lord Liverpool was invited to form a revised version of Perceval's ministry. All was not entirely lost, however. The new government, still weak and tentative, opted to revoke the Orders in Council in the face of overwhelming evidence presented by the committee of inquiry led by Henry Brougham and Alexander Baring into the causes of economic distress. There was an outburst of rejoicing in the ports and industrial regions of the North. Charlotte Brontë was to recall it in *Shirley* (1849), her fable of the Luddite insurrection in the West Riding, 'You know very well – such of you as are old enough to remember – you made Yorkshire and Lancashire shake with your shout on that occasion.' The triumph was tempered by the news, which arrived a month later, that the United States had voted by the narrowest of margins to go to war with Great Britain. The two ships, one carrying overtures towards peace and the other a declaration of war, had crossed in mid-Atlantic. Nevertheless the dismantling of the British trade blockades provided immediate relief for the economy and the remainder of the war years saw relative prosperity. 'Stocks, which had been accumulating for years, now went off in a moment, in the twinkling of an eye,' Brontë remembered, 'warehouses were lightened, ships were laden; work abounded, wages rose: the good time seemed come. These prospects might be delusive, but they were brilliant – to some they were even true.

At that epoch, in that single month of June, many a solid fortune was realized.'

Lord Moira's fortune was hollow. He was left with a sense of bewilderment, having been betrayed by the Prince, whose needy friendship had left him many thousands of pounds in debt. Some supposed that the Regent's distress during this crisis had been brilliant play-acting to rid himself of Whig affiliation. As a consolation prize Moira was offered, and accepted on 12 June, the Order of the Garter with the hint of a lucrative official post in the near future.

The Fitzwilliams did not gain much credit from destitute constituents for their part in the furore over the Orders in Council. Two days after the government conceded defeat, Lord Milton, in his role as a justice of the peace, was stoned at Sheffield by an angry crowd protesting against the extortionate price of flour. One of the protesters had dressed himself up as Earl Fitzwilliam to assure the flour dealers that he would make up the difference if they would agree to sell the flour at half the rate. The country might be awash with banknotes but for the poor, bread was the main unit of value. It was the staple that made the difference between survival and starvation. As in the case of the mutiny in Henry's Oxfordshire Militia back in 1795, the inflated cost of flour or a standard loaf was seen as the violation of a basic right to life. When challenged by soldiers, several of the crowd declared they would go to Wentworth Woodhouse to lay their grievances before the Earl in person. Two days later twenty-three men were arrested. The price of flour remained high.

In Derbyshire it would seem that calm was entirely restored, but the textile workers were encouraged by their victory and continued to organise. Another crisis in 1817 would lead to the last armed rebellion on British soil at Pentrich, allegedly sparked by government agents.

Henry could have gathered something of the inside story of the tumultuous court politics of May and June 1812 from Charles James or other contacts. But for the moment the Austen family, though denied the advantages that a Moira premiership might have brought, went on placidly enough. Henry seemed secure in his fine residence in Sloane Street, rated in June at twice the value of the home of his partner James Tilson in nearby Hans Place. Jane had received another review, this time in the *British Critic*, a journal dedicated to the defence of the Anglican religion and the Crown. The May issue in which *Sense and Sensibility* was approved contained endless articles justifying the Protestant state religion, and a long piece on a book by a Captain Pasley making the case for more belligerent imperialist expansion that made her think of Eliza and Warren Hastings. The book was even published in Harley Street, amid the nabob community. It was expensive, twelve shillings; not one to buy.

On 18 June, the day that Lord Milton was attempting to break up a food riot in Sheffield, Henry took Cassandra on a visit to Godmersham. They received a visit from an old East India Company friend of Eliza's, Mr Hoar, and the following day Henry's Kent banking partner William Stevens Louch came to breakfast and stayed for dinner, along with Mr Hoar. Austen & Co. acquired another regimental agency on 25 July: the Royal West Middlesex. The colonel was Nicholas Bayly, brother of the first Earl of Uxbridge, and the deal was probably facilitated by Charles James. He had once been a captain in this corps, joining in 1788 and then, after a period in France, rejoining in 1795 before transferring to the North York Militia.

Some sense that these were particularly strange disordered times must have filtered through to Jane when she learnt that Eliza's émigré friends, the Comte d'Antraigues and his musical wife, whom she had visited at their charming riverside home in rural Barnes in April the previous year, had been murdered by one of the servants. Although there was no evidence that the murders were politically motivated, the Comte had feared assassination by an agent of the French regime and kept a weapon by his bed. He gave information and advice to the British authorities in return for a pension and cultivated friendships with the opposition Tory George Canning and the Whig leader, Earl Grey.

Closer to home, Eliza's state of health was worsening. Jane may have visited Sloane Street in the autumn of 1812, and witnessed the deterioration, when Henry approached the publisher Egerton regarding the sale of *Pride and Prejudice*. This was not the time to load Henry with protracted negotiations over copyright, or to saddle him with the risks entailed by publishing on commission again. Although the reviews for *Sense and Sensibility* were encouraging, the first edition would not sell out till the summer of 1813 and it wasn't yet apparent that she would make a comfortable profit. She was anxious that Henry might be forced to cover some of the expenses of her first publication. She settled for Egerton's offer of £110 for the copyright, remarking in a letter to Martha, 'I would rather have had £150, but we could not both be pleased, & I am not at all surprised that he should not choose to hazard so much. – Its being sold will I hope be a great saving of trouble to Henry, & therefore must be welcome to me.'[14] Besides, after the tortuous delays to the publication of her first novel, it might be as well if Egerton had more of a financial stake in the success of the second.

Pride and Prejudice did indeed appear with greater rapidity. Its publication on 28 January 1813 was first announced, as *Sense and Sensibility* had been, in the Whig daily, the *Morning Chronicle*, rather than the Tory *Morning Post*. On Friday 29 January 1813 Jane received her author's copy of *Pride and Prejudice*, her 'darling child', by way of Falkner and Lamport's Farnham and Alton Waggon which departed from the George Tavern in Snow Hill near Smithfield Market. *Pride and Prejudice* may have been born in the country but it had been nursed in the City. Jane was now confident that her bond with the metropolis would be permanent.

CHAPTER 6

SPECULATIVE SOCIETY:
MANSFIELD PARK (1813–1814)

Eliza was dying. She had never truly been well since the chest cold Jane had noted during her visit in the spring of 1811. That summer, when she had stayed a fortnight at Chawton Cottage, Cassandra had heartily assured Phylly Walter that 'I never saw her in such good health before', but it was surely suspected in the family that she was suffering from the cancer of the breast that had killed her mother, and there was nothing now to be done but to watch her slow decline.[1] Some in the family behaved as if she was already gone. Her niece Fanny, Edward's oldest child, now a young lady by turns vivacious and censorious, had bristled at Eliza's rare appearance at Godmersham in the autumn of 1811. They were thrown together while the men drove to Canterbury. 'Mrs. H. A. & I got on a little, but we never shall be intimate…' she wrote in her diary. 'Mrs. H. A. & I had a tete-a-tete, how agreeable!' was the sarcastic entry on another day. When Papa took her to stay at Sloane Street in May 1812 they 'dined quietly' one evening, presumably with Henry out on business and Eliza ill upstairs, but no mention of Eliza or her illness was made.[2] On an autumn visit to London they stayed at a hotel and Henry joined them for dinner and a trip to the theatre. Eliza's absence went unrecorded.

And where was Henry as the end approached? Generally attending to his own business or pleasure, as ever. After the visit to Godmersham in 1811 he returned to London while Eliza went to Ramsgate for some restorative sea air. Her dear friend and companion Mrs Perigord, much more than a servant, had stayed with her then and was with her now. As Eliza faded her comfort came from Marie Marguerite Perigord and her mother Françoise Bigeon. Like her, they had been fugitives from the Terror in France. Natives of Calais they fled across the Channel to London where, sometime in the mid-1790s, they had found employment with the widowed Comtesse de Feuillide, a young mother who's disabled child required constant nursing and supervision. Eliza came to have absolute confidence in Madame Bigeon who filled the role of a grandmother to poor Hastings. When Eliza had been forced to go to Cheltenham on business, at a time when her son's symptoms were acute, she had been able to send him to benefit from the clear dry air of the seaside at Lowestoft with Madame Bigeon whom, she told Phylly, 'I consider as more than myself in every thing that relates to him'; she was one 'on whose care you know I can thoroughly depend'.[3] They had grieved together over his death. Now the kind elderly Frenchwoman nursed Eliza as if she were her daughter. Madame Bigeon would not desert her.

For a time it had seemed that Marie Marguerite would leave. On 7 June 1805, aged thirty, she had married Pierre Frayté or Fraytet, aged thirty-five, at the Catholic church in Marylebone. Henry was then at Godmersham but Eliza must have attended the service. The groom went by the name 'Perigord' and Claire Tomalin, the only Austen biographer with sufficient curiosity to seek further details, has suggested that this probably meant he was from the Perigord region of south-west France, and as was often the custom, had adopted the name of his birthplace as his own. Marie Marguerite now became in turn Mrs Perigord (she was referred to using the English title, while her mother was 'Madame'), yet she remained in the household of Henry and Eliza and no further mention of her husband survives.[4]

Madame Bigeon has been described sometimes as a cook and sometimes as a housekeeper, but was in fact the beating heart of the household.

She may at times have looked askance at the indifference with which her beloved mistress was treated by *le maître*, but Henry Austen was charming, cheerful and appreciative and she also had a certain motherly fondness for him. It was her business to create harmony and happiness. For Eliza, who was in constant pain, the presence of Madame Bigeon and Marie Marguerite was her chief consolation. They had become her family, and there was something infinitely soothing in being able to speak with them in French. It connected her to the days of the *ancien régime* when the sun shone on gilded youth, when she had lived in Paris, danced at Versailles, and gained for a husband a handsome captain of dragoons.

Henry, on the other hand, was preoccupied with business. At the end of January 1813 he was in Oxford dealing with tax affairs and militia matters. He could spare a thought for *Pride and Prejudice*, however, dashing off a three-line note to send down to Chawton along with the author's copy, before leaving London. He had matters to discuss with his long-time patron Lord Charles Spencer who, at seventy-three, was as desperate as ever to find the government sinecure that would allow him the lifestyle to which he felt he was entitled as the younger son of a duke. Now his son John Spencer, the Receiver of Taxes for Oxfordshire, found himself in a spot of bother. The London bank in which he was a partner, Boldero, Lushington, & Co. at 30 Cornhill was folding, and the government was owed £17,000 in undelivered tax receipts. Eventually John moved to St Omer in France to escape his creditors, including Henry, to whom he owed £6,500. Yet Henry at this moment readily agreed to offer Lord Charles another loan of £2,000.[5] The receivership was now available, if Henry could find the financial backers demanded by the Revenue Office.

Henry was thinking of continuing on to Adlestrop, presumably to visit Leigh relations, and maybe Warren Hastings at Daylesford on the way, but must have been summoned back to town. Eliza had taken a sudden turn for the worse and in late April he sent news to Chawton that the end was near. Edward and his large family had just arrived and were settling into Chawton Great House for an extended stay of four months. Jane

immediately packed her bag and set off for Sloane Street, accompanied
by her nephew Edward. He returned the next day by mail coach, leaving
her to take her turn by Eliza's bedside and to comfort Henry and the
two distraught Frenchwomen. Eliza passed away two days later, aged
fifty-one, on the evening of 24 April, a 'cold & vile' day according to the
note in Fanny's pocketbook.

Eliza was buried in the picturesque churchyard of St John-at-
Hampstead, in the fields just north of London, in the same grave as her
mother and son. None of the extended family attended the funeral. It
is not clear that even Jane was there, as the same day Fanny records her
return to Chawton bringing Mrs Perigord to recuperate in the country. On that day, 1 May, James's wife, Mary Lloyd Austen, at the rectory
noted that 'Tyger', the Steventon cat, 'had young ones. Mrs. H. Austen
was buried.' The cycle of birth and death rolled on. It appeared that the
memory of what Eliza, Comtesse de Feuillide, had been and meant once
upon a time at Steventon had been obliterated. Her dazzling qualities had
been muted in Henry's keeping. He knew it and it probably troubled his
conscience. The epitaph on her gravestone was an uneasy composition,
including slight inaccuracies, a few mysteries, and no commas:

Also in memory of Elizabeth wife of H. T. Austen Esq. formerly widow
of the Comt. Feuillide a woman of brilliant generous and cultivated mind
just disinterested and charitable she died after long and severe suffering
on the 25th April 1813 aged 50 much regretted by the wise and good and
deeply lamented by the poor.[6]

Who could be included in the category of the 'wise and good' that
lamented the loss of Eliza? And where were her charitable efforts directed?
She would go down in the Austen family tradition as a 'pleasure-loving'
creature who lived only for herself, a spoilt heiress.[7]

With the creation of Elizabeth Bennet, Jane had already paid tribute
to Elizabeth de Feuillide and fearlessly witty women everywhere. But she

too was preparing an epitaph of sorts, one with regenerative powers. The Eliza they had known and been seduced by would be reborn and live for ever as Mary Crawford in *Mansfield Park*. There were also touches of Eliza in Mary's love rival, Fanny Price, the girl transplanted in alien soil. One way or another, as sister, as prospective wife, she would be paired again with a Henry in the form of Henry Crawford, reanimated with the full exuberance of his youth. These days Henry Austen was sometimes only half a Henry, his other guise the careworn servant of Mammon.

Once Eliza had been buried Henry tried to get to grips with the circumstances of a loan to Lord Moira of £6,000. The bankrupted former favourite of the Prince of Wales was on the point of departing British shores and effectively fleeing his creditors, with the alibi of the Governor-Generalship of India. The appointment had first been reported in September and was formally announced at the Court of Directors of the East India Company, along with his accession as Commander-in-Chief of the armed forces in Bengal, on 11 November 1812. Lady Charlotte Campbell, lady-in-waiting in the household of the Princess of Wales, the Regent's hated wife, confided to her diary somewhat spitefully that Moira's 'honourable banishment' was down to the fact that Prinney could not 'bear to have him near his person', horribly aware of his own shabby and destructive treatment of a friend who had given unstintingly of his purse and his political credit. Lady Charlotte had a turn for character analysis and under the name of her second husband, 'Bury', would go on to publish several best-selling 'Silver Fork' novels set in fashionable St James. Moira might have been vain and ambitious, she wrote, 'but his attachment to the Regent was sincere, chivalric, and of a romantic kind, such as the world neither believes in nor understands'.[8]

The details of how Austen & Co. were persuaded to make a large loan to this washed-up grandee as he departed the country are obscure. The post of Governor-General of India carried with it a salary of £25,000 a year, and while this may have raised his credit rating by a fraction, everyone knew that his repayment guarantees were likely to be worthless.

Between 12 and 17 April he was in Portsmouth waiting for his ship to sail. The ship was under the command of Sir Home Popham, his old friend from the days of the great South American speculative bubble of 1807. Lord Moira had persuaded William Adam, another intimate of the Prince of Wales and the principal trustee of his estate, to authorise a loan of £12,000 for the cost of the voyage and the outfitting. Splendid uniforms for Moira and his retinue were essential. At the last moment it was discovered that extra cash was needed to pay for an additional eighteen passengers together with 'his servants' subsistence'. To this end, he 'wrote himself loans upon Austen & Co. totalling £6,000'.[9] What this seems to have meant in practice was that he fell back on his old habit of contacting Charles James to arrange the loan for him.

According to T. A. B. Corley, Charles James went to Austen & Co., and in Henry's absence, 'held several meetings with the erratic Maunde, perhaps applying some blackmail'. Major James knew plenty of secrets about the dealings of the bank, and Henry had been reckless at times when exchanging notes with him regarding payments under the counter for army commissions. Corley adds that, although the details of the transaction are 'far from clear', it appears that 'James went away with £4,000 on the spot', less a discount of 15 per cent. The discount was triple the legal rate of interest and could be classed as unlawful usury, but the two parties agreed on it as the appropriate measure of Moira's 'poor credit record'. 'Francis Austen and Tilson authorised the remaining £2,000 very shortly before Moira sailed in April 1813', still seemingly without Henry's knowledge.[10]

Twenty-six years later, as part of a last-ditch attempt to recover the money from Moira's son and heir, Henry described the chain of events very differently, downplaying the roles of Henry Maunde and Charles James and recounting a face-to-face meeting with Moira in London. 'Your Noble Father', the letter went, had called on Henry 'from time to time' to borrow 'sums of money on his notes of hand. They had always been duly paid up to the time of his departure.'[11] It was certainly true that a repayment of £1,000 from Moira appears in the ledger of Henry and Eliza's account at Drummonds Bank, dated 1 July 1803.

Henry, in his appeal, set the critical meeting in Moira's fine town house overlooking Green Park and quoted his words apparently verbatim,

> Before he sailed, he sent for me into his private cabinet in St. James Place and uttered the following words which I having heard them cannot forget, and which I think you never will when you have read them – 'Mr Austen, be under no anxiety, I would rather cut off my right hand than permit you or any one to lose a farthing by me – I have executed powers and given directions to my trustees, Baron Adam and Mr M'Donald to sell my landed property and pay every demand, although it is like drawing drops of blood from my heart!' – You probably are no stranger to the noble bearing and the irresistible eloquence of your late father, & therefore will not be surprised at my having reposed implicit confidence in his word…

Whatever the truth of matter, the transaction came to assume great importance in Henry's eyes. From Lord Moira's perspective, the sum of £6,000 was just a drop in the ocean of debt. Henry Austen doesn't get a mention in the biography of Moira by Paul David Nelson. The former royal favourite was bound for the East, never again to set foot on English soil.

Henry Austen might have reflected in later years that what goes around comes around. In the 1770s the first Governor-General, Warren Hastings, had bestowed on young Betsy Hancock £10,000 from his Indian fortune; a gift that had eventually benefited Henry. Now the major part of that sum was making the return journey to the subcontinent with Governor-General Francis Rawdon Hastings. As it happened, Warren Hastings approved of the appointment of his namesake. Through the mediation of Sir Charles Hastings, he had sent a series of supportive and instructive letters to Moira when the appointment was first announced.[12]

Eliza was gone, and Henry felt on uncertain ground when he visited Warren Hastings, a few months later, in September. Jane relayed to

Cassandra that Hastings had 'never *hinted* at Eliza in the smallest degree'.[13] It is difficult to know what to make of this remark, seemingly a response to a question raised by Cassandra. It may relate in some way to the wider mystery surrounding the nature of the relationship between Hastings and the Hancock family, or to financial circumstances resulting from her death. Henry was satisfied by his welcome and was able to report to Jane that Hastings greatly admired the heroine of *Pride and Prejudice*.

If Jane and Henry were shocked by Warren Hastings's muted reaction to the death of Eliza, it would have been gross hypocrisy. Try as they might, they could not contain their mutual delight at the two triumphs that quickly followed. *Pride and Prejudice* was a hit, not on the scale of Byron's *Childe Harold's Pilgrimage* the previous spring, but a *bona fide* fashionable success nonetheless. There were again gossipy misattributions, whether to Lady Boringdon or the sister of the celebrated novelist Charlotte Smith or even a man masquerading as 'a Lady', for in the opinion of one male connoisseur it was 'much too clever to have been written by a woman'.[14] But Henry's pride in Jane's achievement kept bursting out. 'The truth is that the secret has spread so far as to be scarcely the shadow of a secret now', Jane was to write to Frank in September. In May came the confirmation of Henry's elevation from deputy to Receiver General of Taxes for Oxfordshire. Jane relayed the 'joyful news' in a 'handsome letter' to Frank at the start of July, over-brimming with affectionate delight. This was something to sweep away anxieties about the loan of thousands of pounds to titled spendthrifts. 'It is a promotion which he thoroughly enjoys; – as well he may; – the work of his own mind.'

Having penned these words Jane became acutely conscious that the note of exultation might jar, coming so soon after the bereavement, and she added in explanation,

Upon the whole his spirits are very much recovered. – If I may so express myself, his mind is not a mind for affliction. He is too busy, too active, too sanguine. – Sincerely as he was attached to poor Eliza moreover, &

excellently as he behaved to her, he was always so used to be away from her at times, that her loss is not felt as that of many a beloved wife might be…[15]

This letter arguably represents the most revealing direct testament to her relationship with Henry. In it she refers to him as 'our own true, lawful Henry', as if he had been recovered to a marriage of true minds, with her. She had returned to Sloane Street on 19 May, and easily slipped into the role of the mistress of the house. Madame Bigeon sat with her at breakfast, Jane reported to Cassandra cheerfully, 'talking of Henrietta St, servants & linen, & is too busy preparing for the future, to be out of spirits'.[16] Henry would be moving to live in the apartment over the bank headquarters in Covent Garden. In the meantime Jane and Henry took tea with the Tilsons on numerous occasions and visited three art exhibitions. They suited each other. They were living at the same emotional temperature at this strange liminal moment. There was talk of a drive to Hampstead, presumably to visit Eliza's grave, and how it might 'interfere' with meeting Miss Burdett, a friend of Mrs Tilson. Miss Burdett was in on the authorship secret and wanted to be introduced to Jane, who shrank from being treated as a literary lion; 'If I *am* a wild beast, I cannot help it.'[17]

'It is a promotion which he thoroughly enjoys; – as well he may; – the work of his own mind': an excess of admiration leads Jane to attribute to Henry a daring creative spirit equivalent to her own. Yet in his case there were a number of co-authors. Henry had assumed the role of Receiver General of Taxes for Oxfordshire, thanks not only to Lord Charles Spencer (in return for a substantial 'loan') but also to his guarantors: his land-owning brother Edward and his wealthy maternal uncle Mr Leigh-Perrot, as well as a second cousin, Thomas Philip Hampson, who together stood surety for Henry's financial integrity to the tune of £73,000 on 24 July 1813. The incentive was rapid and steep profit from the private use of public funds during an interim period of up to two years before receipts must be handed over to the government.

The finances of the various members of the family were interdependent. Each of them had a stake in Henry's different incarnations as army
agent, banker, and tax collector. Edward, with his extensive estates in
Kent and Hampshire – now fully his, since the death of Mrs Knight
in 1812 – was chief among Henry's backers for the receivership. James
Leigh-Perrot's estate, Scarlets in Berkshire, was relatively small, but in the
background was the Barbados property inherited by his wife, Jane Cholmeley, and he too was willing to lend support. James helped to canvas
for army agency business and had stood surety for it. Although details of
these arrangements are lacking, Henry presumably offered a percentage
or some kind of recompense in return for their support.

Frank joined Austen & Co. as a 'sleeping' rather than an active partner
for a seven-year term from 1806 to 1813, sank a good deal of his money
in the bank, and even extended a loan to Lord Moira on his own behalf.
Among the brothers only impecunious Charles was unable to participate
actively, although he kept some savings on deposit at the Henrietta Street
bank.

As things stood, Mrs Austen, Cassandra and Jane were passively reliant
on annual contributions from James, Edward, Henry and Frank, in the
home at Chawton which Edward provided free of charge, along with gifts
of firewood and other essentials. However, through Henry's efforts, Jane
was on the path to gaining a degree of economic independence, through
authorship. He provided a financial guarantee for her enterprise, just as
others provided it for his. Henry's income, as he stated himself at the time
of his father's death, was 'precarious'. If he failed, then the whole house of
cards might collapse. But in 1813, that possibility seemed remote.

The role of Receiver General for Land and Assessed Taxes set the seal on
Henry's apparently irresistible success. He was to state that it was an office
that provided him with '£1,000 a year'.[18] The official level of payment was
acknowledged to be low. In 1814 collectors could expect only £200 from a
yield of £24,000 for land taxes and £440 for assessed taxes, with £270 for
expenses including deputies' and clerks' fees.[19] Consequently, as a bonus,

it was permitted to delay remittance of the taxes in order to profit from interest, extend private credit, or even use it to make short-term loans. The legal limit was a period of two years, but rules were lax and tricks of accountancy were sometimes employed to retain the money for even longer and some maintained a large permanent balance. From time to time concerns were raised about inefficiency in the system, and the way public money was being siphoned off to enable private profit. But there was no will for change, and with the advent of war even more opportunities were opened up for private banking.

Country banks had already played a part in the provision of bills, banknotes and deposit facilities needed for tax collection, and it was not uncommon for bankers to expand into revenue collecting. Henry's background could even be called typical. As receiver general, not only did his experience with country banks come into play, but he found himself assuming some the responsibilities for financing the militia, familiar from his years as a regimental paymaster and army agent.[20]

For Jane, at this stage, Henry's accession to public office seemed a wondrous thing. It was as if his whole career were a literary invention or a theatrical performance; so unexpected and improbable an outgrowth of the quiet shabby-genteel upbringing in rural Hampshire. Now in the aftermath of Eliza's death, he would move the setting entirely to Henrietta Street, devoting himself fully to the persona of banker, with theatre-land on the doorstep to fill the leisure hours. Jane had long been intrigued and amused by his particular cast of mind. Back in 1807, she had seen it in Edward's second son, aged twelve, 'George's enquiries were endless, and his eagerness in everything reminds me often *of his Uncle Henry*.' It is surely no accident that Jane in her letter then mentions introducing George and his brother to the card game Speculation, which 'was so much approved that we hardly knew where to leave off'.[21] The game involved the noisy buying and selling of trump cards, players being at the same time forbidden to look at their own hand. If one word was needed to describe Henry's mind, it would have to be 'speculative'. But the word would need to be understood in its broadest sense, not only inquisitive and risk-taking, but also with shades of romantic enthusiasm and carelessness over matters of hard fact. There is surely a kinship between Henry and the characters of Marianne and Willoughby in *Sense and Sensibility*, both of whom combine a 'captivating person' with 'natural ardour of mind' (I.x). His was not the poised, self-contained good judgement of an Elinor, but rather an 'active imagination', optimistic, questing and visionary (I.xi).

Henry's nature and his business affairs naturally fed into the narrative of *Mansfield Park* as she completed it in the summer of 1813. At its centre it features a scene in which a game of Speculation is played, led by Henry Crawford. With the confidence of greater experience, Jane now explored in greater depth and at greater length the play of economic relations in a higher sphere of life. The book's tone is set and the essence of the plot stated, as so often, in the opening sentence,

> About thirty years ago, Miss Maria Ward of Huntingdon, with only seven thousand pounds, had the good luck to captivate Sir Thomas Bertram, of Mansfield Park, in the county of Northampton, and to be thereby raised to the rank of baronet's lady, with all the comforts and consequences of an handsome house and large income.

Any young lady who is 'out', is also engaged in a speculation on the marriage market. Miss Maria Ward wins the jackpot. The middle sister after a fruitless wait of six years takes the relatively safe and unspectacular course of accepting the hand of a clergyman, like George Austen without 'private fortune' of his own, but able to benefit from the patronage of his wealthy brother-in-law. The youngest Ward sister, Miss Frances, makes a reckless wager 'fixing on a Lieutenant of Marines, without education, fortune, or connections'. With these economic determinants in place, the story begins.

One early reader of the novel, the Honourable John Ward, later the Earl of Dudley, was pleased to find that it 'never plagues you with any chemistry, mechanics, or political economy'. He had read and liked the author's two previous novels and found that this one too was better contrived and had 'a great deal more feeling' than the celebrated fiction of Maria Edgeworth, though 'not so much fine humour'. Edgeworth was guilty of incorporating instructive mini-dissertations on political economy and other useful subjects 'excellent things in their way, but vile, cold-hearted trash in a novel'. He imagined these interpolations must be the work of Edgeworth's learned father: 'By the bye, I heard some time ago that the wretch was ill. Heaven grant that he may soon pop off.'[22] The lordly Ward was in fact no enemy to the so-called dismal science. He had been mentored by the great economist Dugald Stewart and his knowledge in that sphere stood him in good stead during a parliamentary career, first with the Whigs and then with the renegade troop of Tories led by the economic liberal George Canning. He also considered himself an excellent judge of fiction. Under the cloak of anonymity he was the star contributor to the bestselling *Quarterly Review*, and had chided Edgeworth for her daring fictional *exposé* of political corruption, *Patronage*. He was certain that the proper domain of female fiction was feeling and that *Mansfield Park* respected that propriety.

'I do not write for such dull elves as have not a great deal of ingenuity themselves', Jane had written in January 1813, with reference to the oblique presentation of some dialogue in the newly printed *Pride and Prejudice*. Cassandra, being no 'dull elf', would pick up the paraphrase of a line from Walter Scott's hugely popular poem *Marmion*. John Ward was not a dullard, and yet Jane Austen was too subtle for him. He could discern a political-economic agenda when Maria Edgeworth abruptly introduced an enlightened Englishman into her 1812 novel *The Absentee*, who having travelled the length and breadth of Ireland, was in a position to lecture the newly arrived hero about the state of the nation. Ward had probably like many others been up in arms when in *Belinda* Edgeworth had not only included a West Indian plantation owner to be jilted by the sparky heroine, but even a liberated slave who marries a pretty white farm girl. His expectations of fiction were too narrow, however, and perhaps his place too near the seat of power, to see in *Mansfield Park* what many modern commentators have seen: the first 'Condition of England' novel, anticipating the achievements of Elizabeth Gaskell, Charles Dickens and George Eliot.

The dimension of national allegory in the fable of a great house linked to an economically interdependent West Indian estate, its future threatened by a spendthrift heir, is today impossible to ignore. The importance of the colonial background was first proposed by the critic Edward Said, and has since been acknowledged as a key, though offstage, component in the plot. Sir Thomas Bertram is the owner of Mansfield Park in Northamptonshire but he is also the owner of an Antigua estate. The colonial factor enters the equation in the most understated way when, after a period of estrangement, the rash Miss Frances Ward – now become the impoverished and beleaguered Mrs Price married to a drunken invalid – writes a begging letter to her rich brother-in-law while awaiting the birth of her ninth child. She asks if her eldest son, aged ten, might at some point be 'useful to Sir Thomas in the concerns of his West Indian property? ...or how could a boy be sent out to the East' (I.i). It recurs a little later almost as an afterthought during the stand-off regarding the fate of Mrs Price's daughter who has been brought to Mansfield as an act of charity. The Reverend Norris, the clergyman husband of the middle Ward sister, has died. It is now expected that Mrs Norris will want to take the girl into her own household as a companion; she was after all the originator of the scheme. It turns out that she has no such idea. Her reduced budget and imaginary ailments will not allow it. And so Sir Thomas must continue to shoulder the financial burden in spite of his own setbacks, an extravagant elder son and 'recent losses on his West India Estate' (I.iii).

Before long Sir Thomas will be forced to absent himself from the domestic scene to deal with this nagging worry across the Atlantic. After his return two years later, it is his timid niece Fanny Price who brings the reality of the colonial economy to the fore. Having enjoyed her uncle's anecdotes of the West Indies she ventures to ask Sir Thomas during the evening circle 'about the slave-trade'. But although her dear cousin Edmund assures her afterwards that it 'would have pleased your uncle to be inquired of farther', she was met at the time by 'such a dead silence' from the family, that she hastily retreated into silence herself (II.iii). It is mentioned no more, at least not explicitly, during the remainder of the novel. Enough has been said, however, to establish the idea that the greatness of Mansfield Park, as of Great Britain taken as a whole, was in large part derived from colonial enterprise and, not to put too fine a point on it, colonial plunder.

A vigorous case had been made in 1810 for faster and bolder imperial expansion, backed with military force, by Charles William Pasley, a former captain in the Royal Artillery now retired from active service and appointed in 1812 the first Director of the Royal School of Military Engineering. His *Essay on the Military Policy and Institutions of the British Empire* went through four editions in three years, and it was a long article on the occasion of the second edition that Jane had spotted in the *British Critic*, alongside the very short though favourable review of *Sense and Sensibility*. In January 1813 Pasley was chosen by the Chawton reading club and although 'a book which I protested against at first', being hard at work on *Mansfield Park*, 'upon trial' she found it 'delightfully written & highly entertaining'.[23] Jane Austen was among a host of readers captivated by Pasley's idealistic imperial vision and engaging prose style. He seemed to be saying that along with commercial advantage and military strength, empire would also be the means to spread enlightenment and the message of British liberty. Wordsworth was stirred to write an extended fan letter to the author, and Maria Edgeworth placed his treatise with a pencil in it on the desk of Count O'Hollaran in *The Absentee*. The hero Lord Colambre picks it up with the Count's permission and finds 'it was marked with many notes of admiration, and with hands pointing to remarkable passages'. 'That is a book that leaves a strong impression on the mind,' says the Count.[24]

Jane Austen's reaction was, typically, more tongue in cheek. 'I am as much in love with the author as I ever was with Clarkson or Buchanan, or even the two Mr Smiths of the city,' she told Cassandra, 'The first soldier I ever sighed for; but he does write with extraordinary force & spirit.' The ironical inflection is apparent, confirmed by the 'but' and the echo of unworldly Miranda in *The Tempest* encountering Prince Ferdinand on a desert island in the Caribbean, 'This is the third man that e'er I saw, the first that e'er I sigh'd for.' Her other literary heartthrobs are a mixed bag: satirists, missionary explorers, and Thomas Clarkson the abolitionist. She might have no first-hand knowledge of the rapacious cruelty of imperialism, but having read Clarkson's *History of the Abolition of the African Slave Trade*, published in 1808 immediately after the parliamentary ban, she was familiar with the horror of the Middle Passage, had seen the image folded inside showing the way hundreds of captives were crammed into the hold chained lying down. It was a bare diagram and all the more effective for leaving everything to the imagination.

Then there was the endemic greed, corruption, folly and waste reported by the press or lampooned in caricatures on an almost daily basis. The East India Company's monopoly of Asian trade was a constant source of controversy in Parliament, and the activities of the Prince Regent were a never-ending indictment of any notion of the pride of empire. How could a nation with a selfish, gluttonous voluptuary at its head possibly pretend to set a moral example? At Brighton the Royal Pavilion was under construction, a decadent fantasia of imperial supremacy in which the Prince could wallow. In February 1813 a letter from his estranged and compromised wife stating her grievances was published in the *Morning Chronicle*. It was reprinted in the *Hampshire Telegraph* and Jane's opinion of the behaviour of the Prince was damning: 'Poor woman, I shall support her as long as I can, because she *is* a woman, & because I hate her husband.'[25]

At the start of *Mansfield Park* we are given Tom Bertram, the eldest son and heir, 'who feels born only for expense and enjoyment'. He gambles, and has run into debts that require drastic economies. Our first glimpse of the Bertram girls finds them ominously absorbed in 'the favourite holiday sport of the moment, making artificial flowers or wasting gold paper'. This is not a great house in any traditional sense, firmly based in an agrarian economy, its inhabitants securely wealthy and part of a stable social hierarchy. Instead it is at least partly founded on specifically modern forms of trade and commerce, and some of the inhabitants at least display the hedonistic habits of modern consumer society. For that reason the notion that the Crawfords, brother and sister, bring London values to interfere with the rural peace and harmony of Mansfield Park is difficult to support. What they seem to do is to articulate, with delicious epigrammatic wit, the mercenary mentality already present and tempt the younger generation further down the path, like Mephistopheles visiting Dr Faustus.

Even noble-spirited Edmund who plans to be a clergyman from the purest of motives, the best of the next generation of Bertrams, is shown to be familiar with the rules of Speculation. Mary Crawford addles his understanding with her clever paradoxes delivered with an enchanting smile, and leads him by a serpentine route deep into the wilderness on the visit to Sotherton Park. At Henry Crawford's behest, Maria Bertram leaps over the ha-ha, the guard of respectability, and ends a social outcast. Julia, the second Bertram daughter, rebuffed by Henry, throws herself away clandestinely on one of Tom's set, the 'expensive' Mr Yates. Tom requires little in the way of encouragement, and hard drinking with a group of other young bucks at the Newmarket races brings him to death's door.

But, after all, Jane Austen was not writing a medieval morality play. Henry and Mary Crawford are not incarnations of evil and go their way at the end, a little sadder and wiser. Was not Jane's 'own true Henry' an ardent practitioner of the London practice of speculation? Was not she herself an expert at the card game, dismayed when it was overtaken by Brag in popularity at Godmersham; 'it mortifies me deeply because Speculation was under my patronage'.[26] She remains the patron of Speculation in the present-day Oxford English Dictionary, where her reference to the game in *The Watsons* is cited as the earliest example of its usage. The concept of financial speculation itself only dated back to the late eighteenth century, and in the 1770s was still regarded as a neologism. Horace Walpole wrote to a friend in 1774 of the sale of Sir George Colebrooke's art collection after the collapse of the family bank, 'a citizen, and martyr to *what is called speculation*'. In *The Wealth of Nations* published in 1776, the year after Jane's birth, Adam Smith noted that 'Sudden fortunes, indeed, are sometimes made … by *what is called* the trade of speculation.'[27]

Speculation is a financial action with a high degree of risk. What differentiates it from investment is that there is no guarantee of the safety of the original sum committed. The risk generally arises from insufficient information, and this shortage of information is simulated and heightened in the game Speculation by the rule against viewing one's own cards. It is a novelty that dozy Lady Bertram wonders at. When asked if she is 'pleased with the game' she replies 'Oh! dear yes. – Very entertaining indeed. A very odd game. I do not know what it is all about. I am never to see my cards; and Mr Crawford does all the rest' (II.vii).

In spite of Henry Crawford's inherited estate in Norfolk and a family background in the military, he seems to embody the speculative age, amoral, acquisitive, open to risk and sudden changes of fortune. Managing the cards of Lady Bertram and Fanny as well as his own, Henry is 'preeminent in all the lively turns, quick resources, and playful impudence that could do honour to the game'. Gerda Reith, chronicling chance and gambling in Western culture, stresses the close relationship of gambling games to economic development at large, 'speculation and risk in economic life had their corollary in the speculation and risk involved in gambling games'. The craze for gambling in the Georgian period epitomised the 'speculative, numerical spirit of the time'.[28] Mary wins a round by playing boldly, as she declares, 'like a woman of spirit', and by paying for what she wants 'at an exorbitant rate'. Fanny, on the other hand, has none of the right qualities. Henry has to 'inspirit her play, sharpen her avarice, and harden her heart'.

Ultimately, however, it is hinted that the spirit of speculation is universal. Everyone is at it. Although we are told that with the restoration of Sir Thomas's 'government' following Tom's regency 'Mansfield was an altered place', the danger of corruption does not recede (II.iii). Sir Thomas pursues what are later called 'ambitious and mercenary connections', first by agreeing to the union of Maria with the wealthy fool Rushworth, her escape into dissipation following the disappointment of her hopes of Henry Crawford; then by pressuring Fanny to marry Henry in the name of 'interest' (III.xvii). Even Fanny Price, the moral conscience of the novel, ventures a portion of the £10 given to her by Sir Thomas when she returns to her family in Portsmouth: 'wealth is luxurious and daring – and some of hers found its way to a circulating library' (III.ix). She acquires books for her sister Susan with a view to increasing her stock of cultural capital, and the venture pays off when Susan is invited to Mansfield Park to take her place at the end of the novel. The language of financial speculation even infiltrates the closing realignment of Bertram familial relations. Sir Thomas's 'liberality' in raising Fanny as a child, a step he had considered risky at the time, has 'a rich repayment' when upon marriage to Edmund, she becomes the ideal daughter (III.xvii).

While Austen certainly distinguishes between good and bad investments, and good and bad examples of 'luxury', *Mansfield Park* is the product of a time when she felt at ease with the speculative society Henry's career had revealed to her. In a postscript to Frank in July 1813 she told him the pleasing news that 'every copy of S & S is sold'. The net profit was £140, and she still held the copyright, which might bring more. Added to the copyright fee for *Pride and Prejudice*, 'I have now therefore written myself into £250 – which only makes me long for more.'[29] Once she had quipped to Cassandra, 'I write only for fame, and without any view to pecuniary emolument.'[30] Now, if someone were to pose the question Edmund asks in *Mansfield Park*, 'you intend to be very rich?', she might answer along with Mary Crawford, 'To be sure. Do not you? – Do not we all?' (II.iv).

Jane was keen to show that Henry's example and encouragement had inspirited her play and sharpened her avarice. Henry's luck was essentially self-made, not reliant on the pre-established channels of patronage. It was the result of his own strenuous efforts to educate himself in financial dealings and maintain and exploit contacts in the militia and beyond. He emboldened Jane, also, to be more assertive after the submissive underselling of *Pride and Prejudice*. She had received only £110 for the copyright while Thomas Egerton cleared a profit of £450 for two editions of the novel.

Pride and Prejudice was priced by Egerton at three shillings more than *Sense and Sensibility*, even though the second novel was printed on cheaper paper. This annoyed Jane. She had been forced to cover the cost of the better paper for the first novel, since it was published on commission. The publisher had overcharged her for production costs when her own profit was at stake, and this wouldn't happen again. She wrote to Cassandra, 'The advertisement is in our paper to day for the first time; – 18s. – He shall ask £1 – 1s for my two next, and £1 – 8s for my stupidest of all.'[31] She had a growing sense that her economic interests as an author must be guarded.

In September Egerton had gone ahead with a second edition of *Pride and Prejudice* without giving her an opportunity to make corrections or even notifying her. It was made very clear that the novel was his property. At around the same time, he agreed to handle a new edition of *Sense and Sensibility* on the basis of the usual 10 per cent commission with production costs backed by her brother. It was another gamble and until there were more substantial gains, Jane wrote to Cassandra, 'I shall owe dear Henry a great deal of money for the printing &c.'[32] It was thanks to him, too, that with *Mansfield Park* she continued to pursue a bold and independent course, turning her back on the safer, more conventional, but often financially unrewarding sale of copyright.

Commentators have shown little interest in Jane Austen's preference for publishing on commission, and generally assumed that it was forced on her. However it could be said that this approach, by allowing her to retain autonomy at some financial risk, amounted to a one-woman boycott of current copyright practice skewed in favour of publishers. There was something stubborn in her that, in spite of her embrace of speculation, resisted commodification. Although she told Frank the profit from her first novel made her 'long for more', she also said of *Mansfield Park*, 'I have something in hand – which I hope on the credit of P. & P. will sell well, tho' not half so entertaining'.[33] She had scored a notable success with *Pride and Prejudice*. But instead of continuing to milk a marketable formula she had perversely written a follow-up that was certain to be less popular. 'Too light & bright & sparkling', she had half-joked regarding *Pride and Prejudice*; next she would give the public a shade-dwelling reclusive heroine set against two sparkling rogues, and a gracious 'modern built' country house covered in white stucco, but symbiotically joined to the violent darkness of the colonial slave system. She had begun consciously to test the limits of readers' tolerance.

We don't know the details of the contract negotiations for *Mansfield Park*. It has been suggested that Egerton may have made another low offer for copyright because the author was experimenting with this new novel.[34] However, Jane recorded that he rather tepidly, 'praised it for its morality, & for being so equal a composition. – No weak parts.'[35] Perhaps she simply delighted in telling him it was not for sale.

On 14 September 1813, Jane returned to town in the company of Edward and three of his daughters on their way from Chawton Great House back to Godmersham. It was a first chance to see the bachelor *ménage* in Henrietta Street. Of course Jane had visited the office there before and knew the neighbourhood. In May she had spent a hilarious afternoon driving around town with Mr Tilson trying and failing to find Thomas Hampson, who was wanted at the bank. Now Henry had established his residence over the office and it seemed 'like Sloane St moved here', but in a quarter of the space. On the first floor at the front was a 'breakfast, dining, sitting room' and behind a smaller drawing room; on the second floor, the bedrooms. Edward stayed at a hotel but the others were accommodated with Henry, Jane and Fanny sharing 'poor Eliza's bed'.[36] Henrietta Street felt like a homecoming. Jane instantly warmed to its improvised nature, the informality and intimacy, cheek by jowl with loved ones.

They were kindly welcomed the moment they stepped in the door by Henry, his manservant William and Mrs Perigord all crowding round them in the narrow hall at the foot of the staircase, and then stepped up to the dining room where a 'most comfortable dinner of soup, fish, bouillee, partridges, and an apple tart' was presented by Madame Bigeon. The stay was brief and busy, but Jane instantly picked up the threads of her relationship with the two Frenchwomen. The two of them had taken lodgings close by; Madame Bigeon did the grocery shopping and fussed over keeping Henry supplied with jam. With Jane and Fanny in residence she was constantly at Henrietta Street. She asked Jane to meet her one morning at eight o'clock in the kitchen; she 'wants me to see something downstairs'. Jane was gratified to find Madame B in good health, 'wonderfully recovered from the severity of her asthmatic complaint'.[37] The air of Covent Garden seemed to be a tonic.

Jane also found it bracing. Henrietta Street, named after Charles I's Queen, once the address of actress and courtesan Kitty Clive, was at that time a noisy, lively precinct with linen drapers and mercers as neighbours, and just a stone's throw from the pubs and coffee houses of Covent Garden piazza. Outside No. 11 the smells were pungent. A row of horses were stationed opposite and the detritus of the market mingled with household filth in the gutter. Covent Garden was a quarter that had been teeming with multifarious life since its first establishment as a grand public space in the early seventeenth century. The square or piazza, a British experiment in unified neo-classical urban planning by Inigo Jones in the seventeenth century, provided the backdrop to ever-changing scenes of workaday bustle, theatrical splendour and degradation, night and day: vegetables, make-believe, flowers, and sex. In 1813 the wooden stalls and sheds of the market had become so chaotic that the estate owner, the Earl of Bedford, applied for an act of Parliament to regulate it. It was the place of trade for hawkers and shoppers, artists and print-makers, actors from the surrounding theatres, and prostitutes from the brothels, the molly-houses, or the streets. It was the playground of aristocrats, frolicking apprentices and local children, and the resort of the money-men who worked in the private banks that lined the Strand and Fleet Street to the south. This was the place to which Henry's unpredictable adventures had brought her.

Two months later Cassandra would report during her stay in Henrietta Street that William, Henry's manservant, had found he could no longer cope with living amid the hubbub of the crowds. Jane wrote back from Kent, 'I am glad William's going is voluntary, & on no worse grounds. An inclination for the country is a venial fault. – He has more of Cowper than of Johnson in him.' William Cowper was of course a byword for his hatred of urban life, just as Samuel Johnson, who had lived just down the road off Fleet Street, was famed among other things for the aphorism: 'When a man is tired of London, he is tired of life; for there is in London all that life can afford.' What is perhaps less well known is that he coined it in reply to a comment from Boswell, 'Why, Sir, you find no man, at all intellectual, who is willing to leave London.' Much to her own surprise, Jane was beginning to understand that sentiment, to feel it herself. Who would have thought she could grow so fond of 'the full tide of human existence at Charing Cross'?[38]

At this point Jane cast off her cap, the symbolic garb of a middle-aged spinster. James Edward Austen-Leigh recorded that after coming to live at Chawton she always wore a cap 'except when her nieces had her in London and forbade it'. This was the first time she had stayed in London with her nieces, and she reported to Cassandra that Mr Hall the hairdresser had visited her punctually and 'curled me out at a great rate': 'I thought it looked hideous, and longed for a snug cap instead, but my companions silenced me by their admiration.' She was thirty-seven, 'tall and slender; her face was rounded with a clear brunette complexion and bright hazel eyes'.[39]

She was as delighted to see her money-men as they were to see her. Mr Tilson came up from the 'Compting House' to call on them and she enquired after Mrs Tilson, pregnant yet again. She renewed her friendships with Mr Barlowe and Mr 'Philips' or 'Phillips', the clerks. She scolded Henry affectionately for having publicised her authorship on his recent trip to Scotland with Edward's eldest son. There he had scattered banknotes while socialising with highborn clients. He promised to lend Lord Robert Kerr, son of the 5th Marquis of Lothian, £100 and when Lady Robert praised *Pride and Prejudice* in his hearing, simply could not contain the fact that it was the work of his sister, any more than he could stop himself sending a complimentary copy of the novel to Warren Hastings. 'He told her with as much satisfaction as if it were my wish,' Jane complained to Cassandra. She did not want to appear forward, but couldn't help but feel gratified.

Jane also passed on news of Henry's indiscretions to Frank, primly thanking him for better keeping her secret but also condoning the 'brotherly vanity & love' of the 'dear creature'. She then outdid Henry with plans for a new capitalist venture as a spin-off from novel-writing: 'I believe whenever the 3rd appears, I shall not even attempt to tell lies about it. – I shall rather try to make all the money than all the mystery I can of it. – People shall pay for their knowledge if I can make them.' Like Fanny Price, 'I am trying to harden myself.' How appropriate that the party had a chance to see *Midas* at Covent Garden Theatre during the short three-night stopover at Henrietta Street, 'sing song and trumpery' though it might be. In this popular burlesque opera the story of the king with the golden touch was constantly updated with topical jokes, and Jane continued to be tickled by 'remembrances' of it the following day.[40] Midas conducts a comic rivalry with Apollo, but in the Austen family, finance and art seemed to be capable of perfect harmony. Jane had no fear of the 'London maxim', put into the mouth of Mary Crawford, 'that every thing is to be got with money' (I.vi). She had grown so confident of her wealth-creating powers that she could afford to regard money as 'dirt'.[41]

Once in Kent, she began to yearn for London and her friends there. Jane's two-month stay at Godmersham, her first in four years, could be illustrated by an alternating sequence of contrasted scenes: Jane caught up in the hectic round of life in a large family, Edward's eleven children joined by Charles with his brood, streams of visitors coming and going; frozen tableaux of Jane escaped, still and solitary in large magnificently furnished rooms, the scratching of her quill on paper the only sound. Exhausted, drained, a fugitive from the tyranny of country house sociability and the demands of children large and small, she describes her situation to Cassandra as if she were Robinson Crusoe washed up on a particularly luxurious desert island by the raging sea. 'I am now alone in the library, mistress of all I survey.' Or again, 'I am alone ... At this present time I have five tables, eight & twenty chairs & two fires all to myself.'[42] The irony was, that she felt equally alone in both contexts.

There was another mystery: why should she feel so differently about the hurly-burly of Covent Garden? When Cassandra went to stay at Henrietta Street at the end of October Jane's emotions flared up. The first indication was when she uncharacteristically signed off, 'Love to Mr Tilson'.[43] The next letter, on the 26th, began sensibly enough: 'It is a great pleasure to me to think of you with Henry, I am sure your time must pass most comfortably & I trust you are seeing improvement in him every day. – I shall be most happy to hear from you again...' But towards the end she engages in a strange kind of projection, as if her sister could live vicariously the life she wanted.

I long to know whether you are buying stockings or what you are doing. Remember me most kindly to Mde B. and Mrs Perigord. – You will get acquainted with my friend Mr Philips & hear him talk from books – & be sure to have something odd happen to you, see somebody that you do not

expect, meet with some surprise or other, find some old friend sitting with
Henry when you come into the room. – Do something clever in that way.
– Edwd & I settled that you went to St Paul's Covent Garden, on Sunday.[44]

She had shared the more admissible part of this fantasy with Edward,
attending a service at the so-called 'actor's church' through the passage
directly opposite the door of Henry's premises. She had listened to the
bells ringing as she lay in Eliza's bed.

The experience was one she had analysed in her latest novel. Fanny
Price, revisiting her first home at Portsmouth, is taken aback by her own
reaction when she learns of the disasters that have befallen the family at
Mansfield Park,

> Her eagerness, her impatience, her longings to be with them, were such as
> to bring a line or two of Cowper's Tirocinium for ever before her. 'With
> what intense desire she wants her home,' was continually on her tongue,
> as the truest description of a yearning which she could not suppose any
> school-boy's bosom to feel more keenly. (III.xiv)

Fanny recognises that her feelings are perverse. For years she has longed
to be reunited with her own family, and now it is alien Mansfield, the
scene of so much misery and humiliation, that seems like home. The
experience of homesickness can strike like a revelation, an awakening.
How could Jane have imagined she would one day feel a yearning akin to
homesickness for an apartment above a bank in Covent Garden?

Henry was unwell. Jane had referred to his ailments casually while
there; it was the same old thing, 'the pain in the face which he has been
subject to before'. He also had a cold, picked up on the return journey
through Derbyshire, and looked 'thin in the face', through either pain or
the fatigue of the Scottish tour.[45] She had been confident that he would
quickly get better. But Cassandra reported that the symptoms were lingering or even worsening. The idea of losing him may have slid into her

head unbidden. Suddenly Jane became aware that she needed to return to Henrietta Street to be with him, whatever the impracticalities.

Jane was not famed in the family for tenderness towards invalids and convalescents. Her letters contained many a joke against her hypochondriac mother and she was invariably brisk with herself, when under the weather. But in her next letter to Cassandra she begins to fret over Henry's health. The original plan for the return journey was to stop in London for one night, and then continue down to Chawton the next day. But now…

> But now, I cannot be quite easy without staying a little while with Henry, unless he wishes it otherwise; – his illness & the dull time of year together make me feel that it would be horrible of me not to offer to remain with him – & therefore, unless you know of any objection, I wish you would tell him with my best love that I shall be most happy to spend 10 days or a fortnight in Henrietta St – if he will accept me. I do not offer more than a fortnight because I shall then have been some time from home, but it will be a great pleasure to be with him, as it always is.[46]

Three days later she wrote again, 'I long for your letter tomorrow, particularly that I may know my fate as to London.' She made an effort to sound reasonable, 'My first wish is that Henry should really choose what he likes best; I shall certainly not be sorry if he does not want me.' Again she stressed that her main concern was his health, 'Dearest Henry! What a turn he has for being ill! & what a thing Bile is! – This attack has probably been brought on in part by his previous confinement & anxiety'. Then came the longed-for letter from her sister, encouraging her to remain at Henrietta Street: 'I was only afraid that *you* might think the offer superfluous, but you have set my heart at ease. Tell Henry that I *will* stay with him, let it be ever so disagreeable to him.' Jane's offer was superfluous on a rational level, but essential for setting her heart at ease. She knew Henry could not really find her presence disagreeable. Cassandra, having previously read the work-in-progress, may have understood the deeper logic.

Mansfield Park is the most developed and lyrical treatment of a theme
not uncommon in Austen's work, the love between sister and brother.
The bond between Fanny Price and older brother William is placed at
the heart of the story; a touching and unobjectionable feature in itself.
However, the way the boundary between sibling love and romantic love
is then blurred has been found disturbing by some readers. The eventual
match between the cousins Edmund Bertram and Fanny Price is anticipated from the very start of the narrative as a problem. When Mrs Norris
introduces the scheme of 'adopting' ten-year-old Fanny, Sir Thomas
raises a concern about 'cousins in love, &c.' But his fears are dismissed as
'morally impossible'. It is precisely by undertaking to 'breed her up' with
the two sons that such a thing is to be avoided, Mrs Norris insists. Then
Fanny 'will never be more to either than a sister' (I.i).

The process which will disprove Mrs Norris's theory is traced to its
source in a tender scene that takes place soon after Fanny's arrival at the
great house. Edmund, aged sixteen, finds her sitting on the attic stairs
and weeping. His first assumption is that she misses her mother, but in
fact it is William she longs for. He had been her constant companion,
friend and champion. William had said he did not want her to leave
and promised to write to her, but he asked her to write to him first, and
she has no paper. Edmund kindly supplies the writing materials and Sir
Thomas's free frank, so William will not have to pay postage. Edmund
also, in a perfect detail, puts a half guinea under the seal. Guineas and
half guineas were first minted in the 1660s for the British trade in Africa,
Claudia Johnson has noted in her Norton edition of the novel. They were
'handsome gold coins', striking acquisitions in the era of paper money,
discontinued in 1816.

With this small transferral of wealth comes a transference of affection,
or rather, a triangulation. It is not that Fanny loves William less, but that
Edmund is loved equally, encompassed by that glow of sisterly love, with
the difference that he is a 'brother' she could feasibly marry. From this
moment she is devoted to Edmund. Just as significant is the fact that

he now finds her 'an interesting object' (I.ii). Adoration of her brother William irradiates and transfigures this meek, self-effacing creature.

We are shown exactly the same alchemy at work when Henry Crawford sees Fanny, now grown into a pretty young woman, alongside her brother William, a midshipman in the navy on a visit to Mansfield Park. Henry's plan was for an idle fortnight's dalliance with the poor relation, simply because she seems determined to resist his charms. Then he witnesses her 'unchecked, equal, fearless intercourse with the brother and friend'. He too is struck by Fanny's transfiguration, the glowing cheek, the bright eye. The Prices, brother and sister, represent 'fraternal love' in 'all its prime and freshness, wounded by no opposition of interest, cooled by no separate attachment, and feeling the influence of time and absence only in its increase'. Henry's 'moral taste' is kindled; the 'capabilities of her heart' have been revealed; 'It would be something to be loved by such a girl ... His stay became indefinite' (II.vii).

As Celia Easton has said in her investigation of the 'sibling ideal' in Jane Austen's novels, 'Over and over, sibling-style love lays a good foundation for committed relationships.'[47] It could be added that this pattern was also common in her family. Both Frank and Charles married, as their second wives, sisters-in-law who had lived in the family as sisters for years beforehand. Marriage between cousins was also a frequent occurrence in the extended family and circle of friends: Henry's union with his first cousin was no scandal as far as kinship was concerned. Consanguineous pairings might generally appear to lack the excitement and romance of encounters with outsiders, but given the rigid rules governing courtship, love between cousins or in-laws could offer freedom, a relaxing of the social barriers between men and women. Domestic intimacy was the easiest and best route to genuine knowledge of the other and true mutual appreciation and compatibility.

Yet to pretend that a partnership arrived at in this way was without psychological complexities would surely be misleading. Jane Austen, in her fiction, had to negotiate the transition from a sibling or quasi-sibling relationship to one involving romance and sexuality. Such a change must involve, at some stage, a frisson of transgression. There is nothing in her novels like the sensationalism of Gothic fiction – where the threat of incest was rife – or the deliberate taboo-breaking of the poets Byron and Shelley. However, in *Mansfield Park* Fanny's consciousness of her feelings towards Edward coincide with a period of anarchy in the household, when comedy is mixed with guilty secrets.

Cassandra must initially have been taken aback by the negative portrayal of private theatricals in the novel. Why should Jane apparently condemn amateur play-acting and link it to sexual misconduct, when it had been a favourite pastime at Steventon, indulged and even encouraged by their clergyman father? She might then have put together that memorable Christmas of 1788, Eliza enchanting as Violante in *The Wonder! A Woman Keeps a Secret*, Jane's adolescent fascination with the bewitched brothers James and Henry, and Eliza's slow death which had coincided with the process of composition. It was as if the loss of Eliza had revived the configuration of theatrical make-believe and amorous intrigue.

When at Henrietta Street, there was something compulsive about Jane Austen's attendance at the theatre. She would have been happy to see a performance every night, despite her view that the art of acting was 'at a low ebb at present'.[48] Luckily, others in the family were also happy to attend. She was searching for something elusive, a sensation she wanted to recapture. Jane saw the latest star actress and was disappointed, 'I fancy I want something more than can be. Acting seldom satisfies me.'[49] 'Something more than can be'; something more, perhaps, like the seductive power she attributes to Henry Crawford acting the role of Frederick in *Lovers' Vows* or reciting *Henry VIII*.

Cassandra could not help objecting to the ending. It was the only time on record that she intervened in Jane's composition plans. Edmund was too much of a brother to Fanny and Mrs Norris was right for once: the fact that they had been raised together ought to make the conclusion 'morally impossible'. Jane would say it herself, 'I like first cousins to be first cousins, & interested about each other. They are but one remove from brother & sister.'[50] But still she persisted in pairing Fanny with a brotherly cousin. The fact that she named the unsuccessful alternative suitor 'Henry' may have been a playful trade-off. Once *Mansfield Park* was published, Fanny Knight although 'delighted' with her namesake Fanny Price saw the problem from a different angle. Like many readers since, she was 'not satisfied with the end – wanting more love between her & Edmund'. Jane had not successfully bridged the distance from Edmund as brother to Edmund as lover.

As far as Jane was concerned, however, the business of the marriage was an afterthought. Edmund was most a lover when most a brother. Her niece had missed the emotional climax of the story, the real declaration, which takes place at Portsmouth when Edmund arrives to take Fanny home to stricken Mansfield. She hears him entering the house.

> He so near her, and in misery. She was ready to sink, as she entered the parlour. He was alone, and met her instantly; and she found herself pressed to his heart with only these words, just articulate, 'My Fanny – my only sister – my only comfort now.' She could say nothing; nor for some minutes could he say more. (III.xv)

Jane Austen, better than any author, conveyed the financial pressures governing heterosexual love and courtship among the propertied class. The brother–sister bond, at its best, was free of such concerns. As Glenda Hudson has remarked in *Sibling Love and Incest in Jane Austen's Fiction*, it was unsurprising if writers of the time found a different outlet for the depiction of deep and disinterested feeling: 'The rapture of sibling love could be expressed without fear of repercussions, sexual guilt, or social stigma (unless, of course, the siblings overstepped boundaries and actually indulged in a physical relationship).'[51]

In literature, as in a dream, identities are not fixed. Henry Austen was absolutely right to say that his sister had never used 'individuals' as the

models for her characters. Jane's 'power of inventing characters' was 'in-
tuitive' and 'unlimited'.[52] It would be a fool's errand to determine who
is the 'real' Mr Darcy or Henry Crawford or Edmund Bertram. With
her depiction of Mary Crawford and Fanny Price and probably other
characters unidentified, Jane slipped in and out of memories of Eliza.
She, Jane Austen, naturally inhabited every character, even Mrs Norris.
Remembering those days of the theatricals at Steventon, now revived,
distilled, in all their charged and illegitimate glory in *Mansfield Park*, recalling her own complicity as she watched Eliza and her brothers engage
in transgressive flirtations, had she not heard a hectoring voice in her
head saying along the lines of Mrs Norris, 'these are fine times for you,
but you must not be always walking from one room to the other, and
doing the lookings on at your ease, in this way' (I.xviii).

Jane loved Henry more than she could readily admit or express. Tom
Lefroy, Mr Bridges, the admirer at Teignmouth, they were ephemeral,
passing shadows, whereas Henry was becoming ever more present and
important. It is easy to understand why this should be the case. He had
believed in her, he had risked his money for her, he understood and
adored her talent and would do his utmost to promote her success. He
was a wealthy, handsome, well-connected man and he was hers as none
of the other brothers could be, even had their temperaments been equally
compatible. He had no dependants and now no wife.

Missing letters mean that the unscheduled stay in Henrietta Street
in November 1813 remains a blank. We only know from Jane that the
'prospect of being taken down to Chawton by Henry, perfects the plan
to me'.[53] Henry had not yet read the new novel, and nor did she tell him
much about it now; certainly not the conclusion. He was only aware of
the setting. Back in February she had been seeking information about
whether Northamptonshire was a 'country of hedgerows'. Cassandra
and Martha had not been able to ascertain this but Jane knew that Sir
James Langham, a relative of Mr Tilson, had an estate at Cottesbrooke
near Northampton. 'I am obliged to you for your enquiries about

Northamptonshire, but do not wish you to renew them, as I am sure of getting the intelligence I want from Henry, to whom I can apply at some convenient moment "sans peur and sans reproche."'[54]

Henry promised to come to Chawton and bring her back to London in the spring once she had received and corrected the proofs of *Mansfield Park* and was ready to deliver them to Egerton. In the interval the severest winter in living memory closed in. Snow blocked the entrances to towns, no mail could be delivered, and a frost fair was held on the river Thames in London for the last time. Jane turned inwards and began devising her next novel, with a new sort of heroine but also, whether compulsively or mischievously or both, featuring a sister–brother romance that she was resolved to make more compelling than the last.

March came, and snow continued to blanket the fields. On the first of the month Henry duly carried Jane back to Henrietta Street, and on the way, in the closed carriage with sudden blizzards beating against the window, she laid *Mansfield Park* before him. She had nothing to learn about the carriage ride as metaphor. In *Northanger Abbey* she smoothly engineered the confluence of driving, story-telling, and attraction. This time she was Henry and he was Catherine, and along with the unfurling ribbon of the road came the unwinding of the plot; 'Oh! no, no – do not say so. Well, go on' (II.v).

Jane carefully monitored his responses and relayed them back to Cassandra over the next few days, for he had only 'married Mrs R.' in volume II, chapter 3, by the end of the journey. By that stage he had expressed lively appreciation of all the characters, found it 'very different from the other two' but not at all 'inferior' and 'I think foresees how it will all be'. He went on and declared he 'admires H. Crawford – I mean properly – as a clever, pleasant man. – I tell you all the good I can, as I know how much you will enjoy it.' He evidently expected that a charismatic Henry, albeit undersized and not handsome, must be set for redemption by the love of a good woman. But as he got into volume III he 'changed his mind as to foreseeing the end; – he said yesterday at least, that he defied anybody to say whether H. C. would be reformed, or would forget Fanny in a fortnight.' He was liking it 'better and better'. Then in a third letter she underlined the final verdict, 'Henry has finished ... & his approbation has not lessened. He found the last half of the last volume <u>extremely interesting</u>.'[55] Jane felt vindicated.

CHAPTER 7

UNCOMMERCIAL *EMMA*
(1814–1815)

When Henry and Jane arrived at Henrietta Street on that snowy day in March 1814, they were met at the door by 'nice smiling Mr Barlowe', the chief bank clerk, who in answer to their request for news stated 'that peace was generally expected'.[1] The weather might be freezing but the world was in flux. The war with France had begun in 1793, six weeks after Jane's seventeenth birthday. It had continued with one short intermission for twenty-one years. War was normality. Three of her brothers had forged their careers from the exigencies of war. What would peace bring?

In early March, London was still reeling from a financial scandal arising from a false report of Napoleon's death. Rumours regarding the war were rife, creating volatility in stocks and shares. On 21 February conspirators spread the rumour, elaborately staging the arrival of a courier at Dover, a rapid ride to the capital, and the procession of a post-chaise through the City with passengers dressed as French Royalist officers scattering handbills printed with 'Vive le Roi!' and 'Vivent les Bourbons!' The news provoked an ebullient reaction on the Stock Exchange. Government stocks rose to dizzy heights before collapsing when no official confirmation came and the ruse became apparent.

There was immediate suspicion of fraudulent profiteering. The uncle of the celebrated Admiral Lord Cochrane was found to have bought large amounts of Omnium stock preceding the scam, and when he and other associates fled to the Continent with profits of more than £10,000, Cochrane was left to take the fall. Some believed he had been framed. Alongside his naval career he was a Member of Parliament, a radical independent and a loyal ally of Sir Francis Burdett, with a special interest in combating nepotism and corruption in the Admiralty. He pleaded innocent to the charges. The judge appointed to his case in 1814 was Lord Ellenborough, who had sent Leigh Hunt to jail for two years for defaming the Prince of Wales. The sentence he delivered against Cochrane and his co-defendants was one year's imprisonment and a fine of £1,000. Cochrane only narrowly escaped the additional punishment of being publicly displayed in the stocks outside the Royal Exchange. The authorities may well have feared riots. After Cochrane was expelled from the House of Commons he was promptly re-elected as the representative for the radical constituency of Westminster.

Given that the scandal involved Britain's greatest living naval hero, the Austens were bound take a keen interest. Many years later Admiral Frank Austen would read the first volume of Cochrane's *Autobiography of a Seaman* (1859) and write him a warm letter of support which was then cited in a later second volume. Throughout Jane's five-week stay with Henry at Henrietta Street in March and early April 1814, new developments and revelations in the Cochrane case shared space in the newspapers with reports of the final stages of Napoleon Bonaparte's defence of Paris, and the victory of the allies. It was not until 9 April that news of the Emperor's abdication and exile reached England. In the meantime Jane pursued the usual round of socialising with the Tilsons and others from Henry's circle, in addition to a few London relations, and sent *Mansfield Park* to press.

The Great Stock Market Swindle of 1814 contained an element of protest against the emerging economic establishment. This comes out in remarks made by Alexander McRae, one of the fraudsters, who like Henry Austen had earned a living as a London agent, though for the navy rather than the militia. A neighbour, acting as witness, told the court that when he asked McRae why he was assembling fake military uniforms he replied, to 'deceive the flats' – 'flats' being slang for speculators.[2] The following year, from the safety of his Continental exile, he published a self-justifying pamphlet describing the plot as 'a whimsical farce' designed to show up 'the folly or stupidity of over-reaching gamesters' and make them 'the laughing-stock of Europe'.[3] The affair certainly generated unease about the lack of regulation in share trading. An inquiry by the committee of the Stock Exchange was swiftly launched. It led to no substantive remedy but the upshot was that the excesses and dangers of speculation continued to be the talk of the town, and some at least of the first readers of *Mansfield Park*, encountering the allegorical card party featuring Speculation after its publication on 9 May, must have found it strikingly timely.

Change and uncertainty brought remarkable profits to some of the biggest players in finance. Alexander Baring continued to thrive and would eventually finance France's reparation payments, buying the magnificent Greek Revival Northington Grange close to Winchester, and many other estates in the area on the proceeds. In 1815 it was alleged that Rothschild Bank took advantage of a rapid information circuit to profit handsomely from the final defeat of Napoleon at Waterloo. But far more significant were the secret manoeuvrings of the Rothschilds and the British government, hidden from the public. Just as Goldsmid and Baring had bankrolled the war, Nathan Rothschild, head of the English branch of the family enterprise, bankrolled the peace as a private speculative venture. From 1809 onwards he built up his business as a trader in specie and bullion, buying legally and illegally anywhere from Portugal and France to South America, and operating out of Gosport on the Hampshire coast. Rothschild couriers must have passed Jane Austen's door on the Gosport Road in Chawton on dozens of occasions. Following the defeat of Napoleon, Britain agreed to subsidise the peacekeeping troops of its allies to the sum of £11.6 million, the equivalent of 425,000 men, rather than provide its quota of soldiers.[4] The risk taken by the House of Rothschild was terrifying. By mid-May 1814, Nathan Rothschild alone was owed £1,167,000.[5] But the British government was committed to upholding his credit, just as the Rothschilds supported the credit of British sterling on the international exchange. The failure of the banker, remarked the government negotiator John Charles Herries, 'would recoil upon ourselves'.[6]

There was no guaranteed safety net for a small operator like Henry Austen in the economic depression to come. At the start of the year prices stood at double the level of the early 1790s. The re-opening of trade with mainland Europe was welcomed by manufacturers and workers, but damaging for the agrarian economy. The influx of cheap grain from the Continent, added to a good harvest at home, sent the price of provisions plummeting. Farmers were Henry's main customers at his country banks, and they began defaulting on their loans. Another cycle of bankruptcies began in 1814. Twenty-four country banks failed between May and August, mainly in agricultural districts in the west, south and east of England, and like many men of business, Henry braced himself to weather the storm.[7]

The position of Austen & Co. during the banking crisis of 1814, as compared to 1811, was further weakened by the precipitous decline in agency business, halved and then halved again. In 1813 the sum of the regimental payroll was £112,000; in 1814, £63,000; by 1815 it would dwindle to £34,000.[8] The British government was desperate to retrench on military expenditure. Estimates vary, but the National Debt had increased in the war years to as much as £1 billion: between 200 and 260 per cent of GDP. The total cost of the war to Britain has been put at £831 million.

In the grand scheme of things, the bad debt of £6,000 owed to Henry and his partners by Lord Moira might appear relatively insignificant. But it represented a dangerous faultline in the company's credit. In May the previous year his trustee William Adam had convened a meeting of a dozen creditors, owed £15,000 in all by Moira. In exchange for their debts, Adam offered interest-bearing bonds, guaranteed jointly by Moira and his wife, who was independently wealthy. But the bonds were not payable for seven years and all the creditors turned down the option. Instead they reluctantly accepted the promise that they would be repaid within a year, a promise again unfulfilled.[9] The many risky loans to members of the Whig elite made by Austen & Co. in the hope of social and professional advantage now threatened the bank's survival.

The one apparently solid component in Henry's empire was his role as Receiver General of Taxes for Oxfordshire. He had made the first of his quarterly tours, the 'November collection', the previous autumn. In 1814 he collected £24,000 in land tax and £71,000 in assessed taxes, and earned £640 as his percentage.[10] The real value of the post was the prestige and the ability to retain revenue for private investment. But there were hazards here as well. Henry's predecessor, the son of Lord Spencer, had been bankrupted by his inability to handle the balance between public responsibility and private enrichment. The risks were reflected in the high rate of insurance demanded in the bond made with the Exchequer for the receivership: £73,000.

During 1814, even Edward's Hampshire inheritance, including Chawton Cottage, was under threat. It was challenged by a rival claimant and looked likely to result in an expensive legal battle. The Hinton and Baverstock families of Alton and Chawton would have been heirs to the major part of the Knight estate if the entail had not been broken in 1755. This legal device had given Thomas Knight the freedom to name Edward Austen as his heir. But the rivals suggested the disentailing deed had been drawn up improperly. During her London stay in March, Jane adopted some legalese from discussions with Edward and Henry on the prospect of settling the dispute out-of-court with cash compensation. 'Edward has a good chance of escaping his lawsuit,' she wrote to Cassandra, 'His opponent "knocks under". The terms of agreement are not quite settled.'[11] Edward and his family arrived to occupy Chawton Great House from April until late June and oversee the issue, but a clash could not be averted. In mid-October a formal writ was issued and a lawsuit began which would drag on until 1818.

With Henry's business appearing so unsafe it may have been with some relief that Frank Austen stood down as a partner in the bank after the customary seven-year term. The partnership now became known as Austen, Maunde & Tilson. However, Frank continued to make investments along with Henry. They jointly bought a one-fiftieth share in the Westminster Life Insurance Society for £3,000 and Frank loaned Henry his £1,500 share on a promissory note. Frank had left active service for the time being, and would take up occupancy of Chawton Great House with his family in June, while Charles volunteered for guard duty in the Mediterranean following the tragic death of his 24-year-old wife, Fanny, in childbirth.

As ever, even in these straitened times, there was a sharp contrast between the sums dealt with by the Austen brothers and those handled by Cassandra and Jane. The previous year Jane had overflowed with gratitude when 'kind, beautiful Edward' made her a gift of £5 during the September stopover in London. Edward had an annual income of around £8,000, more than any of Jane's fictional landowners, apart from Mr Darcy and Mr Rushworth.[12] However, he also had eleven expensive children, and unmarried sisters were last in the pecking order. From Henrietta Street in March 1814 Jane punctiliously reported to Cassandra that she had repaid Mrs Perigord a shilling for a sheet of plaited willow to make a hat, and that £6 and 15 shillings had been paid into her bank account but that she had 'just signed something' to transfer it to her mother's bank account.[13] She and Cassandra conferred anxiously about the rising price of tea, attempted to save money by re-trimming old garments, and owed Henry money for silk-dying.

Nevertheless, scrimping and saving could for a time be forgotten in Henry's company, and that of Edward and Fanny Knight when they arrived in London on 6 March. There were snug dinner parties with friends from Henry's Oxford and Marylebone days. While the snow continued to fall outside, Jane and her brothers stayed 'delightfully warm' in the two rooms over the bank (II.i). They braved the unremitting 'cruel weather' to visit Drury Lane and see Edmund Kean in the role of Shylock, along with Mr Tilson and his brother General Chowne, who had once taken the lead in an amateur production of *Lovers' Vows*. Jane was impressed by Kean, thought *The Merchant of Venice* a 'good play for Fanny', and may silently also have thought the near downfall of the reckless merchant Antonio, who believes himself to be too lucky to fail, was a salutary fable for Henry.[14] While Henry continued his reading of *Mansfield Park*, Jane was diverted by Eaton Stannard Barrett's *The Heroine*. It was a zany satire on Gothic published the previous year, and as she no doubt mentioned to Henry, must give hope that something after all might be salvaged from the ill-fated, unpublished *Susan*, yet to be rescued from Crosby and re-dubbed *Northanger Abbey*.

The new novel that Jane had been meditating on since January took shape in the course of 1814, during the so-called 'nine months' peace' before Napoleon's escape from his exile on the Mediterranean island of Elba. Aware of the ominous implications for Henry of the current state of economic uncertainty, her creative imagination turned away from global trade, speculative enterprise, and the financial mindset, all of which had featured importantly in *Mansfield Park*. It turned instead towards the non-monetary system of exchange in a sizeable village in Surrey, only sixteen miles from London and yet remarkably self-sufficient. There, an economy of visits, civilities, gossip and gifts prevails.

The tranquil world represented in *Emma* has often been regarded as the epitome of Jane Austen's miniaturist art. But *Emma* is in fact the only one of her works that adheres to the formula recommended to her niece Anna, who was trying her hand at novel writing at the same time: 'three or four families in a country village is the very thing'.[15] The hint may sound like a recipe for conservative nostalgia, but her own treatment was far from unreflective or uncritical. In *Pride and Prejudice* she had championed trade and social mobility, and been rewarded by the applause of liberal high society. Now she would challenge the blithe assumptions of free-trade progressivists by examining the merits of a micro-society organised around different, non-commercial principles.

In *Emma*, the central characters are securely wealthy. We are told in the first sentence that the heroine, Emma Woodhouse, is 'handsome, clever, and rich', and perfectly content at the age of twenty-one to remain in the comfortable home provided by her affectionate father. The family residence, Hartfield, is the largest in the village but has little surrounding acreage. The Woodhouses' income derives from 'other sources', unspecified. Many chapters later Hartfield is described as a 'notch' in the greater estate of Donwell Abbey, belonging to Mr George Knightley. The delayed information is typical of the understated place of money in the narrative. In any of her previous works it would have featured in chapter one and driven the plot. Only at this late stage do we learn that Emma herself is worth £30,000, a millionaire's fortune in present-day terms, which alone would have yielded an ample annual income of £1,500. It is not until midway through the second volume that Mr Knightley's economic status is sketched. Although he is the greatest landowner in the district and the local magistrate, he has 'little spare money' and so does not keep carriage horses; less of a sacrifice in view of his abundant possession, at the age of thirty-seven or thirty-eight, of 'health, activity, and independence' (II.viii).

The same de-emphasising of wealth and the acquisitive spirit can be seen in the more minor characters. Mr Weston, a former militia captain, had joined his brothers in an unspecified branch of trade in London. He was then seeking to repair a fortune hurt by an imprudent marriage to an extravagant great lady who died young, but he has no interest in money for its own sake. After twenty-eight years of steady work he cashes out and achieves his heart's desire: the small estate of Randalls, just outside Highbury, to share with the 'portionless' Miss Taylor, Emma's amiable former governess, as his second wife (I.ii). Mr Weston's son, Frank Churchill, adopted as an infant by his wealthy, childless maternal uncle and aunt in Yorkshire and taking their surname, turns out to be anything but frank in his dealings with the citizens of Highbury. But, like his father, Frank is wholly disinterested and even quixotic in his choice of marriage partner, a penniless young woman otherwise doomed to work for a living.

Among the inhabitants of the village, the Coles have risen through business (again, of an unspecified kind) to a place 'second only to the family at Hartfield'. We are given Emma's suspicious view of them; 'of low origin, in trade, and only moderately genteel' (II.vii). She is at first determined not to mix socially with the Coles, but is eventually won over by their civil manners. The Coles show themselves to be good neighbours, more attentive than Emma herself to the impoverished vicar's widow, Mrs Bates, and her middle-aged daughter, a warm-hearted but tiresomely garrulous spinster. Mr Perry, the local physician, is similarly charitable, willing to treat Mrs Bates and delicate Jane Fairfax, her granddaughter on an extended visit to Highbury, without charge. Mr Perry's income is something of a mystery. By rights, given the extent and nature of his clientele, he should only have an income of around £200 and yet at a crucial point in the narrative it is revealed that his wife aims to keep a carriage, impossible without at least £800 per annum.[16]

The point here is that, for the most part, the cast of named characters feel no material want. They enjoy a sufficiency. The poverty of the Bates ladies serves to highlight the bounty of others, and Miss Bates feels herself 'a most fortunate creature' with 'so many good neighbours and friends, and a home that wanted for nothing' (I.iii). Jane Fairfax feels desperation at the prospect of becoming a governess, but that fate will be providentially averted. It is not the quest for riches or an establishment that moves the story forwards, with one important exception.

The exception is the subplot concerning Mr Elton, the recently installed vicar of Highbury. Emma believes that his clerical vocation and smooth manners are a guarantee of gentility. He has no 'low connections' although after his fall from grace she reminds herself that he is 'without any alliances but in trade' (I. xvi). Her attempt to make a match between Mr Elton and her protégée Harriet Smith is founded on the expectation that he is above vulgar, mercenary considerations. Harriet, aged seventeen, is a blank apparently without monetary value or social credit, 'the natural daughter of nobody knows whom, with probably no settled

provision at all, and certainly no respectable relations'. She is known in
the village only as a pupil, and then parlour boarder, at the school run
by Mrs Goddard, one of Mr Woodhouse's little circle of regular card
players. Mr Knightley's dismissal of Harriet's worth is voiced in anger at
Emma's interference when his tenant, the yeoman farmer Robert Martin,
proposes to the girl and is rejected. Emma, for her part, is infuriated
by Mr Knightley's refusal to recognise the non-mercenary standard by
which she judges Harriet. She accords her an innate value, rather than
an exchange value: Harriet is perfectly beautiful, and her beauty is an
accurate reflection of her sweet nature. Everything declares her to be a
'gentleman's daughter' (I.viii).

In the first act of the comedy of misjudgements and misunderstand-
ings that constitutes the plot, Emma's championing of Harriet is also a
vigilant defence against market attitudes in human relations. It is not
solely snobbery that motivates her disdain of Robert Martin as a suitor.
She scores some valid points in this quarrel with Mr Knightley, and the
reader should give her credit for genuinely believing that as a man of
business Mr Martin must always be 'thinking of profit and loss' and 'too
full of the market' to make a good husband for Harriet (I.iv). Business
'engrosses' him, she observes, with a play on the notion that the profit
motive must brutalise a man's character. The joke is that Emma entirely
mistakes the true mercenary. She wilfully overlooks the indications in
Harriet's chatter of the Martin family's courteous gift-giving propensities,
in harmony with the rest of Highbury society. She is equally blind to
Mr Elton's avaricious designs on her own fortune until she receives his
drunken and blackguardly marriage proposal.

Full of contrition at fuelling Harriet's false hopes, Emma is at least right
in thinking that Mr Elton will be quickly consoled: 'He only wanted to
aggrandize and enrich himself; and if Miss Woodhouse of Hartfield, the
heiress of thirty thousand pounds, were not quite so easily obtained as he
had fancied, he would soon try for Miss Somebody else with twenty, or
with ten' (I.xvi). And so it transpires. Within a few weeks, news reaches

Highbury that he has profited from a period of self-imposed exile in Bath by landing a Miss Hawkins, daughter of a Bristol merchant, with an independent fortune of £10,000 'or thereabouts', as he doesn't hesitate to advertise on his return to Surrey (II.iv).

Most centrally and personally, Emma is determined that she will never submit to becoming a commodity in the marriage market. Early in the novel, Mr Knightley observes in conversation with Mrs Weston that Emma 'always declares she will never marry' (I.v), and Emma herself expands on the point at length in the face of Harriet's incredulity. There is no reason to change her situation, she explains. Nothing is lacking. She already possesses fortune, employment and consequence, and no man could take the place of an adoring father for whom she is 'always first and always right'. Only falling in love could make a difference, and that was unlikely, as to be in love 'is not my way, or my nature' (I.x).

The odds that Emma will become an old maid are increased by the dearth of eligible young men in the neighbourhood. There is never any suggestion that she will make the journey to Bath or any of the other marts for wedlock. There is, however, the prospect that Frank Churchill will visit his new stepmother, Mrs Weston. Frank is one of Highbury's 'boasts', although he has never been there in his life, and the contents of his 'handsome' letters to his father are pored over and discussed by the whole community (I.ii). Mr and Mrs Weston secretly hope that he will be a match for Emma and she is aware of it, looking forward to his arrival with avid curiosity, and prepared to be delighted by him.

Frank fulfils Emma's expectations, and a large part of his charm lies in his constant declarations of attachment to the Surrey community. He calls his father's house his 'home', praises 'airy, cheerful, happy-looking Highbury' to the skies. When they walk together down the High Street, he declares he must buy something at Ford's, the shop, he has been told by his father, 'that every body attends every day of their lives'. It is another touch typical of the novel that a visit to Ford's is not represented as straightforward consumerism or a display of luxury but an act of civic participation. Frank opts for a pair of gloves and Emma praises his 'patriotism' only half-jokingly, adding that while he was already popular as Mr Weston's son, once he has laid out half a guinea at Ford's 'your popularity will stand upon your own virtues' (II.vi). Ford's serves the non-commercial purpose of a place of social cohesion, where Harriet seeks shelter from the weather and begins the process of reconciliation with the Martins. On another occasion its doorway provides a proscenium arch through which Emma can entertain herself with a moving picture of the 'busiest part of Highbury', identifying familiar faces and feeling herself part of the ebb and flow of life there, while waiting for Harriet to decide on a muslin (II.ix).

Robert Hume has observed of *Emma* that compared to the earlier novels 'few specific sums of money are named'.[17] There is, however, a metaphorical instance in the case of the Crown Inn. As the name suggests, the crown, a large silver coin worth five shillings, was itself an emblem of royal sovereignty. The British crown was first minted in 1707 to mark the union of England and Scotland, although its origins lay in the sixteenth century, when it circulated internationally as the equivalent of similar silver coins, such as Spanish pieces of eight. It became rare in the Suspension era from 1797 when the shortage of metal limited the issue of coins, and even when it was re-minted in 1816 its size restricted its use. Highbury's Crown Inn, like its numismatical namesake and the British royal family, has diminished in value and lustre; its 'brilliant days had long passed away'. The spacious chamber which once served as a ballroom is no longer used, and only two post-horses are kept 'more for the convenience of the neighbourhood than from any run on the road'. They are seldom required in the 'confined society' of Highbury (II.vi; I.xviii). But Frank is determined to restore the Crown Inn as a site for social mixing and communal pleasure in order to further his clandestine romance with Jane Fairfax. He persuades his father to host a ball there, a substantial gift to the community, decisively altering the prospects of several other characters in the process.

Miss Bates, for all her verbosity, is often the source of privileged insights. On entering the room at the Crown, in the course of a speech lasting more than a page, she remarks: 'Oh! Mr. Weston, you must really have had Aladdin's lamp', and to Emma, 'This is meeting quite in fairyland! – Such a transformation!' Like the forest in *A Midsummer Night's Dream* the room at the Crown is an enchanted space of changed appearances and changed emotions. Here, the idea of Frank as a suitor will fade into insignificance, as Emma sees her 'brother' Mr Knightley, the friend and mentor she has known all her life, as an object of romantic possibility for the first time. She observes him, standing apart from the dancing and realises that, Frank excepted, 'there was not one among the whole row of young men who could be compared with him'. She admires his grace as he moves slightly nearer to her, catches his eye and forces him to smile, and wonders whether, as he 'seemed often observing her', he was preparing some new criticism of her behaviour (III.ii). Her appraisal of his attractions was not entirely new; even when he had scolded her over Harriet she had had a vividly physical awareness of him rising from his chair 'in tall indignation' (I.viii). And now having seen him joining the dance, generously rescuing Harriet after a malicious snub from Mr Elton, she is filled with 'pleasure and gratitude'.

The sight of Mr Knightley dancing with another woman stimulates a new inclination. There is an interval for supper, a fashionable addition to the festivities which the young people had insisted upon. When Mr Weston urges everyone to dance again, Mr Knightley asks Emma whom she will dance with. After a moment's hesitation, a hesitation in which the shadow line of the quasi-sibling relationship is crossed, she replies 'With you, if you will ask me'. He does, and agrees that they are 'not so much brother and sister as to make it at all improper' (III.ii).

The scene of magical metamorphosis, the triangle of affections that arises, desire born of familial intimacy, even the references to height; all indicated another visit of the imagination to that vital source of emotional intensity, the theatricals at Steventon. Henry was still a handsome man at

forty-three, five or six years Mr Knightley's senior, with his dark curling
hair touched by grey and his bright hazel eyes, 'the true hazle eye – and so
brilliant!', bestowed in the novel on Emma (I.v). He was as tall as ever and
when he smiled or laughed, which was often, the boyish charm was still
apparent. A seemingly inexhaustible supply of enthusiasm kept him young.

In *Mansfield Park* the name 'Henry' was given to the practised seducer
and eventual adulterer Mr Crawford in *Mansfield Park*. In *Emma*, teas-
ingly, Jane went to the other extreme and bestowed it upon the asexual
Mr Woodhouse, who opposes marriage on the grounds that it breaks up
the 'family circle'. Jane had written to Cassandra with deadpan hilarity on
meeting an unlikeable man at Godmersham: 'They say his name is Henry.
A proof how unequally the gifts of Fortune are bestowed. – I have seen
many a John & Thomas much more agreeable'.[18] Anyone could be *called*
Henry, but only her marvellous brother truly deserved the distinction.

It was inevitable that there would be candidates for the honour of becoming Henry's second wife, and Jane during her three visits to London
in 1814 eyed them warily. He, as if seeking her particular consent, was very
determined to make her acquainted with both the front-runners. 'Henry
wants me to see more of his Hanwell favourite,' Jane told Cassandra, '&
has written to invite her to spend a day or two here with me. His scheme is
to fetch her on Saturday. I am more & more convinced that he will marry
again soon, & like the idea of *her* better than of anybody else at hand.'
Miss Harriet Moore was a relation of one of his business acquaintances, Mr
Gordon of Cleveland Row, close to Henry's first office in Mayfair; whether
a niece or a granddaughter has not been ascertained. Another 'favourite'
at Sunning Hill, a Mrs Crutchley mentioned by Jane, has been supposed
to be an eligible match, but was in fact the married daughter of Eliza's
dearest friend, Lady Burrell.[19] Miss Burdett, however, a close friend of Mrs
Tilson, was an alternative and intriguing contender. She was apparently the
youngest sister of the politician Sir Francis Burdett although the details of
her identity, like those of the other favourites, have remained elusive.

If Henry had married Miss Burdett the Austens would have been connected to the family of the most notorious political radical in the country. Branded a demagogue, Sir Francis was a fierce critic of the Tory ministry and adored by the people. He was also an extremely wealthy man of ancient family, married to Sophia Coutts of the banking dynasty; his father-in-law, Thomas Coutts, provided the couple with a splendid establishment in Piccadilly adjoining his own. The misalliance with Burdett was one of the factors which led George III to move his personal bank account from Coutts to Drummonds. The spectacle of Burdett supporters singing revolutionary songs outside Kew Palace following his success in the 1807 Westminster election was the final straw. Thomas Coutts's other two daughters also married into the aristocracy and were appalled when their father chose an actress as his second wife, leaving all his riches, £900,000, to her. Eventually, through a freak of fortune, the money came to the youngest daughter of Sir Francis, Angela Burdett-Coutts, the great Victorian philanthropist, friend of the Duke of Wellington and Charles Dickens.

Henry's Miss Burdett was named Frances, after an aunt, and barely figures in historical records. She was the youngest of Sir Francis's three sisters, and would have been in her mid-thirties. It is evident from the first mention of her by Jane in May 1813 that Miss Burdett was extremely well-connected. Jane wrote to Cassandra that Mrs Tilson 'is in danger of not being able to attend Lady Drummond Smiths party tonight', because 'Miss Burdett was to have taken her, & now Miss Burdett has a cough and will not go'.[20] Mr Drummond Smith was described by a visiting American statesman in the 1790s as 'one of the richest commoners in England'. He was made a baronet in 1805, and his second wife threw London parties of legendary magnificence in their newly built mansion at No. 144 Piccadilly.[21] In 1810, the year before Eliza Austen's musical party was briefly reported in the *Morning Post*, the same newspaper printed a rapturous account of one of Lady Drummond Smith's assemblies:

On Tuesday evening the house was opened with singular *éclat*; the company exceeded 500 persons. In the great gallery a band of chosen musicians

were stationed during the night; the latter was illuminated by radiant
arches and festoons of variegated lamps; glasses of wonderful magnitude
and beauty, some of them exceeding 10 feet in height, were placed in
appropriate situations to reflect every object (particularly the Grecian
chandeliers) *ad infinitum*.[22]

Miss Burdett probably stayed with her brother and his family at No. 80
Piccadilly when in town, next door to the Coutts, around the corner at
No. 1 Stratton Street. An evening at the Drummond Smiths' was the
equivalent of a ball at the Crown in Highbury for Miss Burdett; Mayfair
was her village.

Peace was officially declared on 30 May 1814, and a party season to
outdo all others commenced. The Austens began by celebrating Henry's
birthday at Chawton Great House on 8 June. Fanny Knight recorded in
her diary that a 'holiday' had been declared for the purpose. Five days
later he left for town with Cassandra, and Edward and his older children
also arrived in London in time to see 'the procession going to proclaim
Peace'. Fanny's diary next records, 'Uncle Henry went to Whites Fete at
Burlington House.'[23] News of this astounding coup reached Jane in a
letter from Cassandra in Henrietta Street to Jane in Chawton, conveyed
'By favour of Mr Gray', Henry's partner in Alton, and brought to the
door of the Cottage by another bank partner Mr Louch, who must have
been staying locally on business.

'Henry at Whites! – Oh what a Henry!' was Jane's reaction. His Midas
touch had worked its wonders yet again. At the ball he would have rubbed
shoulders with the Prince Regent and allied heads of state, the King of
Prussia and the Emperor of Russia. In the same breath she remarked 'I
do not know what to wish as to Miss B, so I will hold my tongue & my
wishes.'[24] Miss Burdett must have been present, and the possibility of marriage may have seemed more probable as a result. The event was sponsored
by White's club, a favourite haunt of Tory politicians, while Brooks's was
the Whig equivalent. But at this time of national rejoicing the guest list

was bipartisan and the fête was held at Burlington House, which belonged to the Whig Duke of Devonshire. Lord George Cavendish sometimes used Burlington House as his town residence. Lord George was a former militia commander and client of Austen & Co., and it was probably through the army agency that Henry gained his entry. Betsey Wynne Fremantle, whose husband, a rear admiral in the Royal Navy, was part of a core of progressive Whigs, remarked that she saw there 'almost every body I know in London'. She described for her correspondent the brilliant illuminations 'like a fairy palace' and 'the men in full dress uniforms and the ladies in plumes, and most rich dresses'. There was dancing in the ballroom and a lavish supper beautifully arrayed, to which '2,000 people set down without the slightest inconvenience or confusion'.[25] She stayed until seven in the morning. No doubt Cassandra's letter to Jane contained a similarly awestruck account, which may have fed ironically into the description of the 'fairy-land' Crown festivities in *Emma* (III.ii).

Jane was probably conscious of the irony that many of those, like Henry, who had prospered during the war had been gathered together to toast a peace that held for them uncertainty and possible ruin. As to Miss Burdett, Jane had indicated to Cassandra her perplexity. At the end of June Henry left his bachelor quarters in Henrietta Street and leased a house in Hans Place, two doors from the Tilsons, and therefore in prime position for meeting Miss Burdett, their constant visitor. For the present, Henry was always eager to get Jane to London to stay with him in his new abode, while she demurred. Much as she loved his company, she could not help seeing that she was being used as a pawn in the game of courtship. Like her own Emma Woodhouse, she provided a screen. The presence of a sister, and such a sister, must stand in his favour and ease social intercourse.

Both Miss Burdett and Miss Harriet Moore read Jane's works and were asked their opinions, which the author duly recorded in spite of their insipidity. Miss Burdett 'did not like' *Mansfield Park*, 'so well as P. & P.'; Miss Harriet Moore admired *Emma* 'very much, but M. P. still her favourite of all'.[26] One can imagine that they failed to pass the test.

Jane and Henry had at least one thing in common with Miss Burdett. In their family, too, democratic politics had been combined with riches. Sir Thomas Hampson was the second cousin of Jane and her siblings and of Eliza Hancock. *He* was the grandson of Sir George Hampson who had inherited a baronetcy and was further enriched by his mother's Jamaica wealth, while *they* were grandchildren of Sir George's sister Rebecca Hampson, who married first William Walter and then the impecunious William Austen. According to family tradition, 'owing to his republican principles' Thomas Hampson dispensed with the 'Sir'.[27] Eliza saw him often in London before her marriage to Henry, but although she admired his fine house she was not on the whole favourably impressed by him.

Sixteen years later, Jane shared Eliza's ambivalence. Thomas Hampson was now indispensable to Henry as one of the three guarantors of the tax receivership. He agreed to renew surety along with Edward and Mr Leigh-Perrot on 9 August 1814. But there was more to the connection than this; he lurked about the bank like a bird of ill omen. 'We do not like Mr Hampson's scheme', Jane wrote emphatically to Cassandra in Henrietta Street as the postscript to a letter sent in the autumn of 1813 from Godmersham, where she would have discussed the matter with Edward.[28] It is unknown what the scheme was and whether it was put into effect, but it had become necessary for the Austens to continue to ingratiate themselves with 'Mr' Hampson. Early in Jane's August visit to Henry in 1814 Thomas Hampson came to the bank and was invited to dine at Hans Place the following evening. He 'proposed bringing his son; so I must submit to seeing George Hampson, though I had hoped to go through life without it. – It was one of my vanities, like your not reading *patronage*.'[29] Jane was evidently reluctant to let business dealings develop into a more familial relationship, while Cassandra refused to read the latest work by one of Jane's chief rivals, Maria Edgeworth.

'I certainly do not *wish* that Henry should think again of getting me to town', Jane had written to Cassandra in late June regarding their travel plans. 'I would rather return straight from Bookham; but if he really does

propose it, I cannot say No, to what will be so kindly intended.'[30] Someone had to stay at Chawton with Mrs Austen, now aged seventy-five, and
Jane estimated she could only get away for a fortnight at most. In the
end, she did not go to London straight from visiting the Cooke family at
Bookham near Box Hill, where she was no doubt finalising ideas for the
locations in *Emma*. Instead she went to Henry for a twelve-day visit from
22 August to 4 September, travelling there adventurously on her own by
stagecoach and being met at the bottom of Sloane Street by her brother,
who took her in 'a nice, cool dirty Hackney Cab' to his latest residence.
Hans Place was, and remains, an attractive enclave on an octagonal plan
inspired by the Place Vendôme in Paris and designed by Henry Holland.
Mary Russell Mitford, a contemporary Hampshire author who had attended school there and returned to visit friends at No. 33 in the summer
of 1814, described it as pleasantly surrounded by fields. Henry's abode
was a basic three-storey terraced house, smaller and cheaper than the one
around the corner on Sloane Street, which was now sublet. Jane liked it,
finding 'more space & comfort in the rooms than I had supposed' and
the garden 'quite a love', with the benefit of being able to converse with
the Tilsons at No. 26 'across the intermediate gardens'.[31]

Jane described her bedroom as the 'front attic' but the two bedrooms
on the top storey were probably reserved for the maid, 'a very creditable,
cleanlooking young woman' and the manservant. *Her* room must have
been on the second floor with the luxury of a double bed to herself and
a water closet in the dressing room opposite. It was, she said, the 'bed-
chamber to be preferred'. She and Henry quickly fell into a comfortable
routine. He would ride out to Henrietta Street early, and she would settle
down to a 'long quiet morning' of writing without the distraction of her
housekeeping duties at Chawton. Henry's study opened onto the garden
and she could step outside for a moment of relaxation before returning
to 'solitary coolness' and her literary labours.[32] In the afternoon John, the
manservant, might drive her into town in the barouche, where she would
visit the bank, run errands, see art exhibitions, and sometimes go for an

airing accompanied by Henry. Evenings were sometimes spent quietly together, conversing on their respective work in hand or in consultation over another encounter with a 'favourite'. More often they involved dinner with friends. Edward and his eldest son made an appearance, on another mission to the dentist. There were plenty of the customary Tilson 'tea drinkings'.

Henry had never been in better health, but for once his state of mind was not sanguine, as Jane relayed to Martha Lloyd:

> *His* view, & the view of those he mixes with, of politics, is not cheerful – with regard to an American war I mean; – they consider it as certain, & as what is to ruin us. The Americans cannot be conquered, & we shall only be teaching them the skill in war which they may now want. We are to make them good sailors & soldiers, & gain nothing ourselves. – If we *are* to be ruined, it cannot be helped.[33]

It seems odd that war with America is described as 'certain', when Britain and the United States had already been at war since June 1812. Jane had alluded to the escalation of hostilities in *Mansfield Park*. The action of the novel conforms to the calendar of 1809 and 1810, and she has Tom Bertram glance at a newspaper and then remark, 'A strange business this in America, Dr Grant! What is your opinion? I always come to you to know what I am to think of public matters'.[34] But it was only in the latter half of 1814, with peace in Europe apparently re-established, that ships and troops from the United Kingdom became available to reinforce the military effort hitherto led by British colonists in Canada, and this made an ongoing conflict seem new. Henry and his companions were convinced that Britain, in its exhausted state, would be unable to pursue a long-running, long-distance campaign with any hope of success, and the government under Lord Liverpool so far agreed with them that it negotiated peace terms before the end of the year, with nothing gained by either nation.

Writing to Martha in Bath, however, Jane voiced mischievous dissent: 'I place my hope of better things on a claim to the protection of Heaven, as a religious nation, a nation in spite of much evil improving in religion, which I cannot believe the Americans to possess', and she continues brightly: 'However this may be, Mr Barlowe is to dine with us today'. More chat about war and peace to come no doubt, with another banking friend. Jane imitated for Martha's amusement the earnest religiosity of the Evangelicals who had become so prominent in public life, but she may also have been remembering a striking assertion made by one of her favourite authors, Captain Charles Pasley. In his treatise on empire he had called the United States a 'body whose whole soul seems wrapt up in commerce' and cautioned his British readers against allowing their own 'commercial spirit' to be carried to a similar 'excess', rather than subordinating it to nobler ends.[35]

In the same letter, immediately preceding the talk of politics, Jane described with her characteristic light touch a genuine religious experience; one which chimed with the sense of impending ruin surrounding her brother. She had been to see Benjamin West's celebrated painting *Christ Rejected*, a monumental, life-size representation of the trial of Jesus on long-term display at No. 125 Pall Mall, formerly the site of the Royal Academy. Like the dioramas and panoramas popular at the time, it was designed to overwhelm and immerse the spectator.

> I have seen West's famous painting, & prefer it to anything of the kind I ever saw before. I do not know that it *is* reckoned superior to his 'Healing in the Temple', but it has gratified *me* much more, & indeed it is the first representation of our Saviour which ever at all contented me. 'His Rejection by the Elders', is the subject. – I want to have you & Cassandra see it.[36]

It is not difficult to imagine what would have appealed to Jane Austen in this representation. It is full of narrative details like the carpenter in

the foreground explaining the technicalities of crucifixion to a pair of ur-
chins, and acute character drawing, from the arrogance of the High Priest
Caiaphas at the centre, denouncing Jesus with outspread arms, to the
apostle St Peter, bowed and shamed having denied the Son of God. The
depiction of 'our Saviour' which so pleased her, shows him meek, still and
introspective, very much a 'lamb to the slaughter' as Isiah prophesied.
Christ's feminine vulnerability aligns him with the group that fills the
right foreground: Mary Magdalene, the Virgin Mary, and other 'women
of Galilee'. In particular, the reformed prostitute Mary Magdalene, the
exemplary sinner, dominates the scene. While Pontius Pilate turns away
and the High Priest draws back, she reaches out to Jesus, crawling on her
hands and knees towards him.

Jane would always be the impudent younger sister when corresponding with Cassandra, but she felt able to touch on serious, even spiritual
matters with Martha. 'You are made for doing good', she once told
her.[37] In the three surviving letters addressed to Martha, Jane wanted to
demonstrate her compassionate attentions towards less fortunate neighbours such as Miss Benn, a genteel but destitute spinster, or the labouring
poor of the parish, among whom she and Cassandra distributed a legacy
from Mrs Knight of £20 in 1812, supplementing the usual Christmas
dole from Edward. Or else she tried to show charitable forbearance.
Thanking Martha for Mrs Harry Digwood's 'goodhumoured commu-
nications' during the stay at Hans Place, Jane added, 'The language of
London is flat; it wants her phrase'.[38]

The connection between Miss Benn in Chawton and Miss Bates in
Emma can be readily made, in circumstances if not in character. Mary
Benn's plight was something that concerned the Austen ladies and Martha
Lloyd from the moment they arrived in the village. Aged forty-four in
1814, she was like Miss Bates in 'the middle of life' and entirely without
means (I.iii). Her brother was rector at Farringdon nearby, but all his
money was devoted to raising twelve children. Like the rest of the neighbourhood, the women at Chawton Cottage who might easily have shared

her fate, issued constant invitations to tea or dinner to help her get by. In one letter Jane described Miss Benn's itinerary of dinners in a different household in the village every day of the week. When she was evicted from her draughty hovel in the winter of 1813, 'terrible for her during the late storms of wind & rain', Jane reported to Martha that 'all Chawton' was anxious to get her decently settled. When Martha thought of making Miss Benn a present, Jane and Cassandra conferred, and proposed a shawl 'to wear over her shoulders in very cold weather'. It would replace her tippet, a fur-lined short woollen cloak, which was almost worn out. Jane specified that the new shawl 'must not be very handsome or else she would not use it'.[39] The discarded tippet found its way into the pages of *Emma*, where it is anxiously handed by Miss Bates to Frank Churchill, to place over the shoulders of her fragile niece.

Miss Benn happened to be dining at Chawton Cottage on the very day that newly published *Pride and Prejudice* arrived from London. That evening, Jane and Mrs Austen took it in turns to read it aloud to her. Jane was still trying to keep her authorship a secret and she explained that they had heard from Henry that the work would soon appear and asked him to send a copy; 'I believe it passed with her unsuspected.' By the second evening's reading Jane was irritated by the shortcomings of her mother's delivery, but she compensated for it. Henry was later to remark, 'She read aloud with very great taste and effect. Her own works, probably, were never heard to so much advantage as from her own mouth; for she partook largely in all the best gifts of the comic muse.' It was as good as a play, and succeeded not only in amusing Miss Benn ('poor soul!') but also transporting her into a world of wish fulfilment where a witty but portionless young woman could hold sway; 'she really does seem to admire Elizabeth'.[40]

This was 'mental physick' of the kind that Martha was so adept at dispensing, the sort which 'bears a stamp beyond all common charity'.[41] In *Emma*, when the heroine goes to minister to a poor sick family in the village, her mental attitude is as important as the practical good she does.

It involves patience, intelligence and goodwill, and the absence of offi-
cious interference, sanctimonious superiority, or censorious judgement.
The issue of 'what the poor must suffer in winter' was a topic not only
for Emma and Harriet, but in Jane's life as well. Her birthday in mid-
December served as an annual reminder of her blessings and the lottery
of life. Miss Bates's adaptation of lines from Psalm 16, 'our lot is cast in a
goodly heritage', suggests precisely the arbitrariness of fate (II.iii).

Miss Bates in the novel combines the sad ill fortune of Miss Benn with
the cheerful chatter of Mrs Harry Digwood. Jane had once attempted
a transcription of Mrs Digwood's speech. When asked how she liked a
recent popular publication Mrs D replied, 'Oh! dear, yes, very much; –
very droll indeed; – the opening of the house! – & the striking up of the
fiddles!' And Jane added drolly to Cassandra, 'What she meant, poor
woman, who shall say? – I sought no further...'[42] In *Emma* this distinc-
tive mode of conversation is extended and amplified until it takes on
an epic quality. Miss Bates, like a Sibyl or prophetess, speaks in tongues
for a page at a time, interspersing her elliptical exclamations and cour-
tesies with piercing truths. After briefly raising the clergy in *Mansfield
Park*, Jane now sank it even below the level of Mr Collins in *Pride and
Prejudice*, by introducing Mr Elton, a complete failure as Christ's representative on earth. Instead it is Miss Bates, a holy fool and miracle
worker, who serves as the spiritual centre of the community. Her days are
spent caring for 'a failing mother' and making 'a small income go as far
as possible':

> And yet she was a happy woman, and a woman whom no one named
> without good-will. It was her own universal good-will and contented
> temper which worked such wonders. She loved every body, was interested
> in every body's happiness, quick-sighted to every body's merits; thought
> herself a most fortunate creature, and surrounded with blessings in such
> a mother, and so many good neighbours and friends, and a home that
> wanted for nothing. (I.x)

She disproves the socio-economic law that poverty contracts the mind: 'If she had only a shilling in the world, she would be very likely to give away sixpence of it' (I.x).

The scene of the excursion to Box Hill, when Emma idly insults Miss Bates as she flirts with Frank, witnessed by most of their circle, partakes of the gravity of 'Christ Rejected'. When Frank proposes that each of the party should say one clever thing, or two moderately clever things, 'or three things very dull indeed', Miss Bates in her humility exclaims that three dull things 'will just do for me' looking round good-humouredly for the assent of the others. Emma cannot resist saying 'Pardon me – but you will be limited as to number – only three at once'. Miss Bates meekly turns the other cheek once she registers the rebuke, 'Ah! – well – to be sure. Yes, I see what she means ... and I will try to hold my tongue.' The words are addressed particularly to Mr Knightley, who sits by her, and he swiftly makes it clear to Emma in private conversation that the quip has been a form of sacrilege. He insists that, inversely, it is Miss Bates's material poverty that makes the regard in which she is held so sacrosanct. For Emma, this is a moral awakening, she is more 'agitated, mortified, grieved' than ever in her life, 'forcibly struck'. 'She felt it at her heart' (III. vii). During the carriage ride home her tears flow unstoppably as if in humbled imitation of Miss Bates's inexhaustible flow of words.

Jane Austen explored in the novel her own social and economic situation as an old maid, an exception to the regular traffic in women. Historically, unmarried daughters were often sacrificial figures, yielded up to God. King Theseus in *A Midsummer Night's Dream* offers Hermia, if she refuses to marry the man of her father's choosing, the choice either of death, or of death-in-life in 'the livery of a nun'. In an echo of his speech, Jane Fairfax imagines that at one-and-twenty she must renounce the world, 'complete the sacrifice', and enter into the vocation of governess and 'penance and mortification for ever', a secular version of the 'shady cloister'. Jane's feverish ideas, comparing herself first to a religious novice, later to a slave, are so close to the rebellious attitude of Jane Eyre or Lucy Snowe that it must always be a wonder that Charlotte Brontë did not discover some common ground with Austen. But of course, the latter's chief focus is on Emma Woodhouse, whose proclivity for seeing her cup entirely full rather than half empty masks her own self-sacrifice on the altar of filial piety. It is only after finding that she loves Mr Knightley that she registers the solemnity of her private vow. To even consider abandoning her father was a 'sin of thought' (III.xiv).

Jane Austen, a little less devotedly, shared the burden of tending to her mother's needs. Her vocation, however, was her art; a rare attitude at a time when literary enterprise, among needy female authors especially, was most often a means to an end. She dedicated herself to composing novels, rather than 'Chanting faint hymns to the cold, fruitless moon', as King Theseus would have it.

Mary Mitford, whose mother had been raised near the Austens in Steventon and knew them slightly, discovered the secret of Jane Austen's authorship in December 1814. Her informant was Miss Jane Hinton, who lived opposite Chawton Cottage and was also party to the lawsuit against Edward Austen Knight. Miss Hinton reported that the Reverend Austen's younger daughter:

> has stiffened into the most perpendicular, precise, taciturn piece of 'single blessedness' that ever existed, and that, till *Pride and Prejudice* showed what a precious gem was hidden in that unbending case, she was no more regarded in society than a poker or a fire-screen, or any other thin, upright piece of wood or iron that fills the corner in peace and quietness. The case is very different now: she is still a poker – but a poker of whom every one is afraid.[43]

Mitford, too, alluded to the speech from *A Midsummer's Night Dream* threatening Hermia with a life of fruitless self-sacrifice. But as Jane was to observe in *Emma*, 'intellectual superiority' had its compensations for an ageing single woman. It could 'frighten those who might hate her, into outward respect' (I.iii). Those who might be inclined to despise or ignore her now knew of the 'precious gem' hidden inside.

The first edition of *Mansfield Park*, around 1,250 copies priced at eighteen shillings, sold out in six months. She had gained around £310 to £347, more than for any of her other works, having given strict instructions to ensure low production costs; even thinner paper than that used for *Pride and Prejudice* and more lines per page. Come the spring, she was in a position to purchase £600 of 'Navy Fives', government bonds yielding 5 per cent interest, issued to fund the Royal Navy. She must have put together her recent profits, the £250 from the first two novels, and a further payment of £30 from Egerton arising from the second edition of *Sense and Sensibility*.[44] But Jane was uneasy. The new novel had received no reviews in the journals whatsoever; a most unusual occurrence, and inexplicable after the steady progress in public regard achieved by her first two works. The attribution 'By the Author of "Sense and Sensibility," and "Pride and Prejudice"' was printed on the title page and it seems that after all, as she had airily predicted, *Mansfield Park* had sold on the credit of previous successes alone.

Henry was now urging her to come to town and negotiate a second edition of *Mansfield Park* with Egerton, while Jane hesitated. It was inconvenient; she was in a fine flow of composition. She wrote to him her 'will & pleasure' but still he pressed and soon she relented, remarking to Fanny Knight, 'I am very greedy & want to make the most of it; – but as you are much above caring about money, I shall not plague you with any particulars.'[45] Ten days later, on 30 November, she wrote to Fanny from Hans Place, adopting a cautious note:

> Thank you – but it is not settled yet whether I *do* hazard a 2d Edition. We are to see Egerton today, when it will probably be determined. – People are more ready to borrow & praise, than to buy – which I cannot wonder at; – but tho' I like praise as well as anybody, I like what Edward calls *Pewter* too.[46]

She was bracing herself for disappointment, and it duly came. Egerton either refused to undertake a second edition, or advised against risking one. The worldly wisdom that readers 'are more ready to borrow & praise, than to buy' may have been his attempt to soften the blow before the decisive meeting. He had little to gain or lose, since he did not own the copyright and the 'hazard' would be the author's, but Jane must have been wounded by his lack of confidence after all he'd gained from *Pride and Prejudice*.

She knew perfectly well that the reading public were willing to buy a novel when the right one appeared. *Waverley* had been published in July that year and the first edition of 1,000 copies had sold out in two days. The work was anonymously published, but the author's identity was an open secret. Jane remarked in a letter to Anna in September, 'Walter Scott has no business to write novels, especially good ones. It is not fair. He has fame and profit enough as a poet, and should not be taking the bread out of other people's mouths. I do not like him, & do not mean to like *Waverley* if I can help it – but fear I must.'[47] By November a fourth edition was in the presses and the eminent *Edinburgh Review* had poured forth its praise in a thirty-five page article, proclaiming that it put 'the whole tribe of ordinary novels into the shade'.

Such was the verdict of the public: *Mansfield Park* was one of those 'ordinary novels' struggling in the shade cast by *Waverley*. The case was made worse by the unconcealed enthusiasm of her own family for Scott's bestseller. Mrs Austen told Anna that it had 'afforded me more entertainment than any modern production (Aunt Jane's excepted) of the novel kind that I have read for a great while'. Charles would write to Jane from Palermo the following year telling her that when he had praised *Waverley* an acquaintance there, nephew of Charles James Fox, the legendary radical politician, had insisted that nothing could compare to *Pride and Prejudice* and *Sense and Sensibility*. It was reassuring to know that her Whig fan base was loyal. But Charles spoilt the effect by mentioning that the man in question, Henry Stephen Fox, a charming young attaché at the

Sicilian court and an inveterate gambler like his uncle, 'did not appear to like "Mansfield Park" as much as the first two'.[48] Was it any surprise that she had appealed to Anna, just settled in her new home after marriage to Ben Lefroy, 'Make everybody at Hendon admire Mansfield Park.'[49]

It was during this crisis of confidence, in the absence of any official word from the reviewers, that Jane somewhat courageously canvassed opinions of *Mansfield Park* from family, friends and acquaintances. They were requested to be brutally honest, without fear of the kind of satirical reprisals at which Mary Mitford had hinted. Not only that, but she apparently asked them specifically to rank her works and rate the new cast of characters, and then recorded the often uncharitable findings without editorial comment. Fanny Cage, in Kent, 'did not much like it – not to be compared to P&P. – nothing interesting in the Characters – Language poor...' Mrs Augusta Bramstone, near Steventon, considered 'S & S. – and P & P downright nonsense, but expected to like MP. better, & having finished the 1st vol. – flattered herself she had got through the worst'. Jane's 'own particular little brother' Charles had to admit that he 'did not like it near so well as P. & P.' and 'thought it wanted incident'. There were compliments and insights, but also hair-raising dismissals. Perhaps most damning of all, her old friend and mentor Mrs Lefroy found it 'a mere novel'.[50]

What was the purpose of this exercise? It seems more self-flagellation than a morale boost. Some of the opinions would have appealed to her sense of the ridiculous but overall it was as if she was deliberately thickening her skin and strengthening her resolve. The adverse comments were hoarded like Harriet Smith's 'most precious treasures' as she continued to write *Emma*. They sparked in her a kind of rebellious pride in opposition to the values of the marketplace. They made her both reckless and resolute. There is no doubt that Jane Austen craved commercial and critical success, as any author would; but on her own terms. It would have been easy enough to employ again the *Pride and Prejudice* formula that had proved most lucrative. Instead her approach was becoming fundamentally uncommercial. Her most extreme act of rebellion was to compose a narrative with no 'story', as the earliest readers were to complain constantly of *Emma*. She would narrow the geographic scope in opposition to wide-ranging, crowd-pleasing adventures. She would 'take a heroine whom no one but myself will much like'.[51] It was Jane, rather than Fanny, who was 'above caring about money'.

The only member of the immediate family whose comments do not appear in the list of 'Opinions' of either *Mansfield Park* or *Emma*, was Henry. When it came to the novels, he was too closely identified with her to count as an external judge. With him, she may have comforted herself when she completed the new novel on 29 March 1815, she would be 'always right'. She perhaps also felt increasingly reassured that she would be 'always first'. Henry was busily exploring the possibility of a new and far more prestigious publisher for *Emma*, though nothing was yet fixed. Any thoughts of a second marriage were apparently put on hold, due to the continuing political instability and the threat it posed to Henry's livelihood. Extraordinary events were taking place on the Continent. Napoleon had escaped from exile on the island of Elba and landed on French soil on 1 March, his army rallying to the cause. The allies scrambled to re-assemble an opposing force under the Duke of Wellington. On 18 June, the French Emperor was defeated at Waterloo. But the temporary return to military alert had done nothing to halt the slide of Austen & Co.

The role of receiver general had rebounded on Henry. The tax collected in Oxfordshire and privately invested through the bank had fallen due, and he found himself unable to pay. Failure to deliver taxes was a serious misdemeanour. A writ of Extent-in-Chief was now issued by the Crown, reserving Henry's assets. He in turn issued writs of Extent-in-Aid, a mechanism regularly used as self-protection by tax collectors and country bankers, calling in private debts in order to pay Crown debts. Lord Moira, the most significant debtor, was untouchable in India. Instead on 11 April 1815 the hammer-blow fell first on a Hampshire farmer and maltster, James Harfield, who owed Austen & Co. £3,748. Harfield was declared bankrupt and committed to a debtors' prison with his wife and seven children for the next two years, while petitioning Parliament for relief. The use of Extents was a growing scandal, as it tended to force the emergency sale of assets at reduced value.[52] Jane's thoughts during the first nine months of 1815 are unknown, due to the absence of letters or other documentation, but Deirdre Le Faye has suggested that she visited Hans Place in the spring, and again in August.[53] She must have been party to the troubling talk.

Fanny Knight's diary entries for April 1815, however, depict life at Hans Place continuing in its regular, prosperous way: visits to Covent Garden and art exhibitions, services at the elegant new Belgrave Chapel, a musical party, shopping, tea with Mrs Tilson. On the 24th, Henry took Fanny to see Benjamin West's picture, no doubt at Jane's urging. On the 28th he hosted a ball in the evening for around twelve couples. Two days later he set off for Oxfordshire early in the morning, to attend to his duties as receiver.[54] In August the bond with the Exchequer would be renewed by Henry's backers, but this time the liability was raised from £73,000 to £80,000. Jane began writing the novel that would be published under the title *Persuasion*.

Around this time, Henry commenced discussions in earnest with the rising publisher of the day, John Murray. The son of a Scottish emigrant who had originally set up shop as a bookseller at 32 Fleet Street, Murray moved the business to 50 Albermarle Street in Mayfair in 1812 and promptly scored his greatest hit with the publication of Lord Byron's verse travelogue, *Childe Harold's Pilgrimage*. Another huge success was the *Quarterly Review*, the Tory answer to the liberal *Edinburgh Review*, a journal launched by Murray and edited by William Gifford. Jane had positioned copies of the *Quarterly Review* in the household at Mansfield Park. Was this strategic product placement? Murray was inundated by unsolicited manuscripts and he rarely published novels. But in 1814 Gifford, who also advised Murray on potential signings, wrote a note to the publisher comparing *Mansfield Park* favourably to Frances Burney's latest work, *The Wanderer*. This reference, newly discovered by the scholar

Kathryn Sutherland, suggests that Jane Austen was already on Gifford's radar. He was reading *Pride and Prejudice* 'again' in early autumn 1815, as formal negotiations got underway.[55]

How did Jane Austen, snubbed by Egerton, achieve the coveted place in the Murray stable of authors? It may have been chiefly on merit. Gifford was a shrewd judge of talent. But Henry was evidently instrumental in establishing the initial contact. Kathryn Sutherland has noted a passing reference in the Murray archive, which points to Henry's role. Gifford remarks of another author's work in a note of 1817, 'It comes nearest your banker's sister's novels – more business and incident' but 'less penetration and nature'.[56] Henry was not literally Murray's banker, but the fact that Jane Austen had a banker brother behind her may have been a factor in Murray's eventual agreement to publish *Emma* and the second edition of *Mansfield Park* on commission.

A direct line of continuity between Jane Austen's two publishers was the printer Charles Roworth, who worked for both Egerton and Murray. Henry had been in frequent communication with Roworth while the previous three novels went through the presses. A less direct route to Murray may have been through Henry's business and social contacts. Politically, Murray was allied with the Tory government, but his regular afternoon literary salon in the drawing room at No. 50 Albemarle Street off Piccadilly was inclusive. Some of Henry's titled liberal friends in the neighbourhood of Piccadilly might have brought influence to bear.

On 4 October 1815 Jane left Chawton Cottage with Henry, intending to stay at Hans Place only a week or two, while the deal with Murray was finalised. It seemed that stability was returning. Ben Lefroy, Anna's husband, placed £2,888 in a Bank of England account he had opened jointly in 1814 with Henry Austen. Edward Knight's income from his Hampshire estates of £4,567 gross rolled in, down on the previous year, but by no means ruinously.[57] Henry had been tested by peace twice over but had somehow pulled through again. When Jane left London more than two months later, however, the outlook would be fundamentally altered.

CHAPTER 8

SECOND SPRING:
PERSUASION (1815–1816)

Jane's intention, on arrival at Hans Place at the start of October, was to settle the business with John Murray briskly and return as soon as possible to her writing routine at Chawton Cottage. Ideas for the work that would become *Persuasion* were flowing. But no word came from the publisher and instead, as well as she could in a state of acute suspense, she applied herself to composition and joined in Henry's busy social programme. In addition to the ever-present Tilsons there was the Jackson family, at No. 9 Sloane Terrace. Mr Henry Jackson was married to Sarah Papillon, the sister of the Reverend J. R. Papillon, rector of Chawton, and they had three daughters. Jane had met the eldest when she stayed with her aunt and uncle in the village in 1812. Down from London, Eleanor Jackson had urged everyone to read the latest bestseller, *Rejected Addresses* by James and Horace Smith, a book parodying the leading poets of the period which also delighted Jane. She wrote to Cassandra of the visiting niece, '*She* looks like a rejected addresser'. The remark could be taken a number of ways, but the most obvious would be that she seemed intelligent and capable of being witty, like the Smith brothers. Jane enjoyed the evening with the Jacksons but was not so sure about the father, who seemed something of a glutton and spoke ill of his Papillon in-laws.

The following day, on 15 October, Henry and Jane dined at the home of Colonel Charles Herries, at No. 15 Cadogan Place, the other side of

Sloane Street. There was 'a large family party', Jane wrote to Cassandra, 'clever & accomplished'. The Colonel was the younger son of Sir Robert Herries, a partner at Coutts Bank before founding his own firm, and the inventor of the 'circular exchange note', a precursor of the travellers' cheque. He had established an international exchange network across Europe; Philadelphia Hancock utilised a Herries' branch in Paris in the 1780s. Sir Robert became an influential member of the political establishment, and his son Colonel Herries was a favourite of George III, as head of the most prominent and prestigious volunteer corps in the country, the London and Westminster Light Horse Volunteers. When he lost his fortune in a bank failure in 1798, he was rescued by society friends and a royal pension.

The dinner party may have included the Colonel's very clever and accomplished son, John Charles Herries, who lived a few doors away at No. 21. If so, Jane Austen dined with the man who, behind the scenes, was determining the destiny of Europe. He had been a protégé of the late Prime Minister Spencer Perceval, and was at present commissary-in-chief charged with army finance at the Treasury. Unknown to the public, he had worked with Rothschild Bank to transfer smuggled French gold to the British war chest, financing Wellington's final push from Spain into France in 1813–14 and subsequently providing subsidies and loans for European allies. Herries, like Nathan Rothschild, grew wealthy on early information from the money markets. Among his other talents, he was handy with a pen, frequently defending Tory monetary policy against such critics as William Cobbett, and active in the founding of the *Quarterly Review*.

Henry Austen was used to Whig aristocrats, with their relaxed manners and notionally egalitarian principles. How he adapted to the society of a High Tory like John Charles Herries, who was firmly anti-Catholic and notoriously partisan, is unknown. But the cultivation of the Herries family was in line with Jane's move to the Tory publishing powerhouse, John Murray.

The following morning, Jane visited the Gordons in Cleveland Row. The weather had been strangely sultry, and she found many of the family ill. Henry too was indisposed, after riding over to the Henrietta Street bank in the morning as usual. He returned early that day, and took to his bed suffering from 'a bilious attack with fever'. 'He is calomeling & therefore in a way to be better & I hope may be well tomorrow,' Jane told Cassandra. She found it 'comical' that in the evening she was left to dine with Mr Seymour, Henry's friend and legal adviser, tête-à-tête.[1] It seems there was once an expectation that William Seymour would propose to Jane. Apparently he admired her.[2] Be that as it may, he had been responsible for the sale of *Susan* to Crosby for £10 twelve years earlier, and she must have been pleased to share with him the news that they had finally received Mr Murray's offer of £450 for the copyright of *Emma* along with *Mansfield Park* and *Sense and Sensibility*. She had made some progress in the publishing world and was gratified by Murray's praise, but she was not satisfied by the amount. After all, she had earned more than £310 from the first edition of *Mansfield Park* alone. 'He is a rogue of course,' she commented to Cassandra, 'but a civil one'. She would not part with copyright of her darling children on such terms. 'It will end in my publishing for myself I dare say.'[3]

Henry's illness became more serious on Tuesday, and Jane was worried enough to summon the apothecary from the corner of Sloane Street, a 'young Mr Haydon', the successor to Mr Smith, 'said to be clever' and 'certainly very attentive'. He stated authoritatively that the slight pain in the chest was inconsequential but that the 'general inflammation' required bloodletting; twenty ounces of blood were taken that evening. Mr Tilson stepped in to play host to the Creeds from Hendon at dinner. Mrs Creed had a claim as one of Colonel Herries's daughters, but Jane was too distracted to entertain their guests properly. Mr Tilson too, was anxious about his wife, worn down by frequent pregnancies and a recent miscarriage. 'Poor woman,' Jane wrote of Mrs Tilson, 'she is quite a wretch, always ill'. On Wednesday morning the apothecary took another twenty ounces of blood from Henry, and planned to do so again on Thursday. In an unusually sober mood, Jane signed off the letter to Cassandra with 'God bless you'.[4]

Henry's self-administered doses of calomel and the apothecary's repeated bloodlettings were standard treatments for the diagnosis: the excess of bile, the digestive fluid secreted by the liver, must be purged by evacuating the bowels, and other bodily fluids restored to their proper balance by controlled bleeding. Calomel was mercury in the form of a yellowish powder and highly toxic. It killed bacteria, and taken in sufficient quantity and for long enough it would kill the patient too. Side effects included excessive salivation, gum inflammation and loosening of the teeth, gastrointestinal disorder, and an ashen appearance. Neurological symptoms could include arm and facial tremors, and unusual timidity and personality change (one wonders if the transformation of lively Louisa Musgrove following severe illness in *Persuasion* was down to the perceived effects of prolonged use of calomel). Yet, although a few dissenting voices were beginning to be heard among medics, calomel remained a routine home remedy. Jane had once turned into comic verse a conversation, which she overheard at a pharmacy in Alton, about the use of calomel as a cure for headache.

Said Miss Beckford, 'Suppose
If you think there's no risk,
I take a good dose
Of Calomel brisk.'
'What a praise-worthy notion!'
Replied Mr Newham
'You shall have such a potion,
And so will I too Ma'am.'

In the light of subsequent knowledge, her remark – 'Henry is an excellent patient, lies quietly in bed & is ready to swallow anything' – is alarming.

'Heroic' bouts of bloodletting were also commonplace. The Prince Regent was a great believer, and had large quantities of blood removed to counter a host of ailments that included chronic indigestion, weak nerves, gout and temporary paralysis. There were high-profile disasters. The first American President, George Washington, failed to survive a throat infection in 1799 after being subjected to the removal of more than eighty ounces of blood in sixteen hours, accompanied by vigorous doses of calomel. Lord Byron would die in 1824 under similar circumstances.

Henry's response was at first reassuring. He lived on 'medicine, tea & barley water', felt no acute pain and slept fairly well. Yet the fever did not abate. He couldn't manage a planned visit to Chawton, but Jane still expected he would be able to travel to Oxford shortly to attend to receivership affairs. She put off a visit by two of Edward's sons until the end of the week, having 'a strong idea of their Uncle's being well enough' by then.[5] On Friday, Henry was still not strong enough to sit up. However, he insisted on dictating a letter to John Murray. His indignation about the low terms offered had mixed with the fever, and needed an outlet. Furthermore, Jane felt she must return home soon, and the publication of *Emma* should not be further delayed.

Murray was known for his generosity to authors. In 1819 the poet George Crabbe was staggered to be offered £3,000 for his latest collection and copyright of some previous works. But even good novels were valued less than poetry. William Gifford, Murray's expert reader, had scribbled a favourable judgement on *Emma* and sent it to Murray on 29 September: 'nothing but *good* to say'. But he also appears to have talked down Murray's initial idea of £500 for copyright of *Emma* alone.[6] The fact that the valuable copyright for *Pride and Prejudice* belonged to Egerton led Murray to drive a hard bargain for Jane's other novels.

Henry's reply, in Jane's handwriting, showed the strain of maintaining a courteous tone,

Severe illness has confined me to my bed ever since I received yours of the

15th – I cannot yet hold a pen, & employ an amanuensis. – The politeness & perspicuity of your letter equally claim my earliest exertion. – Your official opinion of the merits of Emma, is very valuable & satisfactory. – Though I venture to differ occasionally from your critique, yet I assure you the quantum of your commendation rather exceeds than falls short of the author's expectation & my own. – The terms you offer are so very inferior to what we had expected, that I am apprehensive of having made some great error in my arithmetical calculation. – On the subject of the expense & profit of publishing, you must be much better informed that I am; – but documents in my possession appear to prove that the sum offered by you for the copyright of Sense & Sensibility, Mansfield Park & Emma, is not equal to the money which my sister has actually cleared by one very moderate edition of Mansfield Park – (You yourself expressed astonishment that so small an edition of such a work should have been sent into the world) & a still smaller one of Sense & Sensibility...[7]

The letter was never completed or sent. In mid-dictation, Henry collapsed. Jane had failed to see just how gravely ill he was, and must have been overwhelmed with guilt and anxiety. She kept the draft with the annotation 'A letter to Mr. Murray which Henry dictated a few days after his illness began, & just before the severe relapse which threw him into such danger.'

Edward was expected at Hans Place on Tuesday, on business connected with the disputed Knight inheritance. Jane sent daily bulletins to Godmersham and Fanny noted Henry's deteriorating state in her diary. Saturday, 21 October: 'indifferent account of Uncle HA'. Sunday: 'worse acct. of Uncle HA'. Monday: 'bad acct. of poor Uncle H'.[8] From Saturday, the signs increased that Henry might die. Jane was alone with the realisation. After the peace, Madame Bigeon and her daughter had returned to France, and were not there to share the bedside vigil. The servants attended to household matters, but Jane had sole responsibility for nursing Henry. Medical men came and went. It is possible that she summoned the eminent physician, Dr Matthew Baillie, who had attended Henry during a previous collapse in the early days of his marriage with Eliza. On Sunday, Jane sent express letters to Godmersham, Steventon and Chawton, and waited in desperation for her sister and brothers to arrive.

Near the start of his indisposition, Jane had written to Cassandra, 'You must fancy Henry in the back room upstairs – & I am generally there also, working or writing.'⁹ Jane now found herself in the position of Elinor Dashwood in *Sense and Sensibility*, watching over her mortally ill sister Marianne. Even the weather had changed and now conformed to the fictional scene; 'the wind roared round the house, and the rain beat against the windows'. Like Marianne, her patient grew increasingly 'heavy, restless, and uncomfortable', painful slumber alternating with 'sleepless pain and delirium', and Jane like Elinor struggled with her fears through the long nights, 'her thoughts wandering from one image of grief, one suffering friend to another'. In the novel she had applied a striking economic metaphor: 'Her apprehensions once raised, paid by their excess for all her former security' (III.viii).

Jane Austen kept the show of religious sentiment out of her fiction and we do not see Elinor praying. But Jane, as the daughter of a parson, must have prayed long and earnestly during this crisis. She may have visualised in the darkness the kind, gentle face of Jesus that had so struck her in Benjamin West's painting. She prayed for the strength to accept and endure the loss, should it come; that was the orthodox way. But it is not unlikely that more fanciful ideas rose up. She may have reviewed her own shortcomings, the ways in which she'd disappointed Henry. If only he survived, she would seize the first opportunity to make more of her modicum of celebrity. He had been so aggravated, when she turned down an invitation to meet the famous author Madame De Stael. Dwelling on the worries over the bank, who could be surprised if she tried to bargain with God: take everything, take the money, but spare Henry's life.

Edward set off for town the moment Jane's express arrived at Godmersham and reached Hans Place on Monday evening. James went to

Chawton to fetch Cassandra, and Jane feared they would be too late. On Wednesday she wrote to the Leigh-Perrots preparing them for the worst. When Cassandra finally entered the house with James later in the day, Jane must have fallen into her arms, wrung out by grief and strain. Then on Thursday, miraculously, there was a slight improvement in Henry's condition, and they dared to hope. The next day James Austen was able to write to the Leigh-Perrots with the news that Henry was recovering. He continued to make progress, and by the following Monday Jane was able to write a cheerful letter to James's youngest child, ten-year-old Caroline, who with her mother was staying at Chawton Cottage.

It was not until Friday 3 November, a full week after the threat had passed, that Jane gathered herself to send a note to John Murray, asking him to come to Hans Place to agree the terms for *Emma*. She referred to Henry's 'severe illness' and continuing weakness to explain the long silence and her decision to take a more direct approach; 'A short conversation may perhaps do more than much writing'.[10] In the event, neither party was prepared to compromise over the price, but Jane was able to persuade Murray to accept her usual terms and publish *Emma* and a second edition of *Mansfield Park* 'on commission', paying the production costs herself and taking any proceeds, less a 10 per cent charge. For Murray, it was an unusual concession. For Jane, it was another gamble against the odds, true to the speculative instincts of her banker brother. She was staking the profits from previous works on the chance of future success, in defiance of the advice of two experienced publishers, and in spite of her own admission that, since *Pride and Prejudice*, she had been deliberately challenging the expectations of her readers.

The period of convalescence was lengthy. Jane put aside any thought of a quick return to Chawton. Edward and James departed in early November, while Cassandra stayed on at Hans Place with Jane, sharing the nursing duties while Jane recommended her work-in-progress and awaited the proof pages of *Emma*. Henry's brush with mortality was to leave its mark on *Persuasion*, which features no less than three 'deaths', none of them irreversible. The working title of the novel was 'The Elliots', and it is the pride of family that dominates the first chapter, with its appraisal of the 'Elliot' entry in the *Baronetage*, a reference work of ancestry. Within this reckoning, the second daughter, Anne, is 'nobody'. While the eldest of Sir Walter's three daughters, Elizabeth, is still considered likely to marry well and ornament the family tree, Anne has been written off. At twenty-seven she has lost her 'bloom' and looks 'faded and thin'. The readers' deepening knowledge of her history adds to the sense that she is a ghostly presence in the house of Elliot. She haunts the places where she briefly experienced happiness at the age of nineteen. Her future was cut off when she allowed herself to be persuaded by Lady Russell, her one friend and the substitute for her deceased mother, to end her engagement with a brilliant but socially inferior young naval officer for the sake of family harmony. The whole narrative arc of *Persuasion* concerns Anne's recovery from a living death. She again meets Captain Frederick Wentworth, now a wealthy war hero who ultimately, after considerable suspense, plays Orpheus to Anne's Eurydice.

Jane had abjured death scenes since the childhood stories with their outrageous casualty rate. Now she was not content to stop at one resurrection. Louisa Musgrove falls from the steps of the Cobb, the stone pier at Lyme Regis, and 'was taken up lifeless!' Although there is no sign of injury, 'her eyes were closed, she breathed not, her face was like death. – The horror of that moment to all who stood around!' Wentworth, whose irresponsibly flirtatious behaviour was a factor in the disaster, suffers the anguish of an accidental murderer, his face 'as pallid as her own'. Louisa's sister faints and the workmen and boatmen in the area 'enjoy the sight' of 'two dead young ladies, for it proved twice as fine as the first report'. But Louisa, 'the poor corpse-like figure', comes back to life and a different love; a direct consequence of this emotional trial with mythic overtones is the reunion of Anne and Wentworth (I.xii).

The third instance initially seems more tangential. The final act of the narrative takes place in Bath, and there Anne seeks out a former school

friend. Once the pampered wife of a profligate man of fortune, Mrs Smith
is now crippled by rheumatism, 'a poor, infirm, helpless widow' confined
to two rooms in Westgate Buildings in the downmarket area of lower
Bath. She has come to the spa town in order to benefit from the nearby
public bath fed by a thermal spring which, thanks to a 1711 law, was free
of charge to the 'diseased and impotent poor'.[11] Wealthier invalids would
seek a cure in more luxurious private baths. Anne expresses amazement
at the cheerful resilience of her old friend in such trying circumstances,
and Mrs Smith explains that there was a time 'when her spirits had nearly
failed'. A cold caught on the journey to Bath led to 'severe and constant
pain' and reduced her to a helpless 'pitiable object'. But the kind care
of the landlady and her sister, Nurse Rooke, had returned her to the
enjoyment of life. This near-death experience had converted her from
her careless and dissipated ways: 'there are so many who forget to think
seriously till it is almost too late' (II.v).

Ideas of the dead restored to life in *Persuasion* had their source in the
story of Lazarus, from the gospel of St John. Lazarus is summoned by
Jesus from the tomb where he has been lying, wrapped in grave clothes,
for four days. This story must have held a special significance for the
Austen girls since it also featured the sisters of Lazarus – Martha and
Mary – and the reference must always have brought to mind their own
dearest friends Martha and Mary Lloyd. The sisters had their own story
of miraculous recovery, and would always bear the scars. Their family had
been struck down by smallpox in the year of Jane's birth, 1775. The only
son had died, the middle daughter Eliza had been spared serious consequences, and Martha and Mary's looks had been permanently damaged
by pitting. In the Bible, it is stated that Jesus knows and loves Lazarus and
his sisters, and tells Martha: 'Thy brother shall rise again.' This miracle
is key to the narrative of the New Testament, since it prefigures in a material way the role of Jesus as the spiritual saviour of mankind and leads
directly to his arrest and trial.

Any such reveries relating to Henry's escape and the themes of the

new work were to be interrupted by a communication from an unexpected and most unwelcome quarter. The Prince Regent's librarian, James
Stanier Clarke, invited Jane to view the royal book collection with many
complimentary flourishes. The Prince was apparently an ardent admirer
of the novels, kept a set in each of his residences, and had been made
aware of her presence in town by one of the physicians attending Henry.
It was Caroline Austen who remembered this connection, when rem-
iniscing fifty years later, having heard all about it at Chawton Cottage
on Aunt Cassandra's return. She couldn't recall the name of the doctor,
but the fact that Henry's illness had led to a royal salute of Jane's genius
strengthens the likelihood that the go-between was Dr Matthew Baillie,
personal physician to the King. Dr Baillie would have taken an interest in
literary ladies, being the brother of one of the most famous in the land,
the playwright and poet Joanna Baillie.

Jane must initially have been stricken by this invitation from on high.
Not only did she shrink from being fêted as an author but, as she had
categorically stated to Martha, she shared the widespread view that the
Regent was a disgrace to the nation. This view was constantly broadcast in
satirical prints, none so powerful as James Gillray's 'A Voluptuary under
the Horrors of Digestion'. Although first published in 1792, time had
only brought the reality closer to the caricature. In Gillray's image Prince
George sprawls at the dinner table, oppressed by his vast stomach. The
print drew attention to the health consequences of the Prince's legendary
self-indulgence. One small pot in the background is labelled 'For the
Piles', while another carries the tag 'For a Stinking Breath'. His financial
incontinence is highlighted. Under an overflowing chamber pot is a long
list of unpaid grocers' bills. In the foreground, on the floor, a dice box and
other items refer to his penchant for gambling, betting, and neglecting
'debts of honour' to friends. Through the window can be seen the facade
of Carlton House, his luxurious town house. Jane disliked the Prince and
did not think a visit to his residence would agree with her – but Carlton
House was to be her destination.

James Gillray, *A Voluptuary under the Horrors of Digestion*, 1792.
© The Trustees of the British Museum.

Jane probably felt she owed Henry something for his constant exertions
on her behalf over the past five years. She may have hoped that what Caroline retrospectively described as her 'little gleam of Court favour' might
be diverted onto him.[12] Jane knew about the unpaid debt of £6,000 owed
to Austen & Co. by the Prince Regent's former favourite and creditor, the
Earl of Moira. There was a possibility that the spendthrift Prince might
scatter some bank bills in their direction, and justice would be served.
After *Pride and Prejudice* her nephew James Edward Austen had written
a teasing poem suggesting the Prince would inevitably reward her work,
once it came to his notice, by making her 'a countess at least' and in due
course, his second wife.[13] On 13 November Jane dutifully turned up to
meet the Reverend Clarke for a tour of the library and some of the other
apartments.

Carlton House no longer exists. After years of expensive renovation and redecorating, it was torn down to clear the way for the Prince's latest scheme, the creation of Regent's Street. But it is possible to reconstruct Jane's route, from Pall Mall to the north entrance beneath a Corinthian portico designed by Henry Holland, and into the large echoing hall, bordered by tall columns and classical statues. Servants passed hither and thither in their livery of dark blue trimmed with gold lace. Mr Clarke would have led her through the octagonal vestibule to the grand staircase. The library was located downstairs in the east wing of the basement, and the tour may therefore not have included the state apartments. But the chambers below were astonishing enough. Jane and her guide passed through a forest of marble columns in the blue, pink and gold vestibule, and turned left into the library, well-lit on the garden side by five large windows, furnished with Gothic oak book cases, busts and figurines, the cornices housing clever spring rollers devised to display historical maps. They probably ventured beyond the library to the dazzling Golden Drawing Room – the theme throughout Carlton House was 'gold upon gold' – and then to the palatial expanse of the Gothic Dining Room, with its travesty of cathedral ornament. Jane may also have been shown the other wing, featuring *another* spacious dining room and a theatrical Gothic conservatory, the tracery of the iron-cast fan vaulting infilled with coloured glass to create a mysterious lighting effect.

It is not known what literary rarities Jane was shown in the library, but she was sure to have been treated to many choice anecdotes by the confiding Mr Clarke, and in the course of their conversation he also let drop the bombshell that she would be 'at liberty to dedicate any future work' to the Prince. She went away reeling at the prospect of *Emma* being subjoined with the Regent and his debaucheries in the minds of the reading public. There was a quick, anxious consultation with Henry and Cassandra, and she wrote to Clarke to ask whether she had understood rightly, and it was 'incumbent' on her to inscribe 'the work now in the press, to H. R. H.' They no doubt helped her frame the question with appropriate tact: 'I should be equally concerned to appear either presumptuous or ungrateful'. Clarke in reply assured her that while it was certainly not 'incumbent' on her, future work might be dedicated to His Royal Highness 'without any more trouble or solicitation on your part'. He restated that the Prince had 'read & admired all your publications', and, rather presumptuously, added that a good topic for a future novel might be a clergyman much like himself: 'Fond of, & entirely engaged in literature – no man's enemy but his own'.[14] Jane could curl her lip contemptuously just as well as Captain Frederick Wentworth. She submitted to the dedication, but trusted that Martha in particular was 'thoroughly convinced of my being influenced now by nothing but the most mercenary motives'; certainly not by idolatry of rank.[15]

At least royal patronage might serve to hasten the publication of *Emma*. She wrote to Murray mentioning the Prince Regent, and Henry also wrote to the printer Roworth complaining about the delays. The proof sheets began to arrive at Hans Place before the end of November and Jane set to work checking and correcting them. By this time Cassandra had returned to Chawton and been replaced by Fanny Knight as assistant nurse. Henry was still weak and for a time only ventured onto the garden balcony or to sit in the greenhouse, and then paid short visits to the Tilsons (Mrs Tilson was also slowly recovering) and the Malings in Hans Place. Mr Haden, the diligent apothecary, checked his progress frequently, and gradually professional visits merged into social calls. Mr Haden was discovered to have other merits: a cultivated and enquiring mind, a sense of fun, and admirable musicianship. Fanny was taking the opportunity of an extended stay in London to advance her studies as a harpist, and musical evenings became an almost daily occurrence with Mr Haden and a choice selection of Henry's closest friends: Mr Tilson, Mr Seymour, Mr Barlow, and Mr Phillips, all of them connected with the bank. Henry was now 'so well' that Jane couldn't think why he wasn't 'perfectly well'.[16]

It was thought advisable for him to pay a short visit to the country house of his friend Mr Gordon at Hanwell, for a change of air. There was no mention of Harriet Moore, his former 'Hanwell favourite'. That particular danger seemed to have passed. But another danger was looming. Henry's absence from town from Tuesday 28 November to Friday 1 December seems to have been taken not only on the advice of his doctor but also, according to a hint from Jane's letter, on the advice of his bank associates. The letter Jane sent to Cassandra on 29 November was destroyed, presumably because it was too explicit about money matters. Her next letter, on 2 December, begins: 'Henry came back yesterday, & might have returned the day before if he had known as much in time. I had the pleasure of hearing from Mr T. on Wednesday night that Mr Seymour thought there was not the least occasion for his absenting himself any longer.'

November the 28th was the date on which the Alton bank failed. Anticipating problems, Henry had abruptly severed his ties with Gray and Vincent in Alton three weeks earlier. The dissolution of the partnership was announced in the *London Gazette* on 8 November. Three surviving £1 notes, all issued on 11 October by Austen, Gray & Vincent at Alton, may be taken to indicate that bankruptcy was looming. Low-denomination banknotes were often used in the payment of labourers' wages, and when a bank failed it was the practice to pay off creditors holding £1 notes first, as they could least bear the loss. But a cluster of unredeemed £1 notes suggests instead the efforts of local tradesmen to keep a floundering country bank afloat by showing confidence and boosting its reserves. On 24 November Henry had written to Edward regarding the grave situation, and read the letter to Jane before sending it. She commented to Cassandra, 'I wonder that with such business to worry him he can be getting better.' He was putting off his receivership business in Oxford, hoping to attend to it before Christmas. On 25 November, Maunde and Tilson went to Alton to notify Gray and Vincent that future transactions would not be honoured by the London bank without an immediate payment of £1,700–£2,000. On the 26th, Gray conferred with his brother Frederick. On the 27th, Austen & Co. ended their dealings with the Alton bank, cutting off its access to the London money market, and it crashed the following day, with just 16 shillings left in the till.[17]

Henry was not personally liable for the debts of Edward Gray and his uncle, William Vincent, the remaining partner at the Alton bank. But his withdrawal from the partnership was so recent that it must have seemed advisable to leave town in order to play down the association and reduce the risk of a run on the London bank. Unknown to him, the affairs of Lord Moira were also reaching crisis point. Charles James, Moira's man of business, wrote to another agent that 'an éclat' was approaching 'which might hurt many well disposed persons', and 'Austen' was mentioned as one of the billholders likely to suffer the consequences.[18] This correspondence suggests that Major James retained a genuine concern for the welfare of his former army agency partner.

Jane, living at Hans Place, visiting Henrietta Street and consorting daily with Henry's colleagues, understood the difficulties, insofar as they could then be seen. It seemed for the present at least that disaster had been averted, and she was far too happy about the progress of *Emma* and her beloved brother's return to health to be downcast. Her letter to Cassandra on 2 December, describing his 'gala' homecoming, is itself a 'gala' composition, with brilliant flights of fancy reminiscent of the nonsense in missives from her youth and early visits to London. Cassandra seems to have been alarmed by previous hints about Fanny's enjoyment of Mr Haden's company:

> ...you seem to be under a mistake as to Mr H. – You call him an apothecary; he is no apothecary, he has never been an apothecary, there is not an apothecary in this neighbourhood – the only inconvenience of the situation perhaps, but so it is – we have not a medical man within reach – he is a Haden, nothing but a Haden, a sort of wonderful nondescript creature on two legs, something between a Man & an Angel – but without the least spice of an Apothecary. – He is perhaps the only person *not* an Apothecary hereabouts.

Jane herself felt joyously rejuvenated. Like Anne Elliot 'hoping that she was to be blessed with a second spring', if not of youth and beauty then, like Henry, of spirits and physical well-being (II.i). She was revelling in the curious onset of spring in early winter: 'I am sorry my mother has been suffering, & am afraid this exquisite weather is too good to agree with her. – I enjoy it all over me, from top to toe, from right to left, longitudinally, perpendicularly, diagonally...'[19] These passages, put together, have given rise to the idea that Jane may have been infatuated with Mr Haden. There is no doubt that she thoroughly enjoyed his company. But the language of the letter gives the clue to his greatest claim to adoration. He had helped to save Henry and was halfway to being an angel. He deserved everything: daily dinners, Fanny, Jane herself if he wanted her, the keys to the kingdom of heaven. Their little coterie, with its music and laughter and earnest private conversations in corners, had something of the delicious intimacy remembered from the distant play-acting times of midwinter.

Through December, Jane's work continued. A regular routine of comings and goings was established at Hans Place. Printers' boys brought proof sheets from Mr Roworth and took them away to Mr Murray. Jane parcelled up dirty linen to send to Chawton for cleaning (either the provision for washing clothes in London was too expensive or unsatisfactory) and had clean linen sent back. Eventually, with reluctant quill she applied herself to the task of the wording on the title page: 'Dedicated by Permission to HRH The Prince Regent'. The abruptness verged on sedition. Emollient Mr Murray suggested something more appropriate, 'royal highness' appearing three times over:

TO HIS ROYAL HIGHNESS THE PRINCE REGENT,
THIS WORK IS, BY HIS ROYAL HIGHNESS'S PERMISSION,
MOST RESPECTFULLY DEDICATED,
BY HIS ROYAL HIGHNESS'S
DUTIFUL AND OBEDIENT HUMBLE SERVANT,
THE AUTHOR

Advertisements for the new novel began to appear, and in this instance as well, there was obeisance to the powers that be. Instead of *Emma* being first announced, as her previous novels had been, in the *Morning Chronicle*, the daily of the Whig opposition, the novel was initially advertised in the government-subsidised *Morning Post* on 2 December.

Jane had also been forced unwillingly to pay for a handsome presentation set of *Emma*, bound in red morocco with gold lettering, to be sent to the cormorant Prince. The eleven other complimentary copies were simply covered in board, all destined for members of the family apart from one for the erstwhile Lady Boringdon. On 29 November 1815 her husband John Parker (Baron Boringdon) became Viscount Boringdon and 1st Earl of Morley, and Frances Parker was now Countess of Morley. The singularity of this gift to a member of the aristocracy has attracted comment in recent years, but not a great deal of illumination. Parker's business connection to Henry Austen has been established, and we know that society gossip had attributed Jane's first two novels to the Countess, that Frances was much amused when an acquaintance declared Mr Darcy was as like Lord Boringdon 'as two peas', and that Jane referred harshly to his first wife, now Lady Augusta Paget, whom he had divorced for adultery.[20]

The Earl of Morley, in these years, tended to vote with the Tory government in the House of Lords, mainly due to an old friendship with the liberal Tory George Canning. He may have owed his earldom in 1815 to this loyalty to the ministry. But he also had close friends among the Whigs, and would move steadily to the left as he aged, having always been a strong supporter of parliamentary reform. The Countess knew the leading lights at the liberal *Edinburgh Review*: Henry Brougham, Sydney Smith, Lord John Russell. Sir George Cornewall Lewis, who became the journal's editor, married the Earl's niece. Morley's ambiguous political position was probably of some service to the Austens, brother and sister, aiding their access to the Tory political and cultural elite, including John Murray. And his wife's circle surely explains the otherwise inexplicable presence of the *Edinburgh Review*'s current editor among those who gave 'Opinions' of *Emma*, collected by Jane. Shamefully the *Edinburgh* did not review any of Jane Austen's works in her lifetime, but Francis Jeffrey 'was kept up' by *Emma* 'for four nights'. The Countess herself professed to be 'delighted' by it, and thanked Jane for the gift copy in a brief message. But to her sister-in-law, Theresa Villiers, she confided that her interest quickly flagged.[21] Frances Parker was self-confident and clever, and like Emma Woodhouse loved charades and riddles. But perhaps she preferred to think of herself as an Elizabeth Bennet, rising socially through force of personality. She was the daughter of a surgeon who had managed to marry far above her station.

Jane stayed on in London in the hope of carrying the printed volumes of *Emma* back to Chawton. Disappointed, she left Hans Place on her forty-first birthday. As she drew away, did she gaze through the 'misty glasses' of the carriage at the neighbourhood which, like Uppercross in Anne Elliot's history, 'stood the record of many sensations of pain, once severe, but now softened' (II.i). She felt changed. She had been forced to take charge, make vital decisions, and draw on resources she never knew she had. Not only had she been pushed to the fore by the family emergency, but she had also successfully handled business face to face with her publisher instead of through a male intermediary.

She returned to Chawton to discover that their friend, Mary Benn, was in the last stages of a fatal illness. On 3 January 1816 she was buried, aged forty-six, and Jane in her heart dedicated *Emma* to her. It had finally been published on 23 December. She wrote a note to Catherine Ann Prowting, a member of the local reading society and another middle-aged spinster, enclosed with her new novel. 'Had our poor friend lived these volumes would have been at her service,' Jane wrote, 'keep them as long as you like, as they are not wanted at home'.[22]

By this time, rumours of irregularities around the closure of the Alton bank were beginning to leak out and the damage to Austen & Co. in Henrietta Street was apparent. Gray was formally declared bankrupt on

21 December. He owed the London bank £6,500 for notes and cash bal-
ances, and £3,200 for other transactions. More gradually it would emerge
that immediately following the meeting with Maunde and Tilson he had
drained the Alton bank of all its remaining liquid assets over the two
days before the crash by transferring funds to friends and family. On 27
November Gray had paid out sums of £140 and £114 to two uncles and
cashed cheques for his brother totalling £342, including one for £60.10s
on behalf of Michael Rivers a local landowner who had already default-
ed on a bank loan of £1,500. On Christmas Day, Austen & Co. issued
an Extent-in-Aid in an attempt to reclaim the money from Rivers, and
the same day Edward shored up Henry's increasingly precarious position
with a promissory note for £10,325. It eventually turned out that Gray's
uncle, William Vincent, had been still more devious. An investigation
into his Newbury bank revealed that it had been insolvent for two years
before it stopped transactions, and that the theft of £20,000 from its
premises was likely to have been an inside job.[23]

There is a possibility that Jane returned to London in the first half of
January and was party to the increasing sense of panic. Her main purpose
would have been to look over the proofs of the new edition of *Mansfield
Park*. It was advertised by Murray in the *Morning Post* and appeared on 19
February. *Emma* had been marketed at the premium price of one guinea
for a three-volume set, with 2,000 copies issued. The second edition of
Mansfield Park cost three shillings less: 18 shillings, the average price for
a three-volume novel at the time, in a small edition of 750 copies. On
4 May Walter Scott's third novel, *The Antiquary*, was published. It had
been originally intended to sell the book at a guinea, but the price was
raised to an unprecedented 24 shillings because his publisher Constable judged that 'the additional profit would be considerable, and we do
not think one dozen less of the book would be sold'. So it proved, with
6,000 copies sold in three weeks, and the author gaining half-profits of
£1,682.[24] Jane meanwhile fretfully awaited her own initial sales figures,
not revealed until October.

If Jane did stay in London in January, it would have been for the last time. From 17 January Henry let the house furnished to a Mr James Stephens or Stevens, and apparently mortgaged the lease. He was anxious to repay Edward for the December loan of £10,325, and by the start of March had reduced the outstanding debt to £4,911.3s.9d. with instalments of £1,000 or more. Surprisingly, he had approved £2,900 of personal loans in December, and between January and mid-March an additional £7,000. Could this have been an attempt to give the appearance of buoyancy? He visited Oxford to fulfil his long delayed receivership duties, and also went into Kent for at least two visits to Godmersham, which must now have involved conferences with Edward regarding damage limitation. James Tilson was similarly struggling and mortgaged the lease of No. 26 Hans Place to his affluent brother General Chowne as security for a £1,100 debt.[25]

Total failure was closing in on Henry. And yet, at some point early in 1816 he finally took the time to go to the office of Richard Crosby and pay £10 to buy back the manuscript that would become *Northanger Abbey*. It was treasure salvaged from the wreckage. Even such a small amount of ready money must have been welcome to Crosby, who was on the point of bankruptcy himself and went under on 2 March. According to Austen family tradition, the transaction was a moment of triumphant revenge. 'When the bargain was concluded and the money paid, but not till then, the negotiator had the satisfaction of informing him that the work which had been so lightly esteemed was by the author of *Pride and Prejudice*.'[26]

Henry probably presented Jane with her long-lost novel at the beginning of March on one of two flying visits to Chawton, to consult with Frank at the Great House. In a letter of 13 March Jane told her niece Caroline there had been 'a great deal of fun lately with post-chaises stopping at the door', including unexpected appearances by 'your Uncle Henry & Mr Tilson' and 'your Uncle Henry & Mr Seymour'. Jane ended the letter, 'Take notice, that it was the same Uncle Henry each time'.[27] But he was not the same Uncle Henry.

On 15 March the Crown issued Extents-in-Chief arising from the

sum of £22,743.8s.10d owing to His Majesty from the Oxfordshire receivership. The following day the bank stopped payments and its name
appeared among the list of bankruptcies in the *London Gazette*, 'Austin
[*sic*], Maunde, and Co.' Henry's financial career was over. A week later
his partner at the Petersfield and Hythe country banks, William Stevens
Louch, was declared bankrupt, and George Goodwin's Buxton and High
Peak Bank also went bust, owing Henry's firm £271.[28]

Henry attended a statutory meeting before the Commissioners of
Bankruptcy on 19 March. Twelve jurors were appointed to investigate
and in the meantime he and his partners faced the possibility of imprisonment. The next step would be for a committee of creditors to realise
his assets and possessions. Failure to disclose assets could result in the
death penalty. All the goods and furnishings at Henrietta Street and Hans
Place were sold. In the inventory were the objects that had become familiar to Jane during her London visits: the Kidderminster carpet and
bedside rugs on the floor of the bedroom where she slept, the needlework
counterpane on the bed, the small hanging mirror and leather-topped
mahogany writing desk with drawer, the japanned tray-top dressing table
and blue and white washing basin and ewer, even down to soap cups,
white carafe, tumbler and brush tray. There was the mahogany *bureau
secretaire* in Henry's office on which she had written parts of *Emma* and
Persuasion. In the dining room and drawing room were the fixtures of
their social gatherings, the blue and white dinner set, and board games
housed in a sofa table, the gilt-framed chimney glass and bronze cupid
lamp stands, the French curtains made of superfine chintz cotton. In the
cellar were dozens of bottles of valuable wine, from the trade established
at the time of the Treaty of Amiens in 1803.[29]

Caroline Austen would recall this 'most serious misfortune' as 'an
entire surprise at our house and as little foreseen I believe by the rest
of the family'.[30] In fact it had been building for many months, but the
bankruptcy was inevitably a shock for Henry's relations. The bank had
been part of the weave of everyday life for all of them; most of them held

deposits there. The pressure on those who had stood surety for his post as receiver general was to be acute. Thomas Hampson, James Leigh-Perrot, and Edward Knight waited to know the extent of the debt to the Crown.

Jane, having lived so much with Henry in London, especially in the past year, could imagine more fully than the others the ramifications of the disaster not only for him but for his partners and employees and their families. She was familiar with literary bankruptcies. Not only had Frances Burney dramatised the plight of Mr Tyrold, visited in Winchester jail by his swooning daughter Camilla, but even more sensationally in *Cecilia*, an 'execution', a forced seizure of assets takes place in the home of the profligate Harrells and is followed by a suicide in the pleasure gardens at Vauxhall. For those involved in the collapse of Austen & Co. there would be real hardship.

Yet after all, no one had died and they had inner resources. Jane fully subscribed to the notion that laughter is the best medicine and may have attempted to bring cheer by taking out *Volume the Second* to read the relevant passages in *Love and Friendship*. Augustus and Sophia 'blush at the idea of repaying their debts', and Augustus is consequently carted off to Newgate Prison. The heroines are faced with the bailiffs: 'To complete such unparalleled barbarity we were informed that an execution in the house would shortly take place. Ah! What could we do but what we did! We sighed and fainted on the sofa.' Unlike Mrs Beverley in Moore's play *The Gamester*, Sophia declines to visit her incarcerated husband, 'my feelings are sufficiently shocked by the *recital* of his distress, but to behold it will overpower my sensibility'.[31]

Two weeks after the bank stoppage, Jane exerted herself. On Monday 1 April she undertook to write two important letters concerning her writing career: one to James Stanier Clarke, the other to John Murray. Judging by the contents, the date at the head of each letter was significant. In England, it was a feature of April Fool's Day that pranks must be played before twelve noon. Jane customarily dealt with her correspondence in the morning.

Clarke seemed to be a kind man, who genuinely appreciated her work and possessed some literary talent himself. However, he had about him enough of the toadying and self-important Mr Collins to make him before long a stock figure of ridicule among the Austens. In answer to his repeated suggestion that she write a fictionalised account of his own life, she had tried self-deprecation. Regarding *Emma* she confided, 'I am very strongly haunted by the idea that to those readers who have preferred P&P. it will appear inferior in wit, & to those who have preferred MP. very inferior in good sense', and insisted that she simply wasn't qualified to write the story of an erudite clergyman, being 'the most unlearned, & uninformed female who ever dared to be an authoress'.[32] She let off steam by writing a *Plan of a Novel* composed in accordance with all the most irritating 'hints from various quarters', in which the thoughts of Mr Clarke took pride of place.

Her satirical plot outline featured many of the clichés of the market-able novel of the day: a perfect heroine, effortlessly accomplished and highly virtuous, living in idyllic retirement with her father, long inset narratives relating past events, a villainous predator, adventures to the furthest reaches of the globe, extremes of good and bad character, scenes of dreadful pathos, and an improbable resolution. Clarke's pompous self-portrait as a chaplain with 'a literary turn' is quoted virtually word for word. He had asked her to illustrate 'what good would be done' if the burden of the 10 per cent tax levied on property-holders were lifted: a cu-rious request to the daughter of a parson. In the *Plan* he's transmogrified into the heroine's father, who eventually 'expires in a fine burst of literary enthusiasm, intermingled with invectives against holders of tithes'.

On 27 March Clarke had renewed their correspondence, tardily conveying the thanks of the Prince Regent for the 'handsome copy' of *Emma*, and now urging her to write a novel about the Saxe-Coburg dy-nasty, in order to capitalise on the marriage of Princess Charlotte, the Regent's only child, to Prince Leopold of Coburg. This time she broadly hinted at her distaste, firmly rejecting the role of novelist-courtier while commiserating with his lot as a royal servant. He was 'very, very kind' to take an interest in her future compositions, but her life depended on being able to 'relax into laughing at myself or other people'. 'No' she concluded, 'I must keep to my own style & go on in my own way; and though I may never succeed again in that, I am convinced that I should totally fail in any other.' It was a declaration of authorial independence. She would never mix her art with the mercenary considerations of 'profit or popularity' that he proposed.

The fool disposed of she turned to the knave, Mr Murray. Jane was returning the latest edition of the *Quarterly Review*, featuring a long anonymous review of *Emma*, and wrote a covering letter thanking him for the loan. Since Murray published the *Quarterly* he had, as she must have surmised, commissioned the piece himself. The review was in-house, but it was certainly not a mere advertising puff. Murray had elicited it from no less a personage than Walter Scott: 'Have you any fancy to dash off an article on *Emma*? – it wants incident and romance & imagination – does it not – none of the author's other novels have been noticed & surely *Pride & Prejudice* merits high consideration.'[33] His casual dismissal of *Emma*, as Claire Tomalin has rightly said, 'consigns him to that circle of the Inferno reserved for disloyal publishers'.[34]

At the same time, there is cause to suspect that Murray was playing a double game. *Emma* had been published with some fanfare: the price, size of edition and dedication all declared it to be a serious contender. By sending it to his friend Scott, the premier novelist of the day, Murray seems to have been experimentally forcing Scott to acknowledge a challenger whose subtle style was an implicit criticism of his own. In the privacy of his journal, Scott ultimately admitted defeat after reading *Pride and Prejudice* a third time: 'The Big Bow-wow strain I can do myself like any now going, but the exquisite touch which renders ordinary commonplace things and characters interesting from the truth of the description and the sentiment is denied to me.'[35] But here, on the public platform of the *Quarterly Review*, his critical integrity was tested and failed. After devoting the bulk of the review to a standard comparison of the realist modern novel and the improbable old romance, Scott damned Austen's novel with faint praise. His opening gambit on *Emma* is that it 'has even less story than either of the preceding novels', and while he lauds the 'force and precision' of the author's characterisations and the 'neatness and point' of her dialogue, the overall tenor is lukewarm at best. Curiously, many commentators have persisted in describing the review as positive. James Edward Austen-Leigh's discussion of it in his 1870 *Memoir of Jane Austen* shows that within the family it was regarded almost as a hatchet job. Sales had been good prior to the review, and demand then slackened. Murray's stock books show that only 150 copies were delivered to booksellers from April through to August.[36]

Jane returned the volume containing the review accompanied by a remark stiff with displeasure: 'The authoress of Emma has no reason I think to complain of her treatment in it – except in the total omission of Mansfield Park. – I cannot but be sorry that so clever a man as the reviewer of Emma should consider it as unworthy of being noticed.' Her work had been undermined with such finesse that attack could be taken for applause. Everyone knew that Scott was involved in the *Quarterly* and she could guess that the review, if not by him, was by a Scott partisan (the silly baronet in her latest novel would not be 'Sir Walter' for nothing). The note to Murray conveyed that she was not fool enough to be gratified by such a disingenuous offering. She signed off with allusion to 'the late sad event in Henrietta St' and a request that post be directed in future to Chawton.[37]

Although the review was galling, there was no denying that the reviewer was a clever man. He had penetration, and her mind dwelt on one of his reservations in particular. Modern novelists, he complained, too often coupled love with 'calculating prudence', at the expense of the 'romantic feelings' that might be excessive in the popular fiction of old, but which nevertheless could teach 'what is honourable, dignified, and disinterested'. The reviewer made an appeal for a revival of what is 'tenderest, noblest, best'. While Scott did not directly state that the author of *Pride and Prejudice* and *Emma* was guilty of promoting mercenary calculation, he did cite pertinently Elizabeth's discovery of her love for Mr Darcy after visiting Pemberley, at which point her 'prudence' begins to 'subdue her prejudice'. And talking of the conclusion of *Emma*, Scott refers to 'the facile affections of Harriet Smith ... transferred, like a bank bill by indorsation'.[38] This is the more cutting aspect of Scott's assessment of Austen: not that her fiction is at times minutely tedious, but that it lacks passion and has a cynical slant. The point is made lightly, but it could not be mistaken by her. She must have wondered whether Murray's apprehension of her as the 'banker's sister' had become the common talk of the *Quarterly* crowd.

Scott had thrown down the gauntlet. No romance in her work? She'd show him. The plan to write a full-scale three-volume satire on the worldly pretensions of a baronet and his unlikeable elder daughter, suggested by the working title 'The Elliots' and the elaborate mockery of the first chapter, was abandoned. Instead *Persuasion* became a pared-down two-volume study of enduring love and a second chance of happiness. Anne Elliot, 'had been forced into prudence in her youth, she learned romance as she grew older – the natural sequel of an unnatural beginning'. The novelist learns romance alongside her. A marriage between cousins or between brother and sister-in-law had proved a barrier to full-blooded passion in the previous two novels. It is averted in this one when Anne turns her back on the possibility of wedding her cousin and her father's heir, Mr William Elliot. She is momentarily seduced by the picture Lady Russell places before her, of becoming 'Lady Elliot' as her mother had been, and returning to her home, Kellynch Hall. But Anne will not preserve 'the noble line' and 'prevent the family fortune from being redistributed', as Lady Catherine insists *her* daughter Anne and Fitzwilliam Darcy must do. Like *Pride and Prejudice*, *Persuasion* features a disruptive exogamous union, this time without the shadow of a doubt over the motives of the heroine. Anne, in marrying Captain Wentworth, will forever 'pay the tax of quick alarm' which belongs to his precarious profession (II.xii).

Shakespeare's late romance *The Winter's Tale* has sometimes been discussed alongside *Persuasion*. Both feature rejected women who symbolically die, and are then regretted, recovered and revalued at their true worth. Both anticipate a restoration of spring, after the blight of winter. But there is a factor that decisively sets Jane Austen's novel apart from Shakespeare's tale of renewal and from the story of Lazarus in the New Testament. That difference is the role of risk in the narrative. Anne undergoes inner death because, at the persuasion of Lady Russell, she refuses to gamble on the success of a poor but aspiring naval officer. He has ability and self-confidence in his favour, but his progress will inevitably depend to a great degree on the vagaries of chance. She regains life and love by embracing risk. Admiral Croft and his wife provide the model for speculative happiness. They go out riding together in their new gig, confident that they will survive the spills that frequently occur, and Anne observes with interest and amusement Mrs Croft's cool interventions, 'giving the reins a better direction' or 'judiciously putting out her hand' to avert the danger of falling into a rut or running 'foul of a dung-cart' (I.x). Anne takes the drive as a good representation of the Crofts' shipboard habits. Women, like men, should not be reckless but should be willing to take the rough with the smooth. It is Mrs Croft, Captain Wentworth's sister, who voices the closest thing to the motto of the story: 'We none of us expect to be in calm waters all our days' (I.viii).

Given the circumstances, Jane's affirmation of faith in luck and providence appears remarkable. In February, poor Charles, patrolling in the Mediterranean Sea, had the ship under his command run aground by a local pilot and was forced to face a court martial. In March came Henry's bankruptcy. Banking resembled the seafaring life in its precariousness. Jane in her literary career could have chosen to take the safe and sensible path of selling the copyrights to her novels outright, but she had opted to share the speculative approach of her brothers, and was now to undergo comparable setbacks. Her first novel had been a reasonably successful wager, and in March 1816 she received her annual portion of profits from

Egerton for the second edition of *Sense and Sensibility*: £12.15s, which nearly offset her losses of £13.7s from the collapse of Austen & Co. But the second edition of *Mansfield Park* was to be a disaster. *Emma* sold 1,248 copies and gained her a profit of £221.6s.4d by October, but due to losses of £182.8s.3d on *Mansfield Park*, she only ever received from Murray £38 and 18 shillings in her lifetime, and for that she had to wait four months due to Murray's practice of post-dating payments. He may even have silently pocketed the extra penny that appears in his ledger, but not in her final reckoning of her earnings.[39]

If *Persuasion* can be taken as evidence, she did not repent having taken the route marked out by Henry. Frederick Wentworth began his naval career without the benefit of family fortune, like Frank and Charles Austen, but in his 'sanguine temper' he most closely resembles her banker brother at the outset of his career. He is 'lucky in his profession'; he spends freely. He is 'confident that he should soon be rich' (I.iv). And this confidence, 'powerful in its own warmth, and bewitching in the wit which often expressed it', enchants Anne, who is naturally more hesitant. When she finally weds him, after the eight-year separation that resulted from her 'over-anxious caution', it is because she is prepared to embrace risk.

The suggestion has been made that the most likely model for Captain Wentworth was Thomas Cochrane. Their careers are strikingly similar, 'too close to be mere coincidence' in Clive Caplan's opinion.[40] Frank Austen greatly admired Cochrane, writing to him years after that he deserved 'the warmest thanks' of his country. The Austens evidently believed his denial of wrongdoing in connection with the Stock Exchange Hoax of 1814, but Jane may have been intrigued by the revelation that he had an interest in financial speculation. Cochrane was a dashing, upwardly mobile naval officer, politically idealistic, and prepared to take chances on land as at sea.

Henry Austen was no courageous war hero. Furthermore, Jane probably noted in Henry the characteristic Anne Elliot observes in the slippery William Elliot: 'His value for rank and connexion she perceived to be greater than hers' (II.iv). But Henry also possessed those qualities which continue to attach Anne to Frederick Wentworth and which she most prizes: 'the frank, the open-hearted, the eager character ... Warmth and enthusiasm did captivate her still' (II.vi).

Persuasion has often been described as a novel in which Jane Austen, in her imagination, leaves behind the stultifying English class system founded on landed wealth and arranges for her heroine the liberation of life at sea. Anne tastes something of that freedom in the company of naval families in their temporary quarters at Lyme Regis, and there is a moment there when Anne and Henrietta stroll by the shore before breakfast when the sense of freedom seems tangible. They 'gloried in the sea; sympathized in the delight of the fresh-feeling breeze' (I.xii). Yet although the sea air brings renewed colour to Anne's cheeks, drawing the admiration of a stranger and consequently of her former lover, and although it is Anne's composure during the crisis at the Cobb that begins to persuade Wentworth of his mistake, it is not at the seaside that the reconciliation will take place. Instead, Jane Austen staged the renewal of their vows in a place she had long connected with the lowest kind of mercenary manoeuvring.

In *Northanger Abbey* the city of Bath had been aptly chosen as the scene of the heroine's first exposure to dissipation, hypocrisy, and greed. Anne Elliot is old enough to know what to expect, and dreads it. But what she actually experiences there is something very different: it is a rebirth, and the rediscovery of true happiness. The reunion with her old school-fellow prepares the way. Mrs Smith is a woman of the world and her years of profligacy have left her with a jaundiced view of human nature as well as a broken fortune. However, the restorative waters of Bath and the kindness of her attendants there make her thankful, generous and even reverent. As Anne makes her way from the Elliots' pretentious residence in the upper town to Mrs Smith's humble lodgings tucked away in a side road near the baths and the Pump Room, her ideas are similarly elevated: 'Prettier musings of high-wrought love and eternal constancy, could never have passed along the streets of Bath, than Anne was sporting with from Camden-place to Westgate buildings. It was almost enough to spread purification and perfume all the way' (II.ix).

The undercutting of the heroine's romantic notions by the narrator is comparable to the teasing remark which follows Elizabeth Bennet's musings on her compatibility with Mr Darcy after Lydia's elopement has apparently made their union impossible ('no such happy marriage could teach the admiring multitude what connubial felicity really was'; *P&P* III.viii).

Walter Scott would probably see such irony as typical, but in *Persuasion* it was self-directed. The author *herself* is engaged in the 'purification' and perfuming of Bath and permits deep feeling to speak in the final chapters of the novel. While in *Northanger Abbey* only the superficial frivolity of the spa town appears, *Persuasion* alludes to its sacred origins. Temples were raised over the endlessly gushing, hot mineral waters by the ancient Britons and then by the invading Romans. Bas-reliefs illustrating the seasons had been uncovered and put on display in the town in the 1790s. In 1809 a Roman altar dedicated to the goddess Sulis Minerva was found in the cistern of the Cross Baths, probably the one used by Mrs Smith for its tepid temperature and free admission.

The word 'spring' appears repeatedly in connection with the cycle of the seasons, during an autumnal walk from Uppercross when Anne inwardly philosophises on the loss of the springtime of her life, and in Lady Russell's observation that she seems to be enjoying 'a second spring of youth and beauty' (II.i; I.x). The narrator's use of the word in the final paragraph of the novel is a clear reference to the revivifying waters of Bath. Mrs Smith's 'spring of felicity was in the glow of her spirits, as her friend Anne's was in the warmth of her heart'. Ultimately, in the novel, Bath is at least partially cleansed of its association with fashion and commerce. Its origin in those mysterious forces of nature, which are beyond calculation and even commodification, is affirmed.

Jane had cause to reflect on such mysteries when she visited Cheltenham

Spa in May, and took the waters for the persistent pains in her back. Her ailment evidently gave her sister and mother concern enough to warrant drawing on their reduced funds. Cheltenham was smaller and could be managed with less expense than Bath. Eliza had been a devotee, as had Warren Hastings, who continued to live nearby at Daylesford. Every day Jane submitted to the ritual morning visit to the Pump Room to drink a pint or two of the vile-tasting saline well water. We don't know if her treatment included immersion, but she had been happy to try sea-dipping at Lyme Regis as a young woman. Jane herself was probably convinced that her ill health and low spirits were down to the relentlessly dismal rainy weather of the summer of 1816, so different from the summer of 1814 recalled in *Persuasion*.

Through a wet July, Jane pushed herself to complete the story. On 18 July she put the last touches on a denouement that owed something to the courtship farces the Austen children had enjoyed presenting at Steventon, and wrote the word at the end of the manuscript '*Finis*'. Admiral Croft tricks Anne into his house, on the pretext of asking her to pay a call on his wife, and then contrives to leave her alone with Captain Wentworth. After she assures him that she has not accepted a proposal from Mr Elliot, the reconciliation takes place almost without words: 'It was a silent, but a very powerful dialogue; – on his side, supplication, on her's acceptance. – Still, a little nearer – and a hand taken and pressed – and "Anne, my own dear Anne!" burst forth in the fullness of exquisite feeling – and all suspense & indecision were over. – They were re-united.'

Would it satisfy the sceptical reviewer from the *Quarterly*? No, she had to admit it would not. She was skimming over the moment of declaration, the culmination of the love story, as she had done in the past. In a final burst of effort, Jane rewrote the crucial chapters, providing Anne with an opportunity to declare her enduring love while debating with Captain Harwood over the relative strength of attachment in men and women. Wentworth reciprocally gives eloquent expression to the intensity of his feelings in letter form, having overheard the debate. It felt like a dangerous act of exposure: perhaps so much so, that she could not envisage sending it to a publisher. Although she was to hide it away in her lifetime, she let this second version stand. Again she had come down on the side of risk.

Benjamin West, *Christ Rejected*, 1814. © Pennsylvania Academy of the Fine Arts.

CHAPTER 9

'THE CHOICEST GIFT OF HEAVEN': *SANDITON* AND *WINCHESTER RACES* (1816–1817)

Decades after the event, Caroline Austen represented Henry's situation in the spring of 1816 in words borrowed from the poignant description of Adam expelled from Eden in Milton's *Paradise Lost*: 'he saw the world before him, to begin again'. Caroline was then a girl of ten living at Steventon Rectory with her parents James Austen and Mary Lloyd Austen. In the early 1870s she remembered being impressed by her Uncle Henry's dauntless good cheer. About a fortnight after the failure of the London bank, he turned up at Steventon '*apparently*, for truly it could *not* have been, in unbroken spirits'. She thought that it must have been around this time 'that I got to like him so very much, as I remember but little of him previously'. Henry's charm would never entirely cease to work its magic. The family at the rectory had marvelled at the way he turned his thoughts to the future 'with all the energy of a sanguine elastic nature'.[1]

Jane explored this quality of resilience in *Persuasion* through the eyes of Anne Elliot, as she wonders at the unbroken spirits of her former school friend Mrs Smith, now a penniless cripple:

> How could it be? – She watched – observed – reflected – and finally de-termined that this was not a case of fortitude or of resignation only. – A

submissive spirit might be patient, a strong understanding would supply resolution, but here was something more; here was that elasticity of mind, that disposition to be comforted, that power of turning readily from evil to good, and of finding employment which carried her out of herself, which was from Nature alone. It was the choicest gift of Heaven; and Anne viewed her friend as one of those instances in which, by a merciful appointment, it seems designed to counter-balance almost every other want. (II.v)

'Elasticity' was a modern word, a coinage of the scientific revolution in the late seventeenth century used to describe material substances which could spontaneously resume their normal shape after having been contracted by an external force. It only began to be applied figuratively to people at the end of the eighteenth century, and was still a striking novelty when, in *Northanger Abbey*, General Tilney admired the 'elasticity' of Catherine's walk with ingratiating gallantry. In *Persuasion*, the idea of 'elasticity of mind' is presented with heartfelt seriousness, and even a sense of religious awe.

Henry dealt with the technicalities of bankruptcy with pragmatic dispatch. At the first statutory meeting on 19 March, he promised on oath to make full disclosure of his estate within forty-two days or suffer the penalty. By 2 April the necessary information had been submitted and Henry's creditors selected from among themselves Joseph Silver and Richard Taylor, army clothiers of Charlotte Street in Bloomsbury, to take over, administer and realise his assets. On 27 April 1816 he attended the last of a series of meetings with the creditors at the London Guildhall. He would be permitted to keep just 3 per cent of the value of his remaining assets, up to a limit of £200. The exact figures and details involved will never be known, as the case file for the bankruptcy has not survived. On a rough balance sheet Henry had estimated his total debts at £58,000 and his assets at £52,000; not a wide disparity. However, his former partners at the country banks had gone bust owing substantial amounts to the London bank: debts totalled £33,000 in outstanding bills and promissory notes, some even going back as far as 1805. He had also underestimated receipts due to the Crown from the tax-collecting role in Oxfordshire.[2]

On 1 May the extent of his debt to the Crown was made known: £44,000. This included receipts for 1814 of £30,600, in addition to £13,600 of the current year's collection. Two of the sureties – Edward Knight and James Leigh-Perrot – were now required to pay £21,000 each in instalments with immediate effect until 18 March the following year. The third guarantor, Thomas Hampson, escaped his responsibilities; how is unknown. In modern-day terms, which can only be very approximate, the debt amounted to at least £3 million.

There were complexities still to be unravelled, but the scale of the damage was now apparent to the Austens. Edward had probably lost money on account at the bank; he opened a new account at Goslings' Bank. He would weather this setback and the blow of the receivership surety, although the timing was bad. The long-running threat posed by the Baverstock lawsuit to his Hampshire properties appeared more dangerous than ever in 1816. The Leigh-Perrots were furious with Henry and irritated by the Austen family's loyalty to him. There was now a question mark over their long-standing intention to leave their estate to James Austen. James and Frank were both liable as guarantors of Henry's militia agency, and this setback came at a time when James's health was suffering and his income was reduced by the failure of a tenant farmer, while Frank was supporting his wife and six children on half pay. It has been assumed that Charles was too hard-up to have invested or deposited anything in the bank, but he referred in his diary on 19 May 1816 to 'the failure of my brother's house which perhaps may have left me with a penny'.[3]

Henry and Frank could no longer afford to contribute to the support of the household at Chawton Cottage and Mrs Austen lost £100 of a fairly meagre annual income. It is probable that she and Cassandra held accounts at Henrietta Street, as Jane did. Just a few weeks after the failure of Henry's bank, old Mrs Austen, as business-like as ever at seventy-six, opened a new deposit account at Hoare's Bank. Cassandra and Jane were to open accounts there in July. Hoare's, cautious and dependable since the seventeenth century, would not go under.

The temptation has been strong among those commentating on this episode in the Austen family history to blame the bank failure on Henry's shortcomings as a man of business. There had undoubtedly been oversights and a degree of irresponsibility; personal loans to the highborn were an obvious weakness. However, Caroline Austen voiced the opinion of the family that he was not personally extravagant; he had 'been living for some years past at considerable expense, but not more than might become the head of a flourishing bank'.[4] Mentions in Jane's surviving letters show that he was diligent. The bank had been strong enough to survive more than one nationwide wave of bankruptcy, but after the war it was damaged, like others, by abrupt structural changes in government finance, fluctuating prices, uncertainty over whether or how the convertibility of banknotes would be restored, and a bewildering array of new financial instruments. Henry's illness in the decisive autumn of 1815 probably played a part in the unravelling of his business affairs. He had suffered from that eventuality he was by nature most incapable of anticipating: bad luck.

In retrospect it seems clear that the acquisition of the post of receiver general was a disaster in the making. Several years later, Henry Austen's name was to crop up during a Parliamentary Select Committee inquiry into the issuing of Extents-in-Aid in bankruptcy proceedings. The question was asked, whether when he was appointed to the receivership it was ascertained that he had sufficient assets to safeguard the interests of his private bank customers, since in cases of insolvency precedence was given to debts to the Crown.[5] The answer was that it had never been a consideration. Eventually the directors of country banks were barred from becoming receivers general, although they continued to act as deputies.

Henry Austen, and his former partners at Henrietta Street, Henry Maunde and James Tilson, were officially discharged from bankruptcy on 6 June 1816, having surrendered all their assets and answered the queries of the court satisfactorily. There were to be very different outcomes for the three men.

By September Henry Maunde was dead, a likely suicide. The obituary column of the *Gentleman's Magazine* for November 1816 records simply 'H. Maunde, esq. late of Henrietta-street, Covent-garden, banker.' The Maunde family lost homes in the Strand and Euston Road and the expectation of a legacy. As late as 1828 Maunde's sister Mrs Anne Jane Skrine wrote to Edward complaining bitterly of Henry's 'defalcation' and 'country speculations' and claiming that money belonging to her family, outside the bankruptcy losses, had been retained by the Austens.[6]

James Tilson had returned to the world of finance after a previous bankruptcy and was to do so again. Relations and friends came to the aid of his sizeable family. Soon his brother John-Henry, formerly of the Oxfordshire Militia, had taken Henry Austen's place as receiver general for the county with James as his deputy. There was no bad blood between the Tilsons and the Austens. The years of neighbourly intimacy were to result in a marriage, thanks to introductions made by Henry, between one of James Tilson's daughters and the Reverend John-Thomas Austen, a second cousin from the Kentish branch of the family.[7] It can be mentioned as an aside that, like Tilson, two of Henry's country bank partners – William Stevens Louch and Edward William Gray – would rebuild their lives and eventually thrive. Louch ended his long life as an art collector in London and Gray became the mayor of Newbury. However, neither Louch nor Gray were to marry, and no mention was made of James Tilson in a family memoir by his nephew. The stigma of bankruptcy could not be erased entirely.

Henry received his Certificate of Discharge from bankruptcy on 8 June 1816. In Lisbon, kind-hearted Charles Austen wrote in his diary, 'This is poor Henry's birthday the most unhappy to him probably of any of the forty-five he has passed. Why should I record the sad reflections this anniversary has filled my mind with.'[8] Mercifully, Charles himself had been fully acquitted at a court martial in April for the sinking of the inaptly named HMS Phoenix. He passed the hours rereading *Emma* for a third time while anticipating a reunion with his family in the summer. The Austens were clannish, and his sympathy for Henry was shared among the siblings. He would not be handed a bailout, as James Tilson had been. It would be inappropriate in any case, since he was a single man without children, restored to health. But the Austen family would offer what support they could, and Henry spent much of the next few months alternately at Godmersham, Steventon and Chawton Cottage.

At Godmersham in late June a plan was discussed for Henry to accompany Edward's sons William and Henry Knight on a trip to the Continent during the summer. But the brothers and sisters conferred over a counter-attack prior to that. Lord Moira's unpaid debt for £6,000 was exposed during the bankruptcy hearings. The Earl's broken promises particularly aggrieved Henry, and the sum if recovered would reduce the burden on Edward and Mr Leigh-Perrot. Henry managed to persuade the Crown prosecutors to pursue the case. Moira was still in India, but his agent could be taken to court.

Jane wrote to her nephew James Edward Austen in July, 'We suppose the trial is to take place this week, but we only feel sure that it cannot have taken place yet because we have heard nothing of it.' Yaldon's coach had taken Frank and Cassandra from Alton to London the previous day 'on some business of Uncle Henry's'.[9] It was not until the beginning of the next week, Monday 15th, that Henry made his way to the Court of Exchequer in London Guildhall, just north of Cheapside in the City of London. The hearing and its outcome was reported in *The Times* the following day in some detail, since there was bound to be public interest in the financial misdemeanours of the current Governor-General of India, the Prince Regent's former intimate friend. Those hoping for scandal would not be disappointed.

Mr Dauncey, representing the Crown, outlined the circumstances of Henry's insolvency and the debt arising from his role as receiver general. The Crown wished, in fairness, to recover his property, rather than force the sureties to pay all of it. The solicitor acting for Lord Moira rejected the claim, on the grounds that Austen & Co. had come into possession of Lord Moira's bills back in April 1813 by usury, charging three times the legal limit of 5 per cent. According to Henry, when the plea of usury was urged, 'a murmur of indignation ran through the Court'.[10] Mr Dauncey insisted that the jury would not believe that 'a man of Mr Austen's experience would be so dishonest and even so rash, as to take more than the legal interest, where he must necessarily be exposed to detection, and to the loss of his money'.

At this point in the trial the skeleton in Henry's closet appeared. Major Charles James, described as 'the confidential agent of Lord Moira', was revealed as the crucial go-between. He confirmed that he had been 'in the habit of raising money for his lordship for several years', and that the transaction had been usurious. Under cross-examination by Mr Dauncey, he admitted that of 'late years his Lordship's credit had sunk considerably in the money market, and bills with only his own signature were not easily negotiated', and not worth their nominal value. The judge, Baron Richards, in summing up advised the jury that their decision hinged on the question of whether or not the transaction was legal. As it happened, the law on usury was at that time under review, being seen by some as a restraint on capitalist enterprise. After half an hour the jury returned a verdict against Lord Moira.[11]

Henry wrote to Lord Moira immediately, demanding repayment. He would have to wait for up to a year for a response from India, and the sum could make only a small difference to his backers, but it was a victory to brighten the gloom. Having purchased a passport on 11 July, Henry set off with his young charges to France en route for Switzerland with a lighter heart.

Jane must also have received from the outcomes of Henry's trial and Charles's acquittal – reported on the same day in the *Hampshire Chronicle* – the lift she needed to complete *Persuasion*. She was bringing to a close a story that begins with a family facing economic ruin. At the outset, Anne

Elliot is dismayed by her father and elder sister's resistance to plans for
reducing their expenses, and voices an attitude to debts that was evidently
shared by the Austen family:

> Every emendation of Anne's had been on the side of honesty against im-
> portance. She wanted more vigorous measures, a more complete reforma-
> tion, a quicker release from debt, a much higher tone of indifference for
> every thing but justice and equity. (I.ii)

This attitude was not by any means a given in Regency society, where
credit was generally considered an entitlement by the well-born and payment was frequently shirked. The rot began, of course, at the very top
with the Prince Regent. Henry, unlike many of his aristocratic clients, had
not squandered money and had faced the consequences of the mistakes
made at Austen, Maunde & Tilson. He was going abroad legitimately, as
mentor for his nephews, having been discharged from bankruptcy, not
like his predecessor in the office of Receiver General for Oxfordshire,
Lord Charles Spencer's son, fleeing the country to evade his creditors,
or Lord Moira, essentially doing the same with the title of Governor-
General as a fig leaf. Henry had not been publicly disgraced like that
swindler Edward Gray, who would be discharged from bankruptcy on 6
August but could never show his face in Alton again.[12]

In *Persuasion* there is a strand in the plot involving financial skul-
duggery which remains only sketchily developed; perhaps, as some have
suggested, because Jane now lacked the physical and mental stamina
to see it through. Henry was to write of her decline, 'The symptoms
of a decay, deep and incurable, began to show themselves in the com-
mencement of 1816. Her decline was at first deceitfully slow; and until
the spring of the present year, those that knew their happiness to be
involved in her existence could not endure to despair.'

The year of 1816 was a year with no real spring, and has since become
known as 'The Year Without a Summer'. The weather was 'sad', as Jane

repeatedly remarked in letters, perpetually cold and rainy. The cause
was an event 7,300 miles away in Indonesia. Mount Tambora erupted
in April 1815, disgorging plumes of gas and particles which plunged
the whole of South East Asia into darkness for days and spread to the
northern hemisphere, obscuring sunlight and causing a three-year drop
in average temperatures. It was the meteorological event of the century,
a global catastrophe, and resulted in crop failure and death by starvation for thousands. In England there were protests and riots. France was
as bad, if not worse. Jane heard from a melancholy Mrs Perigord that
she and her mother had turned their backs on their native land and re-
established themselves in London: 'she speaks of France as a scene of
general poverty & misery, – no money, no trade – nothing to be got but
by the innkeepers'.[13]

Henry and his nephews in Switzerland were at the European epicentre
of the weather emergency. The mountain ice did not melt that summer.
Rain fell for one hundred and thirty days between April and September
and the waters of Lake Geneva flooded the city. The desperation of the
starving resulted in violence. Arriving in late July or early August, the
Austen-Knight party would have coincided at Geneva with Byron and
the Shelleys, and Henry probably heard rumours about his scandalous
compatriots. At the Villa Diodati, Byron's villa just outside the city, Mary
Shelley dreamt up the story of Frankenstein.

The purpose of Henry's travels in 1816 was to shepherd young William and Henry around the sights of Europe and socialise with friends
made by Edward during an extended sojourn in Switzerland during his
youth in the late 1780s. The experience seems to have made a powerful
impression on Henry personally at this turning-point in his life. The
terrible human suffering they witnessed everywhere they went, exposure
to sublime scenes of nature, and the pilgrimage to Geneva may have
played a part in the decision he announced on his return to England. Jane
received a letter from him on 4 September, written from Godmersham,
and she relayed the news to Cassandra: 'Henry does not write diffusely,

but cheerfully; – at present he wishes to come to us as soon as we can receive him – he is decided for Orders &c.'[14] Henry would enter the clergy, and it was later remarked that he became a 'Calvinist-leaning minister'.[15] Calvinism was the creed of Geneva, where John Calvin, one of the founding fathers of Protestantism, had settled in the sixteenth century. Henry never left the Church of England, but nonetheless the Calvinist doctrine that God has pre-determined all things must have been a source of comfort to a man struggling to come to terms with his losses.

Once set on a new course, Henry was as eager and brimming with confidence as ever. According to Caroline Austen the possibility had been in his mind since the bankruptcy, but it was probably now that he went back to his old college in Oxford to enquire into the practicalities. He already had the necessary qualifications and found that 'altogether no difficulties opposed his entrance into the profession'.[16] On 5 November he wrote to the Bishop of Winchester, outlining his career and asking to be accepted as a candidate for ordination and for the position of curate at Chawton. 'Conscious of no criminality', he admitted his 'worldly failure' but blamed it entirely on the mismanagement of his partners in the Alton bank. 'I bow most humbly to the stroke of Providence,' he wrote, 'and am rendered thereby more desirous than ever of devoting the rest of my life and talents such as they may be to the more immediate service of religion.' Henry explained that he had strayed from the clerical path, when not yet of age for ordination, in order to serve his country at the outbreak of war. His colonel in the Oxfordshire Militia, Lord Charles Spencer, 'distinguished by every moral virtue', would be willing to give 'his fullest recommendation under every circumstance'. Henry might have left the world of credits and debits behind, but the 'creditable' connections he flourished in the letter were crucial to advancement in any walk of life.[17]

The Bishop amiably acceded to the request. At the examination the next month Henry was to be tested in, among other things, his knowledge of classical languages, and enthusiastically worked to 'get up his knowledge of Greek once more'. He was consequently rather disappointed when

Bishop North, indicating a Greek Testament lying on a nearby table, remarked wryly 'As for this book, Mr Austen, I dare say it is some years since either you or I looked into it.'[18]

The following day Henry went to Salisbury, where he was ordained a deacon and offered the curacy of Chawton on an annual stipend of 52 guineas. He would be formally ordained a priest on 28 February the following year.[19] The new post represented a very steep drop in social position and income. But it was also a substantial step towards restored respectability. The very fact that the Reverend Papillon was willing to have Henry as his curate is testament to the fact that the Austen family maintained their standing locally after the bankruptcy, and that neighbours who knew the circumstances and may even have suffered losses at Alton were prepared to accept the former banker in his new clerical guise. They accepted his explanations concerning the misdemeanours of Gray and the perfidy of certain noblemen, and agreed that he had been a victim too.

With typical alacrity Henry had begun writing sermons even before the ordination, and Jane was privy to his work. She was able to inform her nephew James Edward Austen in a letter of 16 December that the family were set to gain new literary lustre. James Edward, like his sisters, looked to Aunt Jane for advice in his novel-writing efforts. Now she suggested a new wheeze, incorporating Uncle Henry's 'very superior sermons':

> You and I must try to get hold of one or two, and put them into our novels: it would be a fine help to a volume; and we could make our heroine read it aloud on a Sunday evening, just as well as Isabella Wardour, in the 'Antiquary,' is made to read the 'History of the Hartz Demon' on the ruins of St. Ruth, though I believe, on recollection, Lovell is the reader.

Jane evidently kept a close eye on her arch-rival, Walter Scott, while she made a few changes to the recovered manuscript of her Gothic satire. Scott's third novel, *The Antiquary*, was published in May 1816.

In spite of appearances, Jane knew the bankruptcy had left an indelible mark on Henry. 'London is become a hateful place to him,' she told Fanny, '& he is always depressed by the idea of it.'[20] The roles of brother and sister had been reversed. Instead of Henry providing Jane with an *entrée* to the metropolis, he now had a walk-on part in her lowly and sequestered world. He was often resident at Chawton Cottage, and his mother and sisters cosseted him, collectively making his shirts as 'a complete memorial of the regard of many'.[21]

They looked forward to his debut performance in Chawton Church with anxious pride. Trial runs at Godmersham and, witnessed by Charles, at a chapel in Margaret Street on the way back via London stood him in good stead. On 24 January, Jane wrote to her old friend Alethea Bigg:

> Our own new clergyman is expected here very soon, perhaps in time to assist Mr. Papillon on Sunday. I shall be very glad when the first hearing is over. It will be a nervous hour for our pew, though we hear that he acquits himself with as much ease and collectedness, as if he had been used to it all his life.[22]

This initiation test of the curacy at Chawton passed successfully, and Henry eased into the clerical role that had originally been allotted to him.

Yet Jane certainly didn't regret or renounce her time as the banker's sister. The business of pounds, shillings and pence still occupied her thoughts and imagination. She would, for instance, continue to monitor the activities of the Royal Mint. The habit had begun early. The date of *The Watsons* can be pinned down thanks to the mention of a 'doubtful halfcrown' in the possession of Mr Robert Watson. It was in 1804, at the time Henry was establishing his business, that counterfeit coins of this kind were in the news. In the late 1790s Spanish silver dollars taken from captured ships were stamped with the head of George III, to compensate for the chronic shortage of British coins. But forgery became rife and by the start of the 1800s banks began rejecting the over-stamped coins, and the Mint was forced into issuing new ones to replace them.[23] The aside that Mrs Croft in *Persuasion* is suffering from 'a blister on one of her heels, as large as a three shilling piece' also has precise significance. This coin, known as the 'three shilling bank token', was struck between the years 1811 and 1816 and 'ceased to be legal tender in 1817'. During the Bank Restriction era the hoarding of coins had become a severe hindrance to trade. While the indolent Mint prepared for new issues, the industrialist Matthew Boulton was permitted to step in and manufacture this alternative coinage.[24]

Finally in 1817 the Mint began replacing the debased old coinage and Jane, praising one of Fanny's entertaining confidential letters, proclaimed her 'worth your weight in gold, or even in the new silver coinage', just one week after the Mint's proclamation.[25] On 13 February new half-crowns, shillings, and sixpences stamped with the date '1816' became legal tender, and four offices were opened in London to accept old coins at their nominal rates. The exchange was completed in two weeks, to the value of £2,500,000. It was the beginning of fully regulated and standardised 'modern coinage'.[26] Jane would live to see the new gold sovereign proclaimed on 1 July 1817, but not the half-sovereign which became currency from 10 October.

Coinage was improved in this year, but the state of banknotes remained a matter of infamy. The Bank Restriction Act was maintained at the end of the war, and the spread of paper money continued unabated. This was gratifying for the Portals of Hampshire with their paper mills supplying the Bank of England. But standards of design and printing had not progressed; even genuine notes were of inconsistent quality, and counterfeiting was rife. Naive innocents as well as deliberate malefactors fell victim in ever greater numbers to the laws that punished the 'passing' of counterfeit notes by hanging or transportation.[27] William Cobbett and other radicals were spokesmen for those who blamed the government for its refusal to restore convertibility and reduce the need for paper money, and the directors of the Bank of England for their inhumanity. What with the epidemic of country bank failures and the enduring suspicions regarding the stock market, the policy on banknotes set the seal on an epoch during which the financial profession was dimly viewed by the majority.

Economic controversy was never out of the news. Jane, in spite of the now unmistakable decline in her health, began writing on 27 January a new novel about an upstart seaside health resort called Sanditon, peopled by a large cast of eccentrics and plotters. As she faded away in the opening months of 1817, she somehow conjured up a vividly animated picture of the cheerful entrepreneur Mr Parker and his speculative world. Jane's astonishing inner resilience led the family to describe her in the same terms that she used regarding Mrs Smith, and that Caroline was to use about Henry. Her nephew James Edward in his *Memoir* was to wonder at the way the 'elasticity of her spirits soon recovered their tone' following the severe symptoms in 1816, while Henry commented on the way she supported, in the final stages of the disease, 'all the varying pain, irksomeness, and tedium, attendant on decaying nature with more than resignation, with a truly elastic cheerfulness'.[28]

Sanditon is a tantalising fragment, abandoned after eleven-and-a-half chapters when Jane's strength finally failed on 18 March. It is almost entirely lacking in love interest and full of contemporary reference – including fulsome praise of Scott's poems put into the mouth of a would-be libertine – and amused observation on the commercialisation of illness and the extremes of speculative enthusiasm. Some see it as a new departure and a masterpiece in the making, others as the disappointing product of diminished powers. The resemblance to the wild parodic pieces she wrote in her teens is, at any rate, undeniable. Through February and March, Anna Lefroy visited her aunt frequently and remarked that she 'kept a great deal in her own room, but when equal to anything she could always find pleasure in composition'.[29] Restricted to the society of her loved ones, Jane was reverting to her adolescent role as family entertainer. Those close to her, and she herself, must be kept amused in the face of death.

Sanditon begins with a 'gentleman and a lady travelling from Tun-bridge towards that part of the Sussex Coast which lies between Hastings and Eastbourne, being induced by business to quit the high road, and attempt a very rough lane, were overturned in toiling up its long ascent half rock, half sand'. Their driver begs them to turn back, but the gentleman insists on going forward, and sprains his ankle as a consequence. It was surely inspired by a family anecdote regarding Henry's impatience with the postillion of a post-chaise in which he was travelling, frustrated by the slow progress of the carriage through a rough country lane. 'Get on, boy! Get on, will you?' he shouted. – 'I *do* get on, sir, where I can.' – 'You stupid fellow! Any fool can do that. I want you to get on *where you can't*.' The critic Geoffrey Carnall took it to show the way Henry's temperament 'exemplified the entrepreneurial spirit to excess'.[30] The intemperate language doesn't sound typical of Henry, but the impatient eagerness certainly does.

Mr Parker is soon revealed to be the driving force behind the latest rival to Brighton and Weymouth on the south coast. There is every indication he is riding for a fall; that the carriage crash at the start of the narrative will very likely be matched by a financial crash at the end. He tells his rescuer, Mr Heywood, owner of a house beside the lane, that he is seeking to acquire the services of a surgeon to boost his pet project, having spotted in the newspapers a notice of the dissolution of a medical partnership in the neighbourhood. He has, it transpires, come to the wrong Willingden. The accident leads to an extended period of recuperation with the hospitable Heywoods during which the magnitude of Mr Parker's speculative obsession becomes apparent. To return the Heywoods' kindness, Mr Parker invites one of their daughters, Charlotte, to accompany them back to Sanditon for the season, and the narrative proper begins with her first impressions of the would-be fashionable bathing-place.

Another source of inspiration was almost certainly *The Magic of Wealth* by Thomas Skinner Surr, a novel published in 1815. It concerns, as one of the characters relates, a 'new and rising watering-place, created, as it were, by magic, out of a few fishing huts, by the power and wealth of a rich banker'.[31] Jane, loving satire and burlesque as she did, must have known of Surr's previous great fictional success, *A Winter in London*, which had appeared in 1806 just as Henry Austen was setting up his bank, and satirised Georgiana Spencer, the improvident Duchess of Devonshire. The author was himself a banker, rising from the position of a clerk in the Bank of England to head of its Drawing Office. He had made something of a name for himself in financial circles with his defence of the Bank's paper money policy, a pamphlet published in 1801 with the less than snappy title *A Refutation of Certain Misrepresentations Relative to the Nature and Influence of Bank Notes and of the Stoppage of Specie at the Bank of England upon the Price of Provisions.*

Given Surr's professional role in the credit economy it is doubtful that his mockery of 'the trafficking spirit of the time' was based on ideological opposition, as some have suggested. Rather, he laughs equally hard at those whose ideas about finance remained stuck in the past. 'You surely do not mean to hold, that the profession of a banker is one of hazard?' exclaims one poor old fogey during a lively discussion in the second chapter, which takes place in a carriage entering the precincts of Mr Flimflam's resort, vaingloriously renamed Flimflamton. This naif is instructed that capital must not remain idle: 'the world is awake'.[32] Nevertheless Surr's comedy is crude and Mr Flimflam the tradesman-turned-banker remains a cardboard cut-out villain, his wife a vulgar cliché.

Jane Austen, musing on a subject so close to home, would have felt she could do better. Though *Sanditon* falls short of the subtlety of her finished works, it represents a great advance in sophistication when seen as a response to *The Magic of Wealth*. Speculation is the focus in each; the word appears seven times in the course of the brief *Sanditon* fragment. However, Mr Parker's decision to turn his back on his small landed estate and stake his fortune on a speculative venture is not shown in an entirely negative light. His motives and activities are viewed benignly. He possesses all the irrepressible optimism and irresistible geniality that made Henry

Austen so attractive. He has the merit of being a 'family-man', openly fond of his nearest relations as well as being 'generally kind-hearted; – liberal, gentleman-like easy to please; – of a sanguine turn of mind' (ch. 2).

Jane, like the rest of *her* family, now had cause to feel that the speculative mentality was in need of an occasional curb. Mr Parker, it is implied, is not a man 'of strong understanding', and would benefit from a wife in the Mrs Croft mould to rein him in from time to time. Jane had once called Henry's financial ambitions 'the work of his own mind'. Then she celebrated the strength of his hypothetical vision as something equivalent to her own generative imagination. Even here, retrospectively, she doesn't condemn the quality outright. The Heywoods regard Mr Parker as a man of 'more imagination than judgment', but entrust their daughter to him and have confidence that she can make up any shortfall in regulatory judgement when required.

The description of Charlotte Heywood's impressions as she journeys with Mr and Mrs Parker to Sanditon is a brilliant stretch of cinematic writing that takes Surr's allegorical carriage ride to Flimflamton to an altogether higher level. It begins with Charlotte's enquiry about the 'snug-looking place' outside of town which turns out to be the Parkers' former old-fashioned dwelling. Its merits and disadvantages are discussed while the coach climbs the hills to modern Sanditon. As they near it, Mr Parker gleefully seizes on every sign of 'civilization' – 'females in elegant white' seated on camp stools and 'blue shoes & nankin boots' in the cobbler's window – that might indicate a prosperous season for the resort while also discussing with his wife the practicalities of the kitchen table. Once nearly self-sufficient, they now live according to the cash nexus but altruistically think of it as a way of spreading wealth more widely. As the vehicle ascends the final hill, they pass 'the last building of former days' and 'the modern' begins. Mr Parker is temporarily subdued by less show of fashionable life 'than he had reckoned on'. Soon they arrive at the new abode of the Parker family, Trafalgar House, 'light' and 'elegant' and precariously perched at the most elevated point in the vicinity and on

the edge of a cliff, exposed to every gale. During one recent storm, Mrs
Parker confides, they had been 'literally rocked' in their beds; though her
husband adds reassuringly that, 'We have all the grandeur of the storm,
with less real danger.' The wind 'simply rages and passes on', unlike in the
nook occupied by the old house: 'nothing is known of the state of the air,
below the tops of the trees' (ch. 4).

Jane, confined to her nook in the damp house as the cold and inces-
santly rainy weather continued into the spring of 1817, might well have
reflected that economic tempests could attack the old just as well as the
new. Nowhere was entirely safe, but that was no reason to cling to the apparent security of the past. At the end of the chapter Charlotte Heywood
looks with amusement out of her window at Trafalgar House towards
the sea over the clutter of modernity that is becoming 'the miscellaneous
foreground of unfinished buildings'. As in *Mansfield Park* and *Persuasion*,
there is a brief, lyrical evocation of the sea as a harbinger of the beyond.
The sea and the sea air are the selling-points of Sanditon, commodified
hilariously in Mr Parker's salesman patter. But like the spring waters
in *Persuasion*, the sea also represents something inexhaustible, uncom-
modified, free and precious at the same time. Charlotte looks at 'the sea,
dancing and sparkling in sunshine and freshness. –,' the final dash hanging
in space at the end of the fourth chapter. In *Sanditon* the extended Parker
family were brought forward and allowed to run riot over several chapters
with their baroque and largely imaginary ailments; all but dashing clever
Sydney, potentially the hero, saved for later. West Indian wealth was to
flow into the Sanditon economy more visibly than in *Mansfield Park*, in
the form of the visitor Miss Lambe a 'half mulatto' heiress from the West
Indies, whom the business interests of the resort are preparing to fleece
but who may defeat their expectations.

On 10 March Jane informed Caroline of her 'fine flow of literary
ardour', prompted by receipt of 'nearly twenty pounds' from Egerton for
sales of the second edition of *Sense and Sensibility*. But four days later the
flow stopped. In mid-chapter she laid down the manuscript of *Sanditon*

for the last time. Charlotte Heywood had just entered the domain of Mr Parker's 'colleague in speculation', the wealthiest and most domineering inhabitant of the town, Lady Denham. On the way there she had spied through the morning mist a secret liaison between Lady Denham's rakish nephew by marriage, Sir Edward Denham, and her companion, the beautiful poor relation Clara Brereton, two rivals for the inheritance of her large fortune. But Jane could do no more. She was suffering from fever and sleepless nights and her skin had turned 'black & white & every wrong colour', she later told Fanny; 'Sickness is a dangerous indulgence at my time of life.'[33] The apothecary in Alton didn't know what to make of her, and the symptoms are debated to this day. A widely accepted diagnosis of Addison's disease first put forward in 1964 has now been challenged by the suggestion of Hodgkin's lymphoma. In a letter back in January Jane had assured Alethea Bigg, 'I understand my own case now so much better than I did'. She was convinced her malady was the same one that had nearly killed Henry: '*Bile* is at the bottom of all I have suffered, which makes it easy to know how to treat myself'.[34] This raises the chilling possibility that she was self-administering doses of calomel.

Jane emerged from a bout of terrible debility, when death seemed abruptly closer, to a murky situation comparable to the goings-on at Denham Hall. All her life, the Austens had paid court to their Uncle Leigh-Perrot and his wife, with the expectation that the claims of family would be recognised in the terms of his will. James Leigh had benefited from the unearned luck that not uncommonly came the way of the sole son of a well-connected gentry family. A collateral inheritance had required only that he add 'Perrot' to his name, and a few years down the line, when the Stoneleigh inheritance was in question, he received a handy cash payment for ceding his claim. He was not uncaring when it came to his two sisters. He had given or loaned sums to bail out Mrs George Austen and her family at various points. He was childless, and made James Austen the trustee of his estate, on the understanding that he and his son would be the main beneficiaries. Once the Austen boys were launched he evidently no longer felt that it was down to him to share the support of his widowed sister and her two daughters, but when he died on 28 March at the age of eighty-two they placed their hopes on his benevolence, especially now that their income had been substantially reduced.

When the will was opened, it was discovered that everything had been left to his wife during her lifetime. Only after Mrs Leigh-Perrot's death were Mrs Austen's children to receive £1,000 each, with a reversionary interest in the property for James. It was clear that Mr Leigh-Perrot had not forgiven the Austens for the financial blow inflicted on him by the Crown surety. The will seemed like a rebuke to all of them, on Henry's account. Jane felt most severely the injustice of the 'forgetfulness' of her mother, although Mrs Austen excused it by reasoning that when the will was written her brother had expected to outlive her. Jane told Charles a week or so later that 'the shock of my uncle's will brought on a relapse'. Although she was 'the only one of the legatees who has been so silly' as to suffer a physical collapse, they must all have been sharply conscious of the corrupting effect of the system of inheritance.[35] Charlotte Heywood in *Sanditon* had moralised regarding the way Lady Denham manipulated her poor relations: 'Thus it is, when rich people are sordid' (ch. 7). Mrs Leigh-Perrot, by nature haughty although capable of strong attachment, would remain exacting and capricious in the Lady Denham style, while the attentions of the Austen family towards her would inevitably continue to be inflected by acquisitive motives.

Around this time Jane prepared a memo titled 'Profit from my Novels, over & above the £600 in the Navy Fives', a record of her earnings since March 1816. The 'Navy Fives' were government bonds yielding 5 per cent interest. Three half-yearly dividends had accumulated since the bankruptcy, amounting to £45 in the new bank account at Hoare's. Poignantly, the memo made note of the 'residue' of the first edition of *Mansfield Park*, the £13.7s 'remaining in Henrietta Street', in her account at Henry's bank. Lost but not forgotten, it might be a relatively small sum but was still essential to her professional pride. The additional profits were £71.6s

which, when added to the earned element in the £600 investment, made
a grand total of 'something over £631, perhaps as much as £668 and loose
change' in her lifetime. As Jan Fergus has observed, Austen's income from
writing, even including the £784.11s received after her death from posthumous works and a few last sales of *Emma* and *Mansfield Park*, was 'rather
less than has usually been thought', and well below that of two of the
most successful novelists of the time, Maria Edgeworth (£11,062.8s.10d)
and the less prolific Frances Burney (£4,280).[36]

On 27 April Jane drew up her will:

> I Jane Austen of the Parish of Chawton do by this my last Will & Testa-
> ment give and bequeath to my dearest Sister Cassandra Elizabeth every
> thing of which I may die possessed, or which may be hereafter due to me,
> subject to the payment of my Funeral Expences, & to a Legacy of £50. to
> my Brother Henry, & £50. to Mde Bigeon – which I request may be paid
> as soon as convenient. And I appoint my said dear Sister the Executrix of
> this my last Will & Testament.

All her worldly possessions were left to Cassandra, aside from the two
legacies. These have been passed over with little comment by previous
biographers. The assumption has been that Jane intended to compensate
Madame Bigeon for losses at the bank, but this seems unlikely given that
she and her daughter had moved back to France after the peace and would
presumably have taken their savings with them. They returned to England
several months after the bankruptcy and Jane knew them to be in difficult financial circumstances, but the fault was not Henry's. The idea of
acknowledging Madame Bigeon may have arisen as she cast her mind back
to another lingering death, that of Eliza. She would also have remembered
the intense happiness she had experienced at the homes in Sloane Street
and Henrietta Street, so well-tended by the devoted housekeeper and her
daughter. The legacy for Henry was similarly eloquent. It was, first of all,
a fiercely protective gesture, demonstrating to the whole family and to

Aunt Leigh-Perrot especially that her love for him was unconditional and her forgiveness absolute. It was perhaps also a gesture of thanks, for the practical aid and unwavering belief that had made her career as a writer possible. And if a legacy can be called witty, it was that also. Fifty pounds was precisely the amount he had pledged annually to support his mother and sisters, at the time he began his precarious course as a banker, and it was also the amount he would be paid annually as curate of Chawton. It could be understood by him as a wry reflection on their adventures together among the moneyed beau monde in town, and his new life in Holy Orders. The will was unwitnessed. It would be a surprise.

Henry's financial bad luck pursued him in the meantime. The Court of Exchequer verdict against Lord Moira was reversed on appeal by his agent. Moira, soon to be raised a notch higher in rank by the award of the title Marquess of Hastings, admitted in a letter to Henry that he had accepted the inflated rate of interest as a matter of convenience, but the letter arrived too late to be used in evidence.[37]

The family still desperately hoped for a cure, and it was decided to place Jane in the care of a respected medic in Winchester. On Saturday 24 May, Jane and Cassandra travelled the sixteen miles to the town in a coach loaned by James. Henry and Edward's son William Knight rode alongside on horseback, and Jane was distressed, looking through the carriage window, to see them making their way through the rain. Their friend Catherine Heathcote, sister of Alethea Bigg and widow of a canon of the Cathedral, had found lodgings for the Austen sisters in College Street just outside the Cathedral Close. Henry shuttled constantly back and forth between Winchester and Chawton, carrying news. James, Edward, Frank and Charles could only make brief trips, kept away by ill health or pressing family concerns of their own, although Mary Lloyd Austen stayed and nursed Jane devotedly with Cassandra. Occasionally Jane felt well enough to get up and even take the air.

In raised spirits, Jane sent her last known letter, published in part later that year by Henry in his 'Biographical Notice' and probably addressed to her old friend from the banking years, Mrs Frances Tilson. It contains earnest praise of her immediate family for their devoted care, but also a complaint excised by Henry, about a 'domestic disappointment', probably a reference to Uncle Leigh-Perrot's unfavourable will. It ends on a note typical of the many rattling London conversations between them concerning the trimming of hats and the foibles of town acquaintance. Chawton neighbours kindly took the letter to London: Captain Benjamin Clement (son of the Alton attorney Thomas Clement), his wife and his sister-in-law Catherine-Ann Prowting. Jane explains to her correspondent that the carrier is 'a very respectable, well-meaning man, without much manner, his wife and sister all good humour and obligingness, and I hope (since the fashion allows it) with rather longer petticoats than last year'.[38]

In mid-June there was another frightening relapse. She received Holy Communion from James and Henry and took leave of her loved ones. Once again she pulled back from the brink. Her final month was borrowed time, an unexpected gift. Remembering this brief '*respite* from death', Caroline wrote that 'at times, when feeling rather better, her playfulness of spirit prevailed' and she entertained her companions 'even in their sadness'.[39] On Tuesday 15 July one of those companions was Henry, returned from Chawton and joining his sisters and sister-in-law in the rooms in College Street. It was another rainy day. It also happened to be St Swithun's Day, the feast day of the Anglo-Saxon bishop, miracleworker, and patron saint of Winchester Cathedral.

Anne Elliot, during a distressing moment in the cancelled ending of *Persuasion*, is soothed by 'taking a newspaper in her hand'. Similarly, Jane seems to have welcomed the distraction provided by the *Hampshire Chronicle*. We can't know whether she was amused or disturbed by reports of an inquiry into the opulent refurbishment of the debtors' prison in Jewry Street by the aptly named architect Mr Moneypenny, who had 'enriched' the facade with 'rusticated coins'.[40] Regrettably, the topic did not revive her muse. But another notice, in the 14 July edition, did tickle her fancy. The Winchester Races were to take place at the end of the

month on the steeplechase course at Worthy Down, three miles north of
the city, with lavish rewards for the winners: 'His Majesty's Plate of 100
guineas on Tuesday 29 July, the City Plate of 50 guineas on 30 July, and
the Cup of 90 guineas on 31 July.'[41] She was struck by the coincidence
of the disappointing weather and the old tradition that a downpour
on St Swithun's Day on 15 July meant forty days of rain. She began to
weave a little comic fantasy in galloping dactylic meter around the ill-
omened race meeting, based on the recollection that St Swithun was an
Anglo-Saxon bishop whose remains had subsequently been enshrined in
the cathedral in Winchester (known as 'Venta' in Roman times). A later
Bishop of Winchester, William of Wykeham, was also brought into the
rhyme. One of Jane's companions acted as scribe.

> When Winchester races first took their beginning
> It is said the good people forgot their old Saint
> Not applying at all for the leave of Saint Swithin
> And that William of Wykeham's approval was faint.
>
> The races however were fix'd and determin'd
> The company came & the weather was charming
> The Lords & the Ladies were sattin'd and ermin'd
> And nobody saw any future alarming.
>
> But when the old Saint was informed of these doings
> He made but one Spring from his shrine to the roof
> Of the Palace which now lies so sadly in ruins
> And then he address'd them all standing aloof.
>
> 'Oh! subjects rebellious! Oh Venta depraved
> When once we are buried you think we are dead
> But behold me Immortal! By vice you're enslaved
> You have sinn'd & must suffer. – Then farther he said

These races & revels & dissolute measures
With which you're debasing a neighbouring Plain
Let them stand – you shall meet with your curse in your pleasures
Set off for your course, I'll pursue with my rain.

Ye cannot but know my command o'er July,
Henceforward I'll triumph in shewing my powers,
Shift your race as you will it shall never be dry
The curse upon Venta is July in showers.

Henry, in the 'Biographical Notice', wrote: 'The day preceding her death she composed some stanzas replete with fancy and vigour.'[42] He cherished this burst of irreverent genius as the expression of a native energy and good cheer resembling his own. He even claimed it was composed on her last full day of life, as if it were her final word, when in fact it is dated three days before.

When Henry's biographical sketch was reissued in 1832, the reference was gone. This may have been due to the disapproval of the younger generation. After his nephew James Edward Austen-Leigh scored an unexpected success with *A Memoir of Jane Austen* in 1870, he and his sisters consulted over a request from one aristocratic admirer of her works to include the 'stanzas replete with fancy and vigour' in the second edition along with other manuscript material not previously made public. Caroline was most anxious about the 'hue & cry' that Uncle Henry had 'unluckily' started with his allusion; 'we cannot keep any thing to ourselves *now*, it seems'. James Edward proposed tactful evasion, and she concurred expansively in a letter to him. The effect of 'the joke about the dead saint, & Winchester races, all jumbled together' would be too jarring in a 'closing scene': 'If put in at *all* they must have been introduced as the latest working of her mind'.[43]

The niece and nephew could not tolerate the mixing of genres. A memoir needed its death scene, and the combining of comedy and pathos was altogether too Shakespearian, in a bad way. It was like the clownish gravediggers engaging in badinage following Ophelia's suicide in *Hamlet*. Such scenes had been habitually cut in eighteenth-century theatrical performances as a violation of good taste, and Caroline and James Edward were agreed that *Winchester Races* should be kept out for the same reason.

Moreover, Caroline was troubled by the miscellaneous nature of the subject matter. It represented something problematic in the nature of her revered aunt. The Austens were not averse to an occasional day at the races. But the reference to 'dissolute measures' – gambling, drinking, fashionable parading – put together with a ludicrously peevish saint would raise questions. If this rollicking jumble of the sacred and the profane was indeed the 'latest', that is to say, the last 'working of her mind', it would contradict the image of a Jane Austen retired, domestic, pious and decorous, put forward by the memoir. True, the second edition would publicise for the first time the scurrilous tale of *Lady Susan*. But that was an early work, a minor experiment. *Winchester Races*, on the other hand, would seem like a regression.

Finally, there was the poem's blunt treatment of death, fearlessly named at the very moment Jane Austen faced extinction. 'When once we are buried you think we are dead,' cries St Swithun. Evidently there was discomfort with the line, since in one of the two surviving manuscript copies, 'dead' has been changed to 'gone', ruining the rhyme, and the whole sentence, including the triumphant 'But behold me Immortal!' has been underlined. Henry was to highlight her tough-minded realism as well as stoical resignation when he related her very last words: 'to the final question asked of her, purporting to know her wants, she replied, "I want nothing but death"'.[44] James Edward, re-writing the event fifty-three years later, was compelled to include the words, but softened them by combining her actual death in July with the more seemly leave-taking in June.

Jane died in Cassandra's arms at half past four on the morning of Friday 18 July. Mary, James's wife, was also there. Henry, having spent

several days in Winchester, left for Chawton the previous evening, probably soon after half past five, when Jane slipped into unconsciousness
and, Mary noted in her diary, 'was taken for death'. When he returned
the next day, she was gone. 'His is not a mind for affliction', Jane had
once written. He now relieved his feelings through activity, undertaking
the funeral arrangements and, perhaps with the help of Jane's close friend
Mrs Heathcote, the Dean's widow, somehow securing for her the rare distinction of burial inside the Cathedral, close to the shrine of St Swithun
himself. He, Edward and Frank with James Edward in place of his ailing
father James, attended the coffin through the Cathedral Close to the final
resting place in a brick-lined vault under the north aisle.

Henry Austen has subsequently been criticised for the burial of his
sister at Winchester, rather than in the quiet churchyard at Chawton
where her sister and mother lie. The epitaph he provided has also attracted disapproval for its lack of any mention of the novels:

> In Memory of JANE AUSTEN, youngest daughter of the late Revd
> GEORGE AUSTEN, formerly Rector of Steventon in this County. She
> departed this Life on the 18th of July 1817, aged forty-one, after a long
> illness supported with the patience and the hopes of a Christian. The
> benevolence of her heart, the sweetness of her temper, and the extraordi-
> nary endowments of her mind obtained the regard of all who knew her
> and the warmest love of her intimate connections. Their grief is in propor-
> tion to their affection, they know their loss to be irreparable, but in their
> deepest affliction they are consoled by a firm though humble hope that her
> charity, devotion, faith and purity have rendered her soul acceptable in the
> sight of her REDEEMER.

In both instances, however, Henry was evidently attempting to compensate Jane for the world's failure to recognise her literary stature. He
was determined to bestow on her all the pomp and circumstance he
could muster. She would not lie buried in a country churchyard as if

her sweetness had been 'wasted on the desert air', in the words of Gray's famous elegy for the forgotten dead. To bury her in the Cathedral was an act of faith in her future fame. Novels had been her trade, but to the prejudiced, 'novel' still carried associations of triviality and dissipation. Henry evidently felt that praise for 'the extraordinary endowments of her mind' was a strong enough indication. The epitaph of many of a male writer is not more explicit. He was to boast that the Cathedral 'does not contain the ashes of a brighter genius'.[45]

For almost a month after Jane's funeral there is no sign of Henry in the family records. Only at the end of August does he reappear at Godmersham, and preach in the church there. The reason must have been that he was immersed in the manuscripts of his sister's unpublished novels. Back in March, Fanny Knight had asked Jane about her unpublished novels. 'Miss Catherine', Jane had told her, referring to the manuscript recovered from Crosby, had been shelved 'for the present, and I do not know if she will ever come out'. As for *Persuasion*, perhaps only Cassandra had been privy to it. Jane admitted when pressed by Fanny that it was 'ready for publication', but swore her to secrecy and would only say vaguely that it might come out 'twelvemonth hence'. Henry, her former collaborator, had only recently been made aware of the novel's existence: 'I could not say No when he asked me, but he knows nothing more of it.'[46]

Now, with lightning rapidity, Henry assembled the manuscripts and prevailed on John Murray, who may have been wary due to the diminishing sales of *Emma* and the failure of the second edition of *Mansfield Park*, to publish the works now named *Northanger Abbey* and *Persuasion*. True to the spirit of their previous ventures, this was again to be a gamble. No sale of copyright; they were published on commission at Henry's own risk – and presumably that of the wider family, since he was penniless. Murray's ledgers show that 1,750 copies of the four-volume set were produced in December 1817, at a cost of £238.17s for paper, and £188.5s.9d for printing. By the anniversary of Jane's birthday in December, the novels were being advertised in *The Courier* and *Morning Chronicle* at the price of 24 shillings. This time the speculation was to be successful, though forced to vie with Walter Scott's *Rob Roy*, which appeared simultaneously and sold 10,000 copies in a fortnight. Jane's volumes sold respectably throughout 1818, with only 321 copies remaining by the end of the year.[47]

Sales must have been aided by the 'Biographical Notice of the Author' written by Henry and prefixed to the new publication. It revealed his sister's identity publicly for the first time and the substantial review in the *British Critic* quoted from it at some length. His own inclination had always been to shout her praises from the rooftops, but the portrait that was actually presented bears the mark of more cautious influences. Here was the beginning of meek and modest Jane Austen, unendingly kind and charitable, and herself faultless 'as nearly as human nature can be'. The fact that the sharp and witty novels could not possibly have been written by such a paragon was neither here nor there. There were no references to her extended visits to London, her exposure to fashionable society and its follies, her acute perception of economic imperatives. There was certainly no mention of his career or his part in hers. For the most part, it was buttoned-up sentimental hagiography.

Yet a flash of real feeling, of genuine loss and even physical yearning, escapes the dutiful diction:

> Of personal attractions she possessed a considerable share. Her stature was that of true elegance. It could not have been increased without exceeding the middle height. Her carriage and deportment were quiet, yet graceful. Her features were separately good. Their assemblage produced an unrivalled expression of that cheerfulness, sensibility, and benevolence, which were her real characteristics. Her complexion was of the finest texture. It might with truth be said, that her eloquent blood spoke through her modest cheek. Her voice was extremely sweet. She delivered herself with fluency and precision. Indeed she was formed for elegant and rational society, excelling in conversation as much as in composition.

These lines were written almost immediately after her death, and the attempt to conjure up her living presence is painful. The activity of objectively itemising her attributes, list-like, suggests an attempt to master emotion. Dwelling on the texture of her skin, words fail, and Henry paraphrased an image from the metaphysical poet John Donne, 'her pure and eloquent blood / Spoke in her cheeks'. Donne's elegy for Elizabeth Drury continues, 'one might almost say, her body thought'. From the idea of the body's eloquence Henry is drawn to the memory of her voice, 'extremely sweet'. It is a sensual picture, palpable, intimate, almost that of a lover. At the same time his remark that she 'was formed for elegant and rational society' speaks of his regret that she never took the place in the literary world that her talents had warranted.

EPILOGUE

This has been the story of the banker's sister rather than the novelist's brother. My account of Henry's life after Jane's death will be brief. The debonair banker has disappeared in the sole visual record of her favourite brother. The miniature portrait shows a man in his fifties, wholly identified with his new vocation of clergyman. He wears black 'Geneva robes', the formal garb of a Protestant minister, and a clerical collar with preaching bands. There are the remains of a handsome face and, although the outlines are gaunt, the eyes seem bright and alert, a smile plays about the lips, and the wavy locks of hair convey something of his famed animation.

Portrait of Henry Austen, undated. Reproduced with kind permission
from the Jane Austen Memorial Trust.

Henry was, after all, destined to seek out and occupy 'dead men's shoes'. He wrote in October 1817 to the fortunate cousin on his mother's side of the family who had inherited the Leigh estate at Adlestrop, asking whether he might be considered for the clerical living in Warwickshire after his own brother had passed away. James had been gifted it at the time of his first marriage and paid a curate to carry out the duties. Now he was ailing, and Henry's ill-judged enquiry got short shrift. When James Austen died in December 1819, the incumbency at Cubbington went to another, less needy, clerical relation.[1]

Henry must have feared that he himself would remain trapped in the insecure, demeaning and ill-paid role of curate forever. However on James's death, Edward invited him to take over at Steventon in a care-taking role until one of his sons was qualified to become rector. James's widow, Mary Lloyd Austen, and their youngest child Caroline were forced to vacate Steventon Rectory as unwillingly as Jane and Cassandra had done. Caroline recalled:

> We left Uncle Henry in possession. He seemed to have renewed his youth, *if* indeed he could be said ever to have lost it, in the prospect before him. A fresh life was in view – he was eager for work – eager for pupils – was sure very good ones would offer – and to hear him discourse you would have supposed he knew of no employment so pleasant and honourable, as the care and tuition of troublesome young men ... He was always very affec-tionate in manner to us, and paid my mother every due attention, but his own spirits he could *not* repress, and it is not pleasant to *witness* the elation of your successor in gaining what *you* have lost; and altogether, tho' we left our home with sad hearts, we did not desire to linger in it any longer.[2]

The sentence beginning 'A fresh life was in view' includes Jane's favourite fictional technique of free indirect discourse, and it is as close as we will get to capturing the flavour of Henry's eager voice. He sounds exactly like Mr Parker in *Sanditon*.

There was another reason for Henry's eagerness. No sooner was he installed, than he proposed to Miss Eleanor Jackson, the niece of John Papillon, rector of Chawton. Eleanor was surely the 'Miss Jackson' that Jane had noted as the warm advocate of the satirical bestseller *Rejected Addresses*.[3] They may have been reacquainted in London, when the Parkers invited Jane and Henry for dinner in October 1815 before his severe illness. It is cheering to think that, like Eliza de Feuillide, Eleanor Jackson had something of Elizabeth Bennet about her, based on her literary taste and the 'very good pair of eyes' that a Kentish relation admired.[4] Cassandra made a gift to Eleanor 'as soon as she knew' of the engagement that seems resonant of her awareness that Jane and Henry's relationship had transcended the usual bounds of sister–brother affection: Jane's turquoise ring.[5] They married in Chelsea on 11 April 1820.

Mrs Austen, according to the bank ledger at Hoare's, made what was probably a wedding gift to Henry of £40 in January. Like Jane and Cassandra, she was determined to demonstrate support for Henry. James Edward wrote to his half-sister Anna two years later: 'Domestic telegraph – Mrs Austen of Chawton has lately finished a magnificent piece of patchwork as a present for her son the Revd. H. Austen to be presented to him as an emblem of his own conduct through life – the colours are brilliant, various & strongly contrasted'.[6]

By that time, William Knight had taken over at Steventon, and went on to marry Caroline Portal, a member of the dynasty which provided the Bank of England with its banknote paper. Less hard-up than his predecessors, William tore down the old rectory and built a new one over the road on rising ground less liable to flooding.

Henry meanwhile moved on to another caretaking role at St Andrew's Church in Farnham, a large and prosperous market town just over the border in Surrey. It was worth £75 annually, with the addition of 'surplice fees' of £35 and a vicarage provided with garden and offices.[7] In *Sense and Sensibility*, Edward Ferrars and Elinor Dashwood were 'neither of them quite enough in love to think that three hundred and fifty pounds a year would supply them with the comforts of life' (III. xiii). Henry and his Eleanor had to make do with considerably less than half that amount, but they were prepared to do without some of the 'comforts of life'. Although they were to remain childless, the marriage seems to have been a success. He was to describe her as 'one dearer to me than life, and for whose comfort I am solicitous beyond my own existence'.[8] His tutoring experience led to an additional appointment, and he served as Master of the local Free Grammar School until 1827.

By this time he had taken up a more permanent clerical position, as 'Perpetual Curate' in the village of Bentley, midway between Farnham and Alton, where he remained until his retirement. Although the stipend was still a very moderate one of around £120 per year, he had status on a par with a rector. It is unknown to whom he owed this boon, but it may have been due to connections in Farnham. The tithes of Bentley and three other livings in the neighbourhood were, by a complicated arrangement centuries old, administered by the archdeaconry of Farnham, rather than privately owned.[9]

Henry was now too poor to own a horse, let alone a carriage, but following the move to Bentley he was able to walk to Chawton, and spent much time there during his mother's final weeks in 1827. Afterwards, he continued to visit Cassandra at the cottage frequently. She wrote to Mrs Whitaker, formerly Phylly Walter, in January 1832,

> Henry resides on his little piece of preferment between six & seven miles from me & is a very good neighbour. He makes an excellent parish priest, is indefatigable in his exertions & seems to have nothing to wish for but a trifling increase of wealth & better health to his excellent wife. His own health is on the whole good, as you will suppose when I tell you that he walked over one day this week to breakfast with me.[10]

Eleanor suffered from chronic rheumatism which affected her mobility, and led to visits to the spas at Bath and Clifton.[11]

Such are the bare outlines of Henry's apparently uneventful career in Holy Orders. He was occasionally tormented or tempted by reminders of his former existence, and sometimes his restless tendencies revived. In 1818 the debts to the Crown fell due and the business seems to have ended with Edward paying two-thirds and Mrs Leigh-Perrot one-third. She was forced to sell securities worth more than £8,600, and Edward had to make a payment at the same time as he agreed an expensive settlement with the Baverstocks over the Knight estates in Hampshire. Many of the trees at Chawton were turned into money, as Henry's bank partner Mr Tilson had once urged (not literally, the Portal paper mill used only the finest rag, not wood pulp). Letters remain to indicate that Henry continued to be dogged by debts remaining from the bank and army agency. Not only did he have to fend off repeated demands from the War Office and draw on the goodwill and resources of his brother Edward and his nephew James Edward Austen, but he also found himself unable to repay those who were struggling like himself, notably Charles Austen, and even poor Mrs Perigord to whom he owed £100 in November 1822.

Henry learned in 1818 that his friend and principal patron, Lord Charles Spencer, the man he had described in his letter to the Bishop of Winchester as 'distinguished by every moral virtue', had fled to the Continent at the age of seventy-eight to escape his creditors.[12] At around the same time, by way of his connection with the Earl of Morley, Henry was offered the temporary role of chaplain to the British Embassy in the Prussian capital. After some hesitation, Henry set off in the autumn of 1818, putting his Chawton position on hold, and the upshot was a volume *Lectures upon Some Important Passages in the Book of Genesis, delivered in the Chapel of the British Minister at Berlin*, published in 1820, in which he described himself opportunistically on the title page as 'Domestic Chaplain to HRH the Duke of Cumberland and the Rt Hon. The Earl of Morley'. Ernest Augustus, the Duke of Cumberland, was the fifth of George III's feckless sons, who had married a widowed German cousin to disoblige his mother, and retreated to Berlin where the living was cheaper.

Henry, like Jane, received his 'little gleam of Court favour' as an author, but it seems to have done him just as little good. He was soon back in Hampshire. There would be one more sortie abroad to south-west France in 1825, in another bid to gain compensation for the de Feuillide estate. The claim was rejected.

Henry retained sufficient credit with John Parker, Lord Morley to describe himself, again, on the title page of a printed sermon of 1826 as his 'domestic chaplain'. But a sermon published in aid of the Vaudois the following year suggests he may have been attempting to renounce worldly hopes. The Vaudois, also known as the Waldensians, were a persecuted sect originating in the twelfth century, and allied since the Reformation to the Calvinists. Like the Franciscans, they preached the vanity of material possessions. It is unknown what Henry made of the crisis in the agrarian economy which had particularly severe consequences in Hampshire in 1830. William Cobbett, the local boy who had been the scourge of the 'Paper Aristocracy' and country banks, rose up again as advocate of the farm labourers who protested against tithes, starvation wages, and severe unemployment during the 'Captain Swing' riots. Cobbett, also a fierce critic of the system of political patronage, was elected to the reformed House of Commons in 1832 and died three years later. His remains lie buried in the graveyard of the church in Farnham where Henry Austen had presided.

Henry never let go of his resentment towards the Marquess of Hastings, formerly Lord Moira. In the letter he sent to James Henry Leigh in 1817 regarding the Cubbington living and his own destitute condition, he described the way he had been 'defrauded' of £6,000 as 'unexampled treachery'.[13] The Marquess of Hastings died at sea off Naples in 1826, having exchanged India for a new post as Governor of Malta. Henry, on his retirement from the Bentley curacy in 1839, made a final appeal to Moira's son and heir, George Rawdon-Hastings. In a long letter sent on 23 May from Colchester, where Eleanor had family, he attributed the failure of the bank directly to Moira. News of the default had become known 'and the amount of my loss of course exaggerated, my credit as a banker was impaired – confidence withdrawn and business destroyed – Insolvency ensued in March 1816...I lost everything.' He had been 'totally ruined & reduced to beggary', but nevertheless could claim a clear conscience and the record of twenty-four years of devoted labour as a curate. He had ever since been 'bleeding under wounds' inflicted by the Marquess's father, 'undesignedly we will hope'.

The first letter met with a polite though unsatisfactory response. It can be gathered from a second letter written by Henry, that the Marquess had presented in some detail the embarrassed state of his own finances. Yet still Henry would not let the matter go. He implied some doubt as to Hastings's inability to pay, given that he had inherited entailed estates from his mother and married a rich wife. He also added new information about the loans contracted by Moira at that time. It seems that they amounted to £150,000 in all, owed to a number of creditors including several of Henry's partners and relations. His cousin Thomas Hampson for instance had lent £4,000.

Clive Caplan has described Henry's two missives as 'begging letters', while T. A. B. Corley, more contemptuously still, characterises them as 'fawning'.[14] These judgements seem too disparaging; although there are considerable variations in tone, from Christian meekness to courtly compliment, it doesn't require reading between the lines to see the anger. Henry makes plain that the letters he possessed from Moira promising to repay the debts would attach even 'heavier reproach' to a name already disgraced, though he declared he was above publishing them. In a postscript, a final suggestion that Hastings might stir himself to help his father's creditor 'without pecuniary sacrifice' is casual to the point of insolence. 'Your rank, position, & many other circumstances must give you influence with the Lord Chancellor – He has livings, though seldom of much value, falling vacant every day – I am sixty-eight years old. Not likely to clog his patronage for many years.' In an aside, Henry had referred to his former secret partner Charles James, whom he described to the Marquess as 'a Major James, much in your father's confidence', and smears as 'a papist ... educated in the Jesuits College at Douay'.[15] Although Henry Austen declared his conscience was clear, he had much to regret regarding the dubious foundations of his initial business success.

Losing Jane was an altogether deeper wound, although here there was less cause for self-reproach. He had thrown himself into the production and promotion of her novels, and his own subsequent attempts at authorship could hardly fill that gap in his life. Interestingly, he seems to have encouraged authorial ambition in Eleanor. In 1831 'Mrs Henry Austen' published *An Epitome of the Old Testament in the Form of Question and Answer, written for the Inhabitants of the Parish of Bentley*, dedicated to the Bishop of Winchester and published at Farnham.[16] Eleanor kept up a correspondence with Cassandra when they travelled, and in a letter sent during a brief placement at Yeovilton Rectory near Ilchester in Somerset in the summer of 1837, one gets the sense of a lively invalid along the lines of Mrs Smith in *Persuasion*. Eleanor reported that Henry was popular with the parishioners, and that in spite of poor health she had gone out the previous day for a three-mile airing in her wheelchair. She was excited to have seen a poem praising Jane's works by Lord Morpeth in an issue of *The Keepsake Annual* for 1835, and urged Cassandra to obtain it.[17]

In May 1831 Cassandra had received a letter from John Murray offering to purchase the copyright for the novels which were still in her possession. A few days later, probably after consultation with Henry, she replied stating that the copyrights were not for sale. They wanted to remain true to Jane's spirit of independence, but Cassandra did express an interest in the possibility of new editions. The family must almost have despaired of the survival of Jane's works by this stage. In 1820 Murray had remaindered the 539 unsold copies of *Emma* at two shillings, and the 498 unsold copies of the second edition of *Mansfield Park* at two shillings and six pence. Murray's overture came to nothing. He may have been considering a budget collected edition, but was over-stretched financially and had to drop the idea.[18]

A year later, Henry was in negotiations with another publisher, Richard Bentley, for the sale of the copyrights. This turnaround suggests an anxiety that the novels might remain out of print. The agreed price of £210 for the five novels, less the £40 Bentley had to pay the executors of Egerton's estate for *Pride and Prejudice*, was disappointing. It represented a drastic devaluation when compared with the £450 Murray had offered for just three of the novels in 1815, an offer that had then been dismissed as an insult.

There was also some cause for dismay in the fact that the novels would be reappearing as part of the mass market 'Standard Novels' series. Bentley was not particularly choosy about the copyrights he bought up. Jane Austen's works were merely numbers twenty-three to twenty-eight (*Northanger Abbey* and *Persuasion* again being published together) of the 128 novels in the series. The price policy was standard too: six shillings for one closely printed cloth-bound volume, when the going rate for a novel presented in the more high-class three-volume set typically cost one and a half guineas. Initially the size of the editions was large: around 4,000 copies. Reprints of the Bentley 'Standard' edition would appear as a set in 1833 and then every few years for individual novels until the 1860s, although sales were less than predicted and the number of copies issued each time was reduced.

Bentley asked for more information to add to the previously published 'Biographical Notice of the Author' and for a portrait, to be prefixed to the first of the Austen volumes, *Sense and Sensibility*. Henry demurred:

> I heartily wish that I could have made it richer in detail but the fact is that my dear sister's life was not a life of event. Nothing like a journal of her actions or her conversations was kept by herself or other. Indeed the farthest thing from her expectations or wishes was to be exhibited as a public character under any circumstances.

It was true that Jane had shrunk from public notice, but that hadn't hindered Henry in the past. He may have been sincere when he said

that he wished he could make the biography 'richer in detail'; very likely
Cassandra and other members of the family held him back. The changes
he made when updating the 1817 biographical sketch are in the direction of *removing* animating personal detail. Not only did the reference to
the comic poem composed on her deathbed go, but also the humorous
remark about the length of petticoats quoted from Jane's last letter and
used to end his original account. The Austens probably felt that mass
circulation of the works required even greater discretion when it came
to publicising aspects of her life. The additions were intended to boost
Jane's public credit by citing further praise from the great and the good.

According to the census return of 1841, Chawton Cottage was occupied
by Cassandra, three female servants and one male servant, and also by
Henry and Eleanor Austen.[19] Although after his retirement they had taken
a house at Colchester for a period of three years, they evidently continued
to spend time in Hampshire. There was probably another reunion and
consultation among the siblings when the bankruptcy case of Austen,
Maunde & Tilson was finally wound up in 1843, with 'a total return to
depositors and not holders of just 50 per cent of their losses'.[20] Edward
received about £1,800, and there was something for James's widow Mary.
Henry was active in caring for Cassandra in the days before her death on
22 March 1845, following a stroke. James Edward Austen-Leigh, writing
to his sister Anna of the funeral, remarked that 'Uncle Henry struck me
as very agreeable and not very old' while 'Uncle Charles was kind, grave,
& thoughtful'.[21] Afterwards, Charles, the main beneficiary of Cassandra's
will, went to London on executors' business, accompanied by Henry,
planning to catch 'that night's mail-train' on an unknown mission to
Leamington Spa.

Cassandra left legacies of £1,000 each to Edward, Henry, Frank and
Anna, who was now a widow with seven young children. Her estate was
valued at £16,000. Like her mother she had become adept at investing in
stocks, adventurously staking money on Brazilian Bonds in 1837 as well
as retaining more conservative Bank of England securities. Cassandra

divided Jane's manuscripts among the next generation, and distributed a few valuables, returning some to Henry 'who originally gave them all': 'Jane's gold watch and chain, miniature of Eliza de Feuillide in a green case; very small miniature of Mrs Hancock set with diamonds and mounted as a brooch; a ring, ruby surrounded by diamonds.'[22]

Henry's last years were spent at Tunbridge Wells in Kent, where Eleanor's spinster sister Henrietta Jackson was resident. He died there, at the age of seventy-eight, on 12 March 1850 and was buried at Woodbury Park Cemetery. The once fashionable spa town was an appropriate final destination. His great-grandmother and grandfather lay in the churchyard in neighbouring Tonbridge, and his father had attended school in the town: three Austens who had worked hard to make their way in life and had little to show for it financially at the last. The resort itself had been the favourite destination for Eliza in her giddy youth. She had dazzled at the ball, in a new dress 'most truly elegant, quite distinguished as the richest in the rooms'; she and cousin Phylly dancing until two in the morning.[23] Jane as a child had received an economic education by proxy in reading of the misadventures at Tunbridge Wells of the heroine of Burney's *Camilla*, and Mr and Mrs Parker are travelling from Tunbridge when their carriage overturns.

All Henry's worldly possessions were left to his wife. Frank Austen's granddaughter Mary Purvis came to live with her. Eleanor was residing in Bath at the time of her death in 1864. She took the trouble in her final year to send Caroline Austen the treasured ring that had once belonged to Henry's novelist sister, with an explanatory note. It remained in the family until 2012, when it was sold at auction for £152,450 to the American singer Kelly Clarkson. After a national outcry and export ban, Jane Austen House Museum raised the funds to buy it. It is now on display alongside the note from Eleanor. In her will, Eleanor left her former companion, Mary Purvis, the exquisite miniature portrait of Philadelphia Austen Hancock set in a ring of diamonds, previously bequeathed by Dr Hancock to his daughter Eliza, and later acquired by T. E. Carpenter for the Jane Austen Memorial Trust.

In their lifetimes, Jane Austen's brothers and sisters maintained an admirable unity and accord in the face of pressures that could easily have led to rancour. The descendants of the brothers sometimes less charitable, particularly when it came to Henry. James Edward's son William Austen-Leigh wrote that Henry was 'possessed an almost exasperating buoyancy and sanguineness of temperament and high animal spirits which no misfortune could depress and no failures damp', while admitting that 'the special pairs of brother and sister, both as to personal likeness and attachment, seem to have been Edward and Cassandra, Henry and Jane'.[24] Two years later, in 1913, William and his nephew Richard Austen-Leigh published an important reference work, *Jane Austen, Her Life and Letters: A Family Record*, with a cutting judgement on both Henry and Eliza; 'Though he was endowed with many attractive gifts there was a certain infirmity of purpose in his character that was hardly likely to be remedied by a marriage to his very pleasure-loving cousin.'[25]

By the end of the nineteenth century Jane Austen's reputation was on the rise. A scheme was launched to raise money for a memorial stained glass window to be installed near her grave in Winchester Cathedral. Hoare's, the Austens' financial institution of choice, oversaw the fund-raising and the senior partner Charles Hoare himself contributed £5 to launch the appeal. At least £301 was required, but after eighteen months only £187.3s.6d had been raised and there was dismay among some supporters at the lacklustre response. A collection raised in the United States by Oscar Fay Adams among fellow 'Janeites' helped to boost the takings, and after a final donation of three guineas from Messrs Hoare in July 1900 the target was finally achieved.

The launch of the Jane Austen £10 note in 2017 represents another step in her ascendancy: the first female author to feature on an English banknote. The Bank of England lags behind Mexico, Japan and Turkey in this respect, and has also been somewhat grudging when it comes to literary figures of either sex. Shakespeare appeared on a £20 note from 1970 to 1993, and Charles Dickens, the first novelist, preceded Austen on the £10 note from 1992 to 2003. Scotland has done better. Walter Scott has had his picture on every Scottish banknote nearly two centuries ahead of Jane, just as he trounced her with his sales figures in life. Scott developed a particular interest in the financial sector when the publishing house in which he was a partner went bust during the banking crisis of 1825. Rather than declaring himself bankrupt, he increased his literary output to superhuman levels, and was somehow able to save the independent Scottish banknote as well. A series of influential satirical articles forced the Westminster government to abandon their plan to stop low denomination notes, and the achievement is commemorated to this day.

As my story has shown, there is also much that makes the choice of Jane Austen for the Bank of England note appropriate; not only her keen observation of economic matters in the novels but also her close association with Henry and his banking business. Their lives coincided with tumultuous years in the history of the British economy due to the long-running war with France. It was an expansionist period for money-men like Henry; a time when the use of paper notes was normalised throughout the nation and the massive military effort opened up new opportunities for profit, and an increased threat of sharp downturns and bankruptcy. When Henry's enterprise was at the pinnacle of success and Jane was launching her career as a novelist on the strength of it, the mass of the population were facing cruel hardships that eventually led to armed insurrection. Eventually Henry too fell victim to an unfavourable turn in the economy.

An image of No. 10 Henrietta Street, the London office of Austen & Co., would have made an interesting talking-point as the background for the £10 note design. Edward Austen Knight's country seat at Godmersham will feature instead, and it makes sense in relation to the family's broad economic story. Austen family finances were all backed by the security of the Knight estate which Edward inherited, and indirectly this was also true of Jane's literary endeavours. When disaster struck in 1816, traditional landed wealth allowed the family to survive as an interdependent collective.

Until recently, any new notes issued by the Bank of England would have been printed on paper supplied by descendants of the same Portal family that Jane Austen knew. The business expanded in the course of the nineteenth and early twentieth century until it came to supply colonial governments throughout the British Empire. Regrettably, the link with the Portals was severed in 1995 when the firm was taken over by De La Rue. However the banknote paper is still manufactured in the same part of Hampshire, at Overton close to Steventon, described by Jane as a 'celebrated city' in her early skit, *The Memoirs of Mr Clifford*.

The sum of £10 itself has special resonances in the light of Jane Austen's biography. This was the amount paid to her by the publisher Crosby, when Henry first attempted, unsuccessfully, to get the one of her novels into print. It is the sum that appears on one of the few surviving artefacts of Henry's business, the unissued banknote on display in the cottage at Chawton with the inscription, 'Alton Bank promise to pay the bearer the sum of *Ten Pounds*, here or at Messrs Austen Maunde & Austen, Bankers London.'

'It is better to be lucky than wise', Henry wrote late in life.[26] His career was blighted by the bank failure but one could say that Jane's genius redeemed his losses. We owe her novels to his speculative endeavours. He may have been rash and unscrupulous in some of his dealings, but he was wise with respect to Jane's talent.

Jane Austen is beginning to be seen as a more metropolitan and professional author than hitherto; an important corrective to previous biases. Yet ultimately, as I have attempted to show, it is not all about the money. Jane declared 'I must keep to my own style & go on in my own way … though I may never succeed', and Henry cherished that independent spirit and ensured the public afterlife of the novels. The literary marketplace of Jane Austen's day valued her genius very cheaply. Today she is a major British export, a global brand, and cultural entrepreneurs continue to find new ways of packaging the stories and the image. At the same time, her writings have attained the generality of a natural resource or creative commons. Any of the texts can be obtained free of charge at a public library or on an electronic device. If you want to own a copy of *Pride and Prejudice* or *Emma* you can pick one up amid the flotsam and jetsam of a charity shop, hand over one of the 2017 commemorative Jane Austen £2 coins, and still receive change. Open the creased cover, turn a dog-eared page, and there are worlds within, of laughter, intelligence and feeling. Her works are among those minor miracles that give life value and meaning.

ACKNOWLEDGEMENTS

The first acknowledgement of anyone engaging in research on the biography of Jane Austen must be to Deirdre Le Faye, for the wealth of reference material she has provided through her superb editions of correspondence and diaries, including *A Family Record*, the encyclopaedic *Chronology*, as well as many other informative articles and books. I am grateful, in addition, for her guidance on a number of points and for her willingness to share findings on the accounts of Henry Austen and Eliza de Feuillide at Drummonds Bank.

Warmest thanks are also due to T. A. B. Corley, the author of pioneering articles on the banking career of Henry Austen, who granted me access to unpublished material for a forthcoming article on Henry's 'secret partner', Major Charles James. His generous encouragement, and the practical support of Jeremy Corley and Felix Corley have been vital to my project.

Jane Hurst with her unsurpassed knowledge of Austen connections at Alton has talked me through aspects of Austen, Gray & Vincent and its place in the community, and given valuable food for thought. My thanks to Pamela Hunter for assistance in accessing and navigating Austen family ledgers at Hoare's Bank Archive, Sarah Lewin for aid with the Austen papers at Hampshire Archives and David McClay at the John Murray Archive, National Library of Scotland. For help with images and other matters, I am extremely grateful to Mary Guyatt and Isabel Snowden at Jane Austen's House Museum in Chawton, Gillian Dow and Darren Bevan at Chawton House Library, Tibbie Adams and Robert Clark. Olivia Beattie, Bernadette Marron and the rest of the team at Biteback kept me on track with their enthusiasm and commitment. The book was made possible by the generous support of the Leverhulme Trust, which allowed me to explore a new avenue as part of a project on Romantic-era women writers and economic debate. I also owe a debt of gratitude to my colleagues at the University of Southampton.

Friends and Austen specialists Isobel Armstrong, Robert Clark and Christine Kenyon-Jones have given encouragement and inspiration. Alice Hunt helped me to get started. I have benefited from conversations with Helen Paul in the course of Henry Austen pilgrimages, and from her vetting of some of my economic history. Josie Dixon and Caroline Wintersgill not only advised me expertly on the entire first draft but provided cake and moral support when it was needed most, and I'm forever in their debt. Last but not least, thanks to my dear sons Benjamin and Joshua for their forbearance, curiosity and good cheer during this adventure.

ABBREVIATIONS AND SELECTED BIBLIOGRAPHY

ABBREVIATIONS

Austen Papers – R. A. Austen-Leigh, *Austen Papers 1704–1856* (Colchester: Spottiswoode, Ballantyne & Co., 1942).

Catharine – Jane Austen, *Catharine and Other Writings*, (eds) Margaret Anne Doody and Douglas Murray (Oxford: Oxford University Press, 1993).

Chronology – Deirdre Le Faye, *A Chronology of Jane Austen and Her Family 1600–2000*, rev. edn (Cambridge: Cambridge University Press, 2013).

JAOC – Deirdre Le Faye, *Jane Austen's 'Outlandish Cousin': The Life and Letters of Eliza de Feuillide* (London: British Library, 2002).

Family Record – Deirdre Le Faye, *Jane Austen: A Family Record*, 2nd edn (Cambridge: Cambridge University Press, 2004).

Juvenilia – Jane Austen, *Juvenilia*, in Peter Sabor (ed.), *The Cambridge Edition of the Works of Jane Austen*, vol. 1 (Cambridge: Cambridge University Press, 2006).

Later Manuscripts – Jane Austen, *Later Manuscripts*, in Janet Todd and Linda Bree (eds), *The Cambridge Edition of the Works of Jane Austen*, vol. 8 (Cambridge: Cambridge University Press, 2008).

Letters – Jane Austen, *Jane Austen's Letters*, ed. Deirdre Le Faye, 3rd edn (Oxford: Oxford University Press, 1995).

Memoir – J. E. Austen-Leigh et al., *A Memoir of Jane Austen and Other Family Recollections* (Oxford: Oxford University Press, 2002).

Reminiscences – Reminiscences of Caroline Austen, introduction by Deirdre Le Faye (Jane Austen Society, 1986).

SELECTED BIBLIOGRAPHY

Alberts, Robert C., *Benjamin West: A Biography* (Boston: Houghton Mifflin, c.1978).

Anon., 'Charles Greenwood', www.peerage.org. [Online]

Anon., 'St Clement Dane', in *London Lives 1690–1800: Crime, Poverty and Social Policy in the Metropolis*, londonlives.org. [Online]

Arthur, Brian, *How Britain Won the War of 1812: The Royal Navy's Blockades of the United States, 1812–15* (Woodbridge: Boydell & Brewer, 2011).

Atkins, Peter J., 'The Spatial Configuration of Class Solidarity in London's West End 1792–1939', *Urban History*, 17 (1990), pp. 36–65.

Austen-Leigh, William, and Austen-Leigh, Richard, *Jane Austen, Her Life and Letters: A Family Record* (London: Smith, Elder & Co., 1913).

—, with Montagu George Knight, *Chawton Manor and its Owners* (London: Smith, Elder & Co., 1911).

Barchas, Janine, *Matters of Fact in Jane Austen: History, Location, and Celebrity* (Baltimore: John Hopkins University Press, 2012).

Bearman, Robert, 'Henry Austen and the Cubbington Living', *Persuasions*, 10 (1988), pp. 22–6.

Benchimol, Alex, 'Knowledge Against Paper', *Romantic Circles*. [Online]

Bennett, Stuart, 'Lord Moira and the Austens', *Persuasions*, 35 (2013), pp. 129–52.

Bolitho, H., and Peel D., *The Drummonds of Charing Cross* (London: George, Allen & Unwin, 1967).

Bridge, Thomas, *The Adventures of a Bank-Note* (London: T. Davies, 1771).

Bury, Lady Charlotte, *Diary of a Lady-in-Waiting*, ed. A. Francis Steuart (London: The Bodley Head, 1908).

Byrne, Paula, *The Real Jane Austen* (London: HarperPress, 2013).

Caplan, Clive, 'The brewery scheme is quite at an end', *Jane Austen Society Report* (2010), pp. 92–6.

—, 'Henry Austen's Buxton Bank', *Jane Austen Society Report* (2004), pp. 46–8.

Jane Austen's Banker Brother: Henry Thomas Austen of Austen & Co., 1801–1816', Persuasions 20 (1998), pp. 70–90.

—, 'Jane Austen's Soldier Brother: The Military Career of Captain Henry Thomas Austen of the Oxfordshire Regiment of Militia, 1793–1801', *Persuasions*, 18 (1996), pp. 122–43.

—, 'Lord Moira's debt and Henry Austen's appeal', *Jane Austen Society Report* (2005), pp. 41–54.

—, 'Meryton Revealed: The Derbyshire Militia at Hertford and Ware', *Jane Austen Society Report* (2004), pp. 41–5.

—, 'Military Aspects of *Northanger Abbey*', *Jane Austen Society Report* (2002), pp. 21–4.

—, 'The Missteps and Misdeeds of Henry Austen's Bank', *Jane Austen Society Report* (2010), pp. 103–9.

—, 'Naval aspects of *Persuasion*', *Jane Austen Society Report* (2007), pp. 34–41.

—, 'We suppose the Trial is to take place this week', *Jane Austen Society Report* (2008), pp. 152–9.

Carnall, Geoffrey, 'Early Nineteenth Century: Birmingham – 'Something Dreadful in the Sound' in *The Representation of Business in English Literature*, ed. Arthur Pollard (London: Institute of Economic Affairs, 2000), pp. 35–64

Clark, Robert, '*Mansfield Park* and the Moral Empire', *Persuasions*, 36 (2014), pp. 136–50.

Copeland, Edward, 'Money', *The Cambridge Companion to Jane Austen*, 2nd edn (Cambridge: Cambridge University Press, 2011), pp. 127–43.

Corley, T. A. B., 'The Austen family, the Grays and the Baverstocks', *Jane Austen Society Report* (2010), pp. 96–103.

—, 'Charles James', forthcoming article in *The Oxford Dictionary of National Biography*.

—, 'Jane Austen and her brother Henry's bank failure 1815–16', *Jane Austen Society Collected Reports 1996–2000*, pp. 139–50.

—, 'Jane Austen's dealings with her publishers', *Jane Austen Society Report* (2011), pp. 127–38.

Craig, Sheryl, *Jane Austen and the State of the Nation* (Basingstoke: Palgrave Macmillan, 2015).

Crosby, Rev. J. Malham, *Complete Pocket Gazetteer of England and Wales or Traveller's Companion* (London: B. Crosby & Co., 1807).

Davis, Kathryn E., '"The First Soldier [She] Ever Sighed for": Charles Pasley's *Essay* and the "Governing Winds" of *Mansfield Park*', *Persuasions On-Line*, 35: 1 (Winter 2014).

—, *Liberty in Jane Austen's Persuasion* (Bethlehem, MA: Lehigh University Press 2016).

Davis, Timothy S., 'Ricardo's Macroeconomics: Money, Trade Cycles, and Growth' [Online].

Dick, Alexander, *Romanticism and the Gold Standard: Money, Literature, and Economic Debate in Britain 1790–1830* (Basingstoke: Palgrave Macmillan, 2013).

Easton, Celia, 'The Sibling Ideal in Jane Austen: When Near Incest Really is Best', *Persuasions On-Line*, 30: 1 (Winter 2009).

Edgeworth, Maria, *The Absentee*, ed. W. J. McCormack and Kim Walker (Oxford: Oxford University Press, 1988).

Edwards, Dudley, *The Soldiers' Revolt* (Nottingham: Spokesman Books, 1978) [Online].

Fergus, Jan, 'The Professional Woman Writer', in Edward Copeland and Juliet McMaster (eds), *The Cambridge Companion to Jane Austen* (Cambridge: Cambridge University Press, 2011), pp. 1–20.

Ferguson, Niall, *The House of Rothschild*, vol. 1 (London: Penguin Books, 1998).

Fetter, Frank Whitson, 'The Bullion Report Reexamined', *Quarterly Journal of Economics*, 56: 4 (August 1942), pp. 655–65.

—, 'The Politics of the Bullion Controversy,' *Economica*, 26: 102 (May 1959), pp. 99–120.

Fremantle, Elizabeth, *The Wynne Diaries 1789–1820*, ed. Anne Fremantle (Oxford: Oxford University Press, 1952).

Garside, Peter, 'The English Novel in the Romantic Era', *The English Novel 1770–1830*, vol. 2, pp. 15–103.

Geng, Li-Ping, '*The Loiterer* and Jane Austen's Literary Identity', *ECF* 13: 4 (2001), pp. 579–92.

Gilson, David, 'Henry Austen, Banker', *Jane Austen Society Report* (2006), pp. 43–6.

Grey, J. David, 'Henry Austen: Jane Austen's "Perpetual Sunshine"', *Persuasions. Occasional Papers*, 1 (1984), pp. 9–12.

Harris, Jocelyn, 'Jane Austen and the *Subscription List* to Fanny Burney's *Camilla* (1796)', *Persuasions On-Line*, 35: 1 (Winter 2014).

—, *A Revolution Almost Beyond Expression: Jane Austen's Persuasion* (Newark, DE: University of Delaware Press, 2007).

Heinrich Heine, *The Prose Writings of Heinrich Heine*, ed. Havelock Ellis (Read Books: 2013).

Hessell, Nikki, 'News and Newspapers: Readers of the Daily Press in Jane Austen's Novels', *Persuasions*, 31 (2009), pp. 248–54.

Horn, Pamela, 'The Mutiny of the Oxfordshire Militia in 1795', banbury-museum.org [Online].

Hudson, Glenda A., *Sibling Love and Incest in Jane Austen's Fiction* (Basingstoke: Macmillan, 1999).

Hume, David, *Essays Moral, Political and Literary*, ed. Eugene F. Miller (Indianapolis: Liberty Classics, 1987).

Hume, Robert H., 'Money and Rank', in Peter Sabor (ed.), *The Cambridge Companion to Emma* (Cambridge: Cambridge University Press, 2015), pp. 52–67.

Hurst, Jane, 'Henry Thomas Austen – "Being a Hampshire Man"', *Jane Austen Society Report* (2002), pp. 49–52.

Hutchings, Victoria, *Messrs Hoare Bankers: A History of the Hoare Banking Dynasty* (London: Constable, 2005).

Jarvis, William, 'Jane Austen and the Countess of Morley: A Footnote', *Jane Austen Society Collected Reports 1986–1995*, pp. 6–14.

—, 'Jane Austen and the Countess of Morley: A Footnote', *Jane Austen Society Collected Reports 1986–1995*, p. 79.

—, 'Some Information about Jane Austen's Clerical Connections', *Jane Austen Society Collected Reports 1976–1985*, pp. 11–17.

Jenkins, Elizabeth, 'Birth of a Legend', *Reports*, V (1965), pp. 289–94.

—, 'The Marriage Registers at Steventon', *Jane Austen Society Collected Reports 1949–1965*, pp. 294–5.

Kaplan, Deborah, 'Henry Austen and John Rawston Papillon', *Jane Austen Society Collected Reports 1986–1995*, pp. 60–64.

Kaplan, Herbert H., *Nathan Mayer Rothschild and the Creation of a Dynasty: The Critical Years 1806–1816* (Stanford, CA: Stanford University Press, 2006).

Kaplan, Laurie, '*Sense and Sensibility*: 3 or 4 Country Families in an Urban Village', *Persuasions*, 32 (2010), pp. 196–209.

Knight, R. J. B., *Britain Against Napoleon: The Organization of Victory 1793–1815* (London: Allen Lane, 2013).

Lane, Maggie, 'Brothers of the More Famous Jane: The Literary Aspirations and Achievements, and Influence of James and Henry Austen', *Persuasions*, 31 (2009), pp. 13–32.

Le Faye, Deirdre, 'Jane Austen's Laggard Suitor', *Notes and Queries* ns 47 245.3 (September 2000), pp. 301–304.

—, 'To Dwell Together in Unity', *Jane Austen Society Collected Reports 1986–1995*, pp. 151–63.

—, 'A Tour of Carlton House', *Jane Austen Society Report* (2005), pp. 28–38.

Ledwidge, Bernard, 'The "Strange Business in America"', *Jane Austen Society Collected Reports 1949–1965*, pp. 197–203.

Lefroy, Helen, 'Silkmaking and papermaking in Hampshire', *Jane Austen Society Report* (2007), pp. 90–93.

Levy, Michelle, 'Austen's Manuscripts and the Publicity of Print', *English Literary History*, 77 (2010), pp. 1015–40.

Litz, A. Walton, '*The Loiterer*: A Reflection of Jane Austen's Early Environment', *Review of English Studies*, 12 (1961), pp. 251–61.

Mahoney, Stephen, *Wealth or Poverty? Jane Austen's Novels Explored* (London: Robert Hale, 2015).

Mandal, Anthony, *Jane Austen and the Popular Novel: The Determined Author* (Basingstoke: Palgrave Macmillan, 2007).

Marsh, Rev. W. Tilson, *Home Light; or the Life and Letters of Maria Chowne, Wife of the Rev. William Marsh, D. D. of Beckenham*, 2nd edn (London: James Nisbet and Co., 1859).

Mathias, Peter, *The First Industrial Nation: An Economic History of Britain, 1700–1914* (London: Methuen, 1969).

Midgley, Winifred, 'The Revd Henry and Mrs Eleanor Austen', *Jane Austen Society Collected Reports 1976–1985*, pp. 86–91.

Morrieson, H. W., 'The Centenary of Our Modern Coinage Instituted in February 1817' (1917); http://www.britnumsoc.org [Online].

Morris, Gouverneur, *The Diary and Letters of Gouverneur Morris* (New York: Charles Scribner, 1888); *Online Library of Liberty* [Online]

Muir, Rory, *Britain and the Defeat of Napoleon, 1807–1815* (London: Yale University Press, 1996).

Munch-Petersen, Thomas, 'Count d'Antraigues and the British political elite, 1806–1812', *Napoleonica: La Revue* (2008), 2, pp. 121–35 [Online].

Neal, Larry, 'The Financial Crisis of 1825 and the Restructuring of the British Financial System', *Review* (May/June 1998) [Online].

Nelson, Paul David, *Francis Rawdon-Hastings, Marquess of Hastings: Soldier, Peer of the Realm, Governor-General of India* (Madison, NJ: 2005).

Parker, Keiko, '"What Part of Bath Do You Think They Will Settle In?": Jane Austen's Use of Bath in *Persuasion*', *Persuasions*, 23 (2001), pp. 166–76.

Pasley, Charles W., *Essay on the Military Policy and Institutions of the British Empire* (London, 1811).

Porter, Roy, *London: A Social History* (Cambridge, MA: Harvard University Press, 1994).

Pressnell, L. S., *Country Banking in the Industrial Revolution* (Oxford: Clarendon Press, 1956).

—, 'Public Monies and the Development of English Banking', *The Economic History Review, New Series*, 5: 3 (1953), pp. 378–97.

Reith, Gerda, *The Age of Chance: Gambling in Western Culture* (London: Routledge, 1999).

Richardson, Harriet, and Peter Guillery, 'Speculative Development and the Origins and History of East India Company Settlement in Cavendish Square and Harley Street', *The London Journal: A Review of Metropolitan Society Past and Present*, 41: 2 (2016), pp. 128–49.

Robins, Nick, *The Corporation that Changed the World: How the East India Company Shaped the Modern Multinational* (London: Pluto Press, 2006).

Rush, Richard, *Memoranda of a Residence at the Court of London* (Philadelphia: Carey, Lea & Blanchard, 1833).

Russell, G. L., 'Henry Austen at Bentley', *Jane Austen Society Collected Reports 1966–1975*, pp. 216–18.

Sabor, Peter, 'Brotherly and Sisterly Dedications in Jane Austen's Juvenilia', *Persuasions*, 31 (2009), pp. 33–46.

Salter, H. E., and Mary D. Lobel (eds), *A History of the County of Oxford: Volume 3, The University of Oxford* (London, 1954), *British History Online*. [Online].

Sambrook, James, *William Cobbett* (London: Routledge and Kegan Paul, 1973).

Schorer, Mark, 'The Humiliation of Emma Woodhouse', in Ian Watt (ed.), *Jane Austen: A Collection of Critical Essays* (Englewood Cliffs, NJ: Prentice Hall, 1963).

Slothouber, Linda, *Jane Austen, Edward Knight and Chawton: Commerce and Community* (Gaithersburg, MD: 2015).

—, 'Bingley's Four or Five Thousand, and Other Fortunes from the North', *Persuasions*, 35, pp. 50–63.

Southam, Brian, *Jane Austen and the Navy* (London: National Maritime Museum, 2005)

—, *Jane Austen's Literary Manuscripts: A Study of the Novelist's Development* (Oxford: Oxford University Press, 1964), pp. 144–9.

—, '*Sanditon*: the Seventh Novel', in Juliet McMaster (ed.), *Jane Austen's Achievement* (Basingstoke: Palgrave Macmillan, 1976).

Southey, Robert, pseudo. Don Manuel Alvarez Espriella, *Letters from England* (London: Longman & Co., 1807).

Stevenson, Graham, *Defence or Defiance? A People's History of Derbyshire*. [Online]

Summerson, John, *Georgian London* (London: Barrie & Jenkins, 1988).

Sutherland, Kathryn, 'Jane Austen's Dealing with John Murray and His Firm', *Review of English Studies*, 64: 263, pp. 105–26.

—, *Jane Austen's Textual Lives: from Aeschylus to Bollywood* (Oxford: Oxford University Press, 2005).

Sweetman, George, *The History of Wincanton Somerset, from the Earliest Times to the Year 1903* (London: Henry Williams, 1903).

Thelwall, John, *An Appeal to Popular Opinion Against Kidnapping and Murder; including a Narrative of the late Atrocious Proceedings, at Yarmouth* (London: J. S. Jordan, 1796).

Thompson, James, *Models of Value: Eighteenth-Century Political Economy and the Novel* (Durham, NC: Duke University Press, 1996).

Tieken-Boon van Ostade, Ingrid, *In Search of Jane Austen: The Language of the Letters* (Oxford: Oxford University Press, 2014).

Tomalin, Claire, *Jane Austen: A Life* (London: Penguin, 1997).

Vick, Robin, 'Jane Austen's House at Chawton', *Jane Austen Society Collected Reports 1986–1995*, pp. 388–91.

—, 'Mr Austen's Carriage', *Jane Austen Society Collected Reports* (1999), pp. 226–8.

—, 'The Hancocks', p. 223

Viveash, Chris, 'The Chelsea Pleasure Ground', *Jane Austen Society Report* (2006), pp. 89–93.

—, 'Jane Austen's Early Adventures in Publishing', *Jane Austen Society Collected Reports*, vol. 5, pp. 78–83.

—, 'Jane, Henry and the Crutchleys', *Jane Austen Society Report for 2009*, pp. 129–35.

—, 'Lady Morley and the "Baron so Bold"', *Persuasions*, 14 (1992), pp. 53–6.

Ward, John William, *Letters to 'Ivy' from the first Earl of Dudley*, ed. S. H. Romilly (London: Longman & Co., 1905).

Watson, J. Steven, *The Reign of George III, 1760–1815* (Oxford: Clarendon Press, 1960).

Wells, Roger, 'The Militia Mutinies of 1795', in John Rule (ed.) *Outside the Law* (Exeter: University of Exeter, 1982).

Willoughby, Rupert, *Chawton: Jane Austen's Village* (Sherborne St John: R. Willoughby, c.1998).

NOTES

PROLOGUE: HENRY AND JANE

1   *JAOC*, p. 76.
2   *JAOC*, p. 89.
3   *Austen Papers*, p. 138.
4   *Catharine*, pp. 82, 86, 93.
5   *Catharine*, p. 103.
6   *Catharine*, p. 197.
7   *JAOC*, pp. 19–20.
8   *JAOC*, p. 31.
9   *JAOC*, pp. 30, 43.
10 *Memoir*, p. 13.
11 *JAOC*, pp. 84–5.
12 *Catharine*, pp. 53–4.
13 *JAOC*, p. 86.
14 *JAOC*, p. 68.
15 *JAOC*, p. 155.
16 *Catharine*, p. 31.
17 9 Jan. 1796, *Letters* no. 1, p. 2. See also Lefroy, 'Silkmaking and Papermaking'.
18 Hume, *Essays Moral, Political and Literary*, p. 317.
19 Cit. Thompson, *Models of Value*, pp. 137–8.
20 Cit. Robins, *Corporation*, p. xi.
21 *JOAC*, p. 15.
22 *Austen Papers*, p. 74; cf. pp. 66, 69, 73.
23 *JAOC*, p. 43.
24 *JAOC*, p. 28.
25 *JAOC*, p. 33.
26 Ibid.
27 *Austen Papers*, p. 66, cf p. 72.
28 *Austen Papers*, p. 31.
29 Cit. *Family Record*, p. 55.
30 *Austen Papers*, pp. 32–3.
31 *JAOC*, p. 86.
32 20 July 1817, *Letters* CEA/1, p. 344.
33 *Catharine*, p. 41.

34 Ibid., p. 107.

35 Ibid., pp. 134–8.

36 Ibid., p. 110.

37 Ibid., p. 126.

38 Ibid., p. 127.

39 Ibid., p. 149.

40 *Juvenilia*, p. 362.

41 *Memoir*, p. 175

42 8 April 1805, *Letters* no. 43, pp. 101–2.

CHAPTER 1: DEAD MEN'S SHOES: *LADY SUSAN, ELINOR AND MARIANNE, FIRST IMPRESSIONS* (1793–1800)

1 No. 24, July 11 1789, *The Loiterer* [Online].

2 Cit. Horn, 'Mutiny of the Oxfordshire Militia', p. 240.

3 *Catharine*, p. 71.

4 *Chronology*, p. 171.

5 *Austen Papers*, pp. 153–4.

6 *JAOC*, pp. 121–2.

7 *Later Manuscripts*, p. 11.

8 *JAOC*, p. 116.

9 Ibid.

10 *JAOC*, pp. 128, 130.

11 *Catharine*, p. 80.

12 9 Jan. 1796, *Letters* no. 1, pp. 1–2.

13 *Austen Papers*, pp. 16–17.

14 Ibid., p. 19.

15 19 Dec. 1798, *Letters* no. 14, p. 28.

16 Austen, *Northanger Abbey &c*, 281.

17 18 Sept. 1796, *Letters* no. 7, p. 12.

18 Caplan, 'Soldier Brother', p. 132.

19 *JAOC*, p. 129.

20 Ibid., pp. 127, 129, 135.

21 Ibid., p. 39.

22 Caplan, 'Soldier Brother', p. 133.

23 *JAOC*, p. 151; see Caplan, 'Soldier Brother', p. 135.

24 Ibid., p. 147.

25 Ibid., p. 151.

26 Ibid., p. 153.

27 Thelwall, *Appeal to Popular Opinion*, pp. 4–5.

28 *Chronology*, p. 193.

29 Mandal, *Jane Austen*, p. 57.

30 *JAOC*, p. 150.

31 Caplan, 'Soldier Brother', p. 140.

32 *Letters*: 24 Dec. 1798, no. 15, p. 30; 9 Jan. 1799, no. 17, pp. 33, cf. 34; 12 Nov. 1800, no. 26, p. 59.

CHAPTER 2: MODERN TIMES: *NORTHANGER ABBEY* AND *THE WATSONS* (1800–1805)

1 *JAOC*, p. 154.

2 Caplan, 'Soldier Brother', p. 142.

3   3 Jan. 1801, *Letters* no. 29, pp. 66, 68.

4   5 May 1801, *Letters* no. 35, p. 82.

5   3 Jan. 1801, *Letters* no. 29, p. 69.

6   1 Sept. 1796, *Letters* no. 4, p. 6

7   *Sanditon*, ch. 6.

8   1 Jan. 1807, *Letters* no. 49, p. 116.

9   *Family Record*, p. 122.

10   Barchas, *Matters of Fact in Jane Austen*, p. 57

11   *Letters* no. 102, p. 264.

12   *Letters* no. 45, p. 108.

13   Jarvis, 'Some Information', p. 79.

14   Cit. 'Charles Greenwood', www.peerage.org [online].

15   Caplan, 'Military Aspects', p. 23.

16   Anon., *A Characteristic Sketch of Charles Greenwood, Esq.* (Boulogne, 1826); accessed 06/10/2016.

17   *JAOC*, p. 154.

18   'Charles Spencer, 1740–1820', *History of Parliament Online*.

19   Caplan, 'Soldier Brother', p. 142.

20   *JAOC*, pp. 152–3.

21   25 Jan. 1801, *Letters* no. 33, pp. 78–9.

22   *JAOC*, pp. 159, 155, 160.

23   Caplan, 'Banker Brother', p. 71.

24   Corley, 'Henry Austen in Shady Company.'

25   Bennett, 'Lord Moira and the Austens', p. 133.

26   Nelson, *Francis Rawdon-Hastings*, pp. 133–4.

27   *Austen Papers*, pp. 176–8.

28   *JAOC*, p. 157.

29   *Family Record*, p. 138.

30   Hurst, 'Henry Thomas Austen', p. 49.

31   21 Jan. 1799, Letters no. 18, p. 37.

32   Bennett, 'Lord Moira and the Austens', p. 134.

33   *Later Manuscripts*, pp. 79, 82, 83.

34   *Austen Papers*, pp. 233, 235.

35   *Later Manuscripts*, pp. 116, 122; *Austen Papers*, pp. 233, 235–6.

36   30 June 1808, *Letters* no. 55, p. 138.

CHAPTER 3: HENRY TURNS BANKER: *LADY SUSAN* AND THE POPHAM POEM (1806–1809)

1   Caplan, 'Banker Brother', p. 74.

2   Cit. Pressnell, *Country Banking*, p. 12.

3   Bagehot, *Lombard Street*, pp. 268–9.

4   *Later Manuscripts*, p. 10.

5   30 Nov. 1814, *Letters* no. 114, p. 287.

6   *Catharine*, p. 28.

7   *Northanger Abbey &c.*, p. 311; original emphasis.

8   *Austen Papers*, p. 267.

9   Pressnell, 'Public Monies', p. 378.

10   Mathias, *The First Industrial Nation*, p. 36.

11   Corley, 'Bank failure', p. 141.

12   Gilson, 'Henry Austen, Banker', p. 43.

13 See Caplan, 'Missteps and Misdeeds', p. 106.

14 Bennett, 'Lord Moira and the Austens', p. 142.

15 Southam, *Jane Austen and the Navy*, p. 169.

16 20 Feb. 1807, *Letters* no. 51, p. 123.

17 *Memoir*, p. 71; cf. p. 173.

18 'Charles Spencer 1740–1820', *History of Parliament Online*.

19 *JAOC*, p. 163.

20 15 June 1808, *Letters* no. 52, p. 126. See Caplan, 'The brewery scheme'.

21 1 Oct. 1808, *Letters* no. 56, p. 141.

22 7 Oct. 1808, *Letters* no. 57, p. 144.

23 10 Jan. 1809, *Letters* no. 64, p. 164; Caplan, 'Banker Brother', p. 79.

24 4 April 1805, *Letters* nos. 68 (D) and (A), pp. 174–5.

25 Willoughby, *Chawton*, p. 40.

26 *Memoir*, p. 67.

27 *Later Manuscripts*, p. 311.

28 *Memoir*, p. 168.

29 *Family Record*, p. 181.

30 9 July 1816, *Letters* no. 142, p. 316.

31 29 Jan. 1813, *Letters* no. 79, p. 201.

32 Caplan, 'Missteps and Misdeeds', pp. 105, 106–7.

33 Marsh, *Home Light*, p. 5.

CHAPTER 4: THE SELF-MADE AUTHOR: *SENSE AND SENSIBILITY* (1810–1811)

1   18 Apr. 1811, *Letters* no. 70, pp. 179–81.

2   25 Apr. 1811, *Letters* no. 71, p. 182.

3   1 Oct. 1808, *Letters* no. 56, p. 140.

4   *Memoir*, p. 141.

5   Gilson, 'Henry Austen, Banker', p. 46.

6   Fergus, 'Professional Woman Writer', p. 6.

7   Garside *et al.*, *The English Novel*, pp. 81, 38.

8   25 April 1811, *Letters* no. 71, p. 183.

9   6 June 1811, *Letters* no. 75, p. 193.

10 Mrs George Austen to Mary Lloyd Austen, 13 Aug. 1806, *Austen Papers*, p. 247.

11 Cit. *Family Record*, p. 188, and for two previous references pp. 188, 207.

CHAPTER 5: WHIG HISTORY: *PRIDE AND PREJUDICE* (1811–1813)

1   4 Feb. 1813, *Letters* no. 80, p. 203.

2   Jenkins, 'Birth of a Legend', pp. 289–94.

3   *Critical Review*, New Series 4: 1 (Feb 1812), p. 217.

4   'William Gore Langton, 1760–1784', *History of Parliament Online*.

5   Ibid., p. 319.

6   Ibid., p. 75.

7   Doody, *Jane Austen's Names*, p. 79.

8   Jenkins, 'Marriage Registers'.

9   Southey, *Letters from England*, I, p. 122.

10 Summerson, *Georgian London*, p. 171.

11 Heine, *Prose Writings*, pp. 46–7; Rush, *Memoranda*, pp. 77–8.

12 *Chronology*, p. 422.

13 Creevey, *Papers*, pp. 96–7, 100.

14 29 Nov. 1812, *Letters*, no. 77, p. 197.

CHAPTER 6: SPECULATIVE SOCIETY: *MANSFIELD PARK* (1813–1814)

1 *JAOC*, p. 170.

2 *Chronology*, pp. 411, 422.

3 *JAOC*, pp. 147, 149.

4 Tomalin, *Jane Austen*, p. 191.

5 Corley, 'Bank Failure', p. 142; Caplan, 'Banker Brother', p. 81.

6 *JAOC*, pp. 171–2.

7 Austen-Leigh, *Jane Austen*, p. 76.

8 Nelson, *Francis Rawdon-Hastings*, p. 148; Bury, *Diary*, I, pp. 55, 56.

9 Corley, 'Charles James'; Caplan, 'Banker Brother', p. 80; Nelson, *Francis Rawdon-Hastings*, p. 150.

10 Corley, 'Charles James'.

11 Caplan, 'Banker Brother', p. 80.

12 See Nelson, *Francis Rawdon-Hastings*, p. 149.

13 15–16 Sept. 1813, *Letters* no. 87, p. 221.

14 *Memoir*, p. 149.

15 3 July 1813, *Letters* no. 86, p. 215

16 20 May 1813, *Letters* no. 84, p. 210.

17 24 May 1813, *Letters* no. 85, p. 212.

18 Caplan, 'Lord Moira's Debt', p. 45.

19 Corley, 'Bank Failure', p. 142

20 Cit. Pressnell, *Country Banks*, p. 71, cf. 59; see also Pressnell, 'Public Monies', pp. 384–5.

21 24 Oct. 1807, *Letters* no. 60, p. 152. Original emphasis.

22 Ward, *Letters to 'Ivy'*, p. 250.

23 24 Jan. 1813, *Letters* no. 78, p. 198.

24 Edgeworth, *The Absentee*, p. 117.

25 16 Feb. 1813, *Letters* no. 82, p. 208.

26 10 Jan. 1809, *Letters* no. 64, pp. 163–4.

27 *OED*; emphasis added.

28 Reith, *Age of Chance*, pp. 59–60.

29 3 July 1813, *Letters* no. 86, p. 217.

30 14 Jan. 1796, *Letters* no. 2, p. 3.

31 29 Jan. 1813, *Letters* no. 79, p. 201.

32 3 Nov. 1813, *Letters* no. 95, p. 250.

33 3 July 1813, *Letters* no. 86, p. 217.

34 Fergus, 'Professional Woman Writer', p. 12.

35 *Later Manuscripts*, p. 232.

36 16 Sept. 1813, *Letters* no. 87, pp. 218, 217.

37 15 Sept. 1813, 8 March 1814, 25 Sept. 1813, *Letters* nos. 87, 98, 90, pp. 218, 257, 230.

38 3 Nov. 1813, *Letters* no. 95, p. 250.

39 *Memoir*, p. 70; 15 Sept. 1813, *Letters* no. 87, p. 220.

40 15 Sept. 1813 and 25 Sept. 1813, *Letters* no. 87, pp. 218, 221 and no. 90, pp. 231, 230.

41 26 Oct. 1813, *Letters* no. 94, p. 245.

42 3 Nov. 1813, *Letters* no. 95, p. 249.

43 21 Oct. 1813, *Letters* no. 93, p. 243.

44 26 Oct. 1813, *Letters* no. 94, p. 246.

45 15 Sept. 1813, *Letters* no. 87, p. 218.

46 3 Nov. 1813, *Letters* no. 247, pp. 247–8.

47 Easton, 'The Sibling Ideal' [Online].

48 25 Sept. 1813, *Letters* no. 90, p. 230.

49 To Anna Lefroy, 29 Nov. 1814, *Letters* no. 112, p. 283.

50 29 Nov. 1814, *Letters* no. 283, p. 283

51 Hudson, *Sibling Love*, p. 15.

52 *Memoir*, p. 141.

53 6 Nov. 1813, *Letters* no. 96, p. 254.

54 16 Feb. 1813, *Letters* no. 83, p. 208.

55 2, 5, 9 March 1814, *Letters* nos. 97, 98, 99, pp. 255–6, 258, 262.

CHAPTER 7: UNCOMMERCIAL *EMMA* (1814–1815)

1   2 March 1814, *Letters* no. 97, p. 255.

2   Dale, *'Napoleon is Dead'*, 12.

3   McRae, *Disclosure*, 3.

4   Muir, *Britain and the Defeat of Napoleon*, pp. 320–21.

5   Ferguson, *House of Rothschild*, I, 95.

6   Cit. Kaplan, *Rothschild*, p. 106.

7   Pressnell, *Country Banking*, p. 471

8   Caplan, 'Banker Brother', pp. 83–4

9   Caplan, 'Lord Moira's debt', pp. 44–5.

10 15 Sept. 1813, *Letters* no. 87, p. 221; see Corley, 'Bank Failure', p. 142.

11 5 March 1814, *Letters* no. 98, p. 260; see Corley, 'The Austen family'.

12 15 Sept. 1813, *Letters* no. 87, p. 219; see Slothouber, *Jane Austen*, pp. 19–20.

13 2 March 1814, *Letters* no. 97, p. 256.

14 5 March 1814, *Letters* no. 98, p. 257; 2 March 1814, *Letters* no. 97, p. 256. cf. p. 261.

15 9 Sept. 1814, *Letters* no. 107, p. 275.

16 Hume, 'Money and Rank', p. 56; Copeland, 'Money', p. 132.

17 Hume, 'Money and Rank', p. 52.

18 14 Oct. 1813, *Letters* no. 92, p. 237.

19 23 Aug. 1814, *Letters* no. 105, p. 271; 2 Sept. 1814, *Letters* no. 106, p. 273. See Viveash, 'Jane, Henry and the Crutchleys'.

20 24 May 1813, *Letters* no. 85, p. 21

21 Morris, *Diary and Letters*, I. xiv. [Online].

22 *Morning Post*, 18 May 1810.

23 *Chronology*, pp. 482, 483.

24 23 June 1814, *Letters* no. 102, p. 264.

25 Fremantle, *Wynne Diaries*, p. 526.

26 *Later Manuscripts*, pp. 231, 237.

27 *Austen Papers*, p. 122.

28 6 Nov. 1813, *Letters* no. 96, p. 254.

29 23 Aug. 1814, *Letters* no. 105, p. 271.

30 23 June 1814, *Letters* no. 102, p. 265.

31 23 Aug. 1814, *Letters* no. 105, p. 270.

32 Ibid., pp. 270, 271; see Corley, 'Bank Failure', pp. 139–40.

33 2 Sept. 1814, *Letters* no. 106, pp. 273–4.

34 See Ledwidge, '"Strange Business in America"'.

35 Pasley, *Essay*, pp. 150, 476.

36 2 Sept. 1814, *Letters* no. 106, p. 273.

37 29 Nov. 1812, *Letters* no. 77, p. 196.

38 Ibid., p. 274.

39 29 Nov. 1812, *Letters* no. 77, p. 197.

40 *Memoir*, p. x; 29 Jan. 1813, *Letters* no. 79, p. 201.

41 29 Nov. 1812, *Letters* no. 77, p. 196.

42 24 Jan. 1813, *Letters* no. 78, p. 199.

43 *Family Chronicle*, p. 221.

44 Corley, 'Jane Austen's dealings', pp. 130–31.

45 18–20 Nov. 1814, *Letters* no. 109, p. 281.

46 30 Nov. 1814, *Letters* no. 114, p. 287.

47 28 Sept. 1814, *Letters* no. 108, p. 277.

48 *JAOC*, p. 222.

49 22 Nov. 1814, *Letters* no. 110, p. 282.

50 *Later Manuscripts*, pp. 230–34.

51 *Memoir*, p. 119.

52 Caplan, 'Banker Brother', p. 85; Pressnell, *Country Banking*, p. 69.

53 *Family Chronicle*, pp. xxviii, 223.

54 *Chronology*, pp. 502–5.

55 Sutherland, 'Jane Austen's Dealings', pp. 120–21.

56 Ibid., p. 108.

57 *Chronology*, pp. 470, 471, 495.

CHAPTER 8: SECOND SPRING: *PERSUASION* (1815–1816)

1 17 Oct. 1815, *Letters* no. 121, p. 291

2 See Le Faye, 'Jane Austen's Laggard Suitor'.

3 17 Oct. 1815, *Letters* no. 121, p. 291.

4 Ibid., pp. 292–3.

5 Ibid., p. 292.

6 Sutherland, 'Jane Austen's Dealings', p. 121.

7 ?20–21 Oct. 1815, *Letters* no. 122, pp. 293–4.

8 *Chronology*, p. 518.

9 17 Oct. 1815, *Letters* no. 121, p. 292.

10 3 Nov. 1815, *Letters* no. 124, p. 295.

11 Harris, *Revolution*, p. 174.

12 *Memoir*, p. 175.

13 *Family Chronicle*, p. 202.

14 15 Nov. and 16 Nov. 1815, *Letters* nos. 125 (D) and 125 (A), pp. 296–7.

15 26 Nov. 1815, *Letters* no. 128, p. 300.

16 26 Nov. 1815, *Letters* no. 128, p. 301.

17 Pressnell, *Country Banking*, p. 155; Corley, 'Austen family', p. 100.

18 Bennett, 'Lord Moira and the Austens', pp. 142–3.

19 2 Dec. 1815, *Letters* no. 129, p. 303.

20 Jarvis, 'Jane Austen and the Countess of Morley', p. 7. See also Viveash, 'Countess of Morley', and Caplan, 'Banker Brother', p. 72.

21 *Later Manuscripts*, pp. 237–8.

22 Undated, ?early 1816, *Letters* no. 136, p. 310.

23 Corley, 'Austen Family'; Corley, 'Bank Failure', pp. 143–44; Caplan, 'Banker Brother', p. 85.

24 Garside, 'English Novel', p. 93.

25 Corley, 'Bank Failure', pp. 114–15; *Chronology*, pp. 528–31.

26 *Memoir*, p. 106.

27 13 March 1816, *Letters* no. 137, p. 311

28 Corley, 'Bank Failure', pp. 144–5; Caplan, 'Banker Brother', p. 48.

29 Corley, 'Bank Failure', p. 140.

30 *Reminiscences*, p. 47.

31 *Catharine*, pp. 86, 87.

32 11 Dec. 1815, *Letters* no. 132 (D), p. 306.

33 Murray to Scott 25 Dec. 1815: NLS MS. 3886 (ff. 261–62), Murray MS.

34 Tomalin, *Jane Austen*, p. 255.

35 Cit. Southam, *Jane Austen*, p. 106.

36 Fergus, 'Composition and Publication', p. 14.

37 1 April 1816, *Letters* no. 139, p. 313.

38 Southam, *Critical Heritage*, p. 67.

39 Gilson, *Bibliography*, p. 69.

40 Caplan, 'Naval aspects', p. 40

CHAPTER 9: 'THE CHOICEST GIFT OF HEAVEN': *SANDITON* AND *WINCHESTER RACES* (1816–1817)

1 *Reminiscences*, p. 48.

2 Caplan, 'Banker Brother', pp. 86–7; Corley, 'Bank Failure', p. 145.

3 Cit. Southam, *Jane Austen and the Navy*, p. 333.

4 *Reminiscences*, p. 48.

5 Caplan, 'Banker Brother', p. 87.

6 Corley, 'Bank Failure', p. 146; *Chronology*, p. 634.

7 Le Faye, 'Jane Austen's Laggard Suitor', p. 304.

8 *Chronology*, p. 540.

9 9 July 1816, *Letters* no. 142, pp. 316, 317.

10 Caplan, 'Lord Moira's debt', p. 52.

11 *Annual Register* 1816, pp. 286–288.

12 *Chronology*, p. 544.

13 9 Sept. 1816, *Letters* no. 145, p. 321.

14 4 Sept. 1816, *Letters* no. 144, p. 318.

15 See eText of Brabourne, *Letters of Jane Austen* (1844), section 'Jane Austen's Brothers and Sister', Pemberley.com [Online].

16 *Reminiscences*, p. 48.

17 HRO 21M65/E1/4/2601.

18 *Family Record*, p. 235.

19 Jarvis, Some Information, pp. 15–16; Midgley, 'The Revd. Henry', p. 86; cf. *Chronology*, pp. 550–51,where a different date for the curacy is given.

20 26 March 1817, *Letters* no. 155, p. 337.

21 20 Feb. 1817, *Letters* no. 151, p. 330.

22 24 Jan. 1817, *Letters* no. 150, p. 327.

23 *Later Manuscripts*, p. lxviii.

24 See Deidre Lynch's note in the Oxford University Press edition of *Persuasion*, p. 246.

25 20 Feb. 1817, *Letters* no. 151, p. 328.

26 Morrieson, 'Centenary of our Modern Coinage' [Online].

27 Dick, *Romanticism and the Gold Standard*, pp. 110, 114.

28 *Memoir*, pp. 120, 138.

29 *Family Record*, p. 243.

30 Carnall, 'Early Nineteenth Century', p. 43.

31 Surr, *Magic of Wealth*, I, p. 162.

32 Surr, *Magic of Wealth*, I, pp. 47, 49, 179.

33 23 March 1817, *Letters* no. 155, p. 336.

34 24 Jan. 1817, *Letters* no. 150, p. 326.

35 6 April 1817, *Letters* no. 157, p. 338.

36 Fergus, 'Professional Woman Writer', p. 16.

37 Caplan, 'We suppose the Trial', p. 156.

38 ?28 May 1817, *Letters* no. 161, p. 343.

39 *Memoir*, pp. 130–31.

40 Cit. Honan, *Jane Austen*, p. 400.

41 Selwyn, *Collected Poems*, p. 86.

42 *Memoir*, p. 138

43 *Memoir*, p. 190.

44 *Memoir*, p. 138.

45 *Memoir*, p. 138.

46 13 and 23 March 1817, *Letters* nos. 153 and 155, pp. 333, 335.

47 Gilson, *Bibliography*, pp. 84–5.

EPILOGUE

1   See Bearman, 'Cubbington Living'.

2   *Reminiscences*, p. 57; *Family Record*, pp. 262–3.

3   *Letters*, p. 199; *Family Record*, p. 263.

4   *Chronology*, p. 601.

5   Ibid., p. 681.

6   Ibid., p. 618.

7   Jarvis, 'Clerical Connections', pp. 15–16; Midgley, 'Revd. Henry', p. 86.

8   HTA to JEAL, 22 Nov. 1828, *Austen Papers*, p. 282.

9   Russell, 'Henry Austen at Bentley', p. 216.

10 *Austen Papers*, pp. 284–5.

11 Midgley, 'The Revd. Henry', p. 90.

12 *Oxford Dictionary of National Biography*.

13 Bearman, 'Cubbington Living', p. 22.

14 Caplan, 'Lord Moira's Debt', p. 53.

15 Caplan, 'Lord Moira's Debt', p. 48.

16 Midgley, 'The Revd. Henry', p. 87.

17 *Chronology*, p. 656.

18 Sutherland, 'Austen's Dealings', p. 115.

19 Vick, 'Jane Austen's House', p. 391.

20 Caplan, 'Lord Moira's Debt', p. 41, citing personal communication from T. A. B. Corley.

21 *Austen Papers*, p. 294.

22 *Chronology*, p. 663.

23 *JAOC*, p. 79.

24 Austen-Leigh, *Chawton Manor*, pp. 163–4.

25 Austen-Leigh, *Jane Austen*, p. 76.

26 *Austen Papers*, p. 18.

INDEX